D0072534

Students:
Looking to improve your grades?

SAGE
Premium
Video

BOOST COMPREHENSION. BOLSTER ANALYSIS.

- SAGE Premium Video **EXCLUSIVELY CURATED FOR THIS TEXT**
- **BRIDGES BOOK CONTENT** with application & critical thinking
- Includes short, auto-graded quizzes that **DIRECTLY FEED TO YOUR LMS GRADEBOOK**
- Premium content is **ADA COMPLIANT WITH TRANSCRIPTS**
- Comprehensive media guide to help you **QUICKLY SELECT MEANINGFUL VIDEO** tied to your course objectives

SAGE Outcomes:
MEASURE RESULTS, TRACK SUCCESS

FOR STUDENTS, understanding the objectives for each chapter and the goals for the course is essential for getting the grade you deserve!

FOR INSTRUCTORS, being able to track your students' progress allows you to more easily pinpoint areas of improvement and report on success.

This title was crafted around specific chapter objectives and course outcomes, vetted by experts, and adapted from renowned syllabi. Tracking student progress can be challenging. Promoting and achieving success should never be. We are here for you.

COURSE **OUTCOMES** FOR AMERICAN GOVERNMENT:

ARTICULATE the foundations of American Government, including its history, critical concepts, and important documents and achievements.

EXPLAIN the main institutions of American Government, including their roles and interrelationships.

DESCRIBE the roles and relative importance of major entities and influences in American political life.

ANALYZE the development and impact of important governmental policies.

Want to see how these outcomes tie in with this book's chapter-level objectives?
Visit us at **edge.sagepub.com/amgov** for complete outcome-to-objective mapping.

AmGov

Sara Miller McCune founded SAGE Publishing in 1965 to support the dissemination of usable knowledge and educate a global community. SAGE publishes more than 1000 journals and over 800 new books each year, spanning a wide range of subject areas. Our growing selection of library products includes archives, data, case studies and video. SAGE remains majority owned by our founder and after her lifetime will become owned by a charitable trust that secures the company's continued independence.

Los Angeles | London | New Delhi | Singapore | Washington DC | Melbourne

AmGov
Long Story Short

Christine Barbour
Indiana University

FOR INFORMATION:

CQ Press
2455 Teller Road
Thousand Oaks, California 91320
E-mail:order@sagepub.com

SAGE Publications Ltd.
1 Oliver's Yard
55 City Road
London EC1Y 1SP
United Kingdom

SAGE Publications India Pvt. Ltd.
B 1/I 1 Mohan Cooperative Industrial Area
Mathura Road, New Delhi 110 044
India

SAGE Publications Asia-Pacific Pte. Ltd.
18 Cross Street #10-10/11/12
China Square Central
Singapore 048423

Executive Publisher: Monica Eckman
Development Editor: Elise Frasier
Content Development Editor: Anna Villarruel
Editorial Assistant: Sam Rosenberg
Production Editor: Kelly DeRosa
Copy Editor: Amy Marks
Typesetter: C&M Digitals (P) Ltd.
Proofreader: Scott Oney
Indexer: Joan Shapiro
Cover Designer: Scott Van Atta
Marketing Manager: Erica DeLuca

Printed in Canada

Library of Congress Cataloging-in-Publication Data

Name: Barbour, Christine, 1955- author.

Title: AmGov: long story short/Christine Barbour, Indiana University, USA.

Other titles: American government

Description: First Edition. | Washington, D.C. : CQ Press, [2019] | Includes index.

Identifiers: LCCN 2018047973 | ISBN 9781544325927 (Spiral : alk. paper)

Subjects: LCSH: United States—Politics and government—Textbooks.

Classification: LCC JK276 .B36 2019 | DDC 320.473—dc23 LC record available at https://lccn.loc.gov/2018047973

This book is printed on acid-free paper.

19 20 21 22 23 10 9 8 7 6 5 4 3 2 1

Brief Contents

Detailed Contents

DIGITAL RESOURCES

A Complete Teaching & Learning Package

SAGE course outcomes: Measure Results, Track Success

Outlined in your text and mapped to chapter learning objectives, SAGE course outcomes are crafted with specific course outcomes in mind and vetted by advisers in the field. See how SAGE course outcomes tie in with this book's chapter-level objectives at **edge.sagepub.com/amgov**.

Interactive eBook

AmGov: Long Story Short is also available as an interactive ebook, which can be packaged with the text for an additional $5 or purchased separately. The interactive ebook Includes access to SAGE Premium Video, multimedia tools, and much more!

SAGE Coursepacks

Easily import our quality instructor and student resource content into your school's learning management system (LMS). Intuitive and simple to use, SAGE Coursepacks allow you to integrate only the content you need and require no access code.

SAGE edge

An open-access study site, available at **edge.sagepub.com/amgov**, provides a variety of additional resources to build students' understanding of the book content and extend their learning beyond the classroom.

SAGE Premium Video

AmGov: Long Story Short offers premium video, produced and curated specifically for this text, to boost comprehension and bolster analysis.

ACKNOWLEDGMENTS

We would like to thank the following people who provided feedback in reviews, surveys, focus groups, and class testing.

Alicia Andreatta, Angelina College

Amy Colon, SUNY Sullivan

Angel Saavedra Cisneros, St. Norbert College

Annabelle Conroy, University of Central Florida

Annette Chamberlin, Virginia Western Community College

Bobby Pace, Community College of Aurora

Read This First (or Nothing Else Will Make Sense)

AmGov—IS THAT EVEN A WORD?

Well, in case it isn't obvious, *AmGov* is short for American government.

The story of American government is a very long one indeed. Someday you should read it all—when you have time and the leisure to do a deep dive into the amazing story that is the history of the United States.

The truth is that the American story is awe-inspiring. Not perfect (not even close), but awe-inspiring, even if it doesn't feel that way sometimes. Our origin story—which includes the horror of slavery and the racism that made slavery possible—continues today, built into the fabric of our society. Women still fight to be taken seriously and to reach the upper echelons of power. The talking heads on TV make us want to scream, and it seems like our elected officials care more about their big donors or their big egos than they do about us. These days it can seem more like we are the divided states of America than the opposite.

And yet . . . a quick look around the world shows that we have the ability to push back, the freedom to try to change things, to voice our disgust and frustration, to resist the power that seems unjust. There is something about the United States that has drawn people from around the world to build a richly diverse and prosperous nation. From its birth, the U.S. Constitution has been a magnet and a promise of a more free and prosperous life.

Crafted by a small band of young revolutionaries more than 200 years ago, and still alive and kicking today, the American system is awe-inspiring, even if those revolutionaries would be astonished by (and maybe a little apprehensive about) how their young republic has grown up and matured.

LONG STORY SHORT: TEXTBOOKS IN THE AGE OF TL;DR

So American government, yeah, you should know all about it. The whole, *long* story. But maybe not all of it, not right now.

Look, of course we want this book to teach you the foundations and fundamentals of American politics. We are political scientists. We want you to be *politically literate* so you know what's going on, and we want you to engage in critical thinking so no one can pull a fast one on you. That means we want this to be your go-to handbook, so that you know what you need to know to be smart when an interesting article pops up in your Twitter feed or when a politician reaches out to you by social media or when you decide to cast a vote or when something gets you fired up and you want to speak out in a voice that can be heard.

We also know you have a life and a lot going on, that you are bombarded with information from zillions of sources, and that you are probably not going to have the time to read a long, anecdote-filled textbook—not even if it's filled with super smart information that your instructor says you need to read to get an A. Because who has that kind of time? Especially during a crazy semester, and for a class that probably isn't even in your major but you need to pass it because it's a requirement for whatever your major is? We get it. We hear it from our students all the time.

THE UPSHOT ↗

And yet . . . being busy shouldn't make you ignorant. That's why we created a book whose subtitle is *Long Story Short*. We want you to get to the point fast, sound intelligent, and still have time for all the other things you value.

SO, WHAT IS DIFFERENT ABOUT THIS BOOK?

→ **This book is *short*.** It tells you what you need to know and leaves out the fluff.

→ **This book is *smart*.** The *directional headers* on the left keep you on target, giving you questions to guide your reading, headers to remind you where you are, points to remember, or summaries to be sure you got it all. They include highlights of what you need to know and provide links so you can follow up on what catches your interest, to dig deeper when more context will help you out.

→ **This book is *fun*.** Well, maybe not going-out-on-Friday-night fun, but if you can't enjoy learning, you probably aren't going to learn. So we write with a smile and a light heart. The subject is super serious; the approach to it doesn't have to be.

IN A NUTSHELL

We haven't dumbed down this book to make it short. We've smartened it up. We want you to read lss, learn more (lss = long story short . . . get it?).

#1 POLITICS AND CITIZENSHIP

In this chapter:

1.1 Introduction to POLITICS

Politics is not some mysterious process engaged in by people beyond our reach. It is not something that happens "out there" and then impacts us, as if we were so many oblivious ducks, passively paddling around in our pond, targets of hunters we neither recognize nor understand.

Politics is simply the way we decide who gets power and influence in a world where there is not enough power for all of us to have as much as we'd like. As a famous political scientist, Harold Laswell, once defined it, politics is *who gets what and how they get it*. That sums it up neatly.

Most of our political wrangling is about trying to get rules that treat us or people like us favorably. **Rules** are incredibly important because they can help to determine who will win or lose future power struggles.

An essential element of power is having the ability to tell the controlling **political narrative** about who should have power, how it should be used, and to what end. Telling a political narrative, or a story about power, that other people buy into can give you enormous authority over them.

IN A NUTSHELL

It can seem like a pretty grimy activity sometimes, but consider this: politics is what saves us from being like the other animals on the planet. It gives us ways to solve disputes over power that do not involve violence. Instead, we have options of bargaining, cooperating, collaborating, and compromising. Or even bribing and arm twisting and threatening to pull out of the process. We *can* resort to violence, and of course we *do* at times, but the key point is—*we don't have to!*

WHERE WE GO IN THIS CHAPTER

By the time you finish reading this chapter, you will understand

→ The basic definitions of politics, government, and economics

→ The varieties of political and economic systems and how they help us understand the differences among nations, including the United States

→ The ideas that underlie the U.S. political system and that bring us together

→ The ideas that divide us despite our being bound by a common culture

→ How narratives can perpetuate particular ideas about politics and economics and how living in a mediated world helps to construct those narratives

→ The narratives about citizenship that provide the context in which we navigate politics in the United States

1.2 COMING TO TERMS: POLITICS, GOVERNMENT, AND ECONOMICS

THIS BOOK IS CALLED *AMGOV*. AREN'T POLITICS AND GOVERNMENT THE SAME THING?

Actually, no. The fact that politics is a process is what distinguishes it from government. Although we often use *politics* and *government* interchangeably, they are not the same thing.

We said earlier that *politics* is the process we use to decide who gets power and influence. **Government**, by contrast, is a system or an organization for exercising authority over a body of people. **Authority** is simply power that people consider legitimate, that is, they've consented or agreed to it. If people stop considering government's power to be legitimate (like the American colonists did with the British in the 1700s), they put themselves into a state of rebellion, or revolution against the government.

Politics and *government* are often used interchangeably because they are so closely related. The process of politics—fighting over rules and the power to make rules—can shape the kind of government we end up with. And the kind of government we establish—the rules and the institutions (or arenas for the exercise of power)—can in turn shape the way politics unfolds.

Politics produces different kinds of governments. The key differences among these governments relate to how much power government officials

politics: the way we decide who gets power and influence in a world where there is not enough power for all of us to have as much as we'd like

rules: political directives that help to determine who will win or lose future power struggles

political narrative: a story that is used to persuade others about the nature of power, who should have it, and how it should be used

government: a system or an organization for exercising authority over a body of people

authority: power that people consider legitimate, that they have consented or agreed to have over how people live their lives and how much power individuals retain to push back against or criticize government.

At one end of the spectrum, government makes all decisions about how individuals live their lives and individuals are powerless to push back. At the other end, individuals make the decisions for themselves and government does not exist. Somewhere in the middle is a government that is ultimately controlled by the individuals who live under it and that has processes in place so individuals can challenge the government if they feel it has over-reached its authority.

TYPES OF GOVERNMENTS OR POLITICAL SYSTEMS ➤ Here they are, ranging from most government power/least individual power to least government power/most individual power:

Authoritarian governments are governments where the rulers have all of the power and the rules don't allow the people who live under the rules to have any power at all. The people who live under authoritarian governments are called **subjects** because they are simply subject to the will of the rulers. They have no power of their own to fight back.

Non-authoritarian governments are governments where the rules regulate the people's behaviors in some respects (outlawing murder, theft, and running red lights, for instance) but allow them considerable freedom in others. The individuals who live under these governments are called **citizens** because government doesn't have all the power over them—they retain some power or rights that government cannot take away and that they can use to push back against an encroaching government. Non-authoritarian governments can be democracies or constitutional monarchies or other arrangements where the power of the leaders over the people is limited in some respect.

Democracy is a special case of non-authoritarian government because here the citizens have considerable power to make the rules

. . . .

authoritarian governments: political systems in which the rulers have all of the power and the rules don't allow the people who live under them to have any power at all

subjects: people who are bound to the will of the rulers and who have no power of their own to push back on an abusive government

non-authoritarian governments: political systems in which the rules regulate people's behaviors in some respects but allow them considerable freedom in others

citizens: individuals who live under non-authoritarian governments

democracy: a type of non-authoritarian government wherein citizens have considerable power to make the rules that govern them

that govern them (based on a theory called **popular sovereignty**). The degree of that power may vary. In small democracies, citizens may make every decision that affects them. In large ones, they may only choose representatives who exercise power on their behalf. The point is that, in a democracy, collective decisions are made by counting individual preferences about what citizens believe to be best.

**Anarchy** is no government at all. Individuals are free to do as they wish. The absence of laws means that organizing and transferring power is difficult, if not impossible. We don't have any lasting real-life examples of this type of government.

We can arrange these systems on a continuum of government power to individual power that looks like this:

FIGURE IT!

1.1: TYPES OF POLITICAL SYSTEMS

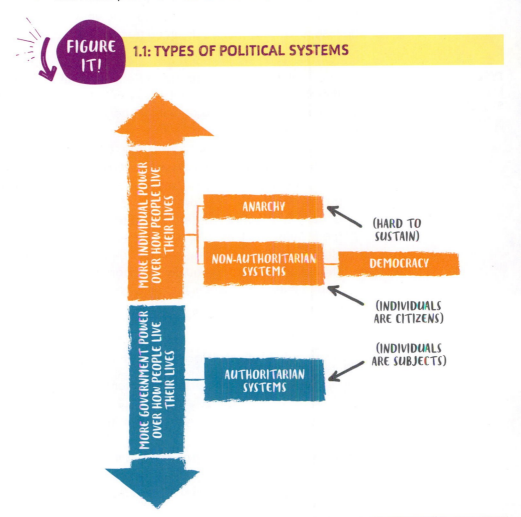

WHY DO DISCUSSIONS OF POLITICS USUALLY END UP BEING ABOUT ECONOMICS ALSO?

Power and influence are not the only scarce resources we have disputes over, of course. We also fight over gold and treasure and Maseratis—that is, material stuff. The process for deciding who gets the material resources and how they get them is called **economics**.

Like politics, economics can also offer us an alternative to a life of violence and mayhem. If we decide to allow an economic system to make decisions about who gets how much stuff, then we will have a narrative to justify the things we have managed to claim as our own. There will be an agreed-upon distributive system that provides predictability and a story about who deserves what.

Politics and economics are closely related. As you can imagine, the more power you have, the easier it will be to push a narrative that gives you more stuff. The more stuff you have, the more power will come with it. It is really impossible to study politics divorced from economics.

TYPES OF ECONOMIC SYSTEMS

Like political systems, economic systems can also vary depending on whether they rely on government power or individual choices to make decisions about the distribution of material goods. Kinds of economic systems include

\# **Socialism**. Socialist systems are economic systems in which the government (a single ruler, a party, or some other empowered group) decides what to produce and who should get the products. Usually in a socialist system the state or the government owns the utilities, the factories, and other essential property (or, perhaps, all property). Government may decide that the goods produced should be distributed equally or according to need or only to a valued elite—the point is that who gets the goods is a political decision.

· ·

popular sovereignty: the concept that the citizens are the ultimate source of political power

anarchy: no government at all, a system in which individuals are free to do as they wish

economics: the process for deciding who gets the material resources and how they get them

socialism: an economic system in which the government (a single ruler, a party, or some other empowered group) decides what to produce and who should get the products

(QUICK HEADS-UP ON USAGE!)

(*Socialism* and *communism* can mean similar things. If you hear references to communism, it probably means something close to what we've described here. To simplify, we'll just go with the term *socialism* in this book.)

\# **Regulated capitalism.** Regulated capitalism is a modified form of **capitalism**, an economic system that relies on the **market** to make decisions about who should have material goods. The market is based on the decisions of multiple individuals about what to buy or sell, creating different levels of demand and supply. When the demand for something goes up, so does its cost until more of it is produced. If production keeps up until the good floods the market and demand is insufficient to buy all that's been produced, then the price goes down.

As with democracy, in regulated capitalism, the fundamental decision-makers are individuals rather than the government. Also as in a democracy, individuals may decide they want the government to step in and regulate behaviors that they think are not in the public interest: the formation of monopolies that restrict competition, for instance, or wild swings that can happen when the market is uncontrolled.

KEY POINT

Just what regulations are appropriate can be a major subject of political debate in democratic countries with capitalist systems.

\# **Laissez-faire capitalism.** Laissez-faire capitalism is what you have when there are no restrictions on the market at all. An unregulated market can be subject to wild swings up and down. Some people like to speculate in that environment, but it turns out most people with money want a little bit more stability and predictability when they invest. Governments also find it costly and difficult to deal with the public catastrophes that can result from market crashes (the Great Depression of the 1930s, for instance, or the Great Recession after the stock market bubble burst in 2008). Consequently, as with anarchy, laissez-faire systems exist in theory but are problematic in practice.

We can also arrange these economic systems on a continuum of more government power over economic decision making to more individual power over economic decision making:

regulated capitalism: a market system in which the government intervenes to protect rights

capitalism: an economic system that relies on the market to make decisions about who should have material goods

market: the collective decisions of multiple individuals about what to buy or sell, creating different levels of demand and supply

laissez-faire capitalism: a form of capitalism wherein there are no restrictions on the market at all

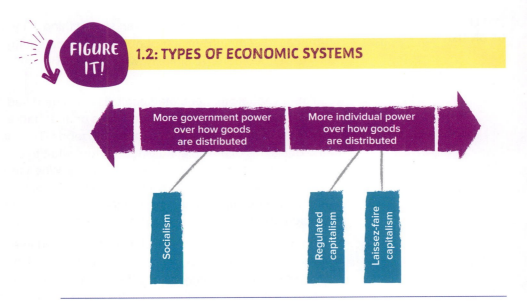

FIGURE IT!

1.2: TYPES OF ECONOMIC SYSTEMS

More government power over how goods are distributed

More individual power over how goods are distributed

Socialism

Regulated capitalism

Laissez-faire capitalism

Note that both forms of capitalism are on the side of more individual power even though government might regulate the economy to achieve social goals, like using taxation to provide benefits for the disadvantaged or to provide universal education. Taxation is just one of the tools politicians might use to regulate the outcome of the market.

1.3 POLITICAL-ECONOMIC SYSTEMS

THE GRAPHIC ADVANTAGE

The advantage of looking at political and economic systems the way we laid them out in the preceding section is that it allows us to understand just how they are different from and similar to each other. And because all nations have a way to manage the distribution of power and material goods, if we layer the two figures from that section on top of each other, we can create a model that will help us understand where most countries are located.

Keep in mind that models are just that—they are not detailed depictions of reality. Instead, they focus on key attributes in order to show relationships or structure. *Models are just tools to help us understand.*

So, take a look. Here we have placed the vertical axis of politics (ranging from more individual control of how people live on the top to more government control toward the bottom) over the horizontal axis of economics (ranging from more individual control of how goods are distributed on the right to more government control on the left). What this creates are four quadrants where we can place most any political economic system in the world:

FIGURE IT!

1.3: A MODEL OF WORLD POLITICAL-ECONOMIC SYSTEMS

Greater individual control over personal lives

Greater governmental control over how goods are distributed

Greater individual control over how goods are distributed

MARXIST UTOPIA

More individual control over personal lives and more government control over the economy

- No existing countries

CAPITALIST DEMOCRACIES

More individual control over personal lives and more individual control over the economy

- Many world countries including the United States, Canada, most European countries, India, Japan, Mexico

TOTALITARIANISM

More government control over personal lives and the economy

- North Korea, Cuba, the former Soviet Union

AUTHORITARIAN CAPITALISM

More government control over personal lives and more individual control over the economy

- Russia, China, Singapore

Greater governmental control over personal lives

FOUR MAIN POLITICAL-ECONOMIC SYSTEMS

> Think about the kinds of systems that fit into each of these quadrants:

\# **Capitalist democracy.** The upper right quadrant includes countries with the most individual control over both political and economic life. These countries have democratic governments and capitalist economies, although they may be found in different parts of the quadrant depending on how much social and economic regulation they endorse.

The United States is in this quadrant, as are the countries of western Europe (although many European countries are willing to have more

capitalist democracy: a political-economic system that grants the most individual control over both political and economic life

regulation of the economy to achieve valued social goals like less poverty or a narrower gap between rich and poor). Japan is also in this quadrant, as are India, Mexico, Canada, and many other nations that value individual choices over a heavy government hand.

\# **Totalitarianism**. Go catty-corner from capitalist democracy and you find totalitarianism. Totalitarian systems include authoritarian governments that tell people how to live and socialist economic systems where the government also decides who gets what material goods. Governments, not individuals, make the important decisions about power, influence, gold, and treasure.

Countries that fit in here are North Korea—and the former Soviet Union. These systems are hard to maintain because you need to keep your population isolated from the rest of the world.

\# **Authoritarian capitalism**. Countries in the lower right quadrant are some of the most interesting. These governments may pretend to have elections, but they are essentially a sham. Individuals have no rights to push back against a government that might determine how many children they can have or how they dress or grow their hair. They have no legal recourse or rights of due process if they are convicted of a crime. As far as how individuals live their lives, authoritarian government is the decider. But increasingly, these governments are choosing to let their subjects have some market freedom. Recognizing that global power is economic power, they take advantage of individual entrepreneurship to help drive their national economic engines.

Some authoritarian capitalist states have evolved from totalitarian systems (like Russia and China), and others were structured that way from the start. Singapore has an authoritarian government (at one time chewing gum was illegal because people threw their gum on the ground and defiled public spaces) but a thriving capitalist economy and tourist trade.

In 1994, eighteen-year-old American Michael Fay was convicted of spray painting cars in Singapore. He was arrested and sentenced to be caned. American claims that his punishment was

DIG DEEPER

Hear Michael Fay talk about his experience.

Go to **edge.sagepub.com/ dig-deeper**

Read about how democracies can become authoritarian systems.

Go to **edge.sagepub.com/ dig-deeper**

totalitarianism: a system that combines authoritarian government with a socialist economic system wherein the government makes all the decisions about power, influence, and money

authoritarian capitalism: a system in which the authoritarian government has strong control over how individuals may live their lives, but individuals do have some market freedom

"cruel and unusual" left Singaporean authorities unmoved since they have no bill of rights that meaningfully limits government action. Bill Clinton's administration was able to intervene to get the sentence somewhat reduced, but the example shows dramatically what it can be like to be in a thriving capitalist economy that doesn't recognize civil liberties.

Note, however, that the evolution can go both ways. Democratic countries can turn in an authoritarian direction, often through populist movements led by strong, charismatic figures. We see that today in Venezuela, the Philippines, Turkey, and Brazil. In recent years, populist movements that feed on a sense of grievance in the population are also picking up steam in Europe and the United States.

\# **Marxist utopia.** This quadrant is tough to describe because there are no real-life examples of what a Marxist utopia looks like. These countries would have extremely free citizens who could choose to live their lives as they please, but not a market economy. The closest we can come to imagining life in this type of system is the society the German theorist Karl Marx thought would emerge after workers had overthrown the capitalist system in a revolution (an event he thought was inevitable but that so far has not happened). After revolution, Marx thought the state would wither away and the economy would operate by requiring that individuals participate according to their ability and receive goods according to their need. Like so many places of imaginary perfection, this one has never survived in the bright sunlight of reality.

1.4 AMERICAN POLITICAL CULTURE

AMERICANS SEEM TO BE FIGHTING ALL THE TIME. DO WE AGREE ON ANYTHING??

Our increasingly media-rich culture gives us many opportunities to hear and participate in political debates, both civil and not so civil. Sometimes it seems like we don't agree on a single thing. But, ironically, it is only because we do agree on some fundamentals that those disagreements can even take place.

FOUR THINGS TO KNOW ABOUT POLITICAL CULTURE

Political culture is a set of *shared* ideas, values, and beliefs that define the role and limitations of government and people's relationship to that

political culture: a set of shared ideas, values, and beliefs that define the role and limitations of government and people's relationship to that government and that, therefore, bind people into a single political unit

government. Because they are shared values and beliefs, they pull people together, making them into a single political unit. Here are four things to know about political culture:

\# Political culture is woven together from political narratives. It is not identical to political narratives, however; political narratives can both unite people and divide them.

\# Political culture is intangible and unspoken. It is very hard to get your hands around it or to find the language with which to discuss it. It is especially difficult to be aware of your own political culture. Like the semi-facetious question of whether fish know they are in water, it is interesting to ask whether people recognize their own political cultures if they have never been exposed to another. People who have not traveled or met many people from other countries are more likely to think that the beliefs we share are objective reality, not just one set of many optional sets of narratives.

\# Political culture is easiest to see when you can step outside of it. Like a fish in water, it is hard to be aware of your environment when you are immersed in it and it's all you have ever known. That is one reason we created the world systems graphic we explored earlier. It allows us to understand our system in relation to others as a first step to understanding the culture that holds it together.

\# Political culture gives people a common set of assumptions about the world and a common political language within which they can disagree. And boy, do they disagree! Remember that to say that Americans share a political culture is not to say that they agree on everything.

SO, WHAT DO AMERICANS BELIEVE?

What does American political culture look like? We know from the world systems graphic that our political culture is found in the upper right quadrant of that figure—defined by a preference for more individual control (that is, less government regulation) of how people live their lives and how they distribute material goods. That means Americans are democratic capitalists whose values are the same Enlightenment values of classical liberalism (which we discuss in the next section).

Within that quadrant there is a fair amount of variation. We said, for instance, that many western European cultures endorse more regulation to bring about valued social goods like a basic standard of living, guaranteed health care, or more equality. The United States is less likely to agree on that kind of regulation (even deciding whether to guarantee access to health care is a struggle here). Here are the fundamentals on which Americans seem to have reached a national consensus:

FUNDAMENTALS OF AMERICAN POLITICAL CULTURE

\# **Limited government** (this goes all the way back to the founding)

\# **Individualism**, which means an emphasis on individual rights rather than on the collective whole

\# A belief in core values of freedom, equality, and representative democracy, in a context of minimal government coercion, so that . . .

- **Freedom** becomes freedom *from* government. That is different, for instance, from some other democratic capitalist countries whose citizens view their freedom as flowing from a strong government that provides basics like medical care and higher education. This gives citizens a level of financial freedom that allows them to focus their time and money elsewhere.

- **Equality** becomes equality before the law; one person, one vote; and equal opportunity—all forms of equality that require minimal government intervention. Americans tend to reject notions of equality like those realized by affirmative action, in which government steps in to create more actual equality of life chances.

- *Democracy* is a decision-making process by which individuals register their preferences for their rulers (and the policies they promise). Democratic capitalism cannot exist without a commitment to a form of democratic choice by individuals.

A WORD OF WARNING!

The thing about political cultures is that they are not eternal. Consensus on the basic elements can weaken, and without a common culture it is hard to maintain national unity. Once a substantial number of colonial Americans had begun to see themselves as a separate people and developed a distinctly

limited government: the Enlightenment idea that the power of government should be restricted to allow for maximum individual freedom

individualism: a political cultural emphasis on individual rights rather than on the collective whole

freedom: in American political culture, individual independence *from* government

equality: in American political culture, forms of political fairness that require minimal government intervention

American political culture, union with the British was hard to maintain. Not all Americans shared the desire to break from England, but eventually the cultural, political, and economic forces prevailed and they severed their ties.

THE UPSHOT

Political culture is a gift: it gives Americans the ability to disagree, within bounds, but also the ability to be united when necessary. The challenge is to make sure that differences among citizens do not become so extreme that the political culture can no longer contain them.

1.5 AMERICAN POLITICAL IDEOLOGIES

AH, YES. THOSE DIVISIONS.

Of course, within the cultural framework of the United States there is plenty of room for disagreement. How limited should government be? How much government regulation should be allowed? How much individualism should citizens endorse? Does government have any role in providing for freedom, education, and equality? Should strongly held ideas, ones that people believe are absolutely true, be enshrined in government policy, or should government allow the maximum range for individual conscience? How much freedom, equality, and democracy should people have, and what should government's role be in guaranteeing it?

The disagreements that citizens have about those sorts of questions are about the boundaries and meaning of the shared political culture. We call the competing narratives we create to explain those disagreements **ideologies**.

THE OLD LEFT–RIGHT DIVISION ON THE ECONOMY

The typical ideological division in the United States has been on the left–right economic dimension, with **conservatives** on the right calling for less regulation of the economy (lower taxes, freer trade, more competition, to name a few) and **liberals** on the left calling for more government regulation (like social welfare programs, universal health care, and free preschool programs).

Over the past century, that economic dimension emerged as the most salient because, in the years after the Great Depression of the 1930s, just making a living was a major concern for people.

. . . .

ideologies: competing narratives that explain various political disagreements

conservatives: Americans on the political right who believe in less regulation of the economy

liberals: Americans on the political left who believe in greater government regulation of the economy

MAKING IT MORE COMPLICATED—THE POLITICAL DIMENSION

Starting in the 1960s and 1970s, however, other noneconomic issues started to motivate voters—issues like racial desegregation; civil rights; women's rights, including reproductive rights; prayer in schools; and crime reduction.

These issues split Americans along a political dimension much like the vertical line we considered earlier, with some Americans saying that government should allow the maximum freedom for all people, regardless of race, gender, religion, or sexual orientation, and others saying it was government's job to enforce a proper, traditional social order.

When you combine the horizontal, economic ideological dimension with the vertical, political ideological dimension, you get four ideological categories that are important for understanding American politics today:

FIGURE IT!

1.4: AMERICAN IDEOLOGIES TODAY

Greater individual control over personal lives

ECONOMIC LIBERALS
- Favor social welfare, universal health care, maximum rights for all regardless of race, religion or creed, or sexual orientation

ECONOMIC CONSERVATIVES
- Favor lower taxes, limited government regulation, maximum rights for all regardless of race, religion or creed, or sexual orientation

Most Americans

SOCIAL LIBERALS
- Favor social welfare, universal health care, maximum rights for all including government action via affirmative action, censorship, and other policies to ensure social equality

SOCIAL CONSERVATIVES
- Favor lower taxes, limited government regulation, government enforcement of a traditional hierarchical social order and religious values

Greater governmental control over how goods are distributed

Greater individual control over how goods are distributed

Greater governmental control over personal lives

Let's take a closer look at each of these:

**Economic conservatives**. These are the people who believe in the narrative that the government that governs best, governs least. They have a fundamental distrust in the government's ability to solve complex problems (President Ronald Reagan once said that the scariest words in the English language were "I am from the government and I'm here to help") and a deep faith in individual ingenuity to do so. They favor getting government out of the boardroom (economic decisions) and out of the bedroom (decisions of personal morality).

In terms of policy, economic conservatives are close to being **libertarians** (those who believe in minimal government) when it comes to social issues. Consequently, they tend to favor policies like gun rights, reproductive rights, civil rights, assisted suicide, and legalized marijuana. They are equally libertarian when it comes to economic issues. Although they generally endorse taxation to provide basic police security and military defense, they are more likely to believe that government should leave many of the other things it currently does (collecting and doling out Social Security and health care benefits, road building, managing the penal system, space exploration, etc.) to the private sector. They are pro-immigration to add to the pool of workers and entrepreneurs. Most want only as much regulation of the economy as it would take to keep competition fair and the market from tanking.

**Economic liberals**. The economic liberal narrative is also founded on the notion that citizens should be able to decide how to live their lives. Where it diverges from the economic conservative narrative is, first, in seeing citizens not just as individuals but as members of groups, some of whom are often not treated equitably by society, and, second, in believing government action may be necessary for all people to reach their full potential. As you would guess, economic liberals don't distrust the government nearly as much as economic conservatives do. They see it as a tool that can be used wisely or foolishly.

Thus, they favor an expansion of civil rights protections—the elimination of racism and the expansion of immigration, women's rights, and gay

- -

economic conservatives: Americans who favor a strictly procedural government role in the economy and the social order

libertarians: Americans who favor a minimal government role in any sphere

economic liberals: Americans who favor an expanded government role in the economy but a limited role in the social order

rights. That means they oppose restrictions on voting rights, penal codes that disproportionately jail people of color, and amendments prohibiting reproductive rights or marriage equality. Economic liberals are very libertarian when it comes to whether individuals get to call their own shots, but their narrative says that for individuals to reach their potential, they might need a boost from the government.

Consequently, economic liberals favor economic policies to provide a basic standard of living to all individuals. They support Social Security, Medicare (health care for the elderly), and universal health care, although they disagree on the form it ought to take. They believe in free college education or at least in requiring favorable terms for student loans. They support free lunch programs, free preschools, and free prenatal care to be sure kids from all backgrounds get a good start in life. They are pro-immigration and pro-diversity for its own sake. They support environmental regulation and using government to provide infrastructure (roads, bridges, dams) to improve life and to provide jobs. Those farthest along the left continuum are referred to as **progressives**, or economic liberals who believe in an even stronger role for the state in creating equality.

\# **Social conservatives.** These people are economically conservative but are often not as far to the right on that continuum as economic conservatives. Many support Social Security and Medicare and even the Affordable Care Act ("Obamacare"), but they often see the allocation of those resources as having to do with "deservingness," where some have rightly earned those benefits and others have taken advantage of the system unfairly. What distinguishes these folks from most other Americans is that their narratives put a priority on government preserving a traditional social order. They see government playing a strong role in creating and enforcing laws that curtail social behaviors they view as corrosive to society.

For some people who have strong beliefs that their vision of the social order (that is, how people should live their lives) reflects absolute truth, it is not unreasonable that they would want to put that vision into law. Social conservatives include several groups who feel that way about their world view. Traditionally, evangelical Christians have believed that the United States is a Judeo-Christian nation (instead

- -

progressives: economic liberals who believe in a stronger role for the state in creating equality

social conservatives: Americans who endorse limited government control of the economy but considerable government intervention to realize a traditional social order; based on religious values and hierarchy rather than equality

of one based on religious freedom) and that its laws should flow from that tradition. Consistent with this perspective are the views that abortion and birth control should be outlawed, prayer should be allowed in school, and marriage equality should be illegal.

Non-Christians can also have concrete ideas about the way people should live. Those who believe that society has a natural hierarchy—whether one that puts men or whites at the top of the heap, or, often, both—also believe there is a particular order that the law should promote. Remember that social conservatives fall in the lower right quadrant—that is, in the less democratic, more authoritarian ideological category. Individual choice is less important than is following an authoritarian leader who endorses their views on the social order.

\#   **Social liberals**. This is a pretty small category in the United States. If you think about it, a country whose culture is in the upper right quadrant (economic conservatives) is less likely to have a lot of ideological commitment to a narrative that endorses both strong government responsibility for the economy and how people live their lives. Social liberals hold views like those of economic liberals on the economy—believing government should intervene to create more opportunity for all individuals and groups.

But social liberals also have concrete ideas about what they think is right, and they don't mind stepping on civil liberties if they need to in order to realize them. If speech is offensive, it should be silenced; if pornography encourages objectification of women, it should be censored. Social liberals also support a lot of science-based regulations that other groups might support including those who don't buy many elements of social liberal ideology. A wide swath of Americans accept environmental regulations or practices like requiring recycling or repurposing, all of which, after all, involve government telling people how to live their lives in accordance with a particular view of the world—probably because that view of the world is based on widely accepted science, not a particular religion or tradition. Similarly, people outside of this quadrant accept protective regulations like seat belt and helmet laws and food and drug regulations, even though these regulations infringe on individual

. . . .

social liberals: Americans who favor greater control of the economy and the social order to bring about greater equality and to regulate the effects of progress

liberties, because they accept as fact that they save people's lives and lower medical costs. Still, as a whole, the social liberal quadrant doesn't grab a lot of adherents because it pushes the limits of Americans' limited government, individualistic culture.

KEY POINT ❯ Political activists may be deeply wedded to their political beliefs. Surely you have that uncle who shows up at the Thanksgiving table firmly fixed in his beliefs and who makes everyone else painfully aware of them. The reason crotchety uncles stand out is that—as you can see in the central circle in the American ideologies graphic—most Americans are in the middle of the ideological scheme. They may be socially liberal on some issues, economically conservative on others. Politics is not equally salient, or relevant, to everyone's lives, so lots of people just ignore it until an election (or Thanksgiving) rolls around. It is true that in recent years Americans have gotten more tribal—more likely to want to hang out with other people who share their views—but for many people these categories are just not personally relevant.

In Chapter 7, on political parties and interest groups, we talk about where these groups fall along the contemporary political spectrum in the United States and how they got there. Here is the short version: At least since the Great Depression, Republicans have traditionally been the party of economic conservatives. Economic liberals were Democrats, the party of President Franklin Roosevelt, whose "New Deal" launched massive new social programs and projects to get the economy on its feet. Plenty of social conservatives followed Roosevelt into the New Deal, but in the 1960s and 1970s, when the Democrats became the party of civil rights under Lyndon Johnson, southern social conservatives split off to the Republican Party.

THE UPSHOT ❯ It's been an uneasy alliance for the Republicans, to house those with libertarian and authoritarian values in one party. They are still trying to find their way through the contradictions inherent in that pairing. Democrats have their own disputes, but they occur mostly within the upper left quadrant (economic liberals), not across quadrants like the Republicans. Theoretically, that should make disputes easier for Democrats to solve, and it's true that the party hasn't been torn apart by internal fighting since the 1970s. No parties are closely aligned with the social liberals. The closest is probably the Green Party, although what they stand for seems to vary with the person heading the ticket.

GEN GAP!

HOW OUR BIRTH YEAR AFFECTS OUR POLITICS

With apologies to The Who (a brilliant rock group prominent from the mid-1960s until the early 1980s), in this series of boxes in each chapter we are talkin' 'bout *your* generation.

Why? Because opinions about public issues are distinctly and measurably different among members of different **generations**—that is, people who were born within the same general time period and share life experiences that help shape their political views. Knowing how different generations think about political issues gives us insight into why certain people are likely to vote the way they do, why politicians make different kinds of policy appeals to different groups, and even what the future of American politics might look like.

Knowing how your own generation experiences American politics can help place your own values and opinions among your peers.

There is no universal agreement on what the political generations are—the exact year they start and when they end. Members of the Greatest Generation fought in World War II, the Silent Generation built the country to postwar prosperity, the Baby Boomers were the hippies and the people who hated the hippies, Gen Xers were the ones without a name who came after the Boomers, and the Millennials (most of you probably fit here or in the next group) were the ones born from about 1980 to the mid-1990s. The post-Millennials, or iGen, or Gen Z, are those of you just picking up where the Millennials left off without a clear identity, except, perhaps, for the distinction that you are the first generation to have lived your whole life with a screen in your hand.

Who You Are: Generations Defined (by Pew Research Center)

Take a minute to study the graphs below and think about the major differences you spot.

One of the reasons the generations have such different opinions is that they live in different worlds. The data in the next graph show that the life of a person aged 25 to 34 has not improved in material ways in the past forty years—and in some ways it is substantially worse. Life for some young Americans must feel

generations: groups of people born within the same general time period who share life experiences that help shape their political views

like it did for Alice in Wonderland: "it takes all the running you can do, to keep in the same place."

BREAKDOWN OF HOW PEW DEFINES EACH GENERATION

GENERATION	BORN	AGE IN 2018	PERCENTAGE OF ADULT POPULATION
Post-Millennials	1997 through the present	18–21	5%
Millennials	1981–1996	22–37	28%
Gen X	1965–1980	38–53	26%
Baby Boomers	1946–1964	54–72	29%
Silent Generation and Greatest Generation	1901–1945	73 and older	11%

FIGURE IT!

1.5: THE NATION'S GROWING DIVERSITY REFLECTED IN ITS YOUNGER GENERATIONS

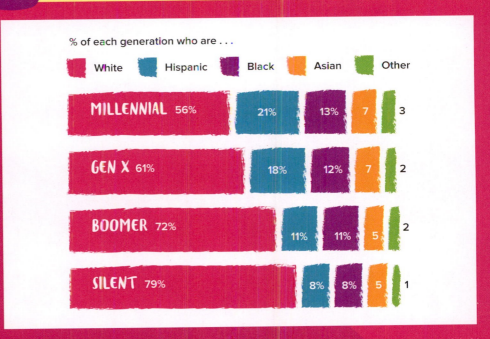

% of each generation who are . . .

White   Hispanic   Black   Asian   Other

MILLENNIAL 56%   21%   13%   7   3

GEN X 61%   18%   12%   7   2

BOOMER 72%   11%   11%   5   2

SILENT 79%   8%   8%   5   1

Source: "The Generation Gap in American Politics." Pew Research Center, Washington, D.C. (March 01, 2018) http://www.people-press.org/wp-content/uploads/sites/4/2018/03/03-01-18-Generations-release.pdf

1.6: POLITICAL IDEOLOGY VARIES ACROSS THE GENERATIONS AND OVER TIME

% with political values that are . . .

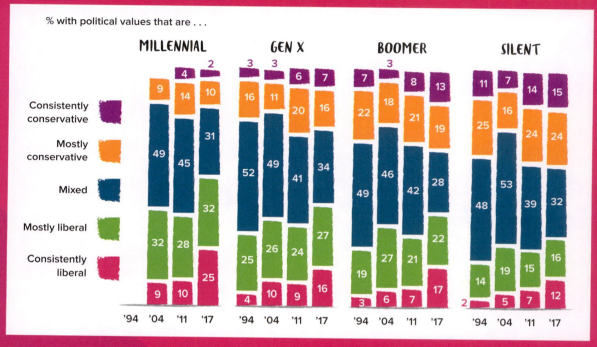

Source: Pew Research Center, The Generation Gap in American Politics, March 1, 2018, http://www.people-press.org/2018/03/01/the-generation-gap-in-american-politics/030118_o_6/ and http://www.people-press.org/2018/03/01/the-generation-gap-in-american-politics/030118_o_5/.

Notes: Whites, blacks, Asians, and other/multiple races include only non-Hispanics. Hispanics are of any race. Asians include Pacific Islanders. Figures may not add to 100 due to rounding. In these charts, Silent and Greatest Generation are grouped together.

TAKEAWAYS

→ **America is becoming more diverse.** Whites have gone from making up 79 percent of the adult population to only 56 percent. Pew projects that by 2065 there will be no single racial or ethnic majority in the United States. How is that likely to change power politics in the US?

→ **Younger generations are increasingly diverse, but less well off financially**, less likely to be married, and less likely to own a home. What does that mean for them down the line?

→ Pew projects **Millennials will be the largest generation in 2019**. How will a country dominated by Millennials differ from one led by Boomers?

→ While older generations tend to be more conservative and have shown little ideological change over time, **Gen Xers and Millennials especially have gotten increasingly more liberal in the past few years**. In what ways might being liberal, an ideology that sees a role for government in improving people's standards of living, be tied to the diversity and socioeconomic plight of younger Americans? How might it reflect their diversity?

1.6 POLITICAL NARRATIVES AND THE MEDIA

THE INTERSECTION OF POLITICAL NARRATIVES AND MEDIATION

This section of the chapter is about the power of narratives, but it is also about the ways we receive them and create them—the channels through which they are disseminated to us and by us. It is about the media through which information passes.

MEDIATION?

Just as a medium is a person through whom some people try to communicate with those who have died, **media** (the plural of medium) are channels of communication. The integrity of the medium is critical. A scam artist might make money off the desire of grieving people to contact a lost loved one by making up the information she passes on. People in power might tell narratives motivated by greed and the wish for personal glory.

Think about water running through a pipe. Maybe the pipe is made of lead, or is rusty, or has leaks. Depending on the integrity of the pipe, the water we get will be toxic, or colored, or limited.

KEY POINT

In the same way, the narratives and information we get can be altered by the way they are mediated by the channels, or the media, through which we receive them.

CONTROLLING THE NARRATIVE = POWER

In every one of the political-economic systems we have been discussing, people with opposing views struggle mightily to control the political narrative about who should have power, how it should be used, and to what end. Controlling the political narrative can give people a great deal of authority over others.

HOW POLITICAL NARRATIVES WORK IN NON-DEMOCRACIES

In authoritarian governments, the narrative is not open to debate. The rulers set the narrative and control the flow of information so that it supports their version of why they should have power. Subjects of these governments accept the narrative, either because they haven't been exposed to alternatives in the absence of free media or communication with the outside world (think North Korea) or out of fear (think Russia). Authoritarian rulers often use punishment to coerce uncooperative subjects into obedience.

MEDIATING POLITICAL NARRATIVES IN THE PRELITERATE AGE

Authoritarianism used to be a lot easier to pull off. In the Middle Ages and earlier, when few people could read, maintaining a single narrative about power that enforced authoritarian rule was relatively simple. For instance, as we see in the next chapter, the narrative of the divine right of kings kept monarchs in Europe on their thrones by declaring that those rulers were God's representatives on earth.

media: channels of communication

Because most people then were illiterate, that narrative was passed to people through select and powerful channels that could shape and influence it. It was *mediated* by the human equivalent of the pipes we mentioned earlier. Information flowed mostly through medieval clergy and monarchs, *the very people who had a vested interest in getting people to believe it.*

Following the development of the printing press in 1439, more people gained literacy. Information could be mediated independently of those in power, and competing narratives could grab a foothold. Martin Luther promoted the narrative behind the Protestant Reformation (1517–1648) to weaken the power of the Catholic Church. The European Age of Enlightenment (1685–1815) gave voice to the multiple narratives about power that weakened the hold of the traditional, authoritarian monarch.

THE NARRATIVES OF CLASSICAL LIBERALISM AND THE FREE FLOW OF INFORMATION

The narratives of **classical liberalism** that emerged from the Enlightenment emphasized individual rights, and non-authoritarianism. (*Note:* "liberalism" in this context does not mean the same as "liberalism" today.)

One of the key classical liberal narratives was that of the **social contract**, a story that said power is not derived from God, but from the consent of the governed. Philosopher John Locke's version of the social contract was that people have natural rights and give up some of those in order to have the convenience of government. However, they retain enough of those rights to rebel against that government if it fails to protect them. In order for it to work, the social contract requires that people have the freedom to criticize the government (that is, to create counternarratives) and also the protection of the channels through which information and narratives could flow (like a press free of influence by those in power).

As we will see in the next chapter, Thomas Jefferson was clearly influenced by Locke's work. The Declaration of Independence is itself a founding narrative of the rights of Americans: it tells a story about how those rights were violated by the British, and was designed to combat the British narrative that America should remain part of its colonial empire.

- -

classical liberalism: an Enlightenment philosophy emphasizing individual freedom and self-rule

social contract: the idea that power is not derived from God but instead comes from and is limited by the consent of the governed, who can revolt against the government they contract with if their rights are not protected if the contract is not kept

HOW WERE NARRATIVES MEDIATED AT THE FOUNDING?

> Even at the time of the founding, literacy among average citizens was very limited. Political elites still played a major role in mediating information, but new channels also started to play a part—newspapers, pastors, and publicans all began to shape narratives.

Even though Americans today still largely adhere to the basic governing narrative the founders promoted, the country is now light years removed from their era, when communication was limited by illiteracy and the scarcity of channels through which it could pass.

AND TODAY?

> Consider this timeline of the development of the media through which we get information, receive narratives, and send out our own information.

1.7: MEDIA TIMELINE

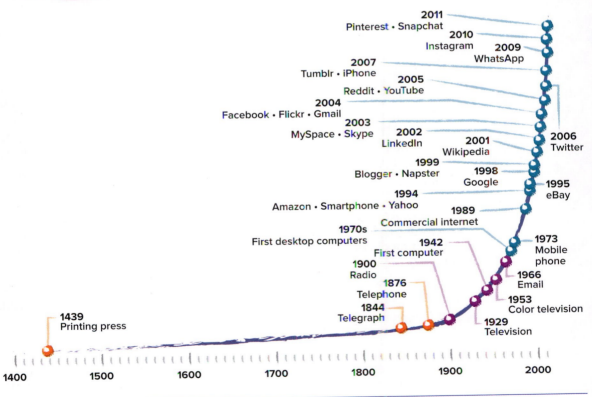

KEY POINT

> A revolution like the one fought by the Americans against the British would look entirely different in today's highly mediated culture. *But remember, it is because of the revolution they fought and the narrative of a free press that followed (and of course enormous technological development) that the mediated world we live in today is even possible.* It is not possible in places like North Korea that isolate their subjects from information, or places like Russia that weaponize social media and kill journalists who are critical of the government.

LIVING IN OUR MEDIATED WORLD

> Unlike the founders, certainly, but even unlike most of the people currently running this country (who are, let's face it, kind of old), people born in this century are almost all digital natives. They have been born in an era in which not only are most people hooked up to electronic media, but they also live their lives partly in cyberspace as well as in "real space." For many of us, the lives we live are almost entirely mediated. That is, most of our relationships, our education, our news, our travel, our sustenance, our purchases, our daily activities, our job seeking—our very sense of ourselves—are influenced by, experienced through, or shared via electronic media. If not for Apple, Google, Facebook, and Amazon, how different would our lives be? How much more directly would we need to interact?

THE UPSHOT

We are conducting our lives through channels that, like the pipe we mentioned earlier, may be made of lead, may be rusty, or may be full of holes. When we do an online search, certain links are on top according to the calculations made by the search engine we use. When we shop online, certain products are urged on us (and then haunt our online life). When we travel, certain flights and hotels are flagged, and when we use social media, certain posts appear while others don't. No one checks very hard to be sure that the information they receive isn't emerging from the cyber equivalent of lead pipes.

Living mediated lives has all kinds of implications for everyday living and loving and working. The implications we care about here are the political implications for our roles as citizens—the ones to do with how we exercise and are impacted by power. We will be turning to these implications again and again throughout this book.

· ·

digital natives: people who have been born in an era in which not only are most people hooked up to electronic media, but they also live their lives partly in cyberspace as well as in "real space"

1.7 MEDIATED CITIZENSHIP

IMAGINE
@JMAD ON
INSTA, #CREATING
A REPUBLIC
#WRITING THE
CONSTITUTION
#GROUP WORK
SUCKS

Being a citizen in a mediated world is just flat-out different from being one in the world in which James Madison wrote the Constitution. It's the genius of the Constitution that it has been able to navigate the transition successfully, so far.

After the Constitution had been written, so the story goes, a woman accosted Benjamin Franklin as he was leaving the building where the founders were working. "What have you created?" she asked. "A republic, madam, if you can keep it," he replied.

The mediated world we live in gives us myriad new ways to keep the republic and also some pretty high-tech ways to lose it. That puts a huge burden on us as **mediated citizens**—as people who are constantly receiving information through channels that can and do shape our political views—and also opens up a world of opportunity.

Among the things we are divided on in this country is what it means to be a citizen. We know what citizens are: they are people who live under a non-authoritarian government that gives them rights to push back against government action and even to overthrow it if it doesn't protect their rights. Anyone born in the United States is a citizen, as are people born to Americans living abroad. There are also various ways for those not born here or to American parents to become **naturalized citizens** if they arrive legally and follow the procedure that the law lays out.

MULTIPLE MEANINGS OF CITIZENSHIP

But once you are a citizen, born or naturalized, what is your role? James Madison had ideas about this. He thought people would be so filled with what he called "republican virtue" that they would put country ahead of self. (Again notice that "republican" does not mean what it means today.)

mediated citizens: people who are constantly receiving information through multiple channels that can and do shape their political views but who also have the ability to use those channels to create their own narratives

naturalized citizens: people who become U.S. citizens through a series of procedures that the law lays out

That is, they would readily put aside their self-interest to advance the public interest. As we will see in the next chapter, this public-interested citizenship proved not to be the rule, much to Madison's disappointment. Instead most people demonstrated self-interested citizenship, trying to use the system to get whatever they could for themselves. This was a dilemma for Madison because he was designing a constitution that depended on the nature of the people being governed.

Today we have that same conflict. There are plenty of people who put country first—who enlist in the armed services, sometimes giving their lives for their nation, who go into law enforcement or teaching or other lower paying careers because they want to serve. There are people who cheerfully pay their taxes because it's a privilege to live in a free democracy where you can climb up the ladder of opportunity. Especially in moments of national trouble—when the World Trade Center was attacked in September 2001, for instance—Americans willingly help their fellow citizens.

At the same time, the day-to-day business of life turns most people inward. Many care about self and family and friends, but most don't have the energy or inclination to get beyond that. President John Kennedy challenged his "fellow Americans" to "ask not what your country can do for you but what you can do for your country," but only a rare few have the time or motivation to take up that challenge.

WHAT DOES CITIZENSHIP LOOK LIKE IN TODAY'S MEDIATED WORLD?

The world today is not the same world that Madison wrote about or designed a government for. Mediated citizens experience the world through multiple channels of information and interaction. That doesn't change whether citizens are self-interested or public-interested, but it does give them more opportunities and raise more potential hazards for being both.

Many older Americans who are not digital natives nonetheless experience political life through television or through web surfing and commenting, usually anonymously. This is not always a positive addition to our civil discourse, but they are trying to adapt. You may have grandparents who fit this description. They want to know why you are not on Facebook.

But younger, more media savvy digital natives—iGens, Millennials, GenXers, and even some tech-savvy Baby Boomers—not only have access

. . . .

public-interested citizenship: citizens who put country ahead of self by putting aside their self-interest to advance the public interest

self-interested citizenship: citizens who are focused on their personal lives and use the political system to maximize their interests

to traditional media, if they choose, but also are accustomed to interacting, conducting friendships and family relationships, and generally attending to the details of their lives through electronic channels. Their digital selves exist in networks of friends and acquaintances who take for granted that they can communicate in seconds. They certainly get their news digitally and increasingly organize, register to vote, enlist in campaigns, and call each other to action that way. We will be following these new patterns of mediated citizenship in the Generation Gap (*Gen Gap*) boxes you will find in each chapter.

THE HAZARDS OF DIGITAL PARTICIPATION

In fact, **hashtag activism**, the forming of social movements through viral calls to act politically—whether to march, to boycott, to contact politicians, or to vote—has become common enough that organizers warn that action has to go beyond cyberspace to reach the real world or it will have limited impact. #BlackLivesMatter, #ItGetsBetter, and #NeverAgain are three very different, very viral, very successful ways of using all the channels available to us to call attention to a problem and propose solutions.

An intensely mediated world does not automatically produce public-interested citizens. People can easily remain self-interested in this world. We can custom program our social media to give us only news and information that confirms what we already think. We can live in an **information bubble** where our narratives get reinforced by everything we see and hear. That makes us more or less sitting ducks for whatever media narrative is directed our way, whether from inside an online media source or from a foreign power that uses social media to influence an election, as the Russians did in 2016. Without opening ourselves up to multiple information and action channels, we can live an unexamined mediated life.

AND THE OPPORTUNITIES . . .

But mediated citizenship also creates enormous opportunities that the founders never dreamed of. Truth to tell, Madison wouldn't have been all that thrilled about the multiple ways to be political that the mediated citizen possesses. For Madison, even public-interested citizens should be seen on election day but not heard most of the time, precisely because he thought we would push our own interests and destabilize the system. He was reassured by the fact that it would take days for an express letter trying to create a dissenting political organization to reach Georgia from Maine. Our mediated world has blown that reassuring prospect to smithereens.

hashtag activism: the forming of social movements through viral calls to act politically

information bubble: a closed cycle in which all the information we get reinforces the information we already have, solidifying our beliefs without reference to outside reality checks

Here's just one example of how mediated citizenship has upset the founders' applecart. At a time when basic political **norms**—the unspoken, unwritten ideas that support the U.S. Constitution and give structure to democratic government—are being challenged as never before, millions of high school students and their supporters recently took to the streets to challenge one of the richest, most powerful groups in America for control of the national narrative on gun safety.

As these young people transfer that battle from the street to the ballot box, they are following in the footsteps of multiple groups who have fought for their rights in American politics. The U.S. government was not born perfect, but it has proved over time to be an ideal open to the efforts of its citizens to perfect it, to become closer to the inspiring image that President Reagan liked to quote: "the shining city upon a hill."

Whether you agree with the students' political activism or not (and there are many people on both sides of the issue), the fact that *high school* students could organize and execute such a movement is a pretty impressive testimony to their own political and digital savviness. It also demonstrates that despite the founders' misgivings about popular government, they gave us a constitutional framework that is strong, adaptable, long lived, and open to citizen action. It has seen the country through a lot.

THE UPSHOT

As the ability of ordinary citizens to create narratives has grown and as the media disseminate them widely, we regularly see and have to evaluate or even participate in these battles about issues that are deeply important to Americans. Throughout this book we will encounter conflicting narratives that define some of our greatest divisions. Read these narratives carefully. Would you frame any of them differently?

Mediated citizens are not only TV-watching couch surfers in the information bubble receiving and passing on narratives from powerful people. We can be the creators and disseminators of our own narratives, something that would have terrified the old monarchs comfortably ensconced in their divine-right narrative. Even the founders would have been extremely nervous about what the masses might get up to.

As mediated citizens, we have unprecedented access to power, but we are also targets of the use of unprecedented power—attempts to shape our views and control our experiences. That means it is up to us to pay critical attention to what is happening in the world around us.

· ·

norms: unspoken, unwritten ideas that support the U.S. Constitution and give structure to democratic government

Big Think

→ Have the advances in media made us freer or less free to create our own stories?

→ Can you make a case for authoritarian over democratic values? What would it look like?

→ What kinds of things could destroy a political culture, and what would be the result?

Key Terms

CONCEPTS

anarchy (p. 5)

authoritarian capitalism (p. 10)

authoritarian governments (p. 4)

authority (p. 3)

capitalism (p. 7)

capitalist democracy (p. 9)

classical liberalism (p. 24)

democracy (p. 4)

economics (p. 6)

equality (p. 13)

freedom (p. 13)

generations (p. 20)

government (p. 3)

hashtag activism (p. 29)

ideologies (p. 14)

individualism (p. 13)

information bubble (p. 29)

laissez-faire capitalism (p. 7)

limited government (p. 13)

market (p. 7)

media (p. 23)

non-authoritarian governments (p. 4)

norms (p. 30)

political culture (p. 11)

political narrative (p. 2)

politics (p. 2)

popular sovereignty (p. 5)

public-interested citizenship (p. 28)

regulated capitalism (p. 7)

rules (p. 2)

self-interested citizenship (p. 28)

social contract (p. 24)

socialism (p. 6)

totalitarianism (p. 10)

KEY INDIVIDUALS AND GROUPS

citizens (p. 4)

conservatives (p. 14)

digital natives (p. 26)

economic conservatives (p. 16)

economic liberals (p. 16)

liberals (p. 14)

libertarians (p. 16)

mediated citizens (p. 27)

naturalized citizens (p. 27)

progressives (p. 17)

social conservatives (p. 17)

social liberals (p. 18)

subjects (p. 4)

#2 THE UNITED STATES' FOUNDING

In this chapter:

2.1 Introduction to THE FOUNDING

BEING A COLONY—
THE GOOD AND
THE BAD

As we can see in Figure 2.1, almost all of the territory in North America was held by European colonial powers prior to independence. To be a colony meant not only being a political subject of the ruling country—England, Spain, France, or others—it also meant being economically dependent on it, and having cultural ties to it as well.

The economic relationship between mother country and colonies was called **mercantilism**. In our case, England provided protection and settlement costs to the colonists, and the colonies sent resources and a cut of the profits from their own trade back to the mother country. Meanwhile, the colonists were denied access to the lucrative markets in which England competed.

THE ULTIMATE POLITICAL ENFORCER

England also had a political culture that understood power to be vested in the king because he was God's representative on earth—a theory known as the **divine right of kings**. Under that narrative, revolution against the king was also a sin against God. It put a great burden on the colonists to come up with a counternarrative to justify independence that didn't make them all sinners.

The colonists originally bought into both the economic and world views of the British—most of them were born British subjects after all. But after living more or less on their own for years, they began to develop an idiosyncratic identity and culture, and their economic and political views began to diverge.

As the American colonists began to see themselves more and more as a separate political entity, independence started to look like a desirable and viable option.

WHY THE COLONISTS WANTED INDEPENDENCE

Essentially there were three reasons the colonies wanted to be independent of England:

→ Political reasons ("You aren't the boss of us.")

→ Economic reasons ("We'll make more money if we can compete with England and England doesn't take its cut of our profits.")

→ Cultural reasons ("We have a new way of looking at government and power, and you, England, are stuck in yesterday's narrative.")

2.1: AMERICA'S BABY PICTURE

Map legend:
- Land claimed by England, 1750
- Land claimed by France, 1750
- Land claimed by Spain, 1750
- Unorganized territory

CANADA

LONDON ENGLAND 3800 MI

ME (Mass.)
NH
MA
NY
RI
CT
PA
NJ
DE
MD
VA
NC
SC
GA

ORIGINAL 13 COLONIES

FRENCH LOUISIANA

California

New Mexico

MEXICO

Texas

Florida

PACIFIC OCEAN

ATLANTIC OCEAN

Gulf of Mexico

THREE THINGS TO NOTICE ABOUT THIS MAP

→ **How many countries claimed land on the continent.** A claim to independence by the thirteen British colonies could have repercussions for the French and the Spanish if their colonists decided they wanted independence too.

→ **How long the British colonies had been in place.** The colonists had been on their own long enough to start to form their own political culture and identity.

→ **How far away from England (and from each other) the colonies were.** In particular, think about how difficult communication must have been without modern technology.

IN A NUTSHELL

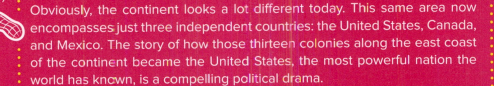

Obviously, the continent looks a lot different today. This same area now encompasses just three independent countries: the United States, Canada, and Mexico. The story of how those thirteen colonies along the east coast of the continent became the United States, the most powerful nation the world has known, is a compelling political drama.

2.2 THE SOCIAL CONTRACT

WAKING UP TO A WORLD VIEW OF INDIVIDUAL RIGHTS AND SELF-RULE

Over time, the American colonists grew impatient with a political system that allowed them minimal input, and an economic system that limited their ability to accrue wealth. But more than anything, while the British were secure in a political culture based on the divine right of kings and mercantilism, the Americans were developing a new way of looking at the world.

In that new world view, derived from the European Enlightenment, power was understood to be held by all citizens, each of whom gave up some of their rights to government in exchange for the right to use the power

mercantilism: an economic system that sees trade as the basis of the accumulation of wealth

divine right of kings: the political culture that understood power to be vested in the king because he was God's representative on earth

they retained safely and securely. The new government was based on the consent of those governed. If government didn't protect the secure use of their remaining rights, they had the right to rebel and form a new government. This idea was called the **social contract**.

2.1: THE SKIMMABLE POLITICAL ENLIGHTENMENT: HOW DOES THE DIVINE RIGHT OF KINGS COMPARE WITH THE SOCIAL CONTRACT?

Two ideas about how government works	The Divine Right of Kings	The Social Contract
Power is held by . . .	The monarch	The people
Power is given by . . .	God	Nature (natural rights)
Government is formed by . . .	Divine right	Consent of the people
How much power is retained by the people?	None	Considerable
What happens if government doesn't protect people's rights?	Doesn't arise; subjects don't have any rights to protect	Citizens can revolt and form (by consent) a new government

The idea of the social contract evolved between the writings of two British philosophers. Thomas Hobbes's (1588–1679) version had a fundamentally different rationale for power than the divine right of kings. He thought free men had the right to subject themselves to a ruler who would protect them. But that did not in the end change the result for most subjects, since Hobbes envisioned an all-powerful government whose subjects had no rights to push back against its power. John Locke (1632–1704) wrote closer to the time that the American founders were contemplating independence, and his ideas were hugely popular. It was Locke who introduced the idea

social contract: the idea that power is not derived from God but instead comes from and is limited by the consent of the governed, who can revolt against the government they contract with if their rights are not protected if the contract is not kept

John Locke: the British philosopher who introduced the idea that the social contract was conditional on the government's protection of rights and could be revoked if the government failed to protect those rights

that the social contract was conditional on the government's protection of rights and that it could be revoked if the government failed to hold up its end of the bargain.

2.3 THE DECLARATION OF INDEPENDENCE

THIS IS WHERE THOMAS JEFFERSON COMES IN

> When the founders picked Thomas Jefferson to write the **Declaration of Independence**, he rested his argument on the ideas of John Locke. If you read Locke's *Second Treatise on Government*, you can see the influence clearly. The following covers the highlights.

FOUR THINGS TO KNOW ABOUT THE DECLARATION OF INDEPENDENCE

> \# The Declaration of Independence is a political document about changing the rules for what makes power legitimate and who should hold it.

\# By relying on the social contract, the Declaration claimed that Americans had **inalienable rights** that they could not give up to government. In doing this, it created the modern notion of *citizens*—people who can claim rights against the government—distinguished from British *subjects*—people who retained no rights against the government at all.

   \# It blamed George III, the British monarch (who was still immersed in a political culture based on the divine right of kings), for breaking a contract he knew nothing about, rather than Parliament, which was responsible for many of the "crimes" they assigned to George. They were trying to discredit the idea of a monarch but knew they would have a "parliament" of some sort and so tried to preserve its legitimacy.

\# Not everyone in the new country was a citizen. Women, African Americans (most of whom were slaves), and Native Americans were not endowed with inalienable rights. The fights of these groups to be included as citizens are the civil rights movements documented in Chapter 3.

DIG DEEPER

Read the WHOLE Declaration of Independence.

Go to **edge.sagepub.com/ dig-deeper**

. . . .

Declaration of Independence: the political document that dissolved the colonial ties between the United States and Britain

inalienable rights: rights that we are born with, that cannot be taken away from us, and that we cannot sell

2.2: THE SKIMMABLE DECLARATION OF INDEPENDENCE

Section of the Declaration	How Jefferson Said It	What It Means
The part everyone remembers	"When in the Course of human events, it becomes necessary for one people to dissolve the political bands which have connected them with another. . . . We hold these truths to be self-evident, that all men are created equal, that they are endowed by their Creator with certain unalienable Rights, that among these are Life, Liberty and the pursuit of Happiness."	Introducing the idea that there is a new paradigm in town and that it is *not* the divine right of kings.
The statement of the contract	"That to secure these rights, Governments are instituted" . . . "That whenever any Form of Government becomes destructive of these ends, it is the Right of the People to alter or abolish it, and to institute new Government. . . ."	Government exists to protect our rights, and if it doesn't, the deal is off.
The public relations paragraph	"Prudence, indeed, will dictate that Governments long established should not be changed for light and transient causes. . . ."	Convincing the world we have no alternative and they should stick with us since we pose no threat to them.
Proof that George III has broken a contract he likely had never heard of	"The history of the present King of Great Britain is a history of repeated injuries and usurpations, all having in direct object the establishment of an absolute Tyranny over these States. To prove this, let the facts be submitted to a candid world."	Out of a total of 1,337 words, 866 are used to detail the sins of the king. To strengthen their case they threw in some things that were in the king's normal job description, and a few things that were actually done by Parliament.
Disclaimer: This is not our fault.	"Our repeated Petitions have been answered only by repeated injury. . . . We have warned them from time to time of attempts by their legislature to extend an unwarrantable jurisdiction over us. We have reminded them of the circumstances of our emigration and settlement here. We have appealed to their native justice and magnanimity, and we have conjured them by the ties of our common kindred to disavow these usurpations, which, would inevitably interrupt our connections and correspondence."	We tried over and over again to warn Britain, but they wouldn't listen.

(Continued)

(Continued)

Section of the Declaration	How Jefferson Said It	What It Means
The final declaration of independence from Great Britain	"That these United Colonies are, and of Right ought to be Free and Independent States; that they are Absolved from all Allegiance to the British Crown, and that all political connection between them and the State of Great Britain, is and ought to be totally dissolved. . . . And for the support of this Declaration, with a firm reliance on the protection of divine Providence, we mutually pledge to each other our Lives, our Fortunes and our sacred Honor."	We have no choice, and, besides, God is on our side.

THE UPSHOT

The ideas contained in the Declaration of Independence sparked a war. The Revolutionary War era lasted from about 1765 to 1783, although the first shots against the British were not fired until 1775.

After the former colonists won, they had the job of creating a new government, just as the social contract had dictated.

2.4 THE ARTICLES OF CONFEDERATION

FIRST, FORM A NEW GOVERNMENT

Declaring independence and winning a war against an established major world power were no simple tasks, but they were only the beginning of the political challenges the Americans faced. Creating a new government from scratch is a remarkable task, and it took more than one try to get it right.

After the Revolution, America was a mix of thirteen states, big and small, slave owning and not. Having just overthrown a king, the one thing they had in common was a dedication to their own sovereignty and a commitment to the idea that any national power should be limited.

Some of the founders, like James Madison, had a lingering hope that if the powers of a national government were kept to a minimum, people would be activated by what they called **republican virtue** to act in the public interest without coercion by a strong government. That hope was doomed.

WHAT DOES A CONSTITUTION HAVE TO INCLUDE?

The founders' main task was to write a constitution, or rule book, that would determine how the new government was to function, who would have power, and how that power would be limited. Although there were colonial and state constitutions, the founders had no immediate example of a national constitution—England had and still has an unwritten constitution, and they didn't want to follow the British model in any case. The founders faced a steep learning curve, but we in turn can learn a lot from the way they pulled it off.

The story of the writing of the Constitution is the story of clashes of interest, power struggles, and **compromise**, a word we will be hearing many times. The document that resulted is a remarkable one. It's not perfect, but neither is it static—it carries within it the means to improvement through its amendment process.

ARTICLES OF CONFEDERATION

The first U.S. constitution, adopted in 1777, was called the **Articles of Confederation**. But because the states viewed themselves as sovereign and didn't want to give up their power, they decided to limit their new constitution to a "firm league of friendship" among the states, rather than being a full union.

HOW DID THAT WORK OUT FOR THEM?

Not very well, actually. As their name suggests, the Articles established a **confederation**, which is a form of government in which all the power lies with the local units, in this case, the states. The national government had only the power the states decided to allow it, and since they were unwilling to allow any entity to have power over them, that meant not very much.

. . . .

republican virtue: the idea that citizens would act in the public interest without coercion by a strong government

compromise: the act of giving up something you want in order to get something else you want more; an exercise in determining and trading off priorities

Articles of Confederation: the first constitution of the United States, adopted in 1777, creating an association of states with a weak central government

confederation: a form of government in which all the power lies with the local units; in the American case, that's the states

DIG DEEPER

Read the Articles of Confederation.

Go to **edge.sagepub.com/dig-deeper**

Economic troubles, drought, and crop failures meant heavy demands for relief were placed on the state governments. The solution—cancellation of debts and contracts—rocked the country's economic stability, and the national government didn't have enough power to steady it.

Here are some other things the national government was not allowed to do under the Articles of Confederation:

\# Draft soldiers (making it difficult to coordinate a response to a threat from a foreign power)

\# Tax citizens (making the government totally dependent on the states for funds)

\# Regulate interstate commerce (leaving the states to create their own markets, economic rules, etc.)

\# Establish a central monetary system (requiring Americans to change their currency if they lived in Virginia but wanted to do business in Maryland)

Historians call the era after the American Revolution "the critical period" because the new government was so close to collapse. Economic chaos and Shays's Rebellion—a march of angry farmers demanding debt relief in western Massachusetts—drove some of the founders to meet in Annapolis in 1786 to discuss fixing the dysfunctional Articles.

TREASON!! Soon some at the gathering in Annapolis decided the Articles were too broken to fix, and they set out to create a whole new U.S. Constitution instead. Under the Articles, this was illegal (just as it would be today if a group of leaders decided to dispense with our current Constitution), and it angered many of the attendees. Some of them declared the undertaking treason (which it technically was), before walking out and later even refusing to sign the new document.

2.5 THE CONSTITUTIONAL CONVENTION

HOW IT STARTED Clearly, if some of the attendees were accusing the others of treason, the **Constitutional Convention** of 1787 was not off to a great start. In fact, while

Constitutional Convention: the assembly of fifty-five delegates in the summer of 1787 to recast the Articles of Confederation; the result was the U.S. Constitution

they were fighting the British, the colonists had been united, more or less. In the absence of a common enemy, all kinds of fault lines started to show among the states that were deeply divided, and not for the last time. (This was not because we were special, by the way—it's a common political tendency to watch for, even in much smaller groups).

THE FIRST BIG DIVIDE

> The biggest fracture came between groups known as the **Federalists** and the **Anti-Federalists**.

FOUR THINGS TO KNOW ABOUT THE FEDERALISTS

> \# The Federalists were those who wanted a stronger national government (though not *too* strong) to be able to handle crises like the one that had erupted under the Articles.

\# They were mostly representatives of large states who felt they could control government power so they were less threatened by the prospect of a vigorous government.

\# They came to be known as Federalists because they preferred to get rid of the confederal system of the Articles, in which the states ultimately held the power, and move to a federal system, where power would be shared between states and the national government.

\# The plan for the new constitution that they favored was called the **Virginia Plan**, a comparatively robust but limited government whose signature institution would be a **bicameral legislature** (meaning it would have two chambers) where representation in *both* chambers would be based on population and taxes paid. Big states win!

FOUR THINGS TO KNOW ABOUT THE ANTI-FEDERALISTS

> \# The Anti-Federalists were against a robust national government because they believed power was best contained when you could keep an eye on it (that is, at the state level).

\# Their preference would have been to tweak the Articles to make them more effective.

Federalists: supporters of the Constitution who favored a strong central government

Anti-Federalists: advocates of states' rights who opposed the Constitution

Virginia Plan: a proposal at the Constitutional Convention that congressional representation be based on population, thus favoring the large states

bicameral legislature: a lawmaking body with two chambers

\#   Mostly representatives of smaller states, they feared a stronger government would roll over them and the big states would always get their way.

\#   The new plan they favored was called the **New Jersey Plan**. It looked like a slightly upgraded Articles of Confederation—a single chamber of the legislature in which every state cast one vote, with a weak executive and a nonexistent court system, but some additional powers for the national government, like the regulation of interstate commerce. Small states hold their own against larger ones.

THE GREAT COMPROMISE

The so-called **Great Compromise** was "great" in the sense that it worked to bring the two sides together, but it was greater for the Federalists than the Anti-Federalists because they got more of what they wanted. The compromise they agreed on called for a bicameral legislature that split the difference between the two sides: representation in the House of Representatives is based on a state's population, but in the Senate every state gets two members. Much of the rest of the compromise looked a lot like the Virginia Plan.

THE SECOND BIG DIVIDE—NORTH VS. SOUTH

Once the outlines of the Great Compromise were clear and it was apparent that representation in one house would be based on population, the question arose of who would be counted as part of that population. The southern states, in order to get more legislative representatives, wanted to include slaves in their population total, even though they were unwilling to give slaves any political power or count them as citizens. The North, not surprisingly, refused to let the South count slaves at all.

The compromise that solved this dispute, the **Three-Fifths Compromise**, is the most disgraceful portion of the Constitution, although it allowed

New Jersey Plan: a proposal at the Constitutional Convention that congressional representation be equal, thus favoring the small states

Great Compromise: the constitutional solution to congressional representation: equal votes in the Senate, votes by population in the House

Three-Fifths Compromise: the formula for counting five slaves as three people for purposes of representation; reconciled northern and southern factions at the Constitutional Convention

ratification to go forward. It says that to determine representation, the population count would be made "by adding to the whole Number of Free persons . . . three fifths of all other persons." Sometimes compromise means you may have to do something against your principles in order to advance your goals.

2.3: THE SKIMMABLE EVOLUTION FROM THE ARTICLES OF CONFEDERATION TO THE CONSTITUTION

Articles of Confederation *Ratified 1781*	The New Jersey Plan *Drafted June 15, 1787*	The Virginia Plan *Drafted May 29, 1787*	The Constitution *Ratified 1789*
State sovereignty	State sovereignty	Popular sovereignty	Popular sovereignty
State law is supreme	State law is supreme	National law is supreme	National law is supreme
Unicameral legislature, equal vote for all states	Unicameral legislature, one vote for each state	Bicameral legislature, representation in each house based on population	Bicameral legislature, representation in one house based on population; two votes for each state in the other
Two-thirds vote to pass important laws	Extraordinary majority to pass laws	Majority vote to pass laws	Majority vote to pass laws
No congressional power to tax or regulate commerce	Congressional power to tax and regulate commerce	Congressional power to tax and regulate commerce	Congressional power to tax and regulate commerce
No executive branch	Multiple executive	No restriction on single strong executive	Strong executive
No national judiciary	No national judiciary	National judiciary	Federal court system (including national judiciary)
Unanimous state passage of amendments	Unanimous state passage of amendments	Popular ratification of amendments	Complex amendment process

Note: These plans are arranged to highlight major similarities. They are not chronological, because the Virginia Plan came before the New Jersey Plan.

This does NOT mean that slaves got three fifths of a vote. They had *no right to vote at all*. The southern states just used their slaves to increase their own power in the House of Representatives.

Both the Great Compromise and the Three-Fifths Compromise reduced the popular control of government by countering it with state control, in particular, by empowering smaller, rural states. The Great Compromise meant that even states with tiny populations (like Montana) will always have at least three members of Congress—two senators as well as the one House member the state gets on the basis of population. That is pretty obvious.

But the desire of southern states to boost their power in relation to the North had another lasting effect on the Constitution. We do not elect the president of the United States by direct popular vote. In part this is because the founders were wary of direct popular power and were concerned that information would not travel throughout all the states in time for people to cast informed votes.

Instead, we have the Electoral College, an unusual constitutional arrangement for electing the U.S. president (see Chapter 5). In this arrangement, the states actually choose the president, and the number of electors a state gets in the Electoral College (that is, the number of votes that state can cast for president) is determined by the total number of representatives the state has in both houses.

The South fought direct popular presidential election because the presidency would have been determined by actual population totals—a metric by which they would have come up short. Creating the Electoral College gave the southern states more power to choose the president, because it replaced the actual population count with the number of representatives, which was inflated by the inclusion of slaves (three fifths of them, anyway) in each state's population total.

So, through the Three-Fifths Compromise, southern states used the institution of slavery to boost their political power in the House of Representatives, but it also gave them and other small states more power in choosing the president through the Electoral College, a power advantage that continues today.

2.6 RATIFICATION

SO THE FOUNDERS FINALLY AGREED ON A CONSTITUTION. ARE WE DONE YET?

No. Once there was a draft, the Constitution's rules dictated that nine of thirteen states had to agree to it in a process called **ratification**. The Federalists supported the new document, but the Anti-Federalists did not. A vigorous battle of ideas about governance was conducted nationwide.

The clearest picture we have of the battle that raged between the Federalists and the Anti-Federalists is in their writings. Because the Federalists won, it is their work that stands as the best record of the arguments for the Constitution.

THE *FEDERALIST* PAPERS

The *Federalist Papers* is a collection of eight-five newspaper editorials published in support of the Constitution by three Federalists—Alexander Hamilton, James Madison, and John Jay—writing under the pseudonym of *Publius*.

DIG DEEPER

Read the *Federalist Papers* #10 and #84.

Go to **edge.sagepub.com/ dig-deeper**

THE UPSHOT

Americans have a remarkable Constitution today but *only* because it is based on compromise, something we said earlier would prove key. At least four key compromises made this document possible:

\# Great Compromise (between large and small states)

\# Three-Fifths Compromise (between North and South)

\# Acceptance of Bill of Rights (between Federalists and Anti-Federalists)

\# Federalism (compromise between confederal and unitary systems, which we will read about in a later section)

ratification: the process through which a proposal (such as the Constitution) is formally approved and adopted by vote

Federalist Papers: a collection of eighty-five newspaper editorials written in support of the Constitution under the pseudonym of *Publius*, whose real identity was three Federalists: Alexander Hamilton, James Madison, and John Jay

2.4: THE SKIMMABLE *FEDERALIST PAPERS*: THREE YOU SHOULD KNOW

Federalist #10	James Madison on the danger of factions	In this essay, Madison refuted the Anti-Federalist concern that the new nation would be too large, with a government too big, to prevent corruption. # Madison argued that, on the contrary, the chief threat to liberty in a republic was not corruption but what he called **factions**, groups of people driven by an interest of their own, other than the public interest, who would try to manipulate the rules to benefit themselves. # To squash these factions would destroy the fundamental liberties the people retained, so Madison believed the best way to control these groups would be to establish government over a large territory in which (a) they would be unable to find each other and organize and (b) they would cancel each other out. # *When we get to interest groups, the modern manifestation of factions, in Chapter 7, we can ask if Madison was right.*
Federalist #51	James Madison on separation of powers, and checks and balances	In an elegant argument, Madison said that government should be based on the type of human nature you have to govern. # Having long since decided that people were not virtuous after all, but, in his opinion, self-interested, jealous, and ambitious, Madison argued that the remedy was to find a system of governance that would take advantage of that nature and turn it to good effect. # His answer was his famous system of checks and balances, where each branch was distinct but able to contain the others.
Federalist #84	Alexander Hamilton on why a bill of rights might end up limiting our rights	This one was written in response to an Anti-Federalist requirement that they would vote to ratify the Constitution only if the government were limited by a bill of rights— in this case, ten amendments to the Constitution that explicitly limit government by protecting individual rights against it. # Hamilton said that the Constitution *already* created a limited government. # The Federalists thought that, if you attached a list of things government was not allowed to do, one day someone would come along and conclude that it *was* allowed to do everything not on the list. That would result in a less, not more, limited government. # *We can ask, in Chapter 4, if Hamilton was right.*

factions: groups of citizens united by some common passion or interest and opposed to the rights of other citizens or to the interests of the whole community

Without any one of these compromises, there would have been no Constitution. The founders wrote the Constitution based on compromise, expecting future compromise, and it has been when politicians compromise that our system works best. They recognized that when purists or ideologues hold out to get their own way without compromise, they are breaking a fundamental norm on which the system depends. Inaction is the result.

2.7 BASIC CONSTITUTIONAL PRINCIPLES

CREATING A GOVERNMENT THAT SOLVED PROBLEMS OF HUMAN BEHAVIOR

> By the time the American founders had compromised on their differences at the Constitutional Convention, they had created a document that was pathbreaking in its innovative approach to human governance. Others have copied the U.S. Constitution, but at the time it was created, there was no model for the American founders to follow. They had to piece together the ideas of philosophers with their own political experience to arrive at the document we have today.

THE GENIUS BEHIND IT?

> *James Madison.* His key idea: design a system that takes human nature *as it is* (self-interested, greedy, and ambitious), not as you want it to be. Create internal mechanisms based on that human nature to produce good laws and policy because of it, not in spite of it.

MADISON'S GREAT SOLUTION

> \# Divide the government vertically into branches: legislative, executive, and judicial. This is called **separation of powers**. Give each layer and branch independent status with some of its own constitutional power. But also give each of them just enough power over the others that their jealousy will guard against the overreach of the others. This is called **checks and balances**.

> \# Divide the government horizontally into layers: national (also called federal) and state. This system is called **federalism**.

James Madison: one of the founders whose key insight was to design a system that takes human nature *as it is* (self-interested, greedy, and ambitious), not as you want it to be

separation of powers: the division of the government vertically into branches: legislative, executive, and judicial

checks and balances: the idea that each branch of government has just enough power over the others that their jealousy will guard against the overreach of the others

federalism: the horizontal division of government into layers: national (also called federal) and state

2.5: THE SKIMMABLE CONSTITUTION

Preamble	*"**We the People** of the United States, in Order to form a more perfect Union, establish Justice, insure domestic Tranquility, provide for the common defence, promote the general Welfare, and secure the Blessings of Liberty to ourselves and our Posterity, do ordain and establish this Constitution for the United States of America."*
Article I **10 sections**	# Establishes the bicameral legislative branch of the government, qualifications, terms, duties, and behaviors of members of Congress. # By far the longest article. Article I, Section 8, lists the specific powers of Congress, called the enumerated powers, concluding with a clause that says Congress can do anything necessary and proper to carry out its duties, which takes some of the limitations out of the enumerated powers.
Article II **4 sections**	# Establishes the executive branch, # lays out qualifications for office, # details how the Electoral College works, # describes powers of the president, and # addresses grounds for impeachment by Congress.
Article III **3 sections**	# Establishes the judiciary, # the general scope and jurisdiction of the court system that Congress may alter, and # lifetime tenure of federal judges.
Article IV **4 sections**	# Establishes states' relations. # Each state gives the full faith and credit of the law to the laws and proceedings of the other states. # Citizens of each state are entitled to the privileges and immunities of the others. # Details the process for admission of new states.
Article V **1 section**	# Covers amendment processes.
Article VI **1 section**	# The Constitution is the supreme law of the land (supremacy clause), # officials are bound by their oath of office to support it, and # no religious tests for office are permitted.
Article VII **1 section**	# Covers the process for ratification.

Madison's great solution became the fundamental theory behind the U.S. Constitution. In the next few sections we will explore each of its components in turn, starting with separation of powers and checks and balances.

Madison's ideas on "republican remedies for the diseases most incident to republican government"—that is, the ways to fix the ills that arise from giving people freedom to control their own government—are a fascinating reflection on human nature and the way government works.

DIG DEEPER

Read *Federalist #51*.

Go to **edge.sagepub.com/ dig-deeper**

2.8 SEPARATION OF POWERS AND CHECKS AND BALANCES

WHAT POWERS ARE WE SEPARATING?

> The Constitution gives the three branches of government their own powers, shared powers, and checked powers.

BRANCHES?

> The different functions of government are referred to in the American system as "branches":

The **legislative branch** is the lawmaking component.

The **executive branch** is the law-enforcing component.

The **judicial branch** is the law-interpreting component.

DO ALL COUNTRIES SEPARATE THESE GOVERNMENTAL FUNCTIONS?

> In some countries these functions are not separated—they might all be combined in the same institution. An example is England, which does not separate its powers but rather *fuses* them. The legislature, executive, and

. . . .

legislative branch: the lawmaking component of the federal government

executive branch: the law-enforcing component of the federal government

judicial branch: the law-interpreting component of the federal government

judiciary are all part of Parliament. In what is called a **parliamentary system** there is no separation of powers so there cannot be the same kind of effective checks on power either. Such systems need to rely on unwritten norms to contain power.

Other parliamentary systems include Germany, Ireland, Italy, Denmark, Sweden, and in fact much of Europe, as well as Japan and some countries that were, at one time, part of the British empire, like India.

DIG DEEPER

Read the WHOLE Constitution.

Go to **edge.sagepub.com/dig-deeper**

FOUNDERS: A PRESIDENTIAL SYSTEM IS A BETTER PROTECTION AGAINST ABUSES OF POWER.

Unlike England's parliamentary system, in the United States we have a **presidential system**, in which the executive as well as the other two branches are constitutionally distinct and are given their own powers according to the Constitution.

WHAT YOU NEED TO KNOW ABOUT SEPARATION OF POWERS AND CHECKS AND BALANCES TODAY

The three key elements laid out in Articles I, II, and III are the legislative, executive, and judicial branches. To ensure that none of these separate branches would get too powerful, the Constitution also *shares* powers by

\#   Giving Congress some executive and judicial powers

\#   Giving the executive some legislative and judicial powers

\#   Giving the judiciary some legislative and executive powers

You can see the complex but ingenious way they relate to each other in Figure 2.2 on next page.

WHY DOES THIS WORK?

Checks and balances are effective partly because of the ingenuity of Madison's insight, based on the writings of Enlightenment thinkers at the time, which was that pitting public officials' self-interest and hunger for

parliamentary system: government in which the executive is chosen by the legislature from among its members and the two branches are merged

presidential system: government in which the executive is chosen independently of the legislature and the two branches are separate

2.2: SEPARATION OF POWERS AND CHECKS AND BALANCES

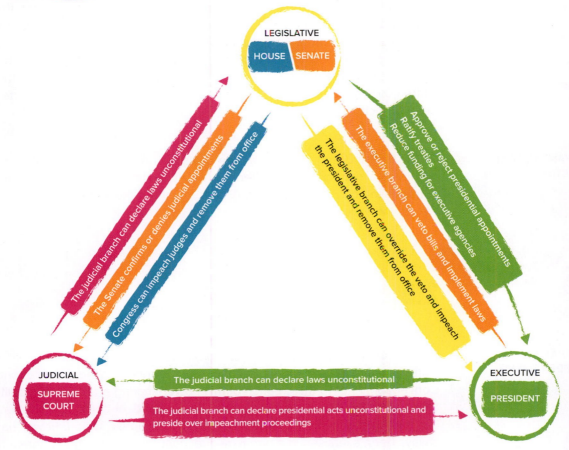

LEGISLATIVE

HOUSE SENATE

The judicial branch can declare laws unconstitutional

The Senate confirms or denies judicial appointments

Congress can impeach judges and remove them from office

The legislative branch can override the veto and impeach the president and remove them from office

The executive branch can veto bills and implement laws

Approve or reject presidential appointments
Ratify treaties
Reduce funding for executive agencies

JUDICIAL

SUPREME COURT

The judicial branch can declare laws unconstitutional

The judicial branch can declare presidential acts unconstitutional and preside over impeachment proceedings

EXECUTIVE

PRESIDENT

power against each other's would keep everyone in check. But, as in parliamentary systems, it also works because most officials traditionally follow unwritten political norms, like respect for the rule of law and a dedication to national security.

Although various members of each branch have at times in our history thought their

DIG DEEPER

Read Emily Bazelon's essay on norms.

Go to **edge.sagepub.com/ dig-deeper**

turf should be supreme, to date the checks designed so carefully by Madison and the other founders have held.

KEY POINT

The Constitution is strong, but a consistent disregard for the norms that support it can weaken it considerably. The system of checks and balances is stable but also more fragile than we like to think since it depends on human wisdom. Madison had specifically wanted to insulate the republic against failures of human wisdom. So far it has lasted longer than any other written constitution in human history, but no political system has ultimately been invincible.

WANT TO TAKE ACTION?

Be vigilant and engaged. Know the Constitution and the norms that are required to support it. Pay attention when politicians break norms, and consider the consequences. Think critically about the significance of their words and actions.

2.9 FEDERALISM AND CHECKS AND BALANCES

WHAT IS FEDERALISM?

Federalism was an experiment, a *compromise* born out of the struggle over states' rights between Federalists and Anti-Federalists at the Constitutional Convention. Prior to the creation of this power-sharing arrangement, political systems had been unitary systems like England, or confederal systems like the Articles of Confederation or today's European Union. Power had always been exercised in a *one-way direction*, from central government to regional units, or the other way around.

CONSTITUTIONAL PROVISIONS CREATING FEDERALISM

Federalism breaks with that pattern, giving separate and independent powers to both national (federal) and state governments and allowing them to share some powers (called **concurrent powers**). A handful of specific constitutional provisions make up the building blocks of federalism in the United States. We turn to them below.

concurrent powers: powers that are shared by the federal and state governments

2.3: UNITARY, FEDERAL, AND CONFEDERAL SYSTEMS

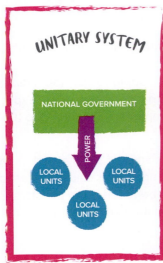

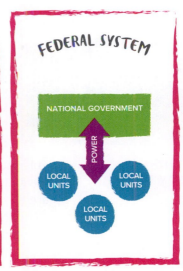

ENUMERATED POWERS

> \# Article I, Section 8. As you saw in the *Skimmable Constitution,* this section is called the **enumerated powers**. It spells out exactly what Congress (and hence the national government) is allowed to do, including things like coining money and managing interstate commerce.

THE NECESSARY AND PROPER CLAUSE

> \# The **necessary and proper clause** coming at the very end of the enumerated powers says Congress can do anything "necessary and proper" to carry out its duties. The Supreme Court has ruled that the necessary and proper clause is elastic (think *stretchy*). That means it can accommodate a lot of extra powers if needed.

enumerated powers: congressional powers specifically named in the Constitution

necessary and proper clause: the constitutional authorization for Congress to make any law required to carry out its powers

WHO GETS THE ADVANTAGE?

Article I, Section 8, limits congressional power to a specific list and then lifts that limitation by saying that Congress can also do those things that are necessary to carry out the duties on the list. Generally, this strengthens the national government at the expense of state power. Limits on it depend on judicial interpretation.

DIG DEEPER

Read Article 1, Section 8.

Go to **edge.sagepub.com/ dig-deeper**

\# The **Tenth Amendment** to the Constitution (the last of the ten amendments in the Bill of Rights that the Anti-Federalists insisted on adding to limit the national government's power) says that any powers not explicitly given to the national government are reserved to the states.

THE TENTH AMENDMENT

This sounds like it keeps a lot of powers safe for the states, but given the judicial opinion that the necessary and proper clause is elastic—are there significant powers left over to be reserved to the states? It all depends on what the Court says, and the Court changes its mind over time.

WHO GETS THE ADVANTAGE?

It's pretty much a tie; the balance of national–state power again depends on judicial interpretation.

THE SUPREMACY CLAUSE

\# The **supremacy clause** in Article VI of the Constitution says that the Constitution itself and national laws made under it are the law of the land.

WHO GETS THE ADVANTAGE?

This doesn't leave too much room for interpretation—if national law clashes with state law, national law almost always wins if the federal government chooses to impose its will.

SIBLING RIVALRY

The founders were well aware that national stability was threatened not only by the tension between the states and the federal government but also by the tensions between the states themselves. The Virginia and

Tenth Amendment: the amendment that stipulates that any powers not explicitly given to the national government are reserved to the states

supremacy clause: a constitutional clause that says the Constitution itself and national laws made under it are the law of the land

New Jersey Plans were evidence of that, as was the Civil War and many aspects of politics today. To try to smooth the edges off the potential clashes, they included the *full faith and credit clause* in the Constitution (Article IV, Section 1), which says that the states have to respect the legal proceedings and public acts of the other states, but also the *privileges and immunities clause* (Article IV, Section 2), which says that a state cannot deny a citizen of another state the rights its own citizens enjoy.

THE UPSHOT

American federalism gives some power to the national government, some to the states, with some to be shared. Where the line is drawn between what belongs to the national government and what to the states is partly spelled out in the Constitution, and partly left up in the air, which means the courts have stepped in to decide what belongs to whom. The balance has changed over time, but generally the national government has gained power at the expense of the states.

WHEN POLITICS FAILS—THE CASE OF THE CIVIL WAR

The one battle the political institutions could not solve was the issue of slavery. In the Civil War the South tried to promote a "states' rights" narrative, but the right the southern states were fighting for was the right to preserve slavery. The Civil War was a national struggle about the moral issue of enslavement.

DIG DEEPER

See what happens when states pass laws that conflict with national law.

Go to **edge.sagepub.com/dig-deeper**

HOW IS FEDERALISM PART OF CHECKS AND BALANCES?

The history of federalism shows that the national government and the state governments have periodically checked each other. For instance, just in the area of civil rights, the national government not only fought the Civil War to end slavery but then, through the passage of the Thirteenth, Fourteenth, and Fifteenth Amendments to the Constitution, also attempted to bring rights to former slaves. National legislation in the 1960s and 1970s attempted to redress racial inequalities (see Chapter 3). That is an example of the national government checking the states. Conversely, in the late 1800s and early 1900s, many states gradually allowed women to vote, with the effect that eventually women could vote in sufficient force to aid the passage of the Nineteenth Amendment in 1920, making women's suffrage a constitutional right.

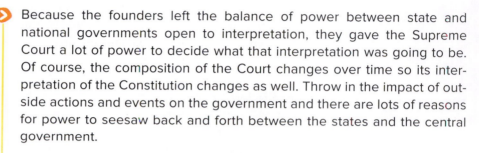

2.10 CHANGES IN FEDERALISM OVER TIME

THE CHANGING BALANCE OF POWER BETWEEN STATE AND NATIONAL GOVERNMENTS OVER TIME

> Because the founders left the balance of power between state and national governments open to interpretation, they gave the Supreme Court a lot of power to decide what that interpretation was going to be. Of course, the composition of the Court changes over time so its interpretation of the Constitution changes as well. Throw in the impact of outside actions and events on the government and there are lots of reasons for power to seesaw back and forth between the states and the central government.

Looking at federal–state power relations over time we can see two trends:

DIG DEEPER

Read the text of *Marbury v. Madison, McCulloch v. Maryland,* and *Gibbons v. Ogden.*

Go to **edge.sagepub.com/ dig-deeper**

\# Changes like industrialization, urbanization, and advances in science and technology have made life more complex and have led citizens to look to government at all levels for assistance, protection, and security in the face of the growing uncertainties and hazards of everyday existence.

\# Even though all levels of government have grown, and despite the fact that the balance of power has swung both ways, there has been an undeniable shift of power over time from the states to the national government.

KEY MOMENTS IN FEDERAL HISTORY

> We can identify at least four major moments in our history that have seen these power shifts from state to national government:

\# **John Marshall's tenure as chief justice of the Supreme Court (1801–1835).** The third chief justice of the Supreme Court, John Marshall believed in the Federalist vision of a strong national government. Several of his opinions (see the *Skimmable Court Watcher*) accounted for major power grabs by the national government in general and, in one case, for the Court in particular.

. . . .

John Marshall: the third chief justice of the Supreme Court; believed in the Federalist vision of a strong national government

2.6: THE SKIMMABLE COURT WATCHER: JOHN MARSHALL'S IMPACT ON THE GROWTH OF NATIONAL POWER AT THE EXPENSE OF THE STATES

	Marbury v. Madison (1803)	McCulloch v. Maryland (1819)	Gibbons v. Ogden (1824)
Ruling	The Supreme Court has the power of **judicial review** and can determine if congressional laws, state laws, or executive actions are constitutional. If the Court decides they are not, it has the power to strike them down.	The necessary and proper clause of the Constitution could be interpreted broadly to include many powers that are not among the enumerated powers of Congress.	This case opened the door to federal regulation of commerce, broadly understood to mean most forms of business. It removed many limitations on the federal regulation of interstate commerce.
Impact on Federalism	In significant ways, this case made the Court the most powerful of the three branches, if it chooses to get involved. What is amazing is that the Court gave itself this ultimate power over the government and the states. A remarkable power grab by the Court.	This interpretation severely limited the clout of states as given to them by the Tenth Amendment. Another seizure of national power by the Court.	Again, a Court ruling took power from the states and gave it to the national government—exactly why the Anti-Federalists had balked at having a national court and why the Federalists were so vague in Article III about the Court's reach.

Marbury v. Madison: the 1803 Supreme Court ruling holding that the Court had the power of judicial review

McCulloch v. Maryland: the 1819 Supreme Court ruling holding that the necessary and proper clause of the Constitution could be interpreted broadly to include many powers that are not among the enumerated powers of Congress

Gibbons v. Ogden: the 1824 Supreme Court decision that opened the door to federal regulation of commerce, broadly understood to mean most forms of business

judicial review: the Supreme Court's power to determine if congressional laws, state laws, or executive actions are constitutional

The Civil War (1861–1865).
Lincoln's Emancipation Proclamation, a final effort to prevent the dissolution of the Union, declared that the slaves of any state leaving the Union would be freed. The eleven states of the Confederacy rejected the idea that the national government could tell them what to do, and in fact they asserted their own sovereignty by claiming the right to void national laws they didn't like. **Nullification** was never the law of the land, but the issue of states' rights to be sovereign and to own slaves was the most compelling force behind a war that had many causes. With the South's defeat in the war, the idea of state sovereignty was forced to the fringes of American politics, where it remains even today.

The New Deal (1933–1942).
After the devastation of the Great Depression that followed the stock market crash of 1929, many people were without jobs, pensions, or other means of support. They turned to the national government, and Franklin Roosevelt came into office promising Americans a "New Deal." Part of that new deal involved taking a firmer hand in regulating the ups and downs of the economy and using government spending on infrastructure building and other projects that private business was not strong enough to handle to stimulate the economy.

Broad interpretation of the Fourteenth Amendment and civil rights.
The Fourteenth Amendment was added to the Constitution after the Civil War (in 1868) to ensure that southern states did not deny those free from enslavement their rights as citizens (although interestingly, as we will see, it ended up also having the effect of incorporating the rights of the Bill of Rights into state constitutions). It took more than 100 years to make good on the promise of that amendment, and that century is the story of a gradual imposition of federal protections of citizens from state governments. We will cover this in more detail in Chapter 3, on civil liberties and civil rights. For now it is enough to know that increasingly the Court interpreted broadly the amendment's promise that "No state shall make or enforce any law which shall abridge the privileges or immunities of citizens of the United States; nor shall any state deprive any person of life, liberty, or property, without due process of law; nor deny to any person within its jurisdiction the equal protection of the laws."

nullification: declaration by a state that a federal law is void within its borders

THE UPSHOT

The compromise of federalism was key to the creation of a Constitution that could win approval of both Federalists and Anti-Federalists. But it signaled a serious division between those who believed in state sovereignty and those committed to national sovereignty. Although the supremacy clause ultimately tilts the balance of power toward the national government, the struggle continues. In many ways the compromise of federalism is renegotiated continually through the course of American politics.

2.11 FEDERALISM TODAY

THE STATUS OF THE COMPROMISE TODAY

In terms of constitutional law, the national government is clearly supreme and has extended its reach to the states in some powerful ways. The debate is not over, however. Advocates of national power tend to be Democrats whose ideology leads them to believe, like the Federalists, that national power is not a threat to individual liberties. They also believe that government can be an effective problem solver, so they are not afraid to test its limits. Republicans tend to be more like the Anti-Federalists in their distrust of national power and their preference for keeping important decisions at the state level. They have long advocated *devolution*, or the returning of power to the states, although their enthusiasm for that position falls somewhat when they are in control of the federal government.

When Republicans control Congress and the executive, many of them are less wary of the reach of the national government because it is doing their bidding. George W. Bush's No Child Left Behind program was a key example. Similarly, when Democrats are out of power, they look to the states to enact their agendas. After Donald Trump was elected president, many states took steps to preserve President Barack Obama's climate action plan and to preserve sanctuary cities as havens for undocumented immigrants.

Today the battle over federalism seems to have less to do with its old framework of limited government versus big government and more to do with the battle for power between two highly polarized parties.

For example, Republicans have fought for state power to regulate the electorate, making it more difficult for voters likely to be Democrats to get to the polls. The Supreme Court recently gave them several wins on that front. In 2013, in *Shelby County v. Holder,* the Court canceled out parts of the

1965 Voting Rights Act that required states with a history of discrimination to have changes in their electoral systems reviewed by the Department of Justice. And in 2018, in *Husted v. A. Philip Randolph Institute*, the Court endorsed Ohio's policy of purging its voting records of anyone who hasn't voted in two years. If the purged voters are aware of what happened, they can reregister; otherwise, they lose the chance to vote in that election, unless they know to ask for a provisional ballot. This action is especially targeted at younger, more transient populations who move a lot.

Meanwhile, many more liberal states are using the courts to try to stop the imposition of Trump administration policies with which they disagree—the banning of sanctuary cities, zero tolerance of immigration violations, the separation of children from their asylum-seeking families, the permission to release plans for 3-D-printed assault weapons, and the loosening of emissions standards on automobiles.

The larger debates aside, most of the policies that affect our lives are created or at least administered by the states. The Affordable Care Act (ACA), for instance, passed during the Obama administration, is a national law that directs private insurance companies to provide certain guarantees of coverage and that directs all individuals to sign up for some level of coverage. The insurance exchanges—marketplaces where people buy health insurance policies under the ACA—are operated at the state level, however. States have the ability to decide whether or not to accept Medicaid funding to extend financial support to people who cannot afford the fees they must pay to buy insurance. The Supreme Court held that the national government cannot force states to accept those federal funds.

State policies matter to us on a day-to-day level, and the national government has a stake in controlling those policies as much as possible. The tools the national government (Congress) has to do that, however, are limited by the powers retained by the states. The chief way Congress can influence what states do is by giving or withholding federal funds.

FOUR OPTIONS FOR THE NATIONAL GOVERNMENT TO EXERCISE INFLUENCE OVER THE STATES

There are essentially four ways the national government can approach the task of getting states to do what it wants them to do:

\# **Do nothing.** When the federal government chooses this option, states can do as they wish.

GEN GAP!

GENERATIONAL ATTITUDES TOWARD THE FEDERAL GOVERNMENT

A big division between the Federalists and the Anti-Federalists was the degree to which they trusted government and wanted to restrict its size and function. Generational data on that topic are interesting.

When it comes to age, there isn't much difference in how much people trust their government. Millennials are a tiny bit less likely to say they trust their government all the time, but altogether, more than 80 percent trust

 FIGURE IT!

2.4: TRUST IN THE FEDERAL GOVERNMENT VARIES LITTLE ACROSS GENERATIONS

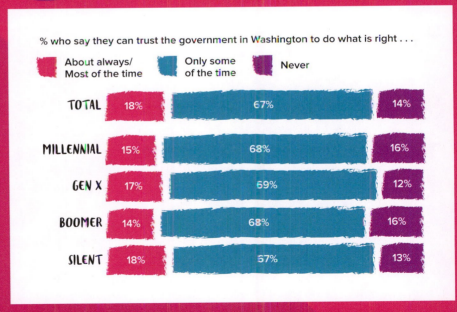

% who say they can trust the government in Washington to do what is right . . .

- About always/ Most of the time
- Only some of the time
- Never

	About always/ Most of the time	Only some of the time	Never
TOTAL	18%	67%	14%
MILLENNIAL	15%	68%	16%
GEN X	17%	69%	12%
BOOMER	14%	68%	16%
SILENT	18%	57%	13%

Source: Pew Research Center, The Generation Gap in American Politics, March 1, 2018. http://www.people-press.org/2018/03/01/2-views-of-scope-of-government-trust-in-government-economic-inequality/.

2.5: CONTINUED GENERATIONAL DIVIDES IN PREFERRED SIZE AND SCOPE OF GOVERNMENT

% who would prefer a bigger government providing more services

	1980	1989	1996	1999	2007	2011	2014	2017
TOTAL	32%	48%	30%	43%	43%	41%	42%	48%
MILLENNIAL	—	—	—	—	68%	56%	54%	57%
GEN X	—	—	53%	54%	51%	45%	46%	50%
BOOMER	45%	52%	24%	41%	33%	35%	35%	43%
SILENT	25%	35%	19%	34%	30%	25%	27%	30%

Source: Pew Research Center, The Generation Gap in American Politics, March 1, 2018, http://www.people-press.org/2018/03/01/2-views-of-scope-of-government-trust-in-government-economic-inequality/.

government at least some of the time and uniform percentages of each generation say they never trust it.

Whether they trust it or not, however, younger Americans are far more likely than older ones to say they would prefer to have a larger government that provided more in the way of services. There could be a couple of reasons for that finding. First, most of the services government supplies (e.g., Social Security and Medicare) are already benefitting older Americans. It is younger Americans who, as we saw in the Chapter 1 GenGap, are not doing as well as older Americans were doing at their age and might need additional assistance with health care, student loan relief, and the like. Second, social services are not the only kind of services that government provides. Younger people are far more likely to want government to clean up the environment or support social justice. So the generations in this figure may not even be talking about the same basic services.

TAKEAWAYS

→ **Very few Americans, fewer than 20 percent, trust their government all the time.** What are the implications of that for government legitimacy?

→ **Millennials were *far* more likely to want to see expanded government services in 2007 than they were in 2011, 2014, or 2017.** What was it about 2007 that could cause that discrepancy?

→ **As those preferring smaller government die off and those preferring more services grow as a percentage of Americans, politicians who promise those services are likely to thrive.** What does that mean for the balance of power in the United States?

\# **Block grants.** When Congress wants to impose a policy goal on the states but wants the states to maintain maximum control, it can provide block grants. Block grants are funds that come with flexibility for the states to spend the money as they wish within broad parameters.

\# **Categorical grants.** These grants give far less autonomy to the states; they are grants of money with specific instructions on how it is to be spent.

\# **Unfunded mandates.** Sometimes Congress tells the states to do something but provides no funds to offset the costs of administering the policy.

block grants: funds that come with flexibility for the states to spend the money as they wish within broad parameters

categorical grants: grants of money with specific instructions on how it is to be spent

unfunded mandates: policies requiring states to do something but without any funds provided to offset the costs of administering the policy

THE UPSHOT

For obvious reasons, states prefer these options in the order listed. They would like to be left to their own devices, but if they have to do the bidding of Congress, they want to do so with maximum flexibility. Their least preferred option is the unfunded mandate, which takes all of their autonomy and offsets none of the cost.

Members of Congress prefer the options in the opposite order. Doing nothing means they don't exercise control and they don't get their way. Members of Congress get no bragging rights when it comes to telling constituents what they have accomplished. Block grants can be a convenient way of shifting responsibility onto the states for hard, possibly unpopular decisions that they don't want to make, but they also have minimal control and bragging rights. Categorical grants are better on both counts, but they have to deal with irate states that dislike them. Unfunded mandates are the least cost and trouble to them, and they allow members of Congress to tout their accomplishments in exercising their will, but the states hate them and the Supreme Court has become increasingly unfriendly to them as well.

2.12 AMENDING THE CONSTITUTION

MAKING A CONSTITUTION FLEXIBLE, BUT NOT TOO EASY TO CHANGE

By endorsing a role for the Supreme Court in interpreting the Constitution, the founders ensured that they built a little bit of flexibility into the system, much as a skyscraper has to give a little in a hurricane so the storm doesn't destroy it. The winds of change haven't destroyed the Constitution in more than 200 years because judicial interpretation allows it to give a little in the face of those winds. How far the Court should go in relying on interpretation instead of the actual words in the Constitution is, as we will see, a matter of some debate.

On the other hand, the founders made it extremely challenging to actually change the Constitution. The **amendment process**, as it is called, is complex and involves both Congress and the states. Getting everyone on the same page about constitutional change has happened so rarely that we have only twenty-seven amendments in total. Ten of those were added right away, and one exists to repeal another. That is not a lot of amendment activity to show for the more than 230 years of the Constitution's existence.

....

amendment process: the process by which the Constitution may be changed

HOW DOES IT WORK?

> The Constitution provides for several ways in which it can be amended. One, beginning in a national convention convened by Congress for the purpose, has never been used, although states have frequently tried to initiate a such a movement. In fact, an effort to create a balanced budget amendment in this way is currently in the works. Twenty-seven of the necessary thirty-four states (all Republican-led) have passed resolutions calling on Congress to hold a constitutional convention to pass a balanced budget amendment. Opponents argue that once a convention is convened, it might be hard to contain the urge to make multiple changes to the Constitution, although three quarters of the states would still need to approve the amendments.

All the amendments that have been passed began with a two-thirds majority vote in both houses of Congress. From there, at least three quarters of the states had to ratify the amendments. This was done once through separate ratifying conventions in each state (that was for the Twenty-First Amendment, which repealed the Eighteenth Amendment that banned the manufacture or sale of alcohol in the United States). All the other amendments were ratified by state legislatures.

FIGURE IT!

2.6: THE AMENDMENT PROCESS

AMENDING THE CONSTITUTION

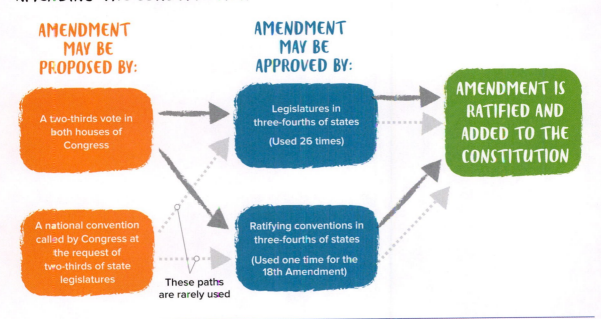

AMENDMENT MAY BE PROPOSED BY:

A two-thirds vote in both houses of Congress

A national convention called by Congress at the request of two-thirds of state legislatures

These paths are rarely used

AMENDMENT MAY BE APPROVED BY:

Legislatures in three-fourths of states

(Used 26 times)

Ratifying conventions in three-fourths of states

(Used one time for the 18th Amendment)

AMENDMENT IS RATIFIED AND ADDED TO THE CONSTITUTION

THE UPSHOT

We may very well owe the longevity of our constitution to the wisdom of its creators. Were it easier to amend, many laws might have taken on constitutional status, only to be changed as times changed (witness the fate of Prohibition). A constitution that is too easy to amend can end up looking like a phone book, and the stature and legitimacy of the constitution can easily be diminished. At the same time, providing for a Supreme Court and letting it be known (via *Federalist Paper #78*) that they were not opposed to judicial review, the founders provided for a method that would allow the Constitution to change more subtly over time and possibly even to change back as conditions and circumstances evolved.

Big Think

→ Do you think anything essential is missing from the basic Constitution? What amendment about how government functions would you add to it?

→ How strong are the checks and balances the founders put in place? Should they also have written down the norms needed to support them?

→ Have Supreme Court rulings strengthened or weakened federal–state relations?

Key Terms

CONCEPTS

amendment process (p. 66)

bicameral legislature (p. 43)

block grants (p. 65)

categorical grants (p. 65)

checks and balances (p. 49)

compromise (p. 41)

concurrent powers (p. 54)

confederation (p. 41)

divine right of kings (p. 36)

enumerated powers (p. 55)

executive branch (p. 51)

factions (p. 48)

federalism (p. 49)

Great Compromise (p. 44)

inalienable rights (p. 38)

judicial branch (p. 51)

judicial review (p. 59)

legislative branch (p. 51)

mercantilism (p. 34)

necessary and proper clause (p. 55)

New Jersey Plan (p. 44)

nullification (p. 60)

parliamentary system (p. 52)

IMPORTANT WORKS AND EVENTS

KEY INDIVIDUALS AND GROUPS

#3 CIVIL LIBERTIES AND CIVIL RIGHTS

In this chapter:

3.1 Introduction to CIVIL LIBERTIES AND CIVIL RIGHTS

AREN'T RIGHTS AND LIBERTIES THE SAME THING? →

Yes, liberties and rights are synonyms in everyday English, which can make the discussion of *civil liberties* and *civil rights* in the context of politics very confusing. It is the word *civil*—having to do with the nonpolitical collective life of citizens—that gives these phrases specific and different meanings. In democracies and other non-authoritarian societies, where citizens hold at least some political power, both civil liberties and civil rights are essential for balancing the power in our public and private lives. In authoritarian societies, there *is* no nonpolitical life for everyday people. Politics can seep into every corner of daily life.

IN A NUTSHELL

Civil liberties are individual rights that come from the *limitation of* government power. By contrast, civil rights *empower* government to give rights to groups of people who share common characteristics. You could say civil liberties are about equal protection *from* the law, and civil rights are about the equal protection *of* the laws.

SO WHAT DO CIVIL LIBERTIES AND CIVIL RIGHTS ACTUALLY MEAN?

Civil liberties, the individual freedoms that limit government, are guaranteed by the Bill of Rights and the text of the Constitution itself. These rights include freedom of speech and of religion and the right not to incriminate ourselves or be subject to unreasonable searches and seizures. Some others, like the right to privacy, come from Supreme Court decisions that have interpreted the Bill of Rights broadly. Those civil liberties stand on shakier ground because the Court can (and sometimes does) overturn or modify them.

Civil rights refers to the freedom of groups to participate fully in the public life of a nation. These groups are defined by particular characteristics—like race, gender, or sexual orientation—that are beyond their members' control. What is protected is the group members' right to do things like vote, get an education, travel, and get married. As we said earlier, rather than limiting government, the protection of civil rights often empowers government to act. Protections of civil rights are guaranteed by the Thirteenth, Fourteenth, Fifteenth, Nineteenth, and Twenty-Sixth Amendments to the Constitution.

We will understand the *civil* aspect more clearly after we have discussed the nature of rights and liberties in general.

By the time you finish reading this chapter, you will understand

→ The meaning of rights or freedoms in a democracy and why we can't always have all the rights we want

→ The value (and cost) of having a Bill of Rights

→ The civil liberties that restrict government action

→ When groups have the right to be treated equally by the law and when they do not

→ How different groups have battled for rights to equal treatment

3.2 RIGHTS EQUAL POWER

ONE BIG THING TO KNOW

> Rights are so important, so sought after, and so controversial because they are fundamentally about *power*: they confer power on people and limitations on government. That's why debates about power have such high stakes.

HOW DO RIGHTS CONFER POWER ON PEOPLE?

> Rights confer power on people in many ways. Here are three of the most important:

\# The ability to claim rights makes one a citizen, not a subject. Rights give citizens power to push back on their government's actions.

\# The ability to deny rights gives citizens power over each other. Historically, some groups of Americans have fought to hang on to the power to deny fellow citizens recognition and protection of their full citizenship rights.

\# The ability to use government to fight back against those who would deny their fellow citizens rights is also a form of power. Civil rights movements (described later in this chapter) are efforts to claim and exercise citizenship rights under government protection.

civil liberties: the individual freedoms guaranteed by the Constitution that limit government

civil rights: the freedom of groups to participate fully in the public life of a nation; protected by the government primarily in the Thirteenth, Fourteenth, Fifteenth, Nineteenth, and Twenty-Sixth Amendments

WHERE DO OUR RIGHTS COME FROM?

Excellent question, and the narrative we tell about this really matters in terms of power. If we believe we have rights because the government or the Constitution or the Bill of Rights or any other amendments give them to us, then those rights can also be taken away.

That's why, in the Declaration of Independence, Thomas Jefferson emphasized his belief that Americans' "unalienable Rights" are conferred by "Nature" and "Nature's God." These unalienable rights are called **natural rights**. In Jefferson's understanding, if one is born with these rights, no government can take them away. Even though a determined government could violate those rights if it really wanted to, the idea of natural rights forms a powerful story to keep the government in check. Any government that wants to be seen as non-authoritarian is confined by that narrative.

ARE AMERICANS' CONSTITUTIONAL RIGHTS UNLIMITED?

Unfortunately not. Rights are some of those scarce resources we talked about in Chapter 1. This makes them ripe for political battles over power.

The rights of American citizens are limited in two main ways:

\# **First, rights become limited when they clash with other people's rights**. Some disputes over rights are zero-sum games. In other words, for someone to win, someone else has to lose. When two people's rights conflict, both can't get what they want. For instance, when an employer refuses on religious grounds to provide birth control to employees through company-funded insurance, the employer's freedom of religion might come into conflict with an employee's right to privacy if she demands birth control as part of her insurance coverage (the courts have ruled the right to privacy includes reproductive rights).

Sometimes clashes over rights happen because a dominant group wants to deny rights to another group that its members see as less deserving or inferior. Denying rights to another group can reinforce the dominant group's power or, if it feels threatened, reestablish it.

\# **Second, rights are limited when they conflict with a collective good that society values**. A classic example is individual liberty and national security. We could live in complete safety if we gave up all our freedom and lived in a locked-down world. We might be safe, but it wouldn't be much fun. On the flip side, we could be completely free if we removed all restraints on personal travel, communication,

natural rights: the idea that one is born with a set of rights that no government can take away

and privacy, but we'd lose a lot of safety. So, we make trade-offs, like taking off our shoes and going through scanners at the airport before we board planes even while we still value freedom of movement. Solving rights conflicts often involves compromise.

AND WHO SOLVES THOSE CONFLICTS?

Since rights conflicts are at heart political conflicts, it should come as no surprise that they are solved through the political process. In the United States, that means through congressional legislation, executive action, individual and group efforts on the part of the people, and most of all, judicial decisions. So these are the key actors to remember:

\# THE COURTS

\# Congress

\# The president and the bureaucracy

\# The people

3.3 THE BILL OF RIGHTS

LET'S REVISIT THE BILL OF RIGHTS.

Remember from Chapter 2 that the **Bill of Rights** consists of the first ten amendments to the U.S. Constitution, which the Anti-Federalists demanded as their price for ratification. Their argument was that if this new national government was to be created, it needed to be restricted by appending to the new constitution a list of the things it could not do.

> ## DIG DEEPER
> Read the WHOLE Bill of Rights.
>
> Go to **edge.sagepub.com/dig-deeper**

SO, A BILL OF RIGHTS IS A GOOD THING, RIGHT?

Maybe. Maybe not. Remember that Alexander Hamilton argued in *Federalist Paper #84* that a bill of rights might be a dangerous thing, because the founders' intent was to create a government that was already powerless to do the things the Bill of Rights ruled out. Future politicians might argue that the Bill of Rights lists the *only* limitations on government and would

Bill of Rights: ten amendments to the Constitution that explicitly limit government by protecting individual rights against it

therefore give government *more* power than the founders wanted it to have. The Ninth and Tenth Amendments are specifically designed to stymie that argument, but Hamilton worried that they would not be sufficient.

3.1: THE SKIMMABLE BILL OF RIGHTS

Amendment number	What it says
1	The "firsts": establishment clause, free exercise of religion, free speech, free press, right to assemble
2	Right to bear arms necessary for a well-regulated militia
3	No forced housing of soldiers in your home during peace
4	No unreasonable searches and seizures
5	Grand jury indictment required for capital crimes, no double jeopardy, no self-incrimination, no deprivation of property without due process of law
6	Right to a speedy trial and right to counsel
7	Guarantee of jury trials for civil cases in which the value in controversy is over $20
8	No cruel or unusual punishment or excessive bail
9	Promise that rights listed in the Constitution don't limit the possession of other rights
10	Declaration that rights not given to the national government are reserved to the states

DIG DEEPER

If you didn't read *Federalist Paper #84* in Chapter 2, this would be a great time to check it out.

Go to **edge.sagepub.com/ dig-deeper**

All of the founders feared a powerful government; they just differed on ways to limit it. The Federalists thought they had created internal mechanisms—separation of powers, checks and balances—that would keep the government from overreach. The Anti-Federalists wanted to spell out restrictions on the government—limiting powers the Federalists didn't think the Constitution conferred.

This is an interesting difference, and, as we will see, there is good reason to believe that Hamilton was right.

WHOSE BEHAVIOR IS THE BILL OF RIGHTS MEANT TO LIMIT?

It's pretty clear when you read it that the Bill of Rights is speaking to the national government and specifically to Congress: "*Congress shall make no law. . . .*" That makes sense since the document they are amending is the *U.S. Constitution.*

But most Americans don't interact with the federal government or commit federal crimes. If they have run-ins with the law, it is far more likely to take place at the state level. The Bill of Rights, however, provides no limits on the states. In fact, the Bill of Rights itself tries to reserve rights to the states that are not given explicitly to the federal government. States may have their own bill of rights, but they don't have to and there are no regulations about what they cover.

THE SUPREME COURT GRABS SOME POWER FROM THE STATES TO MAKE THEM ENFORCE THE BILL OF RIGHTS.

Still, Americans are not helpless if a state denies them a basic right. Protections at the state level have been the result of hard-fought legal challenges. In 1870, five years after the Civil War ended, the Supreme Court got an unexpected new tool in its constitutional toolbox that allowed it to address what it felt were the states' denials of fundamental American rights.

The new tool was the **Fourteenth Amendment**, intended to stop southern states from denying former slaves their citizenship rights after the Civil War. Its authors didn't think they were giving the Supreme Court a way to, for instance, force the state of Florida to provide a poor white man with a lawyer if he was accused of breaking a state law. But that is what happened. Using a process called **incorporation**, the Court was able to fold the guaranteed national rights into required state protections via the Fourteenth Amendment.

Look closely at this portion of the Fourteenth Amendment:

No state shall make or enforce any law which shall abridge the privileges and immunities of citizens of the United States; nor shall any state deprive any person of life, liberty or property without due process of law, nor deny to any person within its jurisdiction the equal protection of the laws.

Fourteenth Amendment: the 1868 constitutional amendment ensuring that southern states did not deny those free from enslavement their rights as citizens

incorporation: Supreme Court action making the protections of the Bill of Rights applicable to the states

That language can be interpreted to mean that no state can deny a citizen any of the rights the federal government guarantees. The Supreme Court didn't go off and incorporate all the rights in the Bill of Rights in one bang. Instead, it did it selectively over time. As of today, just about every right in the Bill of Rights has been incorporated.

THE UPSHOT

With incorporation, the Supreme Court did what it had done in the past with decisions like *Marbury v. Madison,* establishing judicial review, and *McCulloch v. Maryland,* allowing an *elastic* interpretation of the necessary and proper clause. *It expanded the national power at the expense of the states, changing the balance of federal power.*

3.4 CIVIL LIBERTIES—UNDERSTANDING THE FIRST AMENDMENT

THE POWER OF BEING FIRST

Americans' basic civil liberties cover a lot of ground. They include all the rights the founders felt were necessary to keep the state in check. The most important of those rights they packed into the First Amendment because they wanted to indicate their primary importance. A lot of rights are protected in the First Amendment, which reads:

> *Congress shall make no law respecting an establishment of religion, or prohibiting the free exercise thereof; or abridging the freedom of speech, or of the press; or the right of the people peaceably to assemble, and to petition the Government for a redress of grievances.*

This amendment covers so many rights because, for the founders, these were all fundamental to the full functioning of a democracy. Don't underestimate "the power of being first." Being able to say that something comes first gives it prominence and status. For the founders, these rights were all of first importance.

FREEDOM OF RELIGION—FIRST AMONG FIRSTS

Religious freedom was at the forefront of the founders' minds because many of the original colonists had fled England in the first place to avoid an established church. Hence, the first words of the First Amendment: "Congress shall make no law respecting an establishment of religion or prohibiting the free exercise thereof." Those two rights are known as the **establishment clause** and the **free exercise clause**.

ONE BIG CONTRADICTION ❯ The trouble with those words spelling out religious freedom protection is that they contain an inherent contradiction. If *no establishment* of religion means there can be no officially endorsed practice of or support for a religion, and the *free exercise* of religion allows you to practice the religion of your choice, then if, for instance, your religion leads you to want to say a group prayer at the start of your school day or to display religious icons in public places, you are in a fix. Both of those things cannot happen at the same time.

WHY DID THE FOUNDERS OPPOSE RELIGIOUS ESTABLISHMENT? ❯ The founders might have been primarily Christian, but they were members of a variety of denominations that differed in fundamental ways. Any effort to establish one of those denominations as the official state religion would have doomed the new country from the start.

Historical as well as present-day conflicts have shown us what happens when political differences are reinforced with religious differences: every conflict is infused with profound meaning, and compromise is impossible because no one wants to compromise on his or her deeply held spiritual beliefs.

Besides, when a government can put the power of an Almighty behind its laws, it is very hard to resist the government if it overreaches. Aggrieved citizens would be rebelling not only against the state but also against God, and who wants to risk eternal damnation for short-term earthly redress of grievances? The entire notion of *the divine right of kings* was based on the collapse of any distinction between church and state. The founders, in their quest for a limited state, wanted, in Jefferson's words, to build "a wall of separation" between the two.

In addition, historical examples of religious empires show us that not only does it damage the state when religion merges with politics, but it risks damaging religion as well when political power conflates with religious power.

· ·

establishment clause: the First Amendment guarantee that the government will not create and support an official state church

free exercise clause: the First Amendment guarantee that citizens may freely engage in the religious activities of their choice

HOW WELL DO WE LIVE UP TO JEFFERSON'S IDEAL?

In a nation that is largely, but not exclusively, Christian, maintaining a wall of separation between church and state can be hard. Americans and, indeed, members of the Supreme Court are divided on whether we need to keep the two entirely separate, or whether it is okay to allow some state recognition of and support for religion as long as it accommodates all religions.

The trouble with agreeing to accommodate all religions in a predominantly Christian country is that often it is Christianity that is accommodated, leaving nonbelievers and members of other faiths to feel alienated, silenced, or forced to challenge public authorities to have their own rights protected. The efforts of those who want to be more inclusive—by saying "happy holidays" instead of "Merry Christmas," for instance, or by emphasizing the celebration of non-Christian holidays—has often left Christians feeling under attack. Others' insistence on having their religious rights respected has led some Christians to feel that *their* beliefs are disrespected that saying "happy holidays" means there is a "war on Christmas," for instance.

3.2: THE SKIMMABLE COURT WATCHER: *LEMON V. KURTZMAN* AND THE FIRST AMENDMENT

One side of the controversy	The other side of the controversy	What does the Court say?	Problems implementing the decision
People who want to support "all" religions equally—**accommodationists**	People who want a separation between church and state—**separationists**	*Lemon v. Kurtzman* (1971) → *Lemon* test: # Law must have secular purpose # Law must not advance religion # Law must not have excessive entanglement with religion	Hard for Court to decide what "excessive entanglement" means. How much is "excessive?" What is "entangled?"

accommodationists: people who want to support "all" religions equally

separationists: people who want a separation between church and state

Lemon **test:** the three-pronged rule used by the courts to determine whether the establishment clause is violated

What is a constitutional issue—how far church and state can be intermingled—has become a cultural clash that it is almost impossible to solve to everyone's satisfaction. Legal quarrels over something so deeply felt as religious beliefs tend to explode into something divisive and difficult to solve politically, underscoring the founders' desire to keep religious disputes out of the political sphere.

FREE EXERCISE, THE OTHER HALF OF THE EQUATION

The First Amendment not only prohibits the establishment of religion but also says Congress can't prohibit the free exercise of religion. That sounds unobjectionable on its face, but, in practice, exercising your religion can frequently crash into other people's rights. We have already pointed out the internal conflict between the establishment and free exercise clauses, but the free exercise of religion is even more complicated than that.

Americans have an absolute right to believe what they want to believe. It is when their beliefs cross into action that they can conflict with other people's actions or the state's obligation to exercise its police power to protect the health, well-being, and security of all citizens.

CAN THE STATE REGULATE RELIGION?

The question of when and how much the state can regulate religion is a tricky one. The Supreme Court has danced around this issue for decades. For many years the Court had said that the government had to demonstrate a compelling reason to infringe on religious practice, but in 1990 the Court reversed course and put the burden of proof back on religious groups to show that the state regulation violated the groups' rights. In 1993, Congress passed the Religious Freedom Restoration Act (RFRA), which returned the burden of proof to the state. The Supreme Court struck the law down until it was amended to apply only to the federal government. Many states have since passed their own RFRAs. It's been a bit like legal ping pong, which shows you how controversial the issue is.

The issue of religious freedom from state regulation became even more controversial during Barack Obama's administration. Some employers balked at the Affordable Care Act's requirement that they provide their employees with health insurance that included contraception as part of basic coverage. They argued that this violated their deeply held religious convictions. The law had already exempted religious employers from the requirement, but in what has become known as the *Hobby Lobby* case, the Court ruled in 2014 that corporations that were not publicly traded did not have to provide coverage if doing so would violate their owners' beliefs.

MORE FREEDOM FOR SOME MEANS LESS FOR OTHERS?

Another issue that has raised a religious controversy stems from **marriage equality**. In 2015 the Supreme Court surprised many Americans with its ruling in *Obergefell v. Hodges,* which held that the equal protection clause and the due process clause guaranteed gays the right to marry. Furthermore, same-sex marriages had to be recognized as legal in all fifty states. Public opinion had swung sharply toward support of marriage equality in the years leading up to the ruling, but not all Americans agreed that it should be legal.

NOT EXACTLY A PIECE OF CAKE

Some people in the wedding industry (notably, wedding cake bakers) argued that the ruling required them to violate their consciences because it coerced them to provide support for a practice that ran counter to their religious beliefs. This issue of coerced speech arrived at the Supreme Court in 2018. In a narrow ruling in what has come to be called the *Masterpiece Cake Shop* case, the Court didn't resolve the question of whether someone's religious beliefs would allow them to discriminate in whom they served, but it did side with the baker because it found that he had faced a local Colorado process hostile to his religious beliefs. The Court also made it clear that more rulings on this subject could follow in the future.

Although the Court has not yet settled the issue of whether religious liberty could exempt someone from providing services in the marketplace, in May 2017, President Donald Trump issued an executive order protecting religious freedom. In October, then-Attorney General Jeff Sessions fleshed out that order with a memo that said, among other things,

Religious liberty is not merely a right to personal religious beliefs or even to worship in a sacred place. Except in the narrowest of circumstances, no one should be forced to choose between living out his or her faith and complying with the law. Therefore, to the greatest extent practicable and permitted by law, religious observance should be reasonably accommodated in all government activity, including employment, contracting and programming.

Sessions's clear intent was to force laws to accommodate religious beliefs and ignored the "excessive entanglement" concerns of the *Lemon* Test. How far this results in the denial of civil rights to other groups has yet to be seen, but whichever way it turns out, it is an excellent example of how our own natural rights can be limited by the requirement to respect the rights of others.

marriage equality: the idea that marriage should not be reserved for heterosexual couples and that all marriages should be equal before the law

SPEECH, PRESS, AND ASSEMBLY: THE REST OF THE FIRSTS

As important to the founders as freedom from an established religion was **freedom of expression**—including freedom of speech, freedom of the press, and **freedom of assembly** to air one's views. There are a lot more ways for people to express their opinions today than there were in the eighteenth century. At that time, speech, press, and assembly pretty much covered the options.

WHY FREEDOM OF EXPRESSION IS A BIG DEAL

Freedom of expression is important for many reasons but chiefly because it includes the right to criticize the government. If government is going to be accountable to citizens, they have to know what government is doing with the authority they give it, whether it is carrying out their wishes and protecting their rights, or whether it is corrupt or has conflicts of interest. They also need to keep themselves and their fellow citizens informed so they can make (one hopes) wise choices at the ballot box. Furthermore, denying free speech sets a dangerous precedent—if we can stop our opponents from speaking out today, they might stop us from speaking out tomorrow.

IF FREE SPEECH IS SO IMPORTANT, WHY DO WE EVER LIMIT IT?

The Court has allowed the burning of the U.S. flag as protected speech; it has recognized that what is seen as pornographic in a small midwestern town may not be in New York's Times Square; it has permitted the wearing of arm bands and the wearing of a T-shirt protesting the Vietnam War with the words "Fuck the draft"; and it has allowed people not to pledge allegiance to the flag. It has even ruled that giving money to political causes is a form of expression and cannot be limited.

In the United States, *all* rights have limits and speech is no exception. Just like there are limits to religious freedom, there are limits to our freedom of expression. The Supreme Court has at various times ruled that speech (and symbolic speech) can be limited for purposes of national security during war (**sedition**), because it is obscene, because it is intended to start a fight (**fighting words**), or because it maliciously damages a reputation (**libel** when printed; **slander** when spoken).

freedom of expression: the ability to express one's views without government restraint

freedom of assembly: the right of the people to gather peacefully and to petition government

sedition: speech that criticizes the government in order to promote rebellion

fighting words: speech intended to incite violence

libel: written defamation of character

slander: spoken defamation of character

PUTTING SPEECH TO THE SUPREME COURT TEST

The Court has come up with a series of tests (like the *Lemon* test, mentioned earlier) meant to clarify the yardstick it is using for allowing or denying protected status for speech. And like the *Lemon* Test, many of these tests, designed to eliminate ambiguity, introduced even more.

For instance, when regulating political speech, the **clear and present danger test**, first suggested in 1919, was meant to distinguish speech that was immediately harmful from that which posed only a remote threat. The test didn't prove helpful in determining what "clear" and "present" meant, however, and it was eventually replaced with the **imminent lawless action test**, which protected speech unless it was linked with action.

Similarly, obscenity has been the subject of test-making efforts. Defining *obscenity* has given the justices considerable grief because of how seemingly subjective it can be: the late Justice Potter concluded in 1964, but "I know it when I see it." Eventually the Court concluded that obscenity could be restricted so long as it met standards defined by the *Miller* **test**, which refers to local standards and asks whether the work lacks "serious literary, artistic, political, or scientific value." Again, hard to define.

One thing the Supreme Court has been fairly steady on is its refusal to engage in previous or **prior restraint**—that is, censoring and refusing to allow the publication of something, even though it very well might fail one of the Court's tests *after* publication. The Court has held that only a national emergency could justify such censorship, and it rejected President Richard Nixon's effort to prevent the *New York Times*'s publication of a "top secret" document about the Vietnam War, ruling that national "security" is too vague a concept to excuse violating the First Amendment. To grant such power to the president, the Court ruled, would run the risk of destroying the liberty the government was trying to secure.

BE AWARE— LOOMING ISSUES ON THE FREE SPEECH HORIZON

Life was simpler when the printing press was the only mechanism for disseminating information besides the human voice. Electronic communication makes it vastly more complicated. The Internet and the social media that

. . . .

clear and present danger test: the rule used by the courts that allows language to be regulated only if it presents an immediate and urgent danger

imminent lawless action test: the rule used by the courts that restricts speech only if it is aimed at producing or is likely to produce imminent lawless action

Miller **test:** the rule used by the courts in which the definition of obscenity must be based on local standards

prior restraint: censorship of or punishment for the expression of ideas before the ideas are printed or spoken

thrive on it open up legions of questions about the regulation of access, content, and censorship.

An important issue related to the Internet is **net neutrality**. Net neutrality describes how the Internet works now—on the principle that service providers (Verizon, Comcast, AT&T, and the like) cannot speed up or slow down access for customers or make decisions about the content they see or the apps they download. The Federal Communications Commission (FCC) adopted net neutrality rules in 2015, but President Trump appointed a former Verizon employee as chair of the FCC in 2017 and he rolled back the protections. Supporters of net neutrality are urging Congress to reverse the policy.

The existence of the Internet has raised other issues that the authors of the First Amendment could not have anticipated. In 2016 it became apparent that a foreign country, Russia, had launched an attack on the American electoral system with the goal of damaging the chances of one of the candidates and destabilizing the political system as a whole. We were vulnerable to this attack because of our tendency to practice citizenship through various media channels. Among other methods (hacking into private email accounts and into voting systems themselves), the Russians manipulated social media with fake accounts destined to stir social unrest, boost the fortunes of Donald Trump, and damage the reputation of Hillary Clinton. In the wake of the election, Internet giants like Facebook and Twitter, which were used as instruments of the attack, have tried to regulate their own usage rules to avoid facing federal regulation of free speech on the Internet, which they may face anyway. At issue is whether protections of free speech also cover weaponized fake speech, particularly when the consumers of the speech are unaware of its source.

3.5 CIVIL LIBERTIES—UNDERSTANDING DUE PROCESS RIGHTS

WHAT ARE DUE PROCESS RIGHTS?

> **Due process rights** are the rights preserved in the Fourth through Eighth Amendments—the ones that give Americans some rights against being railroaded into jail by the police and the courts, especially for political purposes.

net neutrality: the principle that Internet service providers cannot speed up or slow down access for customers or make decisions about the content they see or the apps they download

due process rights: the guarantee that laws will be fair and reasonable and that citizens suspected of breaking the law will be treated fairly

WHY DID THE FOUNDERS DEVOTE HALF OF THE BILL OF RIGHTS TO DUE PROCESS?

A chief fear of the founders was a government so strong that its leaders could use its police power and the judicial system for political purposes. Rulers who can arrest, jail, torture, and imprison their opponents without cause can secure their own power much more easily than those who have to be accountable to citizens. English history was rife with examples of the denial of due process despite the 1215 Magna Carta, which limited the monarch's powers somewhat, at least over the nobility. The founders were determined that their new republic would not have a president who could investigate or lock up his rivals.

The founders were so focused on these rights that some of them are even in the text of the Constitution itself. Article I provides that Congress cannot suspend the writ of **habeas corpus** (the right to be brought before a judge and informed of the charges and evidence against you) or pass a **bill of attainder** (a law directed at an individual or group that accuses and convicts them of a crime) or an **ex post facto law** (a law that makes something illegal after you have already done it).

If some liberties are so important that they belong in the First Amendment, how important must others be that the founders put them in the Constitution itself, and that the Anti-Federalists devoted half of the Bill of Rights to them?

WHAT DO THE DUE PROCESS RIGHTS INCLUDE?

The due process rights ensure that the police do not become a political weapon. That means Americans have the following protections:

\# Their homes cannot be searched for evidence of a crime without probable cause (and if evidence is obtained illegally, the **exclusionary rule** prevents it from being used against them in a court of law).

\# They have a right to be told why they are being arrested.

\# They cannot be tried twice for the same crime (double jeopardy).

habeas corpus: the right to be brought before a judge and informed of the charges and evidence against you

bill of attainder: a law directed at an individual or group that accuses and convicts them of a crime

ex post facto law: a law that makes something illegal after you have already done it

exclusionary rule: the rule created by the Supreme Court that evidence seized illegally may not be used to obtain a conviction

\# They have rights to an attorney, to resist questioning, and not to incriminate themselves (and to be informed of these so-called **Miranda rights**, named for the case establishing that the police must inform suspects that they possess these rights).

\# They have a right to a fair and speedy jury trial with counsel.

\# They can't be subjected to cruel treatment in their imprisonment.

EXCEPT WHEN THEY DON'T

There are exceptions to all of these protections. Although police do need probable cause, they don't have to get a warrant to search someone's car, for instance (because that person will likely be gone by the time the warrant is obtained). Electronic surveillance raises many issues that the founders never had to face. The question of double jeopardy can run into federalism issues—for example, can you be tried for the same case in federal and then in state court? And many states have the death penalty, which some Americans consider cruel and unusual punishment.

Some courts—tax courts, for instance, or immigration courts—do not have to follow these rules of due process. The separation of families at the border in 2018 and the deportations of parents without their children took place without minimal due process, even though the Court ruled in *Zadvydas v. Davis* (2001) that noncitizens, including undocumented persons, are entitled to civil liberties. President Trump's call to have people deported without court proceedings was a clear violation of the law. The backlog of cases and difficulties in reunifying families torn apart has led to legal shortcuts, however.

These are only a few of the snags run into by the promise of due process, but at least on paper, Americans are protected, and if they are denied due process rights, a lawyer (to which they are entitled, remember, even if they cannot pay) can use that fact to try to secure them.

THE UPSHOT

The Constitution and the Fourth through Eighth Amendments reflect the founders' concern that the police power would be used for political purposes, and they try to protect Americans from that. Although not its original intent, the Fourteenth Amendment has been interpreted to mean that the states must provide that same protection.

Miranda rights: the rights that a person has to resist questioning and not to incriminate oneself; the police must inform suspects that they possess these rights

3.6 CIVIL LIBERTIES—UNDERSTANDING THE RIGHT TO PRIVACY

WHAT RIGHT TO PRIVACY?

In which amendment do we find the **right to privacy**? None of them, as it turns out. It's not in the Constitution, either. One can argue that the founders created a limited government and never intended it to be powerful enough to infringe on the private lives of Americans, but none of them thought it a serious enough threat to put into the document itself.

The right to privacy is a judicial creation of the Supreme Court in the 1965 case of *Griswold v. Connecticut*. In that case the state of Connecticut had passed a law criminalizing the use of contraception. The law was challenged and appealed up to the Supreme Court on the grounds that the decision to use birth control was a private one.

The justices on the Court agreed, but the Constitution didn't give them much to work with as a basis for their argument. Since there was no actual right to privacy in the document or any of the amendments, the justices "found" such a right to be implied in the First Amendment protection of one's beliefs and speech, the Fourth Amendment protection against unreasonable searches and seizures, the Fifth Amendment protection against self-incrimination, and the Ninth Amendment promise that one's rights weren't limited to the ones enumerated in the document. Based on that reasoning, the Court declared the Connecticut law unconstitutional because it violated an implicit right to privacy.

WHY IS THIS RIGHT CONTROVERSIAL?

On its face, there doesn't seem to be a whole lot that's controversial about the right to privacy. Most Americans would agree that the right to plan one's family is a private decision the government should stay out of. Yet, the right to privacy has become one of the fiercest battlegrounds in American politics.

The disagreement arises because the precedent set in *Griswold* was the basis for the landmark 1973 decision *Roe v. Wade,* which held that a woman's decision to terminate a pregnancy in the first trimester was a private one. And although contraception may not be all that controversial (unless we are talking about providing it as part of health care coverage), abortion definitely is.

. . . .

right to privacy: the judicial creation from *Griswold v. Connecticut* (1965) that certain rights in the Bill of Rights protected intimate decisions like family planning from state interference

WHICH BRINGS US BACK TO HAMILTON'S *FEDERALIST PAPER* #84

Underlying this controversy is an interesting constitutional issue: whether the Constitution should be read literally as the founders wrote it or whether it can be read flexibly in the light of contemporary circumstances. The first position, if you recall, is exactly the argument that Hamilton feared would be made if a bill of rights were to be attached to the Constitution—that only those rights that were explicitly written down would be protected. The right to privacy has become a target of those who argue that position.

Legal scholars who take the position Hamilton was wary of believe that the Constitution should be read just as it was written—that the task of the constitutional scholar is to discern the founders' original intent and that their words are to be taken literally. These scholars and judges, known as originalists or **strict constructionists** because they read the Constitution strictly, believe that if Americans want a right to privacy, they need to amend the Constitution to include it.

Those who take the other approach to reading the Constitution, whose number includes seven of the nine justices who ruled in *Griswold*, are called **judicial interpretivists**. This view holds that the founders could not have anticipated all the changes that make the world today different from theirs and, therefore, judges should read the Constitution as the founders would write it in light of modern-day experience. That is, they should interpret what the founders would mean today.

THE POLITICAL SIGNIFICANCE OF THIS ARGUMENT TODAY

Because how you read the Constitution has such clear policy implications, Supreme Court confirmation hearings have often become battlegrounds as well. Republicans want to appoint strict constructionists to the Court, hoping they will overturn *Roe* (by overturning *Griswold* and the right to privacy that interpretivists believe is implied). Democrats, seeking to protect women's reproductive rights and the extension of rights generally, want to put interpretivists on the Court.

ARE REPRODUCTIVE RIGHTS THE ONLY ONES THAT FALL UNDER THE RIGHT TO PRIVACY?

No, actually, they are not. Supporters of gay rights tried unsuccessfully to use the right to privacy to fight laws that criminalized homosexual behavior. As we will soon see, they ended up winning rights not as civil liberties but as civil rights under the constitutional principle of equal protection.

strict constructionists: supporters of a judicial approach holding that the Constitution should be read literally, with the framers' intentions uppermost in mind

judicial interpretivists: supporters of a judicial approach holding that the Constitution is a living document and that judges should interpret it according to changing times and values

The right to refuse life-supporting treatment if one is terminally ill, and the right to have a doctor's assistance in ending one's life in the face of such terminal illness, have also been argued under right-to-privacy grounds. The Court has upheld advance directives determining one's medical wishes and has also allowed states to permit physician-assisted suicide under certain circumstances. Currently six states allow that practice.

3.7 CIVIL RIGHTS—BATTLING POLITICAL INEQUALITY

NOW TO CIVIL RIGHTS . . .

> So far in this chapter we have seen how the protection of our liberties restricts government action, leaving us free to act in various spheres. But sometimes exercising rights requires an active government to step in and create a protected sphere in which a group can exercise its rights.

JUST TO REMIND YOU

> Civil rights refers to the freedom of groups (defined by some particular characteristic—like race, gender, or sexual orientation—that is beyond their members' control) to participate fully in the public life of a nation (for instance, voting, getting an education, traveling, and marrying). Rather than limiting government, the protection of civil rights often *empowers* government to act. Protections of civil rights are guaranteed by the Thirteenth, Fourteenth, Fifteenth, Nineteenth, and Twenty-Sixth Amendments to the Constitution.

THE DILEMMA OF EQUAL PROTECTION

> The difficulty as we study the effort of excluded groups to possess the full array of citizenship rights is that we are studying the inherent problem of discrimination. All laws discriminate in some way. To discriminate is to treat differently—we treat murderers and nonmurderers differently, for instance, and people who speed on the highway differently from people who do not. The trick is to know what kinds of discrimination are okay and what kinds are not. When is it okay to treat people differently?

OKAY, SO WHEN IS IT OKAY TO TREAT PEOPLE DIFFERENTLY?

> The Supreme Court has an answer to that question—similar to the "tests" we looked at earlier. It got there in a strange way.

· ·

discrimination: differential treatment

THE COURT TRIES TO ANSWER.

> Obviously, the United States has a history of treating some people very differently from others, and the Supreme Court generally found a way to approve that differential treatment for people of color or women. But in 1942, the Court was forced to articulate a rule for when it was okay to discriminate and when it was not. During World War II, Franklin Roosevelt issued an executive order that people of Japanese descent, two thirds of whom were citizens, be put in internment camps, where they stayed until the order was suspended in 1944. His reasoning (which was not backed up with empirical evidence) was that, since the United States was fighting Japan, Japanese Americans might betray their own country because of secret loyalties to a country many had never even seen. Many of them lost their homes and their property while they were in the camps.

DIG DEEPER

Read about Fred Korematsu being honored with a Google Doodle.

And, almost as important, watch as he was presented a presidential medal of honor by President Bill Clinton.

Go to **edge.sagepub.com/ dig-deeper**

The order was challenged on equal protection grounds by a man named Fred Korematsu and reached the Supreme Court in 1944.

SKIM IT!

3.3: THE SKIMMABLE COURT WATCHER: *KOREMATSU V. UNITED STATES* AND EQUAL PROTECTION

One side of the controversy	The other side of the controversy	What does the Court say?	Problems implementing the decision
The Fourteenth Amendment guarantees that citizens cannot be denied the equal protection of the laws, and that includes treating them differently because of race.	Japanese Americans pose a serious potential threat to national security.	*Korematsu v. United States* (1944): # Laws that treat people differently because of race are highly suspicious, making race a **suspect classification**. # That means the Court must subject them to a standard of review called **strict scrutiny**. # Strict scrutiny means asking if there is a **compelling state purpose** to the discrimination.	In *Korematsu* the Court held there was a compelling state purpose in national security, but this legal standard of review would from then on be used to evaluate laws that discriminated on the basis of race.

A compelling state interest is a very hard standard to meet, although the justices in *Korematsu* shamefully decided the government had met it. Some good has come out of the compelling state interest test, however. It has been applied to strike down most laws that discriminate by race since the mid-1950s. It is part of a set of standards of review that the Court uses to decide when it is okay for the law to treat classes of people differently.

Through a number of cases the Court has arrived at the following scheme:

TABLE IT!

3.4: LEGAL CLASSIFICATIONS AND SCRUTINY STANDARDS

If the law classifies people by	that classification is	which means the Court subjects the law to a	and asks if there is a	The usual outcome?
race	suspect	strict scrutiny standard of review	compelling state purpose for this classification	The law is usually struck down.
gender	quasi-suspect	intermediate standard of review	important state purpose for this classification	The law may be struck down, or it may stand.
age, income	nonsuspect	minimum rationality standard of review	rational basis for this classification	The law usually stands.

suspect classification: a classification, such as race, for which any discriminatory law must be justified by a compelling state interest

strict scrutiny: a heightened standard of review used by the Supreme Court to assess the constitutionality of laws that limit some freedoms or that make a suspect classification

compelling state purpose: a fundamental state purpose, which must be shown before the law can limit some freedoms or treat some groups of people differently

A FEW THINGS TO NOTE ABOUT THIS SCHEME

Laws that discriminate according to gender do not get the same level of scrutiny that race does. However, had women's groups been able to pass the Equal Rights Amendment in the 1970s, gender may have very well become a suspect class.

Becoming a suspect class sounds like a good thing since it means that laws that discriminate against your group get the strictest level of scrutiny. But it has proven to be *a double-edged sword* for racial groups because it tends to strike down not only laws that discriminate against you but also laws that discriminate in your favor. Thus, some affirmative action plans that try to create more racially diverse student bodies at American universities have been struck down. The practice that allows state legislatures to draw congressional districts to advantage racial minorities has been struck down as well.

One classification that is currently difficult to fit into this scheme is sexual orientation. Not long ago, sexual orientation was a nonsuspect class. It simply required a rational basis to treat members of the LGBTQ community differently. But the Court ruled in 2015 that the Fourteenth Amendment meant that states had to allow people of the same sex to marry. The standard they applied was stronger than the rational basis standard but not yet quite as strong as strict scrutiny. This is a classification that is in flux, and we will have to watch future Court cases to see how it is treated.

It may look cut-and-dried, but groups have had to put grueling effort into getting higher levels of scrutiny applied to the laws that treat them differently. We will look at some of these groups shortly.

Even when the battle is successful and the discriminatory laws are struck down, only one kind of discrimination is ended—**de jure discrimination,** or discrimination by laws. Another, more difficult kind of discrimination has nothing directly to do with laws. Called **de facto discrimination,** it is discrimination that results from life circumstances, habit, custom, or socioeconomic status. It can be just as devastating for a group to be the focus of this kind of discrimination, but it is harder to fix since there is no law to be subjected to scrutiny and changed.

· ·

de jure discrimination: discrimination by laws

de facto discrimination: discrimination on the basis of life circumstances, habit, custom, or socioeconomic status

Many groups have had to wage mighty battles to be included as full citizens in American civil society. From their earliest days, American colonies excluded people from citizenship because of their religion, their lack of wealth, their gender, their status as slaves or Native Americans, or their ethnicity. In the next two sections we will look closely at the specific cases of African Americans and women as those groups struggled for equal rights.

3.8 CIVIL RIGHTS — THE CASE OF RACE

WHY DO SOME PEOPLE CALL SLAVERY AMERICA'S ORIGINAL SIN?

The story of America of course cannot be told without the institution of slavery and the narratives that white slave-owners told to justify owning and forcing the labor of fellow human beings. Adding insult to grievous injury, slaves were denied any rights in the Constitution, but southerners used them—through the Three-Fifths Compromise—to inflate the representation southern states received in Congress. Those narratives created a story of an inferior race that required white mastery and established a set of stereotypes of African Americans—that they were less intelligent, less industrious, and less capable than their masters—that continue to haunt the nation. Slavery has been called the original sin of American politics. It was a tragedy for the human beings who were enslaved and demeaned by the narratives that supported it, and it twisted the minds and moral character of those who did the enslaving. Americans still live with the consequences today.

THE CIVIL WAR

The American Civil War (1861–1865) was fought over slavery and the states' rights to practice it, and even the conclusion of that bloody and tragic moment in our past did not put the issue to rest. Remember—rights equal power. It's not human nature to give up power without a fight.

Immediately after the War and the passage of the Thirteenth Amendment banning slavery, white southerners tried to seize back the power they had lost by passing state and local laws called black codes. Black codes denied freed blacks the right to vote, to go to school, or to own property—they essentially re-created the conditions of slavery under another name.

. . . .

slavery: the ownership, for forced labor, of one people by another

Thirteenth Amendment: the 1865 constitutional amendment banning slavery

black codes: a series of laws in the post–Civil War South designed to restrict the rights of former slaves before the passage of the Fourteenth and Fifteenth Amendments; denied freed blacks the right to vote, to go to school, or to own property, which re-created the conditions of slavery under another name

JIM CROW

In an effort to shut down the black codes, the northern-dominated Congress passed the Fourteenth and Fifteenth Amendments (the Fourteenth extends full citizenship rights and equal protection to "all persons born or natural-ized in the United States," as we read earlier in the discussion of incorpora-tion; the **Fifteenth Amendment** said the right to vote could not be denied on the basis of race). White southerners responded by ushering in the era of **Jim Crow laws**, again trying to re-create the power relations of slavery but this time attempting to do an end run around the amendments designed to give blacks citizenship rights. Jim Crow laws included various ways of stop-ping African Americans from exercising the vote and from using the same schools and other facilities as whites. They were forms of de jure discrimi-nation that created a segregated society in the South.

IN WHICH ARENAS DID AFRICAN AMERICANS FIGHT FOR EQUAL RIGHTS?

When members of a group are as thoroughly barred from mainstream polit-ical life as African Americans were, it can be hard to gain access to a bat-tleground on which they can fight for their rights. The arena of national legislative politics was closed to African Americans after the North turned to its own affairs following the passage of the Thirteenth through Fifteenth Amendments (known as the Civil War amendments). The presidency did not offer any recourse, nor did the state governments, which were the source of the discriminatory laws.

COURTS

Before the Civil War, the precedent on black rights had been set in the 1857 *Dred Scott v. Sanford* case, in which the Court ruled that even a freed slave had no standing to bring a case to the courts. In 1896 the Supreme Court made segregation constitutional in *Plessy v. Ferguson*, ruling that sepa-rate facilities were legal if they were equal. Of course, **separate but equal** wasn't equal at all, and the ruling signaled that the courts weren't going to be a profitable arena for blacks to fight in either. All three branches of government—and government at all levels—seemed filled with obstacles.

The courts nonetheless offered an important strategic avenue. In 1910, African Americans who refused to accept the second-class citizenship of Jim Crow organized the National Association for the Advancement of

. . . .

Fifteenth Amendment: the 1870 constitutional amendment guaranteeing that the right to vote could not be denied on the basis of race

Jim Crow laws: laws passed after the Thirteenth, Fourteenth, and Fifteenth Amendments granted African Americans citizen rights; intended to re-create the power relations of slavery

separate but equal: the legal principle stemming from *Plessy v. Ferguson* (1896) that segregation didn't violate the Fourteenth Amendment unless the separate facilities provided were unequal

Colored People. NAACP lawyers developed a legal strategy to gain access to the arena of the courts by first targeting legal education. Part of their calculation was that, to most Americans, law schools would be a less threatening area for desegregation than primary education, but one where the justices of the Supreme Court were particularly likely to find arguments against segregation to be persuasive. They ended with the political earthquake of *Brown v. Board of Education* in 1954. In *Brown,* the Court finally overruled the separate but equal doctrine that had prevailed in the legal community for more than half a century.

3.5: THE SKIMMABLE COURT WATCHER: FROM SEPARATE BUT EQUAL TO DESEGREGATION

The legal basis for "separate but equal"	The arguments for nondiscrimination	Changes at the Court level	Problems implementing the *Brown* decision
# *Dred Scott v. Sanford* (1857), the last Court case dealing with the rights of blacks, had established the precedent that even a freed slave had no rights in court. # The Court struggled to reconcile the power relationships of segregation with the 14th Amendment and came up with the principle of separate but equal.	# The 14th Amendment said that all Americans were entitled to the equal protection of the laws. # Requiring separate facilities was a violation of that right and thereby unconstitutional.	# *Plessy v. Ferguson* (1896) agreed that if facilities were "equal," it was okay for them to be separated, putting the seal of constitutional approval on segregation for almost 100 years. # *Brown v. Board of Education* (1954) reversed that ruling, holding that segregation itself was unequal.	# *Plessy* became the basis for legalized Jim Crow throughout the South. # It was not until the 1930s—when the NAACP began to use a law school–centered strategy [*Missouri ex rel Gaines* (1938), *Sweatt v. Painter* (1950)]—that *Plessy* was slowly undermined. The Court eventually overturned it in *Brown v. Board of Education* (1954) and set off a decades-long effort to desegregate schools.

Brown v. Board of Education: the 1954 Supreme Court case that rejected the idea that separate could be equal in education

BOYCOTTS

> At the same time that *Brown* was being decided, African Americans found access to another arena that led to changes in discriminatory laws: economic activity. When Rosa Parks refused to vacate her bus seat for a white man in Montgomery, Alabama—launching the **boycott** of the bus system—African Americans realized that their purchasing power could be a considerable political weapon.

DIG DEEPER

Watch the excellent movie about the boycott called *The Long Walk Home*.

Go to **edge.sagepub.com/ dig-deeper**

PUBLIC OPINION

> By the early 1960s, the new technology of television had brought the plight of African Americans out of isolation in the South to the whole country's attention. The court of public opinion was not kind to southern whites.

Peaceful black protest marches met by snarling police dogs, and college-aged black students holding sit-ins at whites-only lunch counters being hauled off by police, made for gripping television viewing in northern states. Driving the point home was horrifying footage—including coverage of the murders of three young men, two white college students and one black, who were participating in the 1964 black voter registration drive called Freedom Summer.

CONGRESS

> In 1964 and 1965, civil rights legislation initiated by President John Kennedy and then pushed through Congress by President Lyndon Johnson after Kennedy's assassination finally removed most of the legal barriers to integration.

Southern whites, most of whom still belonged to Johnson's Democratic Party despite their social conservatism and racist views, (in large part because many still held a grudge against the party of Lincoln) didn't take any more kindly to passage of the new civil rights laws than they had to the Civil War amendments 100 years earlier. Southern congressmen staged a filibuster to prevent a vote on the legislation in the Senate. When they lost, they began a slow process of defecting from the Democratic Party, a process sped up by President Richard Nixon's so-called "southern strategy" of using racial issues to split them off from the Democratic Party.

· ·

boycott: the refusal to buy certain goods or services as a way to protest policy or to force political reform

The combination of these strategies has come to be known as the **civil rights movement**.

DID THE CIVIL RIGHTS MOVEMENT ERADICATE DE FACTO DISCRIMINATION AS WELL AS DE JURE?

Unfortunately, no. One irony of the legislative change accomplished by Congress was that, although it ended the de jure discrimination in the South, it highlighted the shortcomings of legal change as a method to redress de facto segregation in the North. Northern cities didn't have discriminatory laws to change. Instead, segregation in the North arose from long-term economic patterns and demographic changes that left African Americans in the city centers and succeeding waves of newly assimilated white immigrants in the suburbs. Schools and neighborhoods were segregated as a result, and there were no laws to change to reverse the process. Attempts at **integration** involving busing black kids out of the city to attend suburban white schools and white kids back in to attend urban black ones roused fury in white families that had fought their way up the economic ladder to move to places with better schools. De facto discrimination can't be remedied by fixing laws. It requires an effort to fix the outcomes, which strikes many Americans as fundamentally unfair.

But the fact that opposition to busing was not solely race based did not mean that **racism** was vanquished or did not exist in the North as well as the South. Despite the hard-won changes in laws, demeaning racial narratives were still woven into the American story and still determined how African Americans were treated and how they were treated by rules and institutions founded on **white privilege**, that is, the learned tendency to see the world through the context of white culture and power.

DOES THE UNITED STATES STILL HAVE A RACE PROBLEM?

Yes. It would be tempting to believe that, almost a quarter of the way into the twenty-first century, the United States has finally left its race problems behind. We have certainly made strides that the early civil rights marchers

civil rights movement: the group effort of African Americans to claim their civil rights through a variety of means—legal, political, economic, civil disobedience—in the 1950s and 1960s

integration: breaking down barriers (legal, cultural, economic) that keep races apart to allow the creation of a diverse community

racism: institutionalized power inequalities based on the perception of racial differences

white privilege: the learned tendency to see the world through the context of white culture and power

only dreamed of. But race endures as a defining issue in American politics, especially as demographic change forces whites to grapple with sharing minority status with other racial groups.

Systemic racism is built into the American system in a way that gives preference to whites and stacks the deck against people of color. We can see it in the education and income gaps that continue to reflect the different opportunities many African Americans face from birth. We can see it in the fear and prejudice that cause police officers to be quicker to shoot (and kill) unarmed black suspects than their white counterparts. We can see it in young Trayvon Martin's 2012 murder by an armed vigilante who feared a young black kid in a hoodie making a candy run through his own neighborhood. We can see it in a Yale student who called the police in 2018 because she saw a black woman (a fellow student) asleep in a commons area and assumed she had no right to be there.

Groups like Black Lives Matter have picked up the mantle of the civil rights movement, marching in protest and able, for the first time, to use smartphones to capture on video the vitriolic responses and police abuses that black Americans still face, and to let those videos go viral. Like television carrying pictures of southern racism north, social media carries pictures of systemic racism everywhere.

Barack Obama's ascent to the presidency was a huge symbol of the progress this nation has made on race, as well as a sign of the demographic changes occurring in the population. He was not the first president to win without a majority of the white vote—for more than fifty years a majority of white voters have typically supported Republicans. But he won a significant portion of the white vote, and his election night in 2008 was filled with the hopes of many that perhaps Americans had obliterated the stain of racism from the nation's character.

In hindsight, we know that no such thing happened. Obama won the presidency in part on his promise to bring Americans together and to work with both halves of a Congress that had grown to be more polarized than at any time since the Civil War. Of course, that put the keys to his success in the hands of Republican legislators who were united in their effort to deny it to him.

And, of course, there was the election of Donald Trump in 2016 on a campaign that had clear racial and nativist overtones—not only was Trump the most famous of the birthers who denied President Obama's legitimacy because of a bogus claim that he wasn't a U.S. citizen, but he also made denigrating remarks about Hispanics, Muslims, women, Jews, and just about any other group whose members he felt had crossed him in any way. A significant part of Trump's support came from those reacting to Obama's presidency and the coalition that had put him in office. The claim that we had to "take our country back" or "Make America Great Again" was an implicit rebuke to the president who many people felt had diminished America simply because of his skin color.

ARE AFRICAN AMERICANS THE ONLY PEOPLE OF COLOR WHO FACE DISCRIMINATION IN THE UNITED STATES?

We all know the answer to this is "no." People of color who have had to fight for equal treatment by the law include Native Americans, who were forced from their lands by European settlers to live on quasi-sovereign reservations; Latinos, who have regularly crossed the border from Mexico (across land they once owned) to do the cheap agricultural and domestic labor Americans often refuse to do; and Asians, who at various times in history have been refused entry or who have been admitted and then denied basic civil rights or worse, as the *Korematsu* case shows.

The United States is a nation of immigrants. Hardly any American, even direct descendants of the British settlers, can deny that their ancestors came from foreign lands. But immigrants from Europe—despite facing discrimination when they first arrive for talking funny or for eating strange foods or for living in a culture that seems odd to Americans already here—are eventually able to assimilate because they lose the accents, their food becomes Americanized, and *they look like other white Americans*.

But people whose skin color or other facial features continue to mark them as "the other," or different, assimilate more slowly, if at all. The assimilation of European immigrants has traditionally been about their ability to fit in. The assimilation of people of color has depended on the willingness of the white population to give up racist narratives to accept them. As that white-majority status wanes, along with the privilege it has carried, the United States can expect more reaction from those whose numbers are declining, and less patience from those on the receiving end of the racist narratives.

3.9 CIVIL RIGHTS—THE CASE OF GENDER

A QUICK HISTORY OF THE WOMEN'S RIGHTS MOVEMENT

Sexism, like racism, is pervasive, often unrecognized, and has deep cultural roots. Colonial white women had few rights, although those born into wealthy families or married to men with good incomes lived materially comfortable lives. But even after national independence, they had no right to vote, to own property, to get an education, to have a job, to divorce their husbands, or even to keep their children if they were divorced *by* their husbands.

The fact that women went from holding their father's last name to taking their husband's (after being "given in marriage" by their fathers) is indicative of the legal and social status women had. In fact, in English common law, on which much of the American legal system is based, statutory rape was not a sex crime against the woman but a property violation against her father, because it reduced the dowry he could ask for her if she were no longer a virgin.

The women's rights movement is commonly dated from the Seneca Falls (New York) Convention of 1848, when attendees issued a declaration of principles that read, "We hold these truths to be self-evident, that all men and women are created equal. . . ." Even so, although there was general consensus at the convention that women needed more rights, not all attendees agreed that they should vote.

The widely accepted narrative that kept wealthy white women out of public life was that they were too good and pure for the rough-and-tumble corruption of public life. Their territory was the home and their job was to be a "home-maker," creating comfort for their husbands and a respite from the stressful and ugly outside world.

This was a hard story to combat because it required women to deny their own purity, which not everyone, especially comfortable middle-class women, were willing to do. It was also difficult to find an arena to fight in. The U.S. executive branch was no help, nor was the Congress. (One senator declared on the floor, "If women are allowed to vote, every man's life will become hell on earth.") The courts were not willing to hold that the Fourteenth Amendment applied to women.

IN WHICH ARENAS DID WOMEN FIGHT FOR EQUAL RIGHTS?

Women found an unexpected arena in state politics. Not in the settled eastern states, where well-to-do women could argue they had a good life without civil rights, but in the scrambling, dangerous life in states on the western frontier, where women worked side by side with men to carve a life out of the wilderness. The territory of Wyoming allowed women to vote, and when it applied for statehood it refused to yield to the congressional demand that it disenfranchise women. Wyoming was admitted to the union in 1890 as the first state where women could vote.

Although women's rights activists had been pursuing a national strategy without much luck, the state-level effort promised more, but slow, success. Remember that rights equal power! Strong industrial and liquor interests, who bought into the narrative that women were pure and good, feared that saloons would be shut down and women would prevent profitable but exploitative labor practices if they had political power. They waged a fierce battle against women's suffrage, but the state-level effort slowly yielded real results. By 1912, women could vote in states that accounted for fifty-five electoral votes for the presidency.

The **Nineteenth Amendment**, granting women the right to vote, was finally ratified in 1920, the result of

\# The state strategies combined with the national movement

\# The fact that women took on more powerful positions and in some cases largely ran the country while men fought World War I in Europe

\# A growing international sense that the United States was a leading democracy (that still did not allow half its white population to vote)

To give you an idea of the length of the process, only one child who had been brought by her parents to the Seneca Falls Convention was still alive to vote when the national right was guaranteed.

SO THE NINETEENTH AMENDMENT MEANT WOMEN WON EQUAL RIGHTS?

No. The new amendment said only that no state could refuse them the right to vote. More equal rights, including a guarantee of equal treatment by the laws that would have raised gender to the level of a suspect class, would have required the passage of the **Equal Rights Amendment**. Although the ERA made it through Congress in 1972, it had to be ratified by the states, and campaigners never managed to get enough support for it. That is partly because *Roe v. Wade* was decided in 1973, giving women reproductive autonomy, which was one of the things they sought. The Supreme Court, too, began to apply Fourteenth Amendment protections to women, which also took some of the energy out of the movement to pass the ERA. Finally, many people feared the change the ERA would bring. They recognized,

. . . .

Nineteenth Amendment: the 1920 constitutional amendment granting women the right to vote

Equal Rights Amendment: a constitutional amendment passed by Congress but never ratified that would have banned discrimination on the basis of gender

rightly, that strict scrutiny meant that laws that benefited women would be subject to the same scrutiny as those that disadvantaged them. Opponents of the amendment argued, for instance, that women could be drafted and sent to war if the ERA passed. At a time when few women served actively in the military, that seemed like a frightening prospect.

Even though the ERA was not ratified, women's legal status has improved to a large extent. The Lilly Ledbetter Act, signed by President Obama in 2009, requires equal pay for equal work, although a wage gap between men and women remains. There also continues to be a **glass ceiling** that women have not succeeded in breaking, making the majority of the population a minority in boardrooms across the United States, in Congress, on the Supreme Court, and in the other places where power is wielded.

And, of course, one big glass ceiling that women have not yet managed to fracture is the one giving them access to the Oval Office. Regardless of one's views of her politics, Hillary Clinton's two runs for the presidency revealed a good deal of latent sexism in the media and American politics generally. She was criticized for having a shrill voice; for being weak and sickly; and for her choice in clothing, makeup, and hairstyles—none of which had anything to do with her political experience or readiness to be president.

More insidiously, the gendered coverage in the media held Clinton to a different standard than it did her opponents. American ideas of what constitutes leadership are very much based on models provided by the first forty-five presidents of the United States and, therefore, are inescapably based on male role models. When women embrace those characteristics, they are seen as unfeminine, unlikable, and inauthentic, and when they try to define the role differently, they are not seen as leaders.

THE UPSHOT

Cultural attitudes toward woman are undoubtedly changing. Reactions to the openly misogynistic statements made by the current president and the scandals that the #MeToo movement have revealed have signaled a fundamental shift in the kinds of behaviors considered acceptable on the part of powerful men. The #MeToo movement has displaced men of enormous clout in the political, entertainment, news, and sports industries and, maybe more important, empowered women at the individual level to run for office

. . . .

glass ceiling: the invisible but impenetrable barrier that most women face when trying to ascend the corporate or political ladder and try to change the basic rules of the game. The 2016 midterm elections brought over 100 women into the House of Representatives, and rallied record numbers of women to vote for them.

This chapter's GenGap box examines generational attitudes toward racial, ethnic, and gender issues.

3.10 THE PERSISTENCE OF INEQUALITY IN AMERICA

WHY DO INEQUALITIES OF POWER PERSIST?

America is still, in real ways, a nation with pervasive racism and systemic **gender bias** that most citizens often do not recognize, especially in their own selves. Indeed, given the nation's history, it would be amazing if most Americans did not hold racialized and gendered views of each other—that is, if they did not act on the basis of unconscious **stereotypes** or assumptions about other Americans based on their race, ethnicity, gender, or sexual orientation. Some social scientists call the tendency for fleeting thoughts that confirm existing stereotypes to pass through our minds **implicit bias**—those thoughts don't mean that we are racist or sexist, but they do mean that we are subject to social conditioning that helps sort the world into patterns. When those thoughts become the basis for actions, we have crossed a line.

WHAT IS THE EVIDENCE THAT WE ARE EXPERIENCING A REACTION TO SOCIAL AND DEMOGRAPHIC CHANGE?

The United States is at a moment of profound demographic change. By 2050, most of you reading this book will be well into middle age, and the working population you will be part of will be predominantly nonwhite. That means, for the first time in American history, whites will no longer be the majority but rather will be one minority group among other minority groups and will be outnumbered by people of color. Gender patterns are in flux too. Women already outnumber men, and if current trends continue, women will be at least as likely as men (if not more likely than them) to have a college or advanced degree.

gender bias: systemic ways of treating women differently to their detriment

stereotypes: assumptions about other people based on their race, ethnicity, gender, or sexual orientation

implicit bias: the tendency for passing thoughts to confirm existing stereotypes in our minds, even if we quickly catch them

GEN GAP!

GENERATIONAL ATTITUDES TOWARD DISCRIMINATION

Maybe a natural consequence of the fact that younger generations are more diverse and are exposed more frequently to people whose experiences differ from their own is that they are also more likely than older generations to think that discrimination, rather than personal failings, is the major barrier to blacks' progress. Over half of Millennials hold that view; just over a quarter of the Silent Generation do.

FIGURE IT!

3.1: GROWING GAP ON WHETHER DISCRIMINATION IS THE MAIN BARRIER TO BLACKS' PROGRESS

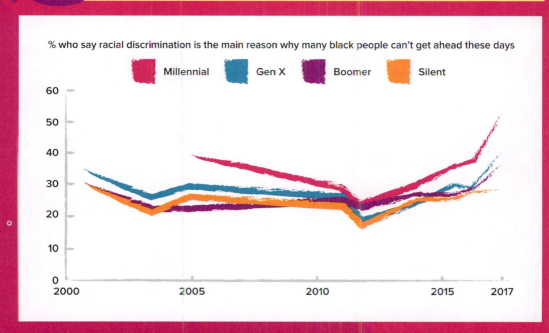

% who say racial discrimination is the main reason why many black people can't get ahead these days

Millennial   Gen X   Boomer   Silent

Source: Pew Research Center, The Generation Gap in American Politics, March 1, 2018, http://www.people-press.org/2018/03/01/the-generation-gap-in-american-politics/.

3.2: ACROSS GENERATIONS, INCREASING SHARES SAY IMMIGRANTS STRENGTHEN THE COUNTRY

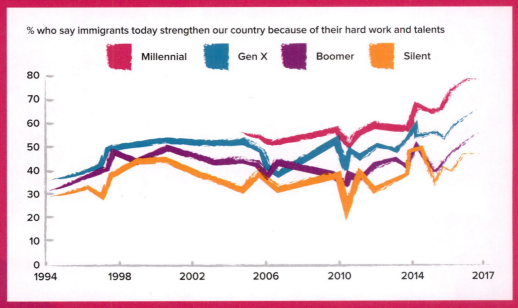

% who say immigrants today strengthen our country because of their hard work and talents

Millennial   Gen X   Boomer   Silent

Source: Pew Research Center, The Generation Gap in American Politics, March 1, 2018, http://www.people-press.org/2018/03/01/the-generation-gap-in-american-politics/.

Perhaps it is not surprising that younger generations are also more open to immigration, with nearly 80 percent of Millennials feeling it strengthens the nation. With the Republican Party taking such a hard line against immigration, it is easy to see connections between these data and those that show younger people tend to be more liberal.

A survey that asked only female Millennials and Baby Boomers about their perceived gains against gender discrimination showed a positive change, but still little support for the notion that women and men are treated the same in the workplace. At best just over a quarter of Millennials think things have changed for the better in the past ten years.

3.3: PERCENT WHO AGREE OR DISAGREE WITH THE FOLLOWING STATEMENTS ("STRONGLY AGREE")

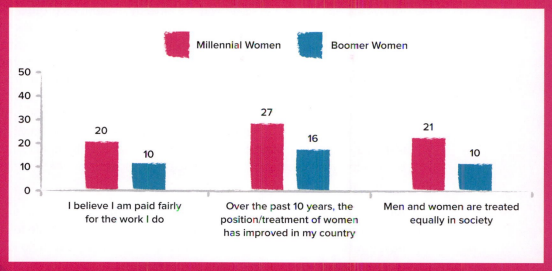

Source: "Want More, Be More: When It Comes to Gender Equality, Millennial Women Are More Optimistic about Closing the Gap," The Nielsen Company, March 8, 2017, http://www .nielsen.com/us/en/insights/news/2017/when-it-comes-to-gender-equality-millennial-women-are-more-optimistic-on-closing-the-pay-gap.html.

TAKEAWAYS

→ **Changes in social attitudes are generally slow, and race and gender are prime examples.** Although public opinions on some issues, like marriage equality, have turned remarkably fast, those that deal with who is perceived as having power in society and who is seen to be losing it can be tightly held and slower to change.

→ **Almost all generations, especially younger ones, say immigration strengthens the nation.** How will these people deal at the ballot box with those who are trying to cut off or limit immigration?

→ **Millennial women really do fare better in the marketplace than their moms did.** And yet, large majorities still perceive bias. How might the frustration behind this perception have helped fuel the Women's Marches, the #MeToo movement, and the number of women candidates running in 2018?

Remember that rights equal power. That means these demographic changes and the rights claims associated with them are likely to cause some social upheaval.

Many of the signs of that upheaval are already evident as groups jockey to hang on to or acquire more rights and privilege. We see it in Barack Obama's election to the presidency and the subsequent challenges to his citizenship and some people's hostility to his presidency. And we see it in the racialized tone of Donald Trump's campaign rallies, in white supremacist marches in response to the removal of Confederate monuments and the growth of the alt-right, in attempts to crack down on immigration from various countries and religious groups, in refusals to support women's reproductive rights or LGBTQ rights in the name of religious freedom, and in the criticism directed at athletes who protest police violence against blacks by kneeling during the national anthem at sports events.

All of these events say something about the turbulence of the times and the inevitable power shifts in a changing society. It is impossible to say right now how those power relationships will end up, but it is useful to look back and see how they have evolved over time.

Big Think

→ Is it possible to keep the divisions that separate religious groups out of politics in a democracy?

→ Will Congress try to regulate social media platforms? And is regulation of tech companies even possible given the degree to which social media are automated?

→ How do your own implicit biases affect your political and social judgments?

→ Can you imagine a nation without systemic power biases? What would it look like?

Key Terms

CONCEPTS

bill of attainder (p. 86)

black codes (p. 94)

boycott (p. 97)

civil liberties (p. 72)

civil rights (p. 72)

clear and present danger test (p. 84)

compelling state purpose (p. 91)

de facto discrimination (p. 93)

de jure d scrimination (p. 93)

discrimination (p. 90)

due process rights (p. 85)

establishment clause (p. 79)

ex post facto law (p. 86)

exclusionary rule (p. 86)

fighting words (p. 83)

free exercise clause (p. 79)

freedom of assembly (p. 83)

freedom of expression (p. 83)

gender bias (p. 104)

glass ceiling (p. 103)

habeas corpus (p. 86)

imminent lawless action test (p. 84)

implicit bias (p. 104)

incorporation (p. 77)

integration (p. 98)

Jim Crow laws (p. 95)

Lemon test (p. 80)

libel (p. 83)

marriage equality (p. 82)

Miller test (p. 84)

Miranda rights (p. 87)

natural rights (p. 74)

net neutrality (p. 85)

prior restraint (p. 84)

racism (p. 98)

right to privacy (p. 88)

sedition (p. 83)

separate but equal (p. 95)

slander (p. 83)

slavery (p. 94)

stereotypes (p. 104)

strict scrutiny (p. 91)

suspect classification (p. 91)

white privilege (p. 98)

IMPORTANT WORKS AND EVENTS

Bill of Rights (p. 75)

Brown v. Board of Education (p. 96)

Equal Rights Amendment (p. 102)

Thirteenth Amendment (p. 94)

Fourteenth Amendment (p. 77)

Fifteenth Amendment (p. 95)

Nineteenth Amendment (p. 102)

KEY INDIVIDUALS AND GROUPS

accommodationists (p. 80)

civil rights movement (p. 98)

judicial interpretivists (p. 89)

separationists (p. 80)

strict constructionists (p. 89)

#4 THE LEGISLATIVE BRANCH

In this chapter:

OH, SNAP. THE FOUNDERS DIDN'T TRUST AMERICANS ANY MORE THAN AMERICANS TODAY TRUST GOVERNMENT.

Congress is the U.S. legislature, the part of government that makes the laws. For the American founders, the legislative branch was the most central of the three branches. It was the subject of Article I, (remember the power of being first!) explained before the executive and judicial branches in the Constitution. But the founders did not trust the legislature to always do the right thing any more than they trusted human nature. So, as we have already seen, while they separated the branches, they also gave each just enough power over the others to keep them in check.

IN A NUTSHELL

Unlike legislatures that are combined with the executive (the British prime minister is a member of Parliament, for instance), the powers of the U.S. Congress are deliberately limited by the founders' institutional design. Once members of Congress were fairly remote from the citizens they represented, but in an age of mediated citizenship, people can have far more contact with the people they elect. Social media, town hall meetings, and video messages from a representative's website all encourage two-way conversation and empowerment of citizens—probably not what the founders had in mind.

The system of checks and balances the founders created was meant to limit power, but it seems to be especially paralyzing for Congress these days. As we will see, additional tensions built into the Constitution and into contemporary politics make it very difficult for Congress to act, and its lack of action often makes it the least popular branch of government. What are the consequences if people lose faith in their legislators?

By the time you finish reading this chapter, you will understand

WHERE WE GO IN THIS CHAPTER

- → How the Constitution structures Congress
- → How the institution organizes itself
- → The congressional role in checks and balances
- → How Congress makes laws
- → The constitutional and political tensions that make it difficult for Congress to act quickly
- → How congressional elections work
- → What kind of Congress those elections produce

4.2 HOW THE CONSTITUTION STRUCTURES CONGRESS

KEY ELEMENTS IN THE FOUNDERS' DESIGN FOR A BICAMERAL CONGRESS

Recall that the founders opted for a **bicameral legislature**, or one with two chambers, as part of the Great Compromise that produced the Constitution. The House of Representatives, in which each state's representation is based on population, has 435 members. The Senate, in which representation is equal, has 100 members (two per state).

The two chambers have different constituencies, membership requirements, and responsibilities. These along with their different organizational structures, as we will see in the next section, show the founders' intention to establish institutional incentives for the two houses to behave differently. Their hope was that these differences would lead the Senate to cool the tempers and check the passions in the House.

WHAT ARE THE DIFFERENT INSTITUTIONAL CONSTITUENCIES?

The founders intended the House and the Senate to have different **constituencies**, groupings of individual constituents or people whom they are supposed to represent. Chief among their constituencies are the geographic regions they represent. Senators were meant to represent the states—in fact, they were originally chosen by members of the state legislatures until that was changed by constitutional amendment. Each state gets two senators by virtue of its statehood—it doesn't matter how big the state is or how many people live there.

Members of the House, by contrast, represent geographic districts determined by population. In the founders' minds, they represented the people, or public opinion.

HOW DO THE MEMBERSHIP QUALIFICATIONS DIFFER?

Candidates for the House must be at least twenty-five years old, whereas Senate candidates must be at least thirty. Since you have to be slightly older to serve in the Senate, and it takes more money to run a statewide campaign, the founders expected senators to be wiser and more stable than members of the House. They gave senators longer, six-year terms, and divided them into three classes, with one third of them coming up for reelection every two years. The founders also gave senators more responsibilities than representatives in the House, especially in approving executive appointments and treaties made by the president.

Congress: the U.S. legislature, the part of government that makes the laws

bicameral legislature: a lawmaking body with two chambers

constituencies: groupings of individual constituents, or people whom an official is obligated to represent

Members of the House, by contrast, always directly elected, serve much shorter, two-year terms. The founders intended that, as representatives of the people rather than the states, they should reflect changes in public opinion. With two-year terms, House members are *always* running for reelection.

WHAT'S IN THE JOB DESCRIPTION?

Both chambers are responsible for lawmaking—something we will see later is not as straightforward as it seems. But as we will also see, they have different responsibilities when it comes to exercising checks on the other branches. Both chambers participate in the impeachment process over executive and judicial officials, but only the Senate approves presidential appointments and treaties with other countries.

The following table shows the different requirements of membership in the two houses and also the different responsibilities each house has.

TABLE IT!

4.1: CONSTITUTIONAL DIFFERENCES IN THE HOUSE AND SENATE

	House	Senate
Term length	2 years, unlimited reelection	6 years, unlimited reelection
Minimum age	25 years	30 years
Apportionment	According to population of state	Fixed: two per state
Impeachment power	Impeaches official	Tries impeached official, reaches verdict
Treaty-making power	None	Requires approval of two-thirds majority
Presidential appointment power	None	Requires approval of simple majority
Size	435	100
Number of standing committees	20	16
Limits on floor debate	Yes (Rules Committee)	No (filibuster)

4.3   HOW CONGRESS ORGANIZES ITSELF

HOW CONGRESS ORGANIZES ITSELF TO DO ITS JOB

Put 435 people together, or even 100, and some internal organization is necessary if you want to get anything done. Congress provides itself with the necessary internal organization by giving leadership roles to members of the majority party and by doing most of its work in committees that then report to the whole. Although both chambers follow this organizational plan, a few more rules are needed for the larger, more unwieldy House. The Senate, at least in theory, is able to give its members more individual freedom.

CONGRESSIONAL LEADERSHIP— IT'S ALL ABOUT THE PARTY!

The role that political parties play in shaping how Congress is organized and does its job is hard to overstate. The leadership of each house is deter- mined by the **majority party** in that house—that is, the political party that wins the most seats in that chamber. The majority party's members choose all the leadership positions and control business in the chamber or cham- bers they dominate. The bigger a party's majority, the more easily the party can impose its will on the chamber.

NUMBER ONE ROLE: THE SPEAKER OF THE HOUSE

The head of the majority party in the House is the **Speaker of the House**, so important a position that it is third in line to the succession of the presi- dency. The head of the majority party in the Senate is the **Senate majority leader**.

The **minority leader** in each house is powerful within his or her party, but it is the leaders of the majority party who call the shots. This is especially true in the House, where there are more members to manage and less of a tradition of mutual respect and deference.

The Speaker of the House's power stems from the potential he or she has to hold the members of the party together and get them to vote in unison

. . . .

majority party: the political party that wins the most seats in a given chamber

Speaker of the House: the head of the majority party in the House

Senate majority leader: the head of the majority party in the Senate

minority leader: the head of the minority party in either the Senate or the House

for the party's priorities. In that effort, the Speaker can rely on the help of the party *whip*, a member who has been elected by the party to generate support for the party's position on key bills. An adept Speaker with a cohesive party, like Republican Newt Gingrich (1995–1999) or Democrat Nancy Pelosi (2007–2011; 2019–), can really advance his or her party's agenda.

If a party has deep internal divisions, as today's Republican Party does, the job of Speaker can be a difficult and thankless task. After years spent trying to get members of his own party on the same page on basic legislation, Speaker John Boehner (2011–2015) seemed almost jubilant when he left the job and retired from Congress, and finding someone to replace him was a challenge for the Republican Party. Speaker Paul Ryan faced the same challenges bridging the gap between centrist and right-wing Republicans and announced his retirement in 2018. The more the conservative Freedom Caucus members challenged the more moderate establishment legislators, the more Congress seems deadlocked, within a single party. After the 2014 election, Nancy Pelosi, returned to the Speaker's Chair, faced her own rebellion among newly-elected Democrats eager for leadership change. She has proved more adept at keeping her troops in order than her predecessors, possibly because the schisms in the Democratic Party don't run as deep.

BUT DON'T UNDERESTIMATE THE SENATE MAJORITY LEADER

The Senate majority leader is generally not as powerful as the Speaker because the Senate is smaller than the House and because Senate traditions give each member more autonomy. As a result, the Senate is not as tightly organized as the House. Even so, a determined majority leader can still wield considerable clout. For example, when Supreme Court justice Antonin Scalia died in February 2016, Majority Leader Mitch McConnell refused to hold hearings or allow a vote on President Barack Obama's nomination to replace him. McConnell's hope, which was fulfilled, was that a Republican would win the presidential election in November and appoint a more conservative nominee than would Obama. McConnell's strategy may have changed basic norms of acceptable behavior in a majority leader.

The majority leadership in each chamber also assigns the chairs of all the committees, which as we will see is where the work of Congress gets done. They also choose a majority of the members on each committee. That helps solidify party control of what happens in Congress.

Figure 4.1 illustrates the leadership structure.

WHERE MOST OF THE WORK GOES ON: THE CONGRESSIONAL COMMITTEE SYSTEM

If you have ever been involved in a group project, you know that it would be difficult to get a lot of work done effectively in a group of 100 people

4.1: THE STRUCTURE OF THE HOUSE AND SENATE LEADERSHIP

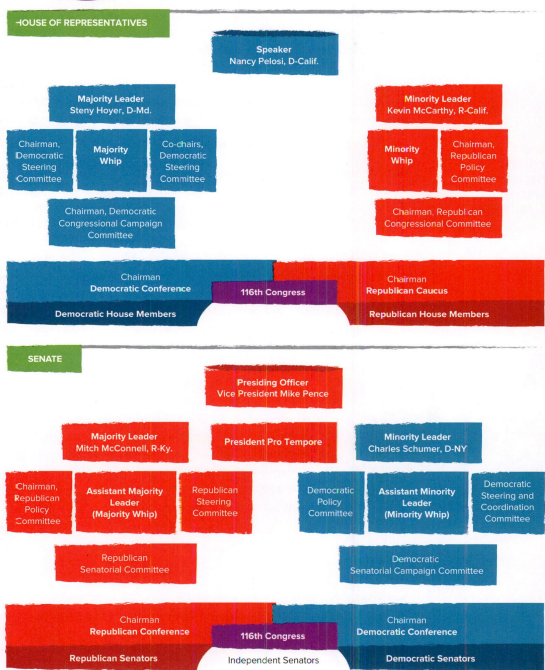

and impossible in a group of 435. It is hard to have deep, deliberative discussions with that many people. It would also be asking a lot to expect every member of Congress to be specialists in every policy area on which they need to make decisions.

So both houses do the logical thing: they divide up the work and allow themselves to specialize in the policy areas on which they focus. Most of the work in Congress gets done in **committees**. So challenging is the job of navigating the constitutional hurdles, juggling the tasks Congress has to perform, and responding to the various constituencies it has to answer to that passing legislation is an incredibly challenging activity. In fact, most of the bills introduced into either house never come out. The committee is often their graveyard.

> Committees fall into several different categories:

WHAT THE COMMITTEE SYSTEM LOOKS LIKE: FIVE MAIN TYPES

\# **Standing committees** focus on basic policy areas (for example, transportation, foreign relations, finance). Committees on these policy areas exist from one session of Congress to another. Members of both houses want to be on the standing committees that will let them do the most work for the people who elected them, their primary constituencies, so they jockey for the best positions. A member of Congress from a rural district or state might hope to get on the Agriculture committee, for example. Ultimately leadership decides who gets to be on a committee, and the majority leadership selects the chairs. The standing committees cover such large ranges of policy issues that they are divided into subcommittees as well.

\# The **House Rules Committee**, as its name suggests, exists only in the House of Representatives and is a function of the large membership. The Rules Committee exists to provide a rule for every bill that says how long it can be debated, how it can be amended, how much time each member can speak, and the like. It's a powerful committee because determining the rules can determine who wins and who loses legislatively. The Rules Committee is controlled by the majority party.

\# **Select committees** exist to cover issues that fall outside the standing committees' jurisdiction or are considered important enough to need

DIG DEEPER

Check out the committee structure for the 116th Congress.

Go to **edge.sagepub.com/ dig-deeper**

committees: small groups oriented around policy or procedural issues where the real work of Congress gets done

standing committees: permanent committees responsible for legislation in particular policy areas

House Rules Committee: the committee that determines how and when debate on a bill will take place

select committees: committees appointed to deal with an issue or a problem not suited to standing committees

a committee of their own. There was some debate, for instance, about whether Russian interference in the 2016 election should be the focus of a select committee investigation, similar to the committee investigation that looked into the federal government's response to 2005's Hurricane Katrina. Speaker Pelosi established a Select Committee on the Climate Crisis in 2019. The select committee disbands after it issues its report.

TABLE IT!

4.2: STANDING COMMITTEES OF THE 115TH CONGRESS

House	Senate
Agriculture (46 members)	Agriculture, Nutrition, and Forestry (21 members)
Appropriations (52 members)	Appropriations (31 members)
Armed Services (62 members)	Armed Services (27 members)
Budget (36 members)	Banking, Housing, and Urban Affairs (25 members)
Education and the Workforce (40 members)	Budget (23 members)
Energy and Commerce (55 members)	Commerce, Science, and Transportation (27 members)
Ethics (10 members)	Energy and Natural Resources (23 members)
Financial Services (60 members)	Environment and Public Works (21 members)
Foreign Affairs (47 members)	Finance (27 members)
Homeland Security (40 members)	Foreign Relations (21 members)
House Administration (9 members)	Health, Education, Labor, and Pensions (23 members)
Judiciary (41 members)	Homeland Security and Governmental Affairs (15 members)
Natural Resources (43 members)	Judiciary (21 members)
Oversight and Government Reform (42 members)	Rules and Administration (19 members)
Rules (13 members)	Small Business and Entrepreneurship (19 members)
Science, Space, and Technology (39 members)	Veterans' Affairs (15 members)
Small Business (24 members)	Senate Special or Select Committees
Transportation and Infrastructure (61 members)	Aging
Veterans' Affairs (24 members)	Ethics
Ways and Means (40 members)	Intelligence
House Select Committee on Intelligence (21 members)	

\# **Joint committees** draw their members from both the House and the Senate to avoid duplication of effort (although all the standing committees duplicate effort anyway). They are focused on such topics as economics and taxation.

\# The most important of the joint committees is the **conference committee**. Since the Constitution dictates that all laws be passed in the exact same form in both chambers and, as we will see, the legislative process can be like a meat grinder, yielding two very different bills, it is the conference committee whose difficult job it is to bring them together. This committee has a lot of clout since it decides on the final content of the bill. Bills in the conference committee are subject only to an up or down vote in each chamber, which means that no more tweaks or amendments are allowed.

DO THESE FOLKS HAVE ANY HELP?

The work of Congress is substantial, even when it doesn't seem to be turning out much product. Each member of Congress has an office and staff at home and in Washington who do the bulk of the routine work and research. Members of the House average eighteen staff members each, and senators average about twice that many, depending on the size of the state.

DIG DEEPER

Get a feel for what a day in the life of a member of Congress is like.

Go to **edge.sagepub.com/dig-deeper**

In addition to individual members' staffs, Congress has several organizations that provide backup and support: the Congressional Research Service provides in-depth information and analysis; the Government Accountability Office helps keep tabs on the executive; and the Congressional Budget Office runs the numbers, tells Congress what various plans will cost, and provides advice about the budget.

4.4 THE CONGRESSIONAL ROLE IN CHECKS AND BALANCES

IS LEGISLATING THE ONLY THING CONGRESS DOES?

No. In keeping with checks and balances, Congress has some powers over the executive branch and over the judiciary. We saw these in the figure on p. 55, but you'll get a clearer idea of how the branches work together here.

joint committees: combined House-Senate committees formed to coordinate activities and expedite legislation in a certain area

conference committee: temporary committees formed to reconcile differences in House and Senate versions of a bill

THREE KEY CONGRESSIONAL CHECKS ON THE EXECUTIVE

> Congress has three main tools at its disposal to balance and control the power of the presidency:

\# **Oversight.** The primary check on the executive branch is called **congressional oversight**. Congress has to keep an eye on the executive to be sure that the laws it makes are faithfully carried out. It does this through hearings and investigations.

These investigations often have a partisan flavor. After all, the majority party would rather dig into the transgressions of a presidential administration of the other party. One example here is the extensive investigation the Republicans held on the death of a U.S. ambassador in Benghazi, Libya, while Hillary Clinton was secretary of state under Democratic president Barack Obama. At the same time, if the administration's behavior is hard enough to ignore, a party will investigate its own. The investigation into Russia's interference with the 2016 U.S. election and whether there was collusion with the Trump administration is a case in point although the Republicans did not dig very deeply. The Democrats' investigation will no doubt be more thorough.

Congress also conducts oversight into the bureaucracy to ensure that agencies implement the laws as Congress intended and to make sure those agencies aren't beholden to the interests of the industry they are supposed to regulate. For example, since 2017, the House Committee on Oversight and Government Reform has held a series of bipartisan hearings looking into how executive agencies can better manage the opioid crisis in the United States and hold the pharmaceutical industry accountable for its role in the problem.

\# **Impeachment.** A second congressional check on the executive that can easily take on a partisan tone is **impeachment**. Impeachment is a two-step process: the House votes to impeach a president, and the Senate votes to convict. Two American presidents have been impeached (Andrew Johnson [1868] and Bill Clinton [1998]), but neither was convicted and both remained in office. A third president, Richard Nixon, on the brink of being impeached and on being told by senators in his party that they didn't have the votes to save him, resigned in 1974. Articles of impeachment are frequently introduced

. . . .

congressional oversight: efforts by Congress, especially through committees, to monitor agency rule-making, enforcement, and implementation of congressional policies

impeachment: a formal charge by the House that the president (or another member of the executive branch) has committed acts of "Treason, Bribery, or other high Crimes and Misdemeanors," which may or may not result in removal from office by members of Congress, usually for partisan reasons, but it is rare for them to be taken up.

\# **Advice and consent.** Finally, Congress, or at least the Senate, has the job of providing **advice and consent** on a host of federal appointments the president makes: cabinet secretaries, ambassadors, and judges (or justices) in the federal court system. Senators can use their confirmation power to slow down or block a president's appointees from taking office. We've already mentioned Mitch McConnell's blocking of President Obama's final nominee to the Supreme Court (and many of his judges), but senators can easily obstruct all presidential nominees to all the federal courts. Presidents can find dealing with the Senate incredibly frustrating when it deadlocks their agenda. The courts suffer because a backlog of cases results when judgeships remain unfilled. Even the Chief Justice has scolded them for this.

CONGRESSIONAL CHECKS ON THE JUDICIARY

Of course, the power to confirm members to the federal bench is a check not only on the executive but also on the judiciary. Presidents try to create a legacy by appointing judges and justices who share their view of the Constitution, but senators can either support or thwart that effort, giving them some power over the courts as well. Indeed, they have the power to impeach not just presidents, but federal judges as well. Furthermore, the Constitution gives Congress the power to organize the lower federal courts, set judicial salaries, and determine some issues of jurisdiction (that is, what cases can be heard where). Finally, Congress has the power to pass laws that circumvent court decisions, and to initiate amendment processes when it cannot.

EXECUTIVE AND JUDICIAL CHECKS ON CONGRESS

The founders ensured that checks and balances worked both ways. Congress not only checks the other two branches but also is checked by them and by itself.

Presidents' ability to veto laws they don't like and, informally, to leverage their stature as the head of their party are powerful checks on Congress. As we will see, Congress can override the veto with a two-thirds vote in each house, but that is difficult to pull off.

Of course, the judiciary can check Congress as well. Although Congress makes the laws, recall that in *Marbury v. Madison* (1803) the Supreme Court decided it held the power, via judicial review, to determine whether those laws are constitutional. It is difficult to underestimate the power this gives to the Court or, should we say, that the Court gave to itself.

advice and consent: the Senate's constitutional obligation to approve certain executive appointments

CONGRESSIONAL CHECKS . . . ON CONGRESS

> Finally, Congress can check itself. The founders designed the two houses to respond to different constituencies: the Senate was to represent the states and the House of Representatives, the people. The older and (they hoped) wiser Senate would check the hot-headed populist tempers of the House. In reality, it is just the fact that bills must be passed in the same form in each house that does the checking. The Senate checks the House, certainly, but the House can check the Senate as well. Only if they cooperate can laws be passed through the legislative process.

4.5 DOING THE HARD WORK OF MAKING LAWS

SO HOW DOES ANYTHING EVER GET DONE?

> As we have seen, Congress is part of an elaborate political scheme designed to keep governmental power in check. But that doesn't mean the founders wanted the system to be immobilized. Just slow and cautious. When we look at Congress's core function of making laws, we see that they may have gotten more than they bargained for.
>
> The process of lawmaking is simple on paper but infinitely complex in real life. Congress has to operate within the institutional constraints imposed by the Constitution and unspoken norms. On top of that, members of Congress must respond to a diverse world of groups and individuals who seek to influence congressional agendas and actions. And there is the always-looming imperative of being accountable to one's constituents so that one can be reelected.

SAUSAGE MAKING!

> Some scholars have likened democratic lawmaking to what goes on in a sausage factory—a process that in many ways is so messy that one does not want to watch. If you want to see a streamlined version of the legislative process, it goes like this, but remember that the real thing is much less tidy:

HOW A BILL BECOMES A LAW

> \# **Out in the political world.** Lawmaking starts when a policy idea gets on the legislative agenda—that is, it has to get onto Congress members' radar screens. Maybe the issue is something one or more of them care about, or maybe it has been brought to their attention by the president, a constituent, an interest group, or outside events.

. . . .

legislative agenda: the slate of proposals and issues that representatives think it worthwhile to consider and act on

\# **In both houses.** Once there is an actual bill, it has to be formally introduced into Congress and assigned a number (like H.R. 932 or S. 953). Bills can be introduced and go through both houses at the same time or one before the other, but *they must eventually pass in both houses and in the exact same form*.

\# **In committee.** The bill gets assigned to a standing committee according to its subject matter. If it can fit in more than one substantive category, the Speaker of the House can decide where it goes. In the Senate all members get to chime in eventually, so initial committee assignment confers less power on the leader.

\# **In subcommittee.** Once in committee, the bill is assigned to a subcommittee. Truth to tell, that is where most bills go to die. Members can hold hearings, inviting people to testify about the bill and provide information. Only a small fraction of bills are "reported out" of committee to get on with the business of becoming a law. For various political reasons, most get tabled or stalled and are never heard from again.

\# **Back in committee.** If the bill does get out of subcommittee, it goes back to the committee to go through a revision process called *markup*. Then the committee votes on whether to send it to the floor. If the bill gets out of committee, it faces a different fate in the House and the Senate.

\# **In the House.** The bill has to be submitted to the House Rules Committee, which attaches a rule that determines how long the bill can be debated, how long members can speak, and what the amendment process will be. An *open rule* gives members lots of freedom to debate and amend a bill, but more often the leadership will keep tighter control over it. Once out of the Rules Committee, the bill is then debated on the floor of the House according to the rule and voted on.

\# **In the Senate.** Because the Senate has fewer members than the House, there is no need to attach a rule. The Senate has a tradition of open debate that gives rise to the Senate tradition of the **filibuster**, which means essentially that a member or members of the Senate prevent a bill from ever coming up for a vote by holding the floor

filibuster: a practice of unlimited debate in the Senate in order to prevent or delay a vote on a bill and "talking it to death." Filibusters were once dramatic events, often involving the reading of phone books and the provision of cots for senators to nap on while waiting their turn to speak, but these days they usually amount to no more than a minority telling the leadership that they intend to filibuster. A filibuster can be ended only by sixty or more senators voting for **cloture** to end the debate. Unless the majority has sixty votes in its pocket, it just puts aside the bill. Frustration about parties blocking presidential appointments has led to something called the **nuclear option**, which means those appointments can proceed with a simple majority, but the filibuster is still in play for regular legislation. If the vote escapes the filibuster—something that is used almost routinely in these partisan times—the bill goes to the Senate floor for a vote.

\# **In both chambers**. If the bill manages to get through both houses, the two versions are unlikely to look very much like each other. But the Constitution says they need to pass in the exact same form. So bills must head to a conference committee, where they are hammered into identical shape. A lot of political haggling can take place at this point, making this committee a very powerful one to be on.

\# **In the White House**. If the revised and identical bill is passed in both houses, it heads to the president's desk for a signature. The president can sign it, at which point it becomes law, or he can **veto** it, at which point both houses can override the veto if they can muster a two-thirds vote in each house. The president can also simply leave the bill on his desk, taking a more passive approach to the lawmaking role. If the congressional session ends within ten days, the bill is automatically vetoed with what is called a **pocket veto**. A pocket veto is handy if the president wants to veto a bill without drawing a lot of attention to it. Similarly, if the president wants the bill to become law without a lot of fanfare and flourishes, he can leave it on his desk and if Congress is still in session in ten days, it automatically becomes law without his signature.

. . . .

cloture: a vote to end a Senate filibuster; requires a three-fifths majority, or sixty votes

nuclear option: a controversial Senate maneuver by which a simple majority could decide to allow a majority to bypass the filibuster for certain kinds of votes

veto: the presidential power to reject a piece of legislation by not signing it into law

pocket veto: the presidential authority to kill a bill submitted within ten days of the end of a legislative session by not signing it

Bill is referred to Senate committee or subcommittee

Committe marks up the bill with changes

Voted on by full committee

Bill introduced in **SENATE**

Inaction graveyard

Tabled

START HERE

Bill introduced in **HOUSE**

Tabled

Inaction graveyard

Bill is referred to House committee or subcommittee

Committe marks up the bill with changes

Voted on by Full Committee

Committee reports and bill is put on Senate calendar

Senate reading and debate, amendments are added

SENATE FULL VOTE

Vote in opposite chamber if no similar bill

If other chamber has similar bill, joint committee resolves differences

PRESIDENT

VETO

LAW

HOUSE FULL VOTE

Committee reports and bill is put on House calendar

Bill is referred to House Committee on Rules before reaching the floor

House reading and debate, amendments are added

HOW CONGRESS MAKES ITS JOB EVEN MESSIER THAN THE FOUNDERS INTENDED

> The trouble with creating a simple flowchart is that Congress has a number of workarounds, shortcuts, and catchall maneuvers that allow it to avoid institutional checks. Here are examples of the unorthodox lawmaking that legislators sometimes use:

If they are feeling political pressure, congressional leadership may craft bills out of the public view, bypassing committee hearings and producing legislation for a vote that in some cases members of Congress have not had time to read. This minimizes opportunities for the opposition to organize and for constituents to lobby their legislators, perhaps costing leadership necessary votes.

At budget time, you may hear talk about laws being passed through reconciliation. Reconciliation is a legislative process that allows certain budgetary laws to pass with a simple majority in the Senate and with limited debate. In other words—*the Senate cannot use the filibuster during reconciliation.* The Democrats used reconciliation to pass the Affordable Care Act (ACA) when they lost their filibuster-proof majority in the Senate in 2010. The Republicans used it to end the ACA's universal mandate and pass large tax cuts in 2017. In both cases the opposite party would have filibustered in the Senate without the legislative sleight of hand provided by the rules of reconciliation.

Another mechanism for members of Congress to get items passed that might not have majority support or might be subject to presidential veto is the use of omnibus legislation—large bills stuffed with often unrelated pieces of legislation that get voted on all at once. If the bill is big enough to include something everyone wants, no one will want to torpedo it to get rid of the parts they don't like.

- -

unorthodox lawmaking: lawmaking tactics—such as omnibus legislation or reconciliation—that bypass usual committee processes to ease the passage of laws

reconciliation: a legislative process that allows certain budgetary laws to pass with a simple majority in the Senate and with limited debate

omnibus legislation: large bills stuffed with often unrelated pieces of legislation that are voted on all at once

4.6 TENSIONS THAT CHALLENGE CONGRESS'S ABILITY TO DO ITS JOB

CONSTITUTIONAL DESIGN SHAPES THE WORK OF CONGRESS

We have mentioned several times that Congress's job of passing real-life legislation is complex. And it is. Partly that is by the founders' design. Haunted by the specter of the speedy lawmaking and political instability that resulted under the Articles of Confederation, the authors of the Constitution were determined to put the brakes on. We can see that in the checks and balances on Congress that we discussed earlier.

THE THREE MASTERS CONGRESS HAS TO ANSWER TO

There are other pressures on members of Congress that make it particularly difficult for them to do their jobs well, however. We have already talked about the pressure lawmakers feel to respond to their constituencies, but constituents aren't necessarily just the people who vote for you. Members have to respond to three different constituencies: the people who elected them, the nation as a whole, and their party. Let's take a look at how each of these constituencies makes the legislator's job more complex.

ONE: THE LOCAL CONSTITUENCY AND THE JOB OF REPRESENTATION

The most obvious obligation of a senator or member of Congress is **representation**. Representation refers to the job of looking out for the interests of the people who elected you. Members pay attention to the interests of those people in part because it's in the job description but also because they want their constituents to be happy with the job they are doing so that they will be reelected. Senators have to look out for the interests of people in their state, and members of Congress have to pay attention to the people who live in the **congressional district** that elected them. Congressional districts are geographic regions that states are divided into by state legislators. Each district can elect one member to represent it in the House of Representatives.

representation: the efforts of elected officials to look out for the interests of those who elect them

congressional district: a geographic region into which state legislators divide their state for purposes of representation

**MAJOR FORMS OF
REPRESENTATION**

Pretty obviously, representation is high on the list of congressional responsibilities. We can think of the job as taking several forms:

\# **Policy representation** is what most of us probably associate with the Congress member's job. It refers to the obligation of members to try to pass legislation that benefits the economic and social interests of their constituency. If you represent a coal-producing state, you try to pass laws that increase dependence on coal. If you are from an agricultural district, you might want to pass laws that give subsidies to farmers. It makes sense that passing legislation that helps your constituents is one way to convince them you are doing your job so that they keep reelecting you.

\# **Allocative representation** refers to the passage of laws that benefit the district in a material way—maybe new highway funds or funding for a research center or approval to keep a military base open. This kind of representation is called **pork barrel** because it "brings home the bacon" (meaning it brings money or resources back to the area) or **earmarks** when general taxpayer funds are used to pay for some special benefit for your district. Constituents love this and are likely to reelect the member who successfully sends goodies to his or her district. But because it can seem like a type of favoritism—constituents in one district get something that others don't—the practice generally frustrates taxpayers as a whole, makes it even harder to balance the budget, and gives Congress a bad name.

\# **Casework** is a kind of representation that refers to taking care of one's constituents' needs and problems—tracking down a lost Social Security check, for instance, arranging a visit to the state capitol for a high school class, arranging an internship, assisting a student to get into a military academy, or helping a constituent clear up a federal student loan issue. This kind of representation, performed in part by congressional staffers, also helps members get reelected because it leaves constituents with warm and positive feelings about them.

policy representation: congressional work to advance the issues and ideological preferences of constituents

allocative representation: congressional work to secure projects, services, and funds for the represented district

pork barrel: public works projects and grants for specific districts paid for by general revenues

earmarks: a type of legislative representation in which general taxpayer funds are used to pay for some special benefit for a member's district

casework: representation that involves taking care of one's constituents' needs and problems

\# **Symbolic representation** is less well defined than the other types of representation. It refers to the public role of showcasing the values of public service and patriotism. It might include agreeing to give a commencement address at a local college or to show up at county fairs and other gatherings to remind constituents that their district is represented in the nation's capital by a person who demonstrates democratic values.

TWO: THE NATIONAL CONSTITUENCY AND THE JOB OF NATIONAL LAW MAKING

Although senators and members of Congress will inevitably be closely attuned to the needs of the folks back home, they are also expected to make laws that benefit the nation as a whole. This job, called **national law making**, includes passing national budgets and voting on nationwide policies like health care or tax cuts or gun regulations.

The problem with making laws for the national good is that it often conflicts with representation. What one's state or district wants is not usually the same as what is good for the nation. Higher taxes, for instance, mean the nation can repair its infrastructure (bridges, roads, and the like) and eliminate debt that will plague future generations. That's good for the whole country. But geographic constituents tend to be very focused on their own lives. Back home, higher taxes will just make voters angry because they see their own taxes rise. Passing gun regulations might mean that the nation suffers fewer mass shootings, but for the gun owners at home far removed from the violence, such regulations feel like a limit on their freedom.

Because of these conflicts between lawmaking and representation, it can take special circumstances to pass legislation that will be unpopular with constituents. A national emergency will sometimes provide an opportunity to pass something that is not going to be a hit at home. Sometimes a congressperson on the brink of retirement or who is willing to take an unpopular stand will be inspired to go against the wishes of his or her voters. The push–pull relationship between representation and lawmaking can make a legislator's job stressful and challenging. Also, because representation often wins out, it contributes to a negative national attitude about Congress. Citizens tend to admire their member of Congress or their senator, and vote to reelect them once they are in office (called the **incumbency advantage**), but they are not very happy with an institution that seems to ignore pressing national problems. Even so, this conflict among constituencies was at least part of the founders' design.

symbolic representation: the public role of showcasing the values of public service and patriotism

national law making: the creation of policy to address the problems and needs of the entire nation

incumbency advantage: the electoral edge afforded to those already in office

FIGURE IT!

4.3: CONGRESSIONAL APPROVAL RATINGS ARE LOW . . . BUT REELECTION RATES ARE HIGH

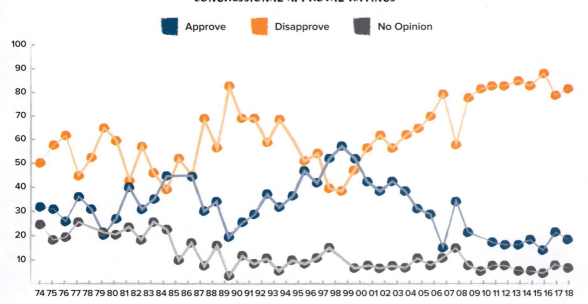

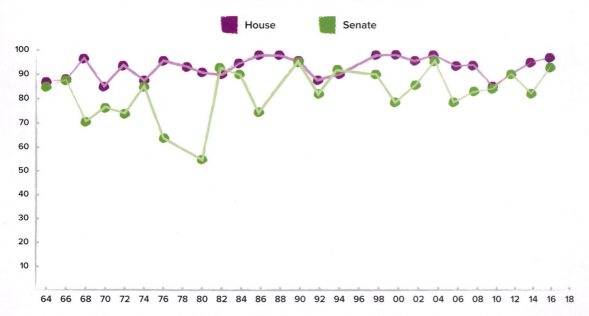

Sources: Data for congressional approval ratings are from Gallup, "Congress and the Public," https://news.gallup.com/poll/1600/congress-public.aspx. Data for House and Senate reelection rates are from Open Secrets, "Reelection Rates over the Years," https://www.opensecrets.org/overview/reelect.php.

THREE: THE PARTISAN CONSTITUENCY AND THE JOB OF BEING A TEAM PLAYER

What the founders did not count on was one force that makes the job even tougher for legislators. Madison hoped that they had dealt successfully with the problems posed by factions by designing Congress the way they did. But factions are alive and well in American politics, and in the form of political parties they can complicate the legislative process.

Not only do legislators have to represent their districts well enough to keep their jobs and try to cope with national issues without alienating their constituents, but they also have to be good party members. At other times in our history this has not been such a potent force. **Partisanship** (one's allegiance to one's party) is always important and even healthy. As we saw earlier, it defines the power structure in both houses. Despite those partisan differences, laws used to be passed by various combinations of Democrats and Republicans compromising and working together on issues they cared about.

HOW MUCH PARTISANSHIP IS TOO MUCH?

Increasingly, in the past twenty-five years or so, partisanship has intensified, making it harder for Congress to reach compromises across party lines. Parties in Congress have sorted themselves out so that they are more consistently internally liberal or conservative, meaning that Republicans in Congress now mostly vote only along party lines with other Republicans, and Democrats do the same within their own party.

At the same time, Congress members' average policy positions have moved further away from each other. This trend is called **polarization**. American parties are more polarized now than they have been at any point since the Civil War in the mid-1860s. These increases in partisanship and polarization today mean that members' loyalty to party rivals their loyalty to nation or even their constituencies (although increasingly these overlap). This state of **hyperpartisanship**, loyalty to party over nation, is what caused former Republican senators like Maine's Olympia Snowe, Arizona's Jeff Flake, and Tennessee's Bob Corker to leave the

DIG DEEPER

Read Olympia Snowe's article, "Why I Am Leaving the Senate."

Go to **edge.sagepub.com/ dig-deeper**

---

partisanship: one's allegiance to one's party

polarization: the ideological distance between the parties and the ideological homogeneity within them

hyperpartisanship: a commitment to party so strong that it can transcend other commitments, including that to the national interest

READ THIS!

SENATOR JOHN MCCAIN ON BIPARTISANSHIP

I've known and admired men and women in the Senate who played much more than a small role in our history, true statesmen, giants of American politics. They came from both parties, and from various backgrounds. Their ambitions were frequently in conflict. They held different views on the issues of the day. And they often had very serious disagreements about how best to serve the national interest.

But they knew that however sharp and heartfelt their disputes, however keen their ambitions, they had an obligation to work collaboratively to ensure the Senate discharged its constitutional responsibilities effectively. Our responsibilities are important, vitally important, to the continued success of our Republic. And our arcane rules and customs are deliberately intended to require broad cooperation to function well at all. The most revered members of this institution accepted the necessity of compromise in order to make incremental progress on solving America's problems and to defend her from her adversaries.

That principled mindset, and the service of our predecessors who possessed it, come to mind when I hear the Senate referred to as the world's greatest deliberative body. I'm not sure we can claim that distinction with a straight face today.

I'm sure it wasn't always deserved in previous eras either. But I'm sure there have been times when it was, and I was privileged to witness some of those occasions.

Our deliberations today—not just our debates, but the exercise of all our responsibilities—authorizing government policies, appropriating the funds to implement them, exercising our advice and consent role—are often lively and interesting. They can be sincere and principled. But they are more partisan, more tribal more of the time than any other time I remember. Our deliberations can still be important and useful, but I think we'd all agree they haven't been overburdened by greatness lately. And right now they aren't producing much for the American people.

Both sides have let this happen. Let's leave the history of who shot first to the historians. I suspect they'll find we all conspired in our decline—either by deliberate actions or neglect. We've all played some role in it. Certainly I have. Sometimes, I've let my passion rule my reason. Sometimes, I made it harder to find common ground because of something harsh I said to a colleague. Sometimes, I wanted to win more for the sake of winning than to achieve a contested policy.

Incremental progress, compromises that each side criticize but also accept, just plain muddling through to chip away at problems and keep our enemies from doing their worst isn't glamorous or exciting. It doesn't feel like a political triumph. But it's usually the most we can expect from our system of government, operating in a country as diverse and quarrelsome and free as ours.

This excerpt is from one of the last speeches given before Senator John McCain's death.

Senate. They believed that tribalism, their party's will to win for the sake of beating the other side, was overriding national and constituent interests. For an example of this sentiment, see the box on the late Arizona senator, John McCain's, speech on the Senate floor in 2017.

THE UPSHOT

These three conflicting constituencies make the job of legislating these days complicated and increasingly tense as members try to juggle considerations that do not fit well together. If the institutions succeed in doing what John McCain suggested and return to more **bipartisanship**, to a more compromising approach to the job, lawmaking would get easier and recruiting candidates to run for office would probably be easier. Even if that were to come to pass, the essential tension between lawmaking and representation would remain as the legacy of the founders who believed it would help the two chambers of Congress to check each other and put the brakes on hasty, dangerous legislation.

4.7 CONGRESSIONAL ELECTIONS

WHAT DOES IT TAKE TO GET A JOB IN CONGRESS?

 Of course, any member of Congress will tell you that it doesn't matter how bipartisan you are, or how civic minded, or what a skilled legislator, if you

---

bipartisanship: an effort that incorporates work from both sides of the aisle and produces a solution to a problem both sides can live with

don't have a job. For the House member or senator, the first challenge of the job is getting it, and that means running for election. Imagine a job interview where you have to meet the expectations of a whole district or state full of people!

SENATE AND HOUSE ELECTIONS COMPARED

Senators and representatives face different obstacles to being elected to office. Senatorial elections are fairly straightforward—each state gets two senators and the borders of those states don't change. One third of the Senate comes up for reelection every two years as its members finish their six-year terms. Running statewide is generally more expensive than running in a smaller district, but six-year intervals between elections give senators plenty of time to raise the funds they need.

House elections are another story. All members are up for reelection every two years, so they are always running for their seat and always raising money.

IT STARTS WITH A HEAD COUNT

Remember that there are 435 members of the House, each of whom is elected to represent a congressional district in a state, and that representation in the House is determined by a state's total population. Each state's number of representatives is based on the number of people who live there. According to an important Supreme Court case, *Baker v. Carr* (1962), although the states are responsible for determining how their elections are held, within each state the congressional districts need to hold roughly equal numbers of people. The process by which House districts are drawn up is partly formulaic and partly political.

NEW DISTRICTS ARE DRAWN BASED ON CENSUS RESULTS

According to the Constitution, the U.S. government needs to count the people who live within its borders every ten years, something we call the **U.S. Census**. Among other things, what the census reveals is how the population has shifted among the states and within them as well.

NUMBERS ARE NOT NEUTRAL!

Traditionally, the census has been a fairly neutral process—as neutral as trying to get a head count of millions of people can be. Questionnaires go out, many people fill them in and return them, and the results are counted. But if people do *not* return their census forms—if they do not have documents proving they are here legally, or if they are afraid that information given to

U.S. Census: a constitutional mandate requiring the U.S. government to count the people who live within its borders every ten years

the government could be used against them, or even if they have more people living in their home than are legally allowed to reside there—then the count will be inaccurate.

4.3: THE SKIMMABLE COURT WATCHER: *BAKER V. CARR* AND ONE PERSON, ONE VOTE

One side of the controversy	The other side of the controversy	What does the Court say?	Problems implementing the decision
Population shifts in Tennessee had changed the composition of districts, leaving rural districts overrepresented because there were fewer people per district. The plaintiff in the case sued, claiming that districts had not been regularly redrawn since the 1900 census; equal protection of the laws required equally populated districts.	The attorney for the state argued that this was a political question and thus not one for courts to get involved in.	In *Baker v. Carr* (1962), the Court decided to intervene, ruling that the Constitution required "one person, one vote"—that is, districts should have roughly equal numbers of constituents.	This is a classic example of an interpretivist ruling. Strict constructionists said the Constitution could be amended to include "one person, one vote," but the principle did not exist as the founders wrote the document.

Democrats have proposed using statistical estimation to get a better picture of who lives where (not unlike the weighting of public opinion polls we will describe in Chapter 8). This approach would give a better count of typically undercounted groups who tend to vote Democratic and would bolster the number of representatives in Democratic areas.

Not surprisingly, Republicans oppose this approach. The current Republican administration has sought to alter the questions on the census and reduce funding for it, which will make it less comprehensive. Democrats oppose changes that they fear will intimidate immigrants who are not yet citizens and discourage them from filling in the forms, reducing their representation. They also feel a less comprehensive census will count fewer Democrats, who can be harder to track down, and reduce the number of representatives they get.

It should be obvious that the process of taking the census is full of political implications—each party wants to count people in a way that will beef up the numbers of representatives in the places where their constituents live and possibly reduce the numbers of representatives in other areas.

REDISTRIBUTING SEATS ACROSS STATES = REAPPORTIONMENT

Because the basis for House representation is population, and since the number of seats in the House is capped at 435, how the population is counted will determine how many representatives each state gets. Growing states get more representatives; states with shrinking populations lose seats. This process of reallocating seats based on population is

FIGURE IT!

4.4: APPORTIONMENT IN THE HOUSE, 2012-2020

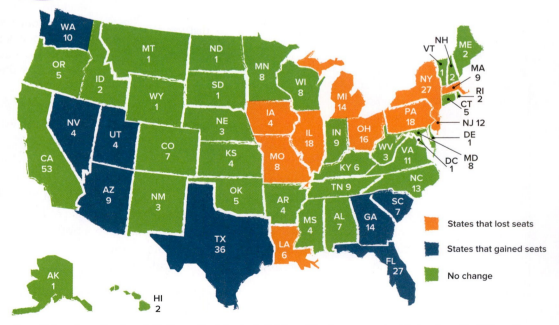

Source: U.S. Census Bureau, "Apportionment of the House and Senate Based on the 2010 Census," https://www.census.gov/population/apportionment/files/2010map.pdf.

called reapportionment, and it happens every ten years following the census. Over the years we can see shifts in population, removing seats from northern Rust Belt states and moving them to the faster-growing southern Sun Belt.

REDRAWING DISTRICT LINES INSIDE STATES = REDISTRICTING

Once the states have found out how many seats they have to distribute—which is already a political process due to the disputes over how the census should be counted—they engage in another political exercise called redistricting. Through that process, they draw new district lines to accommodate the allotted number of seats and any shifts in population within the state so that the districts stay equal (as required by *Baker v. Carr*). It is the state legislature's job to undertake redistricting after each census.

Here the politics heats up even more. Within each state legislature, it is really the majority party that generally controls the process. The way the legislature draws the districts can be done to achieve certain political results.

REDISTRICTING WITH POLITICAL INTENT = GERRYMANDERING

The process of redistricting with political intent is called gerrymandering. Gerrymandering entails drawing districts in odd shapes to try to concentrate the votes of a group of people in just a few districts or to distribute them so that a group has a majority in as many districts as possible.

ISN'T "GERRYMANDERING" A REALLY WEIRD WORD?

Yes, it is. It's derived from the name of Massachusetts governor Elbridge Gerry, who in 1812 drew the state districts so oddly that one resembled a sala*mander* (kind of a lizard-like animal). Gerry + mander = gerrymander. The name stuck.

DRAWING DISTRICTS TO AFFECT RACIAL COMPOSITION

Historically, gerrymandering was done to ensure that black and other minority voters did not control the votes in any district. This was accomplished by splitting up minority votes across two or more districts. After the civil rights movement, the same process was used to create districts with a majority of minority voters so that they had a better chance of sending minority representatives to Congress. Both forms of gerrymandering—diluting minority

. . . .

reapportionment: the process of reallocating seats in the House of Representatives based on population

redistricting: the process of dividing states into legislative districts

gerrymandering: the process of redistricting with political intent

4.5: THE ORIGINAL GERRYMANDER . . . AND ITS OFFSPRING

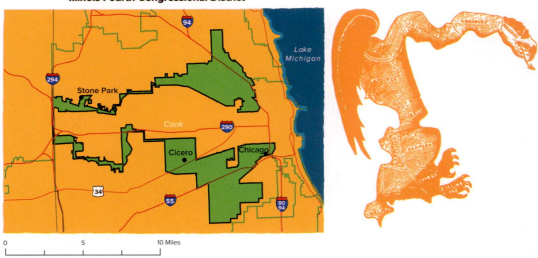

Illinois Fourth Congressional District

Back in 1812, district lines in the state of Massachusetts were drawn to concentrate Federalist support in a few key districts. A contemporary cartoon likened one particularly convoluted district to a long-necked monster, nicknamed the "Gerry-mander" after Massachusetts governor Elbridge Gerry. Redistricting after the 2010 Census proved that the gerrymander is alive and well, as evidenced by the new map of the Illinois Fourth Congressional District, nicknamed the "earmuffs" district, which joins two predominantly Latino areas in Chicago.

Source: "Congressional District 4," NationalAtlas.gov; Library of Congress.

votes and concentrating those same votes—is called **racial gerrymandering**. The practice of racial gerrymandering has been struck down by the Supreme Court since the early 1990s. Recall from our discussion in Chapter 3 that race is a suspect category, which means that when laws discriminate on the basis of race, the courts must ask if there is a compelling state purpose for the discrimination. In most instances, such cases fail to pass that strict scrutiny test.

DRAWING DISTRICTS TO AFFECT THEIR PARTY COMPOSITION

But even though racial gerrymandering is off the table, **partisan gerrymandering**—drawing the districts to enhance the political fortunes of one party over another—is alive and well though the subject of increasing scrutiny and criticism. The last redistricting in 2010 took place after Republicans had won control of many state governments in that year's midterm election. They gerrymandered the districts in enough states that although Democrats received 1.4 million more votes for the House of Representatives than did

racial gerrymandering: redistricting that either dilutes or concentrates minority votes

partisan gerrymandering: redistricting that enhances the political fortunes of one party over another

Republicans in the 2012 elections, Republicans held a majority of 234 to 201 seats. That advantage has continued to hold and will until the 2020 census, before which Democrats are hoping to redress the electoral imbalance. Even with the built-in advantage, however, Republicans lost the House majority in 2018 and some of the ability to call the shots in 2020.

In three cases concerning gerrymandering in 2018, the Supreme Court delivered a mixed bag of rulings. In two, partisan gerrymandering cases in which Democrats challenged maps that gave disproportionate numbers of representatives to Republicans, the Court essentially ruled that only people damaged by the actual gerrymandering (that is, people in the district) could bring a case, so they threw out the broader cases. In a third case concerning racial gerrymandering in Texas, they upheld the districting plan, ruling that the plaintiffs had shown an intent to discriminate only in one district but failed to show such an intent in the others. Note that the Court did not disagree that Democrats or blacks were underrepresented in the districting plans—they upheld the plans for procedural reasons.

DIG DEEPER

Check out FiveThirtyEight's series "The Gerrymandering Project" to see possible solutions to gerrymandered districts.

Go to **edge.sagepub.com/ dig-deeper**

THE UPSHOT

Politics is about trying to control the rules so that you win. Redistricting for the purposes of congressional House elections offers a good example of what that looks like. Current demographic trends do not favor the Republican Party. Republican voters tend to be older, whiter, male, southern, or rural people—a demographic that is not growing. Democrats, by contrast, are more likely to be more diverse, younger, more urban, and female—all demographic categories that are expanding. Although both parties use gerrymandering when they get the chance, Republicans today use gerrymandering as a means to retain power that shrinking numbers would otherwise deny them.

4.8 WHO RUNS AND WHO WINS? DOES CONGRESS LOOK LIKE AMERICA?

WHAT POTENTIAL CANDIDATES ARE THINKING

What makes people run for Congress? Quality candidates don't want to go through the expense and stress of an election, not to mention the interruption to their careers, unless they are going to get something valuable out of it—that is, unless they think they are going to win or at least will get enough name recognition that they may win in the future.

GENGAP!
GENERATIONAL ATTITUDES TOWARD THE PARTIES

Data gathered before the 2018 midterms indicted that there were giant generational discrepancies in how people of different ages viewed the parties and the Blue Wave bore that out. Younger people are indeed more likely to support Democrats—not necessarily because young people by their nature are so much more liberal but because younger people are more diverse non-white populations are more liberal.

FIGURE IT!

4.6: MOST MILLENNIALS FAVOR DEMOCRATS FOR CONGRESS

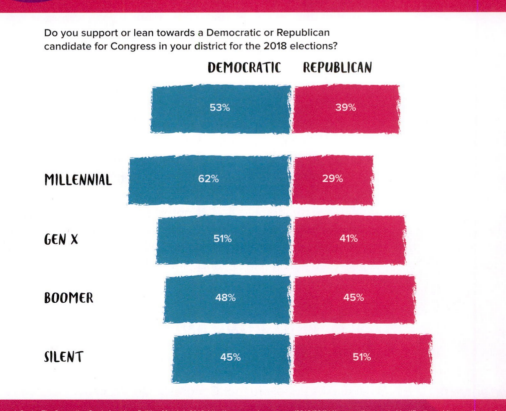

Do you support or lean towards a Democratic or Republican candidate for Congress in your district for the 2018 elections?

	DEMOCRATIC	REPUBLICAN
	53%	39%
MILLENNIAL	62%	29%
GEN X	51%	41%
BOOMER	48%	45%
SILENT	45%	51%

Source: Pew Research Center, The Generation Gap in American Politics, March 1, 2018, http://www.people-press.org/2018/03/01/1-generations-party-identification-midterm-voting-preferences-views-of-trump/030118_1_2/.

4.7: IN 2018, THE GENERATIONAL GAP IN PARTY PREFERENCE APPEARED TO WIDEN FURTHER

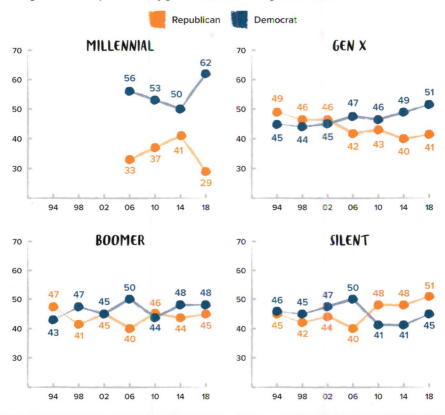

Congressional vote preference, by generation, based on registered voters . . .

■ Republican   ■ Democrat

MILLENNIAL

GEN X

BOOMER

SILENT

Source: Pew Research Center, The Generation Gap in American Politics, March 1, 2018, http://www.people-press.org/2018/03/01/1-generations-party-identification-midterm-voting-preferences-views-of-trump/030118_1_3/.

TAKEAWAYS

→ As the country becomes increasingly diverse it is becoming increasingly Democratic. Why are young people, people of color, and diverse populations attracted to the Democratic Party?

→ The populations that tend to vote Republican are getting older and dying. What can strategies can Republicans employ to stem their losses?

→ The trend toward the Democratic Party among millennials is dramatic—clearly the Democratic identification of these folks is picking up steam. Why?

Consequently, most potential candidates look at several factors in making the decision. In considering their own viability as a candidate, they will often test the waters with donors to see how easy it will be to raise money. They also sound out potential supporters to see if they will be willing to endorse them publicly.

In addition, they consider more systemic indicators of their likelihood of winning:

\#   The first consideration is probably whether there is already an incumbent in the seat. Due to the advantages members of Congress give themselves as well as the benefits they reap from being good representatives, once they are elected they have a good chance of holding the seat. As noted earlier, we call this the incumbency advantage. (For example, 93 percent of House members and 93 percent of senators were reelected in 2018.) In 2018 there were a lot of open seats; an unusual number of Republicans, knowing the winds were not blowing heir way, had already decided to retire. An **open seat** (one with no incumbent) is a much more attractive opportunity for a new candidate than is running against an incumbent.

\#   Of course, whether the district has been gerrymandered to be safe for the candidate's party is another important consideration. If a member of one party has no realistic chance of winning, then it is difficult to find a quality candidate willing to run. What was striking about 2018 was that the Democrats had found reasonably strong candidates to run in almost every district, so they were ready for opportunities that came their way.

\#   The election cycle's place in the bigger picture of things is also important. If the election is a **general election** with a strong presidential candidate on the ballot, that might help to sweep fellow party members into office by increasing turnout. We call this the **coattail effect**.

\#   By contrast, if it is an off-year election, a congressional candidate might want to assess the president's popularity. In most elections in which the president is not actually on the ballot, the election can serve as a sort of referendum on the president, and presidential parties rarely come out ahead. In fact, losses by the president's party

open seat: an election with no incumbent

general election: an election cycle in which presidential candidates are on the ballot

coattail effect: the added votes received by congressional candidates of a winning presidential party

FIGURE IT!

4.8: WHAT DOES CONGRESS LOOK LIKE?

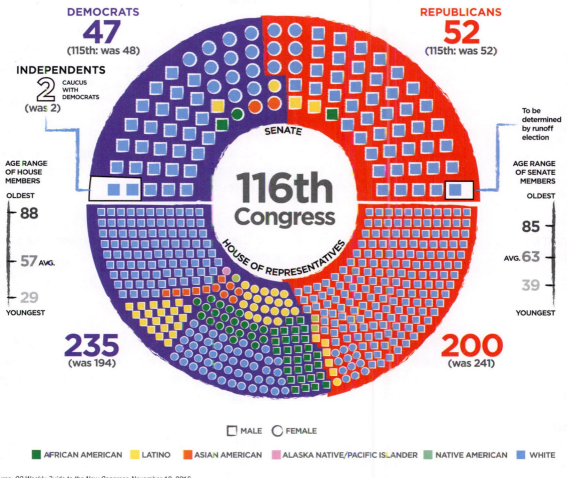

DEMOCRATS
47
(115th: was 48)

INDEPENDENTS
2 CAUCUS WITH DEMOCRATS
(was 2)

REPUBLICANS
52
(115th: was 52)

To be determined by runoff election

SENATE

116th Congress

HOUSE OF REPRESENTATIVES

AGE RANGE OF HOUSE MEMBERS

OLDEST
88
57 AVG.
29
YOUNGEST

AGE RANGE OF SENATE MEMBERS

OLDEST
85
AVG. 63
39
YOUNGEST

235
(was 194)

200
(was 241)

☐ MALE ◯ FEMALE

■ AFRICAN AMERICAN ■ LATINO ■ ASIAN AMERICAN ■ ALASKA NATIVE/PACIFIC ISLANDER ■ NATIVE AMERICAN ■ WHITE

Source: CQ Weekly Guide to the New Congress, November 10, 2016.

Note: Includes likely winners of races not settled at press time.

in off-year elections are so common they are known as a **midterm loss**—a reduction in the number of seats the party holds in Congress. In recent years, only 1998 and 2002 broke the midterm loss pattern, and both were under unusual circumstances. In 2018, President Trump put himself on the ballot, holding rallies and campaigning as if it were

midterm loss: the tendency for the presidential party to lose congressional seats in off-year elections

a general election. In areas he was popular he undoubtedly excited his base to turn out, but his problem was that his popularity, despite a strong economy, was unusually low and the Democrats picked up 40 seats in the House.

Despite the growing diversity of Americans, Congress still looks out of kilter with the rest of the population. It is largely white, male, and rich, whereas most of America is not although the 2018 midterms went a long way toward changing that. Nearly half of the new members of Congress were women or people of color, although almost exclusively on the Democratic side of the aisle. Newly elected Republicans were all white men except for one woman. Although what we call descriptive representation—how much a legislature looks like the population it represents—is better than at any time in our history, white males still make up 80 percent of Congress, even though they comprise only 40 percent of the population.

WHAT DO YOU THINK?

> Does it matter if members of Congress look like most Americans? What might be the advantages of descriptive representation?

4.9 THE 116TH CONGRESS

Midterm elections rarely prove to be winners for the president's party, and 2018 proved the rule. Observers had predicted a "Blue Wave" (major Democratic win) and that was what they got.

TSUNAMI!

> The House win for the Democrats was bigger than many had anticipated as they picked up 40 sets and the House majority, putting Nancy Pelosi back in the Speaker's chair. It happened because Republican exposure was high and Democrats took the unusual (for them) step of fielding candidates in almost every district, no matter how remote their chances were. Often a party will leave a seat uncontested if they don't think they will win but the enthusiasm to take on President Trump gave them good candidates to take advantage of retirements, scandals, or luck. More than a hundred women headed to the House in 2019, and at least 23 to the Senate. We also saw the first of many—the youngest member ever to be elected (Alexandria Ocasio-Cortez, 29), the first two Muslim women, and the first two Native American members.

· ·

descriptive representation: the degree to which a legislature looks like the population it represents

OK, WHAT HAPPENED IN THE SENATE?

As far as the Senate goes, the blue wave was limited by the fact that the Republican Senate had limited exposure—they were not defending many seats. Even though Democrats picked up seats in Arizona and Nevada and hung on to red states like Montana, the Republicans had gained a couple of seats when the dust settled.

WHAT ISSUES DID DEMOCRATS CAMPAIGN ON?

The legislative agenda in the House is headed by health care, the issue Democratic voters said most concerned them. Because Obamacare has become an albatross around the necks of Republicans, it is possible that some compromise could succeed in taking the issue off the table. Additional states voted for Medicaid expansion in the midterms which means that the ACA is not likely going anywhere; it's just a matter of whether the Trump administration can paralyze it by allowing low cost, high deductible plans that can charge a premium for pre-existing conditions.

Immigration is another issue the Democrats really want to move on but while there are clearly Republicans who would like to join them in a compromise solution, President Trump has made blocking immigrants and refugees a key part of his agenda and Republicans are not likely to challenge his base unless his popularity ratings sink further.

BUT THE CHAMBERS ARE SPLIT - WHAT DOES THIS MEAN FOR POLICYMAKING?

The new Congress coming in will have, more or less, the same Senate. The House is more demographically diverse than ever. The House will be led by a Speaker who has a history of holding her caucus together better than either of her two predecessors. While the House can't pass laws without the Senate it is likely, if patterns hold, there will be little cooperation between the two chambers.

SO, WHAT'S GOING TO HAPPEN?

Oversight! What the Democrats can do is to engage in congressional oversight. They have already promised to look carefully at the Russian involvement in the 2016 election, Trump's financial relationship with Russia, and his efforts to hamper freedom of the press, and you can expect them to be much more cooperative with the Special Prosecutor's Office than the Republicans were.

Big Think

→ Can you think of any way to ease the sometimes crippling tension between representation, lawmaking, and partisanship that legislators face?

→ What forces might bring the norm of bipartisanship back to Congress?

→ Think of arguments for and against giving every state two senators, regardless of state size. Does doing so advance or limit equal representation between the parties?

Key Terms

CONCEPTS ....

advice and consent (p. 122)

allocative representation (p. 130)

bicameral legislature (p. 113)

bipartisanship (p. 135)

casework (p. 130)

cloture (p. 125)

coattail effect (p. 144)

committees (p. 118)

conference committee (p. 120)

Congress (p. 112)

congressional district (p. 129)

congressional oversight (p. 121)

descriptive representation (p. 146)

earmarks (p. 130)

filibuster (p. 124)

general election (p. 144)

gerrymandering (p. 139)

House Rules Committee (p. 118)

hyperpartisanship (p. 133)

impeachment (p. 121)

incumbency advantage (p. 131)

joint committees (p. 120)

legislative agenda (p. 123)

majority party (p. 115)

midterm loss (p. 145)

national law making (p. 131)

nuclear option (p. 125)

omnibus legislation (p. 128)

open seat (p. 144)

partisan gerrymandering (p. 140)

partisanship (p. 133)

pocket veto (p. 125)

polarization (p. 133)

policy representation (p. 130)

pork barrel (p. 130)

racial gerrymandering (p. 140)

reapportionment (p. 139)

reconciliation (p. 128)

redistricting (p. 139)

representation (p. 129)

select committees (p. 118)

standing committees (p. 118)

symbolic representation (p. 131)

unorthodox lawmaking (p. 128)

veto (p. 125)

KEY INDIVIDUALS AND GROUPS ....

constituencies (p. 113)

minority leader (p. 115)

Senate majority leader (p. 115)

Speaker of the House (p. 115)

IMPORTANT WORKS AND EVENTS ....

U.S. Census (p. 136)

#5 THE EXECUTIVE BRANCH

In this chapter:

5.1 Introduction to THE EXECUTIVE BRANCH

WHAT *IS* AN EXECUTIVE, ANYWAY?

You are probably most familiar with the word *executive* from the business world. An **executive** is one who has the power to carry out plans, strategies, or laws. Executive action is decisive, managerial, and administrative.

In some countries, as we said in Chapter 2, the chief executive is called a prime minister—first among ministers in the parliament. A *parliamentary system* is one in which the executive is merged with the legislature—no separation of powers there! England is an example of a parliamentary system.

IN A NUTSHELL

The United States has a presidential system as part of a structure of separation of powers and checks and balances. Here, the chief executive is the **president**. But since managing a country the size of the United States is a mammoth undertaking, the president is but the head of what has become a vast network of departments, agencies, and boards and commissions called the **federal bureaucracy**. All of them together make up the federal executive.

WHERE WE GO IN THIS CHAPTER

By the time you finish reading this chapter, you will understand

- ⇒ The roles and powers of the American president
- ⇒ The way the president works with Congress and the Courts
- ⇒ How the expectations and roles of the president have changed over time
- ⇒ The reasons for having bureaucracies to execute the law
- ⇒ How the federal bureaucracy is organized
- ⇒ How and why the bureaucracy has grown
- ⇒ The politics of the bureaucracy in a checked and balanced system

5.2 THE JOB OF THE AMERICAN PRESIDENT

KEY ELEMENTS OF THE JOB DESCRIPTION

The American president has been said to have the most powerful job in the world. You wouldn't guess that from the job description the founders set out in the Constitution, which gives the president less power than is possessed by many other chief executives around the world. It's the reputation, economic heft, and military might of the United States that gives the president's office its cachet.

As far as the Constitution goes, the requirements for office are few. Article II provides that the president must be

\# At least 35 years old

\# A natural-born citizen of the United States

\# Resident in the country for at least fourteen years

\# Chosen by the Electoral College to serve a four-year term

\# Succeeded in the event of death or incapacity by the vice president elected at the same time

\# Removed from office only for "high crimes and misdemeanors" by the House and the Senate (which, recall, have different roles in the process)

\# Unable to receive "emoluments" (that is, profit beyond his normal salary) from the country or any of the states (and Article I prevents him from profiting from "any King, Prince, or foreign State" as well)

THE JOB DESCRIPTION AMENDED . . .

The Constitution didn't cover everything, so several amendments modified the job description:

\# The Twelfth Amendment (1804) modified the Electoral College process to prevent the president and vice president from being in opposing parties by electing them on separate ballots. Previously there was a single ballot—for the presidency alone; the winner of the most votes became the president and the runner-up became vice president. Americans passed the amendment just sixteen years after the ratification of the Constitution to allow the election of party members running on the same ticket.

executive: one who has the power to carry out plans, strategies, or laws

president: the chief executive in a presidential system

federal bureaucracy: the network of departments, agencies, and boards and commissions that make up the executive branch at the federal level; characterized by hierarchical structure, explicit rules, worker specialization, and advancement by merit

\# The Twentieth Amendment (1933) set the official term of office to begin on January 20 and provided for the vice president to take over if the president dies before taking the oath of office.

\# The Twenty-Second Amendment (1951) limits the number of terms to which the president can be elected to two. This followed the four elections of Franklin Roosevelt to the office.

\# The Twenty-Fifth Amendment (1967) clears up some ambiguities about presidential succession and also allows for the removal of the president by the vice president and a majority of the cabinet or the Congress if they determine he cannot do his job.

WHO DOES THE PRESIDENT'S JOB WHEN THE PRESIDENT CAN'T?

Finally, though not an amendment, the Presidential Succession Act of 1947 added to the language of the Constitution further detail on who does the president's job when the president cannot.

Some of the people in the chain of succession are members of the president's **cabinet**, an advisory group composed primarily of the heads of the major departments of the federal bureaucracy. (These are numbers four through eighteen in the table.)

WHY THESE PEOPLE?

The order of succession is kind of odd. First come the vice president and the Speaker, which make sense, but they are followed by the president pro tempore of the Senate who is likely to be quite elderly. After that come the secretaries of state, treasury, defense, the Attorney General, and the secretaries of the interior, agriculture, commerce, labor, health and human services, housing and urban development, transportation, energy, education, veterans affairs and homeland security. There is an excellent chance that these members of the cabinet have never held elected office and know nothing about running a whole country. What line of succession might make more sense?

THE EXECUTIVE ROLE IN A SYSTEM OF CHECKS AND BALANCES

Remember the principles of separation of powers and checks and balances. The president is the executive and as such is not part of either the legislature or the judiciary. But checks and balances ensure that the president has just enough legislative and judicial power to hold the other branches in check.

TWO CONFLICTING RESPONSIBILITIES MAKE THE U.S. EXECUTIVE'S JOB HARD TO DO WELL.

To be the nation's chief executive, the president generally has to fill two pairs of shoes that make the job particularly difficult.

The president serves as **head of state**, which is a largely ceremonial, apolitical role that rallies the country together. Especially after a national tragedy

cabinet: an advisory group to the president composed primarily of the heads of the major departments of the federal bureaucracy

head of state: the president's largely ceremonial, apolitical role in rallying the country together

like a terrorist attack or a destructive storm, the president is the one who helps the nation grieve and find a common purpose.

That job is complicated by the other shoes the president has to fill, those of the head of government. The **head of government** is a partisan role: head of the president's own party, twister of arms, maker of deals, and pusher of the party's agenda.

It is hard to pull off being good at both of those jobs. For one thing, different presidents' talents might naturally suit them for one or the other of those tasks. Ronald Reagan was a trained communicator, a natural at speaking for the nation in emotional moments. When it came to policy, he preferred to delegate. Bill Clinton, by contrast, was a total policy wonk, but it took him months to get the hang of being an effective head of state. So far, Donald Trump has spent less time rallying the nation as a whole as head of state, preferring instead to appeal to his voting base. As a head of government, he has been adept at moving the Republican Party to pay lip service to his own agenda, but he has not done much to bring the rest of the country with him, nor as he gotten Congress to pass many of his signature goals.

Other countries avoid the challenges of having the executive fill two such mismatched roles by having two different people do it. The Queen of England, for instance, is the head of state, high above the political fray. Meanwhile, the prime minister can be as deep in the weeds of partisan politics as she wants without having any citizens feel betrayed because she represents her party.

DIG DEEPER

Watch President George W. Bush addressing rescue workers at Ground Zero and President Obama signing "Amazing Grace"—both efforts to pull the country together!

Go to **edge.sagepub.com/ dig-deeper**

BREAKING DOWN EXECUTIVE POWER ❯ As far as the Constitution goes, the president's job consists of the following executive powers:

\#   **Chief administrator**. The Constitution says that the president "shall take care that the laws be faithfully executed." That makes the president the head bureaucrat—in charge of making sure that the

head of government: the president's partisan role as head of his own party, twister of arms, maker of deals, and pusher of the party's agenda

chief administrator: the president's role as head bureaucrat, in charge of making sure that the departments, agencies, and boards and commissions charged with enforcing the laws do their jobs

departments, agencies, and boards and commissions charged with enforcing the laws do their jobs. As chief administrator, the president also wields the appointment power. With the approval of a majority of the Senate, the president is responsible for appointing the heads of the departments (the cabinet), as well as more than 3,500 federal employees: administrative officers, military officers, federal judges, and diplomats. Presidents cannot necessarily fire all of these people, which limits their control, but the appointment power goes a long way toward shaping the bureaucracy the president leads.

Commander in chief. The president is the civilian head of the armed forces of the United States. That doesn't mean the president can *declare* war—the Constitution gives that power to Congress (see how checks and balances work?)—but the commander in chief has the practical ability to *wage* war. Since the beginning, presidents and Congress have battled over who has power here, and checks and balances keep all of them from having too much.

Chief foreign policy maker. The president negotiates treaties, with the approval of two thirds of the Senate, which means the holder of the office has extraordinary power to set the direction of foreign policy. In addition, as administrator of treaties already passed, the president can issue executive agreements with other countries to fill out the details of those treaties. No Senate approval is necessary for them at all. Only about 1,000 treaties have been approved since 1970, but more than 10,000 executive agreements have been issued to put those treaties into effect.

CHECKS AND BALANCES MEANS THE PRESIDENT *ALSO* HAS SOME LEGISLATIVE POWERS.

The president has just enough legislative power to keep Congress from running the show. In England, parliament is sovereign, but the United States is built on popular sovereignty, which means that Congress is not the ultimate power. The president, along with the judiciary, keeps it that way by exercising some legislative power.

appointment power: the president's power to select the heads of the departments (the cabinet), as well as more than 3,500 federal employees

commander in chief: the president's power to act as the civilian head of the armed forces of the United States

chief foreign policy maker: the president's power to formulate foreign policy and negotiate treaties

treaties: formal agreements with other countries; negotiated by the president and requiring approval by two thirds of the Senate

executive agreements: presidential arrangements with other countries that create foreign policy without the need for Senate approval

THE DESIGNATED SURVIVOR ❯

\# The **State of the Union address**. The Constitution says that the president will regularly inform Congress of the state of the union and recommend the measures he considers useful or necessary. In the modern day, this has turned into a huge televised spectacle in which the president, with the vice president and Speaker of the House standing behind him, addresses both chambers of Congress, members of the Supreme Court, almost all the cabinet members (one designated survivor is not permitted to attend so that, if disaster strikes the Capitol, the entire line of succession to the presidency will not be wiped out), and various guests invited by the president.

The State of the Union address is a chance for the president to lay out a policy agenda and attempt to shape the narrative around it by addressing the nation directly, without a media filter.

\# **Presidential veto**. Recall from Chapter 4 that after a bill is passed by Congress it goes to the president's desk for a signature. The Constitution gives the president the option of refusing to sign. The veto power is a considerable legislative check to keep Congress from doing something the president doesn't like. If Congress can summon a two-thirds majority it can override the veto, but that is difficult to do with our current highly partisan and polarized politics. If a president's party holds the majority in one or both houses of Congress, a veto might not need to come into play that often, but it is a potent element in the president's toolbox. Even the threat of a veto can lead Congress to accommodate the president's wishes.

\# **Executive orders**. Just as presidents can issue executive agreements to implement treaties that the Senate has approved, they can issue executive orders to fill in details and enforce the laws passed by Congress. Technically, executive orders are only points of clarification of existing law, but they can have major policy impact, as did President Truman's executive order to integrate the military in 1948.

Executive orders do not go unchecked, however. Congress cannot override an executive order as they can a veto, but they can pass a law that contradicts the order. And the Supreme Court can hold an executive order unconstitutional through judicial review.

. . . .

State of the Union address: the president's constitutional obligation to regularly inform Congress of the state of the union and to recommend measures considered useful or necessary

presidential veto: a president's authority to reject a bill passed by Congress; may be overridden only by a two-thirds majority in each house

executive orders: clarifications of congressional policy issued by the president and having the full force of law

AND SOME JUDICIAL POWERS, TOO.

> Along with checks on the legislature, the Constitution provides the president with three important checks on the judiciary by giving the executive some judicial power, too.

\# **The appointment power**. Included in the appointment power we mentioned earlier is the president's ability to appoint, with the advice and consent of the Senate, the entire federal judiciary. This gives presidents the ability to shape not just the Supreme Court but also all the lower federal courts (from whom the SCOTUS justices are usually chosen) by careful choice of their nominees. Although a Senate majority of the opposing party can stymie a president, as the Republicans largely did to President Barack Obama, the president's judicial power is huge when his party is in charge of the Senate. In just his first two years in office, President Trump had already had a definitive impact on the courts with two Supreme Court justices and innumerable appointments to the lower courts.

\# **The solicitor general**. The solicitor general (also appointed by the president) is the legal officer who argues cases before the Supreme Court when the United States is a party to the case, as it often is. For many lawyers, arguing a case before the Court is a major and nerve-wracking event, but the solicitor general does it routinely. Whether it is because of all the practice or because the Court tends to be deferential to the administration, the solicitor general typically wins a disproportionate number of cases.

\# **The pardoning power**. The president can also check the judiciary with the power to pardon those accused or convicted of crimes. This is not just a presidential power—many governors (state executives) share it as well—but it is a major check. Not only can the president use it to pardon those who petition that they have been unfairly convicted or sentenced, but more than once presidents have used it to spare members of their own administrations from punishment for being involved in administration scandals.

5.3 THE EVOLUTION OF THE AMERICAN PRESIDENCY

ONE THING TO KNOW ABOUT HOW THE PRESIDENT'S ROLE HAS CHANGED

> The America we know today is much larger and more complex than the thirteen-state nation the founders created the Constitution for, and the job

solicitor general: the legal officer who argues cases before the Supreme Court when the United States is a party to the case

pardoning power: a president's authority to release or excuse a person from the legal penalties of a crime

of the president who oversees it has gotten more complex, too. George Washington had only three federal departments represented in his cabinet. President Trump has fifteen.

AND ONE THING ABOUT HOW IT HASN'T

What is essential to know about the presidential role, however, is that although citizens' expectations of the presidency have grown over time, the formal powers of the job have not. In fact, the only constitutional change to affect presidential powers is the Twenty-Second Amendment, which reduces the power of the office by imposing term limits on it.

THE FOUNDERS ENVISIONED A PRESIDENCY WITH LIMITED POWERS . . .

In the early days of the republic, the presidency had limited powers because the federal government was a limited government. The founders feared unleashed executive powers and were determined to have neither a monarch nor a hereditary aristocracy.

In what is known as the **traditional presidency**, there wasn't all that much to administer. For over a hundred years, the office was pretty much consistent with the founders' intentions. When presidents did step outside that limited executive vision, they excused it by saying they were relying on the **inherent powers** of the presidency—powers that were not explicitly laid out but rather were implied in their constitutional duty "to take care that the laws be faithfully executed"—or that their actions were necessary for national security. But mostly, they didn't stray too far from the founders' original plan.

BUT EVENTS DEFEATED THEIR INTENTIONS.

That limited vision of the executive changed dramatically, however, when the stock market crashed in 1929 and sent the nation into a depression. Unable to find work or financial security, citizens began to look to government to help them out of the disaster. President Franklin Roosevelt's **New Deal** program did just that, turning the government into an employer to build infrastructure and public works and creating social insurance programs like Social Security to ensure that a safety net existed for the elderly, disabled, and orphaned. In the process, it launched the era of the **modern presidency**.

. . . .

traditional presidency: the founders' vision of limited executive power

inherent powers: presidential powers implied but not stated explicitly in the Constitution

New Deal: under Franklin Roosevelt, a series of programs that encouraged people to turn to the government for the solution to social and economic problems; made the government larger and more unwieldy and reignited a debate about the role of government

modern presidency: the trend toward a higher degree of executive power since the 1930s in response to more complex social problems

CAN'T BE SAID TOO OFTEN: HIGHER EXPECTATIONS, SAME OLD LIMITED EXECUTIVE TOOLBOX.

The modern presidency began a new relationship between the president and the public. Government grew at all levels as the services it provided to citizens increased and Americans became dependent on those services. As government's role grew, those running for office began to promise more benefits and services to solve voters' problems, and voters began to choose among candidates based on those promises.

The irony, as we said, is that though the presidential candidates started promising to do more and more, the powers of the office stayed the same. There is no magic wand in the president's pocket that fixes the economy, provides health care, or, indeed, gets any part of the presidential agenda passed.

The newest tool at the president's disposal is Twitter. But even though it has enabled Donald Trump to communicate directly with the American public and to keep his base at a fever pitch of excitement, it has not helped him achieve his policy goals.

Trump's lavish use of Twitter highlight the mediated world in which the president does business today—providing more opportunities for him to communicate with Congress and citizens, and for citizens to respond, not always politely either.

SO WHAT TOOLS DOES THE PRESIDENT HAVE TO GET AROUND THE LIMITS ON EXECUTIVE POWER?

In general, the president's ability to get things done depends on his ability to convince Congress to support his plans—the so-called **power to persuade**. The power to persuade is the modern president's effort to use tools of bargaining, horse-trading, and arm-twisting to get Congress to bend to his will. Needless to say, skillful heads of government are better at this than less politically adept presidents. It can help if the president has voters on his side so that he can take his agenda on the road, **going public** to drum up support that can then be used for leverage with Congress. Mediated citizenship gives presidents a much larger playing field on which to try to make this happen, although they don't always take effective advantage of it. In some cases, notably Obama's, a polarized Congress can afford to ignore the popular pressure generated by the president because the majority may not need support from the president's party.

power to persuade: the president's ability to convince Congress to support his plans

going public: a president's strategy of drumming up support with the public on an issue, with the hope of using public pressure as leverage with Congress

THE UPSHOT

As politics have become more partisan and divisive, we have seen legislators become increasingly less willing to cooperate even with a popular president of the other party if that refusal will defeat the president's policies. Most recently, a Republican Congress strategically denied President Obama any legislative victories, correctly banking on the fact that a failure to get legislation passed would be perceived to be as much his fault as theirs. And going public can have its limits. For all that Trump relishes the pomp of the office, he has in a way made it less dignified by his public squabbles on social media.

THE CASE OF THE WEAK PRESIDENT

But even a president with a congressional majority of his own party can run into problems of cooperation if he is not perceived to have control over the mechanics of governing. If a president is considered by his party to be weak—that is, unable to control the bureaucracy, his cabinet, or other senior staff, and if his approval ratings are low, then Congress won't be persuaded to enact his agenda. **Weak presidents**—Jimmy Carter and Donald Trump—have difficulty getting their priorities through even a friendly Congress. President Trump got his tax cut passed only because it was a top Republican congressional priority. Congress has ignored or sidestepped most of the rest of his agenda, like the building of his wall and actively opposed some of it, like his trade policy. Effective presidents have the administrative and political skills to manage their staffs and the competing actors around them.

HOW DIFFERENT INTERPRETATIONS OF PRESIDENTIAL POWER HAVE PLAYED OUT IN THE MODERN AGE

Since Franklin Roosevelt, the modern presidency is clearly more powerful than the traditional office, apparent in the sheer size of the governments they manage, if nothing else. But the force of the modern presidency has also experienced some ups and downs.

In the 1970s, Lyndon Johnson's handling of the Vietnam War and Richard Nixon's belief that "it's not illegal when the president does it" (a conviction that led to the Watergate scandal and Nixon's own resignation from office) pushed the boundaries of presidential power to such lengths that both Congress and the media began to exercise greater checks on and scrutiny of the president.

The trend, begun after Watergate, continued into the 1990s, when Bill Clinton found that the office could not protect him from being sued for sexual harassment from his days when he was governor of Arkansas.

- -

weak presidents: presidents who have difficulty getting priorities through even a friendly Congress

5.1: THE SKIMMABLE COURT WATCHER: *UNITED STATES V. NIXON* (1974)

Facts presented and arguments made by the United States	Facts presented and arguments made by Nixon	Action by the courts
# Five burglars working for the Committee to Re-elect the President (CREEP) broke into the Democratic National Committee offices in the Watergate Office Building (fun fact—the publisher of this book has offices that include that very room!). # As the scandal became public, Nixon attempted to cover it up, ordering his aides to lie and hiding the methods by which those involved were paid. # In the investigation, a grand jury indicted seven of Nixon's aides for being involved in the cover-up. In the process, it was revealed that Nixon kept tape recordings of all his conversations in the Oval Office. The special prosecutor subpoenaed those recordings.	# Nixon believed he was protected from the subpoena power by virtue of **executive privilege**, the ability of the president to keep confidential certain documents concerning the executive branch or national security. # Nixon ordered his attorney general to fire the special prosecutor appointed to investigate the scandal. He refused and resigned, as did the second in command in the Justice Department. The third person ordered to fire the prosecutor did so. (This series of events is known as the Saturday Night Massacre.) Nixon, however, was forced by public outrage to hire another prosecutor, who subpoenaed the tapes.	# In the District Court of Washington, D.C., Nixon's lawyer attempted to quash the subpoena with these instructions from Nixon: "The President wants me to argue that he is as powerful a monarch as Louis XIV, only four years at a time, and is not subject to the processes of any court in the land except the court of impeachment." # The lower court didn't agree and ordered the tapes turned over. Nixon appealed to the Supreme Court. In a 9–0 ruling, the Court held that *the president's claim to executive privilege is not unlimited.* Nixon had to turn over recordings and other subpoenaed information to the special prosecutor. # Nixon resigned several weeks later, on August 9, 1974.

Reacting to the reduction in stature of the presidency, George W. Bush and his vice president, Dick Cheney, tried to create a more muscular office. Relying on a theory called the **unitary executive**, which held that the executive, not the legislature, was at the core of American power, they pushed back on congressional attempts to limit the president's power.

executive privilege: the president's ability to claim that some materials relevant to his job must be kept confidential to enable him to perform his duties or for national security reasons; a right with limits, according to the Supreme Court

unitary executive: the theory that the executive, not the legislature, is at the core of American power

Barack Obama did not share Bush and Cheney's view, but he used more direct executive action than some of his predecessors because Congress refused to work with him. His critics viewed his executive orders as presidential overreach.

Donald Trump has chafed at the limits of checks and balances since taking office, pushing against the notion that the president is bound by the rule of law or traditional political norms. This is partly because, without a political background, Trump doesn't know how to work with the other branches or, indeed, with the rest of the executive branch. Trump occasionally wished, for instance, that the Department of Justice would "protect" him and attempted to use the department to prosecute people he saw as his political enemies. In 2018, he tweeted an order to his then-attorney general, who had previously recused himself from the matter, to fire special counsel Robert Mueller. The tweeted order was disregarded although the Attorney General, Jeff Sessions, was later fired. His second nominee to the Supreme Court, Brett Kavanaugh, is known for his views that the president is protected from facing the judicial process.

5.4 PRESIDENTS, POPULARITY, AND CONGRESS

IS THE PRESIDENCY A GIANT POPULARITY CONTEST?

To have any chance to effectively exercise their power or to go beyond the constitutional limits of their job description, presidents need to be popular with the public, and to transfer that popularity into political capital they can use to persuade Congress. Recent history shows us that even that may not be sufficient, but it is a minimum requirement. Popular presidents may not get everything they want, but unpopular or weak presidents can end up being seen as irrelevant.

WHAT FACTORS MAKE A PRESIDENT POPULAR?

Presidential popularity can be influenced by several factors, few of which the occupant of the White House can control:

\# **Cycle effect.** The cycle effect refers to the fact that presidential popularity tends to start out strong and decline over time, barring national disasters that may give it a boost. If a president wants to accomplish a policy agenda, the time to strike is during the first

cycle effect: the predictable rise and fall of a president's popularity at different stages of a term in office

5.1: PRESIDENTIAL APPROVAL RATINGS, FROM EISENHOWER TO TRUMP

Average quarterly presidential approval ratings

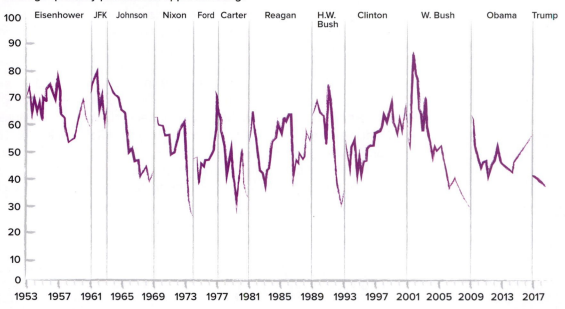

100 days, the so-called **honeymoon period**, when the press is likely to be kindest and when most of the public is still giving the new president the benefit of the doubt. Not all presidents get a honeymoon, and not all use it to good effect, but those early days of the administration remain the likeliest time for a president to get big things done.

 # Economy. Although in truth the president has very little control over how the economy does in the immediate sense, the public responds as if their economic well-being is in his hands. A prosperous economy generally keeps a president popular (and may well have saved Bill Clinton's job for him: the economy was booming while he was undergoing impeachment proceedings), whereas a struggling economy is seen as the president's fault. This is in part because presidential candidates have trained us to think this way by promising economic good times if we elect them, but they can also suffer for it.

. . . .

honeymoon period: the first 100 days following an election when a president's popularity is high and congressional relations are likely to be productive

\# **External events**. Of course, a president's approval ratings are also affected by other, non-economic events that happen during their tenure. George W. Bush had record-high approval ratings after the terror attacks on the United States on September 11, 2001, as Americans rallied around their president in a show of national unity. By the same token, presidents who are seen as divisive or who are president during difficult times (like Lyndon Johnson during the Vietnam War) can take a hit in their ratings.

\# **Polarization**. In our current age of hyperpartisanship, a president's approval ratings can be tied to his party's fortunes. This is one reason why losing the Republican majority in the House was so devastating to President Trump in 2018. A Democratic House can be expected to block his legislative priorities and to begin oversight and even impeachment hearings.

HOW CAN THE PRESIDENT COOPERATE EFFECTIVELY WITH CONGRESS?

A major point of worrying about presidential popularity is obviously to maximize one's chances of getting get reelected, but remember that it is also important to have political capital to convince Congress to do what the president wants.

Working with Congress is key for the president. Although executive orders can accomplish some specific goals, real, comprehensive change requires congressional cooperation. Even a president working with a Congress headed by his own party can face challenges. As Obama found out, a president facing **divided government**, with a majority in at least one house different from his own party, can find his agenda brought to a standstill.

To maximize chances that they can cooperate, presidents appoint **legislative liaisons** whose chief job is to coordinate with Congress, try to find points of potential agreement, and ease the way forward.

The legislative liaison, like other parts of the White House establishment dedicated to supporting the president's work, is also part of the bureaucracy that constitutes the federal government. Before we look at the bureaucracy inside the White House, as well as out, we should take a look at the idea of bureaucracy itself and why, despite being the butt of a thousand jokes, it is indispensable to getting things done.

· ·

divided government: the situation that exists when political rule is split between two parties, in which one controls the White House and the other controls one or both houses of Congress

legislative liaisons: executive personnel who work with members of Congress to secure their support in getting a president's legislation passed

GEN GAP!

PRESIDENTIAL PREFERENCES ACROSS THE GENERATIONS

One of the widest gaps between the generations is in their evaluations of President Trump. After Trump was in office for one year, only 27 percent of Millennials approved of his job performance, compared with 46 percent of the Silent Generation. Of course, as we have seen in this chapter, his average approval is very low for a new president, but the Millennial numbers are striking, especially since their approval of Obama was quite high during the same time frame in his first administration (the first one in which they voted). Before the Millennials were part of the electorate, we did not see the really large generation gaps that we see now.

FIGURE IT!

5.2: WIDE GENERATION GAP IN EVALUATIONS OF TRUMP'S JOB PERFORMANCE IN FIRST YEAR

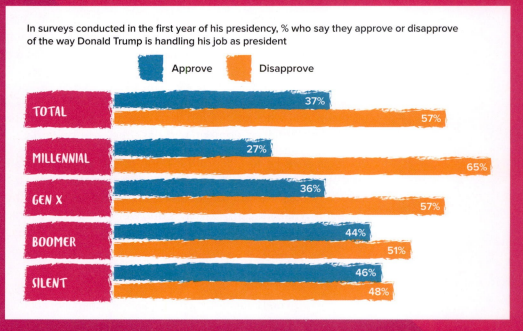

In surveys conducted in the first year of his presidency, % who say they approve or disapprove of the way Donald Trump is handling his job as president

Approve   Disapprove

TOTAL — Approve 37%, Disapprove 57%
MILLENNIAL — Approve 27%, Disapprove 65%
GEN X — Approve 36%, Disapprove 57%
BOOMER — Approve 44%, Disapprove 51%
SILENT — Approve 46%, Disapprove 48%

Source: "The Generation Gap in American Politics." Pew Research Center, Washington, D.C. (March 01, 2018) http://www.people-press.org/wp-content/uploads/sites/4/2018/03/03-01-18-Generations-release.pdf

5.3: GENERATIONAL DIFFERENCES IN JOB APPROVAL MUCH WIDER FOR BOTH OBAMA AND TRUMP

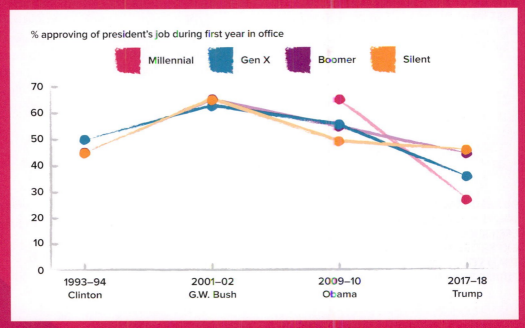

% approving of president's job during first year in office

Millennial   Gen X   Boomer   Silent

| 1993–94 Clinton | 2001–02 G.W. Bush | 2009–10 Obama | 2017–18 Trump |

Source: Pew Research Center, The Generation Gap in American Politics, March 1, 2018, http://www.people-press.org/2018/03/01/1-generations-party-identification-midterm-voting-preferences-views-of-trump/030118_1_5/ and http://www.people-press.org/2018/03/01/the-generation-gap-in-american-politics/030118_o_1/.

TAKEAWAYS

→ **Millennials came of political age during the Obama administration, and they were his largest supporters.** What about his agenda would have appealed to them?

→ **As much as Millennials liked Obama, they dislike Trump.** Since very little of Trump's agenda is directed to young people (and much of Obama's was), perhaps that is not a surprise.

→ **The generation gap in Trump's presidential approval, while nonexistent for the Silent Generation and the Baby Boomers, also shows up in Gen X.** They are slightly more approving of Obama than are older Americans but are quite a bit less approving of Trump. Why is this president so sharply divisive by age?

5.5 WHAT IS BUREAUCRACY, AND WHY DO WE NEED IT?

WHY CAN'T WE JUST MAKE ALL OUR DECISIONS DEMOCRATICALLY?

> If you are flying in an airplane and an engine suddenly flames out, do you want your fellow passengers to vote on what to do, or would you rather that the experts in the cockpit make a decision quickly and professionally? No question, right? Although it can be difficult for Americans to accept, democracy is not always the best way to make decisions. It is time-consuming and cumbersome to find out what everyone wants to do, and everyone just might be wrong. They might be experts on what they personally want, but not on technical or specialized matters.
>
> That's why we have bureaucracy.

BUREAUCRACY— WHEN YOU NEED EFFICIENCY AND EXPERTISE MORE THAN YOU WANT PUBLIC BUY-IN

> **Bureaucracy** is a hierarchical decision-making structure in which unelected officials answer to the layer of people above them, who in turn answer to the people above them, and on up to the very top. Think of a pyramid— ultimate power is at the peak; the least power is at the base. That is the *opposite* of how we expect democracy to work, but it is the essence of bureaucratic decision making.
>
> Much of the private world is organized bureaucratically (large corporations, for instance), but even in a government where many of our leaders are chosen and many decisions are made democratically, there is a big role for bureaucracy.

OKAY, BUT ISN'T BUREAUCRACY USUALLY PRETTY CORRUPT?

> Bureaucracy tends to have a bad reputation, but as a way to make decisions it is neither good nor bad. It can be good at some things—making decisions quickly and consistently and maximizing expertise—but it can also easily be corrupted because of the lack of transparency and democratic accountability.

KEY POINT

> One way to think about government bureaucracy is that it can serve the interests of the power-holders, or it can serve the interests of the public.

. . . .

bureaucracy: a hierarchical decision-making structure in which unelected officials answer to the layer of people above them, who in turn answer to the people above them, and so on

At times in our history—for instance, during the administration of Andrew Jackson—U.S. governmental bureaucracy has served the powerful, allowing them to appoint cronies and supporters to key positions (a practice called **patronage**) and keeping and promoting people who demonstrate loyalty, all of which helps them to consolidate power. This practice of creating a bureaucracy to serve the president's interest was called the **spoils system**, based on the notion that the right to staff government with people loyal to you is part of the spoils of victory. It generally results in government that serves the interests of the elected officials, not of the people who elected them.

REFORMING POWER-SERVING BUREAUCRACY

Because it is just a form of organization and decision making, bureaucracy can be safeguarded with rules and procedures that help to ensure it serves the public.

Legislators of the late 1880s passed **civil service reform** to make the federal bureaucracy serve the interests of the public rather than the powerful. The government hasn't completely depoliticized the bureaucracy or ended all patronage positions, but it has attempted to bring the federal bureaucracy into line with the principles of neutral competence.

FOUR KEY CHARACTERISTICS OF NEUTRAL COMPETENCE

Neutral competence is an ideal bureaucratic structure in which (a) power is *hierarchical*, (b) power is *rule-based*, (c) people are appointed because of their *expertise*, and (d) people are promoted on the basis of *merit*.

The closer a bureaucracy comes to the standard of neutral competence, the less internal politics there will be, the fairer it will be, and the more efficient and consistent it will be.

. . . .

patronage: a system in which people in power reward friends, contributors, and party loyalists for their support with jobs, contracts, and favors

spoils system: the practice of creating a bureaucracy that serves the president's interest

civil service reform: efforts begun in the 1880s to ensure that the federal bureaucracy serves the interests of the public rather than the powerful

neutral competence: an ideal bureaucratic structure where power is hierarchical and rule-based, and where people are appointed because of their expertise and promoted on the basis of merit

WHY PREFER BUREAUCRACY?

> A neutral bureaucratic organization can accomplish many things much better than democratic decision making can. It can be much quicker than tabulating all the preferences of a large group of people, and it has recourse to expert judgment, not just the opinions of a bunch of citizens. There are some things, like the contents of a bottle of antibiotics, that we don't want our fellow voters to weigh in on.

WHAT ABOUT ACCOUNTABILITY AND TRANSPARENCY?

> Precisely because bureaucrats are not elected and thus not accountable to voters, civil service laws try to make them somewhat accountable by requiring them to follow rules designed to treat people fairly, to refrain from politics on the job, and to fill out paperwork (the dreaded red tape that comes with our own bureaucratic interactions, say, at the motor vehicles bureau or when applying for a student loan). Red tape may be a pain, but it also provides supervisors with a paper trail if they want to see how a decision got made, and it ensures that all decisions have been made consistently.

> Remember that, even though bureaucratic decision making is sometimes good or even inevitable, it always means turning over power to people whose actions are not transparent and who are not accountable to voters. We can take steps to make bureaucracy more transparent and more accountable, but the more we do that, the more we hobble bureaucracy and keep it from doing what it does best. Getting the balance right is part of why we have checks and balances, even though the founders could not have imagined a government as large as ours is today.

PARTS OF THE FEDERAL BUREAUCRACY SERVE THE PRESIDENT AND OTHERS SERVE THE PUBLIC.

> Probably the best way to think about the bureaucracy of the executive branch is that the president has his own White House bureaucracy, what some political scientists call the presidential branch, to help him do his job, and part of that job is to manage the larger federal bureaucracy that implements and enforces the laws that Congress and the president make.

> The White House bureaucracy serves the president's interest in doing his job and is less subject to civil service guidelines than is the federal bureaucracy, which serves the country, not the president personally.

red tape: the complex procedures and regulations surrounding bureaucratic activity

presidential branch: the bureaucracy within the White House that serves the president

5.6 THE PURPOSE AND ORGANIZATION OF THE WHITE HOUSE BUREAUCRACY

ALL THE PRESIDENT'S PEOPLE

The 1974 book about the Watergate scandal that forced President Richard Nixon's resignation, written by the two young reporters who broke the story at the *Washington Post*, was called *All the President's Men*, an allusion to the *Humpty Dumpty* nursery rhyme. Kings, and even elected executives, have always had "men"—members of the royal court or, these days, more ordinary staffers who help them do their jobs. Except these days, of course, the "men" are also women. "All the president's people" may be less catchy, but it is a better description of today's presidential staffers.

EXECUTIVE OFFICE OF THE PRESIDENT: BORN IN THE NEW DEAL EXPANSION OF FEDERAL POWER

In 1939, as the range of issues dealt with by the president was expanding rapidly with his New Deal programs designed to pull the country out of the Great Depression, Franklin Roosevelt created the **Executive Office of the President** (EOP) to help him do his job. Previously the White House had been managed by various staffers and advisers to the president, but the modern presidency demanded something more organized.

The EOP is home to agencies that the president appoints to help him manage the huge range of issues that the White House has to deal with every day. These people are the president's advisers and they serve at his will, although they are managed by the **chief of staff**. Few need Senate approval (exceptions include the director of the Office of Management and Budget, the U.S. trade representative, and the Council of Economic Advisers). The president can fire these staff if he wants.

There are about a dozen agencies in the EOP, most organized along policy lines. The most important include the Council of Economic Advisers, the National Security Council, the Office of Management and Budget, the Office of the United States Trade Representative, the Office of the Vice President of the United States, and the White House Office.

. . . .

Executive Office of the President: the agencies and advisers that help the president manage the range of issues that the White House has to deal with every day

chief of staff: the person who oversees the operations of all White House staff and typically controls access to the president

THE WHITE HOUSE OFFICE—IN-HOUSE ADVISERS

The heads of some of these agencies, along with other essential advisers who work with the president, are in the **White House Office**—an in-house group of advisers that includes the Office of the Chief of Staff (who also oversees the White House Office); the Communications Office, including the press secretary; the National Economic Council and the Domestic Policy Council; the Office of the First Lady; and various political advisers.

THREE KEY TAKEAWAYS ABOUT THE EOP AND WHITE HOUSE OFFICE

There are three important things you should know about the EOP and the White House Office:

Unlike the members of the federal bureaucracy, these people work for and are largely loyal to the president. In fact, the offices developed largely because, as we will see, the cabinet secretaries, the departments they manage, and other federal agencies have different constituencies and the president cannot count on them to have his back.

These positions are numerous and slightly redundant, in part because the administration is responsible for so many things but also because these jobs are often held by people the president has worked with before or who have helped elect him and whom he wants to reward with a White House job. In that sense, they are truly vestiges of the pre-reform patronage system.

Because there is minimal Senate vetting of these positions, there is no certain way to determine what qualifications, experience, or problematic baggage they may bring with them. Usually it is the presidential transition teams who start to vet these staffers early, even before they know they will win. The first years of the Trump administration were marked by historic levels of staff turnover due in large part to issues with vetting.

White House Office: an in-house group of advisers that includes the Office of the Chief of Staff (who also oversees the White House Office); the Communications Office, including the press secretary; the National Economic Council and the Domestic Policy Council; the Office of the First Lady; and various political advisers

5.7 THE PURPOSE AND ORGANIZATION OF THE FEDERAL BUREAUCRACY: THE REST OF THE EXECUTIVE BRANCH

WHAT EXACTLY IS INCLUDED IN THE FEDERAL BUREAUCRACY?

Many more people are federal bureaucrats than you probably realize, including the person who delivers your mail, your cousin who serves in the army, and the office worker who processed your student loan. In all, more than four million people work for the federal government. Not everyone sets out to be a bureaucrat, but, clearly, many people end up there.

Besides the president, the Executive Office of the President, and the White House Office, the executive branch consists of the president's cabinet, the departments for which the cabinet members are responsible, and all the agencies, boards, and commissions that it takes to put the laws of Congress into action, as well as everyone serving in the U.S. military and public corporations like the U.S. Postal Service.

WHY IS THE FEDERAL BUREAUCRACY SO BIG?

Not everyone agrees on how big the government should be, but no one can deny that it has gotten much bigger since the New Deal changed many people's views of the role of government.

BECAUSE WE MAKE BIG DEMANDS

The bureaucracy is so big today in large part because we ask the government to do so much. These days the scope of the federal government is generally defined by our demands that it

\# Perform central functions like diplomacy, defense, and watching the national piggybank.

\# Meet changing national needs, like managing the westward expansion of the country's borders and the challenges first of industrialization and then of automation, computerization, space exploration, the creation of a digital world, and an aging population.

\# Respond to **clientele groups**, like veterans, farmers, teachers, or other groups who feel that they have particular concerns that the government needs to address.

clientele groups: groups of citizens whose interests are affected by an agency or a department and who work to influence its policies

Keep people safe. One of the main jobs of the federal government is to create and enforce regulations—restrictions on businesses and individuals to ensure public safety and welfare—like limitations on allowable air pollution from factories or the requirements that cars have airbags or that people not have unfettered access to certain classes of drugs or overstay their visas.

Of course, it is Congress that makes laws about most of those things, but members of Congress cannot be expert on conditions in veterans' hospitals, or the building of a space station, or the appropriate dosage of Tylenol a child should take, or what constitutes a toxic level of lead in drinking water. The federal bureaucracy exists in large part to take laws passed by Congress and operationalize them—turning them into rules that can be enforced or tasks that experts can execute.

THREE MAIN BUREAUCRATIC JOBS

Accordingly, the jobs of the bureaucracy usually fall into three categories:

Administration—running the nation's parks, investigatory services, military, and student loan programs, to name just a few.

Rule-making—filling in all the technical details in the laws Congress passes so they can be enforced, including the regulations we mentioned earlier. When the bureaucracy exercises legislative power delegated to it by congressional law, it is called bureaucratic discretion.

Judgment—adjudicating violations of tax law or immigration law, for instance.

HOW IS THE FEDERAL BUREAUCRACY ORGANIZED?

There is nothing more fun than a good organizational chart (kidding), but sometimes that is the best way to show something as large and complex as the federal bureaucracy. So take a look. You don't need to memorize it, but just see how the different parts fit together.

regulations: limitations or restrictions on the activities of a business or an individual

rule-making: filling in all the technical details in the laws Congress passes so that they can be enforced

bureaucratic discretion: when the bureaucracy exercises legislative power delegated to it by congressional law

FIGURE IT!   5.4 THE ORGANIZATION OF THE EXECUTIVE BRANCH

Executive branch departments handle key functions and policy demands, covering major policy areas and responding to important constituencies. Independent agencies address concerns not covered by the cabinets. Independent regulatory boards create and enforce regulations.

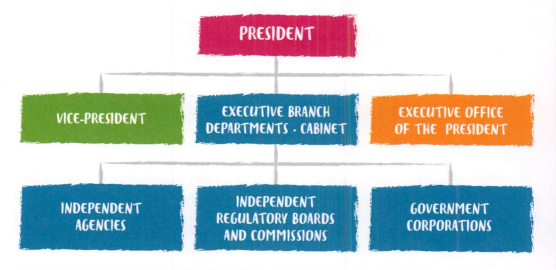

DEPARTMENTS What you see is that there are four kinds of organizations:

\# At the top is the president, the EOP, and the vice president, which we have already discussed.

\# The president works closely with his cabinet, who head up the fifteen **departments** of the federal government. These departments cover essential government functions or policy areas where clientele groups have been effective at lobbying for representation at the executive level.

The heads of the departments are called secretaries, except for the head of the Justice Department, who is called the attorney general. Cabinet members are political appointments, nominated by the president and subject

departments: one of the major subdivisions of the federal government, represented in the president's cabinet

to approval by the Senate. Unlike the members of the presidential branch, these appointees are supposed to serve the national interest and the interest of the groups they were designed to represent. For this reason, cabinet secretaries can have political agendas other than those of the president who nominated them and can work against the agenda of a weak president whose cabinet neither fears nor respects him.

INDEPENDENT AGENCIES

Congress has created many agencies to execute the law that are separate from the departments, even though they are structured similarly with a presidential appointee at the top (some of whom can be fired by the president, and some of whom cannot). These are called independent agencies and include such diverse groups as the Federal Election Commission, the Social Security Administration, and the Office of Management and Budget.

INDEPENDENT REGULATORY BOARDS AND COMMISSIONS

The regulations we discussed earlier are in the hands of independent regulatory boards and commissions. Among the thirty-eight of these agencies are the Food and Drug Administration and the Securities and Exchange Commission. Heads of regulatory agencies are appointed by the president with senatorial approval, but they cannot be fired by the president. Although they are independent of presidential displeasure, they are not always independent of the cabinet departments—the Food and Drug Administration, for instance, is in the Department of Health and Human Services.

GOVERNMENT CORPORATIONS

A final type of federal bureaucracy is the government corporations. Government corporations are set up to fill some commercial function that is important but not profitable enough for private industry to supply. The U.S. Postal Service, for instance, exists because there is not financial incentive for private companies to guarantee pickup and delivery to every remote outpost in Alaska, for instance. Similarly, trains are not money-winners in today's economy, but the United States values its rail system, so it is run by the government corporation Amtrak. Government corporations are generally independent of both the president and Congress. When these functions

independent agencies: organizations within the executive branch that execute the law and that are separate from the departments

independent regulatory boards and commissions: government organizations that regulate various businesses, industries, or economic sectors

government corporations: organizations that fill some commercial functions that are important but not profitable enough for private industry to supply

do become profitable, they tend to get competition from the private sector (think about UPS, FedEx, and other shipping companies challenging the postal service), which can make it hard for them to stay viable.

5.8 POWER PLAYS IN THE BUREAUCRACY

TRYING FOR NEUTRALITY DOESN'T MEAN ELIMINATING POLITICS

> Just because we take all kinds of steps to ensure that the federal bureaucracy stays neutral, that doesn't mean there aren't any internal politics, or that bureaucratic relationships with the other branches of government are always free of power struggles.

THREE MAIN DRIVERS OF POLITICAL TENSION *INSIDE* THE BUREAUCRATIC WORLD

> Power struggles within and among bureaucratic agencies can break out in three main areas:

\# **Bureaucratic culture.** The intra-bureaucratic culture to conform and cover up errors inside an agency tends to push members onto the same page. But sometimes individual members leak what is going on inside the agency. They can do that for political purposes (perhaps to influence how the public views their job) or to bring public awareness to misbehavior or mistakes within the agency. The latter leakers are known as *whistleblowers,* and there is often considerable internal blowback when they go public. Congress passed the Whistleblower Protection Act in 1989 to ensure that whistleblowers are not punished inside the agency, but fellow agency members can often make life difficult for those who break the cultural code of silence.

\# **Career vs. political staff.** Another area of intra-bureaucratic political tension is between political appointees and the permanent career civil servants. Political appointees often have their own agendas—ambitions of their own to run for higher office or to accomplish some particular goals that are at odds with the agency's mission. Career civil servants are in place year after year, from one presidential administration to the next. Their loyalty is likely to be to the agency rather than to a political or ideological program. When goals clash, civil servants have time on their side—stalling techniques can

bureaucratic culture: the accepted values and procedures of an organization hold off change they see as detrimental to the agency until a new administration brings new leadership.

\# Inter-agency tension. As well as political tension within an agency, there can also be clashes between agencies as they vie for budgetary funds, public support, and clientele groups, all of which can be linked together. When Congress is looking to save money, shaving funds from an agency or eliminating it altogether can be an effective strategy. Agencies know this and in their quest to survive, they want to be seen as indispensable or to have such loud backers that they will not be undermined by the budget. One way they do this is by cultivating powerful special interests, but that can cause a conflict for the agency, which ends up indebted to an interest group even as it is supposed to be serving the public interest. **Agency capture** refers to an extreme case of this phenomenon, when the agency begins to identify the interests of the groups they regulate as their own.

AND EXTERNAL POLITICS BETWEEN THE BRANCHES

Earlier we said that the tension between bureaucracy and democracy, between hierarchical decision makers and decision makers accountable to the voters, is accomplished in part by checks and balances. In fact, bureaucracies do interact politically with the president, the Congress, and the courts on a regular basis.

\# The bureaucracy and the president. Presidents share the executive branch with the federal bureaucracy, and they can use it effectively to accomplish large parts of their agenda. They can issue executive orders to direct agencies on how they want laws to be implemented, they can make their nominations for leadership posts in the bureaucracy with an eye to their ideological goals, they can make budgetary plans that enhance or limit the scope of an agency, and they can attempt to reorganize the bureaucracy.

The various agencies are not without defenses of their own. We have already mentioned foot-dragging, a strategy of trying to wait out the administration, hoping for a friendlier one next time. They can leak information to the press about internal changes the president attempts to make, and they can try to get powerful defenders outside the bureaucracy to plead their case.

agency capture: when a government agency begins to identify the interests of the groups they regulate as their own

\# **The bureaucracy and Congress.** Remember that the bureaucracy exists to put the laws of Congress into effect and that doing so often means leaving parts of some laws to bureaucratic discretion. In reality, though, members of various agencies often forge close relationships with members of Congress and with the different industries or sectors

FIGURE IT!

5.5: POLICY RELATIONSHIPS AND THE IRON TRIANGLE

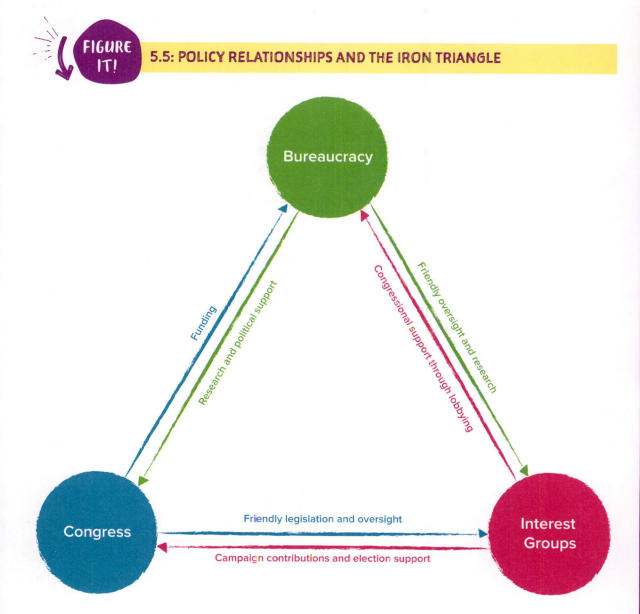

over which they have regulatory or other authority. Because the bureaucracy, congressional committee members, and interest groups work so closely together, they tend to share interests and to come closer to looking out for each other than they do to looking out for the public's interest. Thus, for example, members of the Agriculture Committee in the House and the Senate, the Food and Drug Administration, and the different food-producing industries it regulates often end up making policy that benefits those industries more than it does the food-consuming public.

This kind of informal policy-making relationship is known as an **iron triangle**—*triangle* because of the three points of bureaucracy, Congress, and interest group, and *iron* because it is almost always impenetrable to groups representing the public. Some scholars see the iron triangle as a defining policy-making relationship, but others say **issue networks** better describe the relationship. Issue networks are more complex arrangements of clusters of interest groups and policy makers. In both cases, it is the bureaucracy working with Congress and policy professionals that define the policy outcome, not the voters who put the members of Congress in office.

\# **Bureaucracy and the courts**. While individuals can and do sue agencies for not following the law, it is only a partly successful strategy. Courts tend to defer to bureaucratic expertise unless a flagrant violation of the law occurs. Courts also, by congressional law, do not have jurisdiction over all parts of the bureaucracy. And some parts of the bureaucracy, like those dealing with taxes (the IRS) and immigration, have their own court systems whose decisions cannot be appealed.

THE UPSHOT

Checks and balances can help make the bureaucracy more accountable, but they can also make the other branches less accountable, to the extent that executive, legislative, and judicial power is wielded by unelected bureaucrats.

. . . .

iron triangle: close policymaking relationships among legislators, regulators, and the groups being regulated that tend to exclude the public

issue networks: complex systems of relationships among groups that influence policy, including elected leaders, interest groups, specialists, consultants, and research institutes

Big Think

→ Should the president be above the law? Why or why not?

→ What should the relationship between Congress and the president look like? Should one have more power than the other? Which and why?

→ What roles do you think should be part of the federal government's job?

Key Terms

CONCEPTS

agency capture (p. 176)

appointment power (p. 154)

bureaucracy (p. 166)

bureaucratic culture (p. 175)

bureaucratic discretion (p. 172)

civil service reform (p. 167)

cycle effect (p. 161)

departments (p. 173)

divided government (p. 163)

executive (p. 150)

executive agreements (p. 154)

Executive Office of the President (p. 169)

executive orders (p. 155)

executive privilege (p. 160)

federal bureaucracy (p. 150)

going public (p. 158)

government corporations (p. 174)

head of government (p. 153)

head of state (p. 152)

honeymoon period (p. 162)

independent agencies (p. 174)

independent regulatory boards and commissions (p. 174)

inherent powers (p. 157)

iron triangle (p. 178)

issue networks (p. 178)

modern presidency (p. 157)

neutral competence (p. 167)

pardoning power (p. 156)

patronage (p. 167)

power to persuade (p. 158)

presidential branch (p. 168)

presidential veto (p. 155)

red tape (p. 168)

regulations (p. 172)

rule-making (p. 172)

spoils system (p. 167)

traditional presidency (p. 157)

treaties (p. 154)

unitary executive (p. 160)

weak presidents (p. 159)

White House Office (p. 170)

IMPORTANT WORKS AND EVENTS

New Deal (p. 157)

State of the Union address (p. 155)

KEY INDIVIDUALS AND GROUPS

#6 THE JUDICIAL BRANCH

In this chapter:

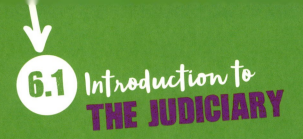

6.1 Introduction to THE JUDICIARY

THE WEAKEST BRANCH?

Seeking to reassure anxious Anti-Federalists who did not want court rulings that would be binding on all the states, Alexander Hamilton played down the threat of a strong judicial branch. Don't worry, he told them in *Federalist Paper #78*. The judiciary will be the weakest and thus the "least dangerous branch" of government because it has "no influence over either the sword or the purse."

WHAT *IS* A JUDICIARY?

The purpose of the **judiciary** is to interpret and apply the law and to solve disputes involving citizens and other government actors. Its decisions are indeed binding. An **appeal** can be made to a higher court for a new judgment (more on that later), but when you reach the Supreme Court, the court of highest appeal, you have exhausted your options. It doesn't need the sword or the purse to make its influence felt.

IN A NUTSHELL

Hamilton was probably right about the judiciary being the least dangerous branch, in that the courts may not be able to take the country to war or spend it into debt. But the judiciary has become an enormously powerful branch nonetheless through *the power of the pen*. In fact, in the case ***Marbury v. Madison*** (1803) that we discussed in Chapter 2, the Supreme Court gave itself the ultimate power of deciding what the Constitution means. You don't get much more powerful, or in some cases more dangerous, than that. We saw the impact that John Marshall's court, wielding the power of judicial review, had on establishing state and federal relations early in our history.

WHERE WE GO IN THIS CHAPTER

By the time you finish reading this chapter, you will understand

→ What it means to live in a lawful society and what kinds of laws there are

→ The kind of judicial system the United States has

→ What happens if you get involved in the legal system

→ What equal justice really means

→ How the Constitution arranged the court system and the role it left for Congress to fill in the details

→ The political nature of the highest court in the land and how that court works and affects our lives

6.2 KINDS OF LAWS

LAWS, WHAT ARE THEY GOOD FOR?

> In a democracy, laws rule. As we saw in Chapter 1, in authoritarian systems people live under the will of a tyrant—unpredictable, self-interested, and final. In a democracy, by contrast, the concept of the social contract means we can agree to live under the rule of law, not under the will of a tyrant. Under the **rule of law**, laws are known in advance, they apply the same way to everyone, and if we feel they have been unjustly applied we can appeal to a higher authority. In a democracy, we say no one is above the law. The basic premise is that we are all equally responsible for living under the Constitution and the rules made in accordance with it.

IF LAWS ARE SO ESSENTIAL, WHY DO WE GRUMBLE ABOUT THEM AND WHY DO WE SOMETIMES BREAK THEM?

> We usually notice laws when they get in the way of what we want to do. Hit the highway at 90 mph? Don't be too surprised to find a flashing red light following behind you. Take a fancy to a stranger's car and slip behind the wheel to see how you look? You might end up behind bars. Let your friend know you have an insider tip that is going to blow up the stock market and the time to sell is now? You can end up with more time on the inside than you want. The laws we notice most limit our behavior and stop us from acting on impulses that are damaging to other people. Laws can feel like they ruin all the fun, but they often keep us from creating a mess.

CAN'T WE ALL JUST GET ALONG?

> We could also look at laws from a collective perspective. Laws allow the traffic to move along without too many jam-ups (and, in fact, they let most of us keep our cars safely, unstolen, in our driveways); laws allow people to take medicines and be reasonably confident that the bottles hold what they are supposed to and that the dosage is correct; and laws keep most of us safe in our homes. Laws are what make collective life possible and even comfortable.

judiciary: the law-interpreting component of the federal government

appeal: rehearing a case because the losing party in the original trial argues that a point of law was not applied properly

Marbury v. Madison: the 1803 Supreme Court ruling holding that the Court had the power of judicial review

rule of law: a system in which laws are known in advance, they apply the same way to everyone, and if we feel they have been unjustly applied we can appeal to a higher authority

A QUICK LOOK
AT DIFFERENT
KINDS OF LAW

But not all laws are intended to make life easier or safer. Sometimes they are created to build the structure of government. The Constitution is filled with laws, too, and they don't have much to do with your car or your safety (at least not directly).

We are accustomed to thinking a law is a law, but actually there are several kinds, so it's helpful to distinguish among them. These are not mutually exclusive—a substantive law can also be a criminal or civil law—but this will help us think about the roles they play:

THERE IS A LOT TO
ABSORB HERE:
NOTICE THAT
THE CATEGORIES
OVERLAP AND THEY
HAVE TO DO WITH:

- WHETHER THE
  LAW TELLS YOU
  WHAT TO DO OR
  HOW TO DO IT

- WHO IS
  DAMAGED BY
  THE BEHAVIOR

- WHAT THE
  BURDEN OF
  PROOF IS

- WHO MAKES
  THE LAW AND
  THE STATUS
  THAT GIVES IT

\# **Substantive laws** define what we can or cannot do.

\# **Procedural laws** define how the laws are used, applied, and enforced. Our founders were big on procedural guarantees to keep tyranny at bay. Hence, the emphasis in American law on procedural due process, which guarantees that the laws will be applied faithfully and fairly. (If you go on to law school, you'll take a civil procedure class early on.)

\# **Criminal laws** are a form of substantive law that prohibits behavior that makes collective living difficult or impossible: theft, murder, rape, disrupting the peace, etc. A broken criminal law is a **crime** against the state and is prosecuted by the state, which must prove you are guilty beyond a reasonable doubt. The penalty for being found guilty is a payment to society—a fine, jail time, or public service, for example.

\# **Civil laws** are laws that regulate interactions between individuals. If someone damages your property or breaks a contract or causes you physical harm and you sue them, it is for damage to you, not to the state. The burden of proof is lighter—you must show the person responsible by a preponderance of the evidence. If the burden of proof is met, the person will not be found guilty of a crime; instead he or she will have committed a **tort**. The payment will not be to society but to you in the form of damages. Medical malpractice law is a form of civil law.

substantive laws: laws that define what people can or cannot do

procedural laws: laws that define how the laws are used, applied, and enforced

criminal laws: a form of substantive law that prohibits behavior that makes collective living difficult or impossible (for example, theft, murder, rape, disrupting the peace)

crime: a broken criminal law, a violation against the state

civil laws: laws that regulate interactions between individuals

tort: a broken civil law, a violation against an individual

\# **Constitutional laws** are the laws we have been focusing on in this book. They establish the legal infrastructure—how the branches relate to each other—and determine how the drama of politics is played. At a macro level they structure the system so that certain people are more likely than others to win. Malpractice laws might be of concern primarily to physicians and patients, whereas everyone has a stake in negotiating constitutional laws. Constitutional laws are not just what is in the Constitution. They also include laws passed by legislatures to support or interpret the Constitution, and they are the body of Supreme Court decisions telling us what the Constitution means and what legislative or executive acts are consistent with it. When a court rules, the ruling becomes **precedent** with the force of constitutional law. Future justices are bound to follow the ruling unless it is overturned or the Constitution is amended.

\# **Statutory laws** are made by legislatures. Legislatures are lawmaking bodies, and that's what they do. If they pass a law prohibiting theft, it is a criminal law. If they pass a law limiting the power of the executive, it's closer to a constitutional law. If they pass a law limiting damages for medical malpractice, it is a civil law.

\# **Administrative laws** are the laws created when a legislature passes a law stating a general policy intent—to have cleaner air, for instance, or a space program. Because federal and state legislators don't have the expertise needed to fill in all the laws that need to be made for a given policy to work, they delegate to the bureaucracy, which in turn makes administrative laws on their behalf. Since Americans don't elect their bureaucrats, these laws are a little harder to check.

\# **Executive orders**, as we saw in Chapter 5, are laws made by the executive alone. They are technically clarifications of existing law and are subject to review by the courts. If a new executive entering office doesn't like them, out they go.

constitutional laws: laws that establish the legal infrastructure in the United States—how the branches relate to each other—and determine how the game of politics is played

precedent: a previous decision or ruling that is binding on subsequent decisions

statutory laws: laws made by legislatures

administrative laws: laws created by the bureaucracy after legislation has been passed stating a general intent

executive orders: clarifications of congressional policy issued by the president and having the full force of law

THE UPSHOT

So, it's not true that a law is a law is a law. Laws take many forms, but the overall point is that together they organize Americans' collective lives and let us live in harmony on a small piece of this planet. Laws can stray from that purpose, clearly, but that is why we have them. And the fact that they are made by us, by people appointed by us, or by people appointed by the people appointed by us is what makes our government a democracy, and it's what makes us citizens.

6.3 THE AMERICAN LEGAL SYSTEM

DO ALL LEGAL SYSTEMS IN THE WORLD WORK THE SAME?

> Of course not. They are heavily influenced by political culture. We know, of course, that authoritarian systems work differently from democratic systems. Even democratic systems differ. The U.S. system in particular is based on common law, adversarial, and litigious. Let's take a quick look at what each of those mean.

A COMMON LAW TRADITION

> Even among democratic systems that otherwise share a lot of similarities, there are differences in how law is created and practiced worldwide. Like England, the United States (and all the states within it except Louisiana) is based on a **common law tradition.** That means the decisions of judges become part of the legal tradition and those precedents (prior decisions) have the standing of law. In a **civil law tradition** (which, just to keep you on your toes, doesn't really have anything to do with the civil law we just spoke of), laws are codified (passed by a legislature and written down), which gives judges less leeway in their decision making. The American system is really a hybrid of common and civil law—it has codified law, but it also relies heavily on precedent. In contrast, consider England, a pure common law system, where even the constitution is not written down and parliamentary rulings have constitutional status.

common law tradition: a legal system in which the decisions of judges become part of the legal tradition and those precedents have the standing of law

civil law tradition: a legal system in which laws are passed by a legislature and written down, which gives judges less leeway

AN ADVERSARIAL SYSTEM Another distinction has to do with whether different legal systems emphasize the principle of fairness or truth. Think carefully about this—they are not always the same thing. The United States has an **adversarial system**. In line with the constitutional commitment to procedural due process, Americans are primarily concerned that the trial will be fair (where all the rules are carefully followed), trusting that a just judgment will result from a just trial. You could have a fair trial, however, and still come up with an incorrect verdict. By contrast, some European democracies use an **inquisitorial system**. In inquisitorial systems, the truth is the goal, and if it requires that the judge leave his or her neutral perch to ask questions and investigate, then so be it. There are different roles for judges and lawyers in both systems, even though their settings are similar. This is due to the differences in political culture we discussed in Chapter 1.

6.1: THE SKIMMABLE COMPARISON OF LEGAL SYSTEMS

	Adversarial	Inquisitorial	Authoritarian
Role of the judge	Neutral arbiter	Fact-finder	Leader of show trial
Role of the lawyers	Skilled advocates for each side	Relatively secondary roles of bringing information to the judge	Lawyers? No, since there are no civil liberties to be guarded
Goal of the proceeding	Due process and equal treatment for each side with a result that is just because the rules that are followed are just	The truth	Off with their heads, usually a verdict with a political purpose
Example	United States	France	Nazi Germany

adversarial system: a legal system concerned primarily with fairness (that is, whether a trial will be fair), trusting that a just judgment will result from a just trial

inquisitorial system: a legal system concerned primarily with finding the truth

AND LITIGIOUS, TOO!

> The United States also has a **litigious system**. That means Americans like to settle their differences in court. They are quick to sue each other and often look to the courts for compensation for damages from medical procedures gone wrong, car wrecks, or reputational attacks. It is not clear that Americans sue one another a great deal more than their counterparts in other countries, but some evidence suggests that is the case. Many other developed countries have secure health care and other social systems in place to take care of those who are victims of misfortune. Because the safety net in the United States is not as strong, litigation is often the only way people can protect themselves against risk.

THE UPSHOT

To understand the U.S. legal system, remember that it is based heavily on the notion of due process, that precedent counts, that Americans often find themselves working out disputes in the courtroom, and that relations there can be contentious. Probably all of us hope never to find ourselves in a courtroom, but the odds are that we will, even if it's for something as innocuous as small claims court, traffic court, or jury duty service.

6.4 WHO'S WHO AND WHAT'S WHAT IN A COURT OF LAW?

LET'S HOPE YOU DON'T NEED THIS INFORMATION, BUT . . .

> None of us intends to end up in court, but it happens for all kinds of reasons—traffic court over a minor infraction, civil court over a roofer who left your house without a tarp while it was pouring rain (just to pick a not-so-random example). It happens. It's a good idea to know who is who and what is what before someone goes and tears the roof off *your* house!

A criminal justice perspective on what happens during this process would focus on the three elements of the criminal justice system: law enforcement, adjudication, and corrections. We can't really cover the first and third here except to say that anyone who gets arrested in this country has rights. Not all police forces (or individual officers) across the country enforce those rights equally across all demographic groups, but they should. Let your phone be your witness. Chapter 3 covers much of what due process entails; refresh your memory there so that you know your rights. For our purposes in this chapter, **adjudication**, the process of resolving disputes in court, takes center stage.

litigious system: a legal system in which parties typically settle their differences in court

adjudication: the process of resolving disputes in court

ADJUDICATION— WHO IS WHO AND WHAT IS WHAT

Where adjudication is concerned, who is who depends on what kind of court you are in—criminal or civil. Remember: criminal = crime against society as a whole = penalty paid to the state; civil case = a tort or a wrongful injury to an individual = damages paid to the injured. Let's skim.

6.2: THE SKIMMABLE GUIDE TO GOING TO COURT

	Criminal Court	Civil Court
What is at issue?	Crime against the state (e.g., murder); state brings charges	Tort—wrongful injury to an individual (e.g., wrongful death in a car accident); claim is filed
In which court is the case brought?	State court for state crime; federal court for federal crime	Either
What is a negative verdict called?	Guilt	Liability
Burden of proof: jury must be convinced . . .	Beyond a reasonable doubt	By a preponderance of the evidence
Repercussion of a negative verdict . . .	Pay penalty to the state in form of prison time, fines, or service	Pay damages to an individual or fulfill a contractual obligation
Who brings the case?	Plaintiff (the government or the United States)	Plaintiff (person claiming to be damaged)
Who represents the plaintiff?	The government's lawyer is called the prosecutor (the formal part of the government legal system that brings claims)	Attorney hired by the plaintiff, or the plaintiff himself or herself
The accused is called . . .	Defendant	Defendant
Who represents the accused?	An attorney—either privately hired or, if the defendant cannot afford it, a public defender	An attorney hired by the defendant, or the defendant himself or herself
What does the jury do?	The Constitution guarantees us a jury of our peers. The lawyers pick the jurors according to complicated rules and the jurors listen to the cases on both sides and *decide on matters of fact.* Grand juries can be called to decide if there is enough evidence to bring a case to trial; trial juries decide if the evidence meets the burden of proof.	

(Continued)

(Continued)

	Criminal Court	Civil Court
What does the judge do?	# In trials with juries, the jury is the decider of what is factually true. # *The judge decides questions of law* and explains the law to the jury so that they know how to apply it to the facts. If there is no jury, the judge assesses both facts and law. # Judges also impose sentences, although in some state courts juries do so when the death penalty is involved.	
If the case is appealed . . .	# In an appeal, the loser in the lower court asks a higher court to review the process and ensure that the lower court handled everything properly. The loser is called the petitioner (or the appellant). # The opposite party is the respondent or appellee. Because there can be multiple appeals, roles can switch back and forth. The prosecutor rarely appeals.	
How does an appeal work?	# If one party believes there has been a procedural error or that the judge has applied the law incorrectly, he or she can appeal (becoming the petitioner). Appeals do not involve facts, witnesses, or any of the familiar aspects of a trial. Rather, judges hear oral arguments and check to make sure the law is constitutional and has been applied properly. # The prosecution generally does not appeal in a criminal case since, even though it is technically not a retrial, it might seem to violate the constitutional prohibition of double jeopardy. # The final court of appeal in the legal system is the Supreme Court.	

JURY DUTY—THE CLASSIC CASE OF THE FREE RIDER

The other way people find themselves in court is by being called to serve on a jury. For many people the arrival of that summons in the mail spells a giant pain the rear end—having to disrupt one's schedule to get off work, go through the process of finding out if you are even chosen to sit on the jury, and then sitting through hours of testimony on a case that's probably pretty mundane. Jury duty is one of those jobs that feels pretty unrewarding unless you remember the ultimate purpose it serves—if you are arrested for something, you are guaranteed a trial by a jury of your peers. If none of your peers can be bothered to show up, justice will not be done. It's a collective action problem—we all want to share in the outcome, but many of us try to avoid the effort that makes that outcome possible.

6.5 EQUALITY AND THE CRIMINAL JUSTICE SYSTEM

EQUAL JUSTICE FOR ALL?

The process of getting arrested, going to court, receiving a verdict, and all that comes with it seems pretty straightforward. One of the hallmarks of American political culture, as we saw in Chapter 2, is that everyone should be treated the same.

We have also seen enough now to know that that the procedural value that everyone be treated the same is often not the way things actually work in America—it may be a goal, but it is a goal that the system often fails to fulfill.

SCRUBBING AWAY AT THE STUBBORN STAIN OF OUR RACIAL PAST

From its beginnings, the United States has had what amounts to separate criminal justice systems for black and white Americans. Often the former was no more than vigilantes looking for a victim to punish for an alleged crime. As late as 1955, Emmett Till, a fourteen-year-old boy, was caught and lynched in Mississippi for allegedly offending a white woman who later admitted she lied. The white men who killed Till were acquitted by a white jury. The case shook the nation but stood as an iconic example of how, at the start of the civil rights movement (it was shortly after attending a memorial service for Till that Rosa Parks refused to give up her seat on the bus), justice for black people—especially young black men—was not the ideal enshrined in the Constitution. The incidents that prompted the formation of the Black Lives Matter movement, and the controversy that movement has generated, stand as testimony to the fact that whites, blacks, and to an increasing degree Latinos and dark-skinned immigrants still experience the criminal justice system in very different ways.

DIG DEEPER

In 2018, Emmett Till's case was reopened, although it is not clear whether the action will be anything other than symbolic. Read about the reopening of the case.

Go to **edge.sagepub.com/ dig-deeper**

DUAL NARRATIVES ABOUT WHO ARE THE "GOOD GUYS"

As a consequence of their experiences, African Americans and whites have developed very different narratives about the role the criminal justice system plays in their lives. Young black men are often "profiled" by police because they live in high crime areas or because they fit someone's

DIG DEEPER

Read about the challenges of police reform.

Go to **edge.sagepub.com/ dig-deeper**

culturally crafted mental image of what a criminal looks like. **Racial profiling** is not just a violation of civil rights; too often it has ended in tragedy with only the police left to tell their version of the story.

But here is one of the pluses of mediated citizenship. Cell phones have enabled witnesses to racial harassment by law enforcement to document what they have seen. New narratives that are told and strengthened by visual evidence are borne by social media. Many police officers now wear body cams to capture their part of the interaction. When law enforcement violations of civil rights are video-recorded and posted online or streamed in real time, often going viral before an official report has been made, it is harder for narratives that blame black people and exonerate whites to take hold. That doesn't mean there is universal acceptance of the evidence or the narratives, however, as the debate between Black Lives Matter and Blue Lives Matter demonstrates.

The country was sadly reminded of that fact in the summer of 2014 through the very different reactions whites and blacks had to the shooting of Michael Brown, an unarmed teenager, by a police officer in Ferguson, Missouri. In the week following the killing, amid riots and demonstrations, curfews and the calling in of the National Guard by the governor, 80 percent of African Americans said they thought the incident raised important ideas about race. In contrast, 47 percent of whites said the issue of race was getting more attention than it deserved.

TAKING A KNEE: PROTEST OF SOCIAL INJUSTICE OR LACK OF PATRIOTISM? ❯ For African Americans, Brown was the latest and not the last young man to be shot by police in suspect circumstances, highlighting the fear that many have that their sons are often targeted by the police out of fear or prejudice. Whites, by contrast, are accustomed to seeing the police as a source of safety rather than danger, and often fail to understand what such incidents look like from the other side of the racial divide. In fact, as Ferguson struggled for calm, sympathy for the police officer who shot Brown generated several online efforts to raise support and funds for him and his family.

As a way to register his outrage and frustration with a part of the system that doesn't seem to be changing, NFL football player Colin Kaepernick

racial profiling: when law enforcement officers base their decision to investigate a person's activities on the individual's apparent race or ethnicity

6.1: RACIAL DIVISIONS AFTER FERGUSON

Do you think the police shooting of an African American teen in Ferguson, Missouri . . .

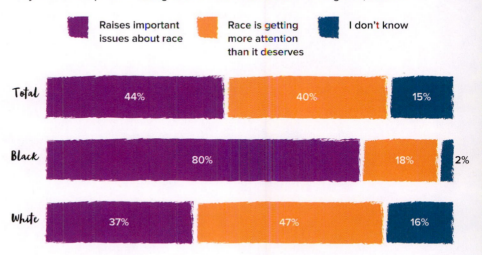

Source: Pew Research Center, "Stark Racial Divisions in Reactions to Ferguson Shooting," August 18, 2014, http://www.people-press.org/2014/08/18/stark-racial-divisions-in-reactions-to-ferguson-police-shooting/.

decided not to stand during the playing of the national anthem before a game in 2016, deciding before the end of the season to kneel rather than to stay sitting. That action lit a firestorm of controversy as other players followed his lead and took a knee during the anthem to protest police behavior.

Soon, two narratives developed around the protests—the players' own, that the kneeling was not in opposition to the flag or the anthem, but strictly a way to call public attention to egregious violations of justice. Critics, chief among them President Donald Trump, insisted on seeing the kneeling as a mark of disrespect for the country and the flag. Because that has proved to be a profitable campaign line for Trump, exciting the racial animus that is part of his appeal, he doesn't seem to be willing to let it go soon. Meanwhile, Kaepernick remains unemployed years later and involved in litigation with the NFL. Several other African American sports figures, notably LeBron James and Michael Jordan, got into a brief Twitter battle with the president over this, showing just how much the methods of our social discourse and narrative building have changed.

GEN GAP!

GENERATIONAL ATTITUDES TOWARD JUSTICE IN AMERICA

As the dispute continues about athletes kneeling during the national anthem to protest mistreatment by police, it is interesting to look at how the generations view justice in America and how much trust they have in police. The results are striking—trust in police is low among young people, who are also less likely to have faith in the justice system.

As you consider these numbers, don't forget that the demographics of the country are changing. Those younger generations are much more likely to be people of color, who have fundamentally different experiences with law enforcement than do older, white Americans. Note especially the last graphic here, which shows that unarmed racial minorities are almost twice as likely as unarmed whites to be shot by police.

FIGURE IT!

6.2: PERCENT OF EACH GENERATION THAT THINKS THE JUSTICE SYSTEM IN AMERICA IS FUNDAMENTALLY JUST OR UNJUST

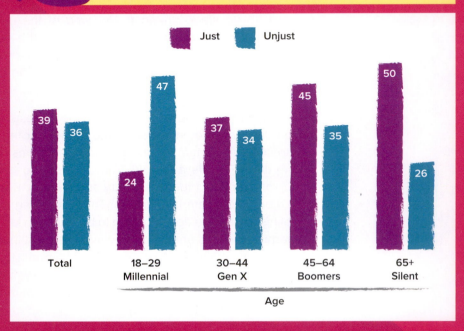

Source: Peter Moore, "Millennials Lack Trust in American Justice," *YouGov*, February 9, 2016, https://today.yougov.com/topics/politics/articles-reports/2016/02/09/millennials-lack-trust-american-justice.

6.3: PERCENT OF EACH GENERATION WHO SAY THEY DO OR DO NOT TRUST THE POLICE

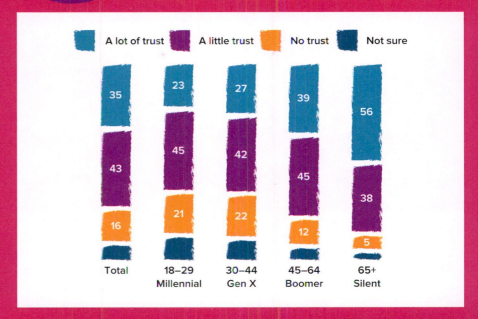

A lot of trust **A little trust** **No trust** **Not sure**

	Total	18–29 Millennial	30–44 Gen X	45–64 Boomer	65+ Silent
A lot of trust	35	23	27	39	56
A little trust	43	45	42	45	38
No trust	16	21	22	12	5

Source: Peter Moore, "Millennials Lack Trust in American Justice," *YouGov*, February 9, 2016, https://today.yougov.com/topics/politics/articles-reports/2016/02/09/millennials-lack-trust-american-justice.

6.4: HOW OFTEN UNARMED INDIVIDUALS ARE SHOT BY POLICE, BY ETHNIC GROUP

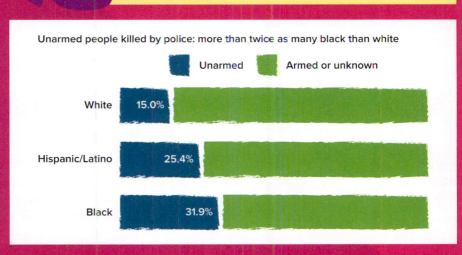

Unarmed people killed by police: more than twice as many black than white

Unarmed **Armed or unknown**

	Unarmed
White	15.0%
Hispanic/Latino	25.4%
Black	31.9%

Source: Data are from U.S. Census, compiled by Jon Swaine, Oliver Laughland, and Jamies Lartey, "The Counted," *The Guardian*, June 1, 2015, https://www.theguardian.com/us-news/2015/jun/01/black-americans-killed-by-police-analysis.

TAKEAWAYS

→ **Compared with older generations, younger generations are more likely to feel that the legal system is fundamentally unjust.** What role do you think social media has in these changing attitudes toward justice in society?

→ **Younger generations have less trust in the police than do older generations.** Your readings have discussed the competing narratives about systemic racism and the essential job of the police. In what ways can this generational gap about attitudes toward the police be exploited politically?

→ **Unarmed minorities are more likely to be the victims of police killings than unarmed whites.** Is there a way to heal this tragic disparity? What will it take?

DIG DEEPER

Read about the controversy surrounding kneeling during the national anthem.

Go to **edge.sagepub.com/ dig-deeper**

When we talk about systemic racism, we are referring to these kinds of differences in treatment. Racism isn't just tweeting a nasty name or making a negative reference—it isn't just what you say. It is also an acceptance of the different rules of treatment according to race that are built into the norms of the system. When we talk about equality in the criminal justice system, the issue is *equal treatment*; in the civil justice system, it is *equal access*. Citizens are treated differently by these systems according to their race, their income level, and the kinds of crimes they commit.

Race, income, and education all predispose us to have different experiences at the hands of the law. The court system that the Constitution and Congress established is only as fair and equitable as we make it.

6.6 THE CONSTITUTION, CONGRESS, AND THE DUAL COURT SYSTEM

THE FOUNDERS' WIGGLE ROOM STRATEGY

❯ The American legal system can seem confusing because much of it is not spelled out in the Constitution. Because it was such a hot-button issue, the founders tended to gloss over the question of whether there would be a national court system with **jurisdiction** over the states—that is, with

jurisdiction: a court's authority to hear certain cases

the power to hear cases pertaining to them. It might have been smart politics, but it didn't give much guidance to Congress, which had to develop an entire legal system out of thin air. Although the founders discussed the powers of the courts in the *Federalist Papers*, they danced around the subject in the three short sections of Article III. Meanwhile, states set up their own court systems, which they were entitled to do under federalism, creating a dual court system but one in which state courts were inevitably under national courts.

ARTICLE III, SECTION 1

Here's the section of the Constitution that describes how the courts will be set up:

> *The judicial power of the United States, shall be vested in one Supreme Court, and in such inferior courts as the Congress may from time to time ordain and establish. The judges, both of the supreme and inferior courts, shall hold their offices during good behaviour, and shall, at stated times, receive for their services, a compensation, which shall not be diminished during their continuance in office.*

WHICH MEANS . . .

The Constitution provides for

One Supreme Court

Lower courts established by Congress as necessary

Judges of federal courts, who hold their jobs as long as they behave themselves and who get paid a salary, which cannot be cut while they are in office

WHAT ARE LOWER COURTS?

In other words—and with due respect to the founders who have otherwise done a really terrific job—they kicked this can down the road and left it for Congress to clean up the mess.

Most court systems—local as well as state and national—are structured so that there is an entry level court to which you first bring your case or in which you are first tried before a jury. That, as we have seen, is a fact-finding court. Most cases end their days with a judgment or verdict in these courts. But the right to appeal makes the court structure more complicated. In a three-tier system, like most states and the national government have, there is essentially an appeals court after the initial court, and then some sort of final court of appeals. The fact that these courts go by different names in different systems does not make your job as a court watcher any easier.

STATE COURT SYSTEMS

Fortunately for the founders, they didn't have to worry about state courts. Don't forget that the states already had court systems of their own in place and some were highly jealous of the idea that the new federal government could create a court system that would instantly have jurisdiction over them. Most citizens end up dealing with the state courts anyway—the crimes and civil matters we are most likely to get involved with are at the state level.

Most state court systems are pretty similar to each other—every state basically has three levels of the sort we just mentioned. The entry-level courts are the trial courts, although they have all kinds of names—municipal court, district court, and so on, depending on whether they are major or minor trial courts. *Most cases are settled at that entry level and never move up the ladder.*

The state appeals courts (level two) take a variety of forms and names, and their procedures vary. But each of them is topped by a third tier—a state supreme court (although they have different names, too).

At the supreme court level, no questions of fact can arise and there are no juries. Rather, a panel of five to nine justices—as judges on the state supreme courts are called—meet to discuss the case, make a decision, and issue an opinion. All these decisions are final unless a federal question is involved. If that happens, the case goes on to the U.S. Supreme Court.

HOW STATE JUDGES ARE CHOSEN

Judges in state courts are chosen through a variety of procedures specified in the individual state constitutions. The procedures range from appointment by the governor or election by the state legislature to the more democratic method of election by the state population as a whole.

Thirty-nine states hold elections for at least some of their judges. This procedure is controversial. Critics argue that judicial elections can create a conflict of interest, that few people are able to cast educated votes in judicial elections, and that the threat of defeat may influence judges' rulings. Also, people who know they may have a major case coming up before a court can give lots of money to help elect the judges they think will be most sympathetic to them.

CONGRESS'S JOB AT THE FEDERAL LEVEL

Congress, left with the founders' direction to "from time to time ordain and establish" such inferior courts as it thought fit, had a complex task on its hands.

THREE TIERS AGAIN

The federal system is also three-tiered. There is an entry-level tier, called the district courts; an appellate level; and the Supreme Court, at the very

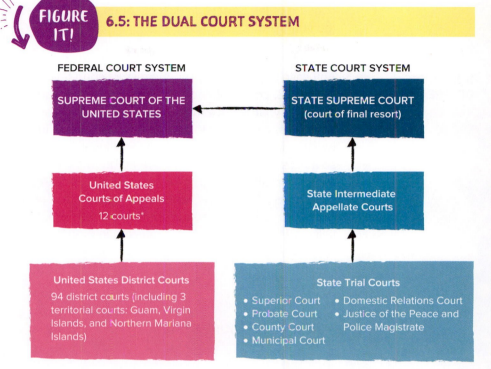

FIGURE IT!

6.5: THE DUAL COURT SYSTEM

FEDERAL COURT SYSTEM

STATE COURT SYSTEM

SUPREME COURT OF THE UNITED STATES

STATE SUPREME COURT (court of final resort)

United States Courts of Appeals 12 courts*

State Intermediate Appellate Courts

United States District Courts

94 district courts (including 3 territorial courts: Guam, Virgin Islands, and Northern Mariana Islands)

State Trial Courts

- Superior Court
- Probate Court
- County Court
- Municipal Court
- Domestic Relations Court
- Justice of the Peace and Police Magistrate

*There are 12 U.S. circuit courts of appeals with general jurisdiction. In addition, the U.S. Court of Appeals for the Federal Circuit handles specialized cases (e.g., patents, international trade).

top. In this section, we discuss the lower two tiers and how the judges for those courts are chosen. Given the importance of the Supreme Court in the American political system, we discuss it separately in the next section.

FEDERAL DISTRICT COURTS

The lowest level of the federal judiciary hierarchy consists of ninety-four U.S. federal district courts. These are like the state trial courts. They are distributed so that each state has at least one and the largest states each have four. The district courts have original jurisdiction (meaning they see these cases first) over all cases involving any question of a federal nature or any issue that involves the Constitution, Congress, or any other aspect of the federal government.

The district courts hear both criminal and civil law cases. In trials at the district level, evidence is presented, and witnesses are called to testify and are questioned and cross-examined by the attorneys representing both sides. In criminal cases, the government is always represented by a U.S. attorney.

U.S. attorneys, one per district, are appointed by the president, with the consent of the Senate. In district courts, juries are responsible for returning the final verdict.

U.S. COURTS OF APPEALS

Any case appealed beyond the district court level is slated to appear in one of the U.S. courts of appeals. These courts are arranged in twelve circuits, essentially large superdistricts that encompass several of the district court territories, except for the twelfth, which covers just Washington, D.C. This twelfth circuit court hears all appeals involving government agencies, and so its caseload is quite large even though its territory is small. (A thirteenth federal circuit court hears cases on such specialized issues as patents and copyrights.) Cases are heard in the circuit that includes the district court where the case was heard originally. Therefore, a case that was tried initially in Miami, in the southern district in Florida, would be appealed to the Court of Appeals for the Eleventh Circuit, located in Atlanta, Georgia.

6.6: THE CIRCUIT COURT SYSTEM

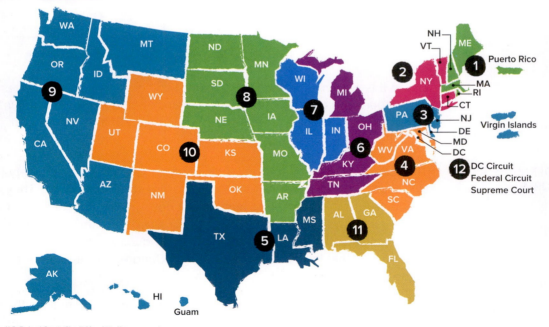

Source: U.S. Federal Courts Circuit Map, http://www.uscourts.gov

CONFUSED YET?

The sole function of these courts is to hear appeals from the lower federal district courts and to review the legal reasoning behind the decisions reached there. As we have seen with other appeals courts, no evidence is presented, no new witnesses are called, and no jury is impaneled. Instead, the lawyers for both sides present written briefs summarizing their arguments and make oral arguments as well. The legal reasoning used to reach the decision in the district court is scrutinized, but the facts of the case are assumed to be the truth and are not debated.

HERE COME THE JUDGES

The decisions in the courts of appeals are made by a rotating panel of three judges who sit to hear the case. Although many more than three judges are assigned to each federal appeals circuit (for instance, the Court of Appeals for the Ninth Circuit, based in San Francisco, has twenty-two active judges), the judges rotate in order to provide a decision-making body that is as unbiased as possible. In rare cases when a decision is of crucial social importance, all the judges in a circuit will meet together, *en banc*, to render a decision. Having all the judges present, not just three, gives a decision more legitimacy and sends a message that the decision was made carefully.

QUALIFICATIONS OF JUDGES—MORE SILENCE FROM THE CONSTITUTION

The Constitution is silent about the qualifications of judges for the federal courts (as it is silent about so much about the court system). It specifies only that they

- Shall be appointed by the president, with the advice and consent of the Senate

- Serve lifetime terms provided they have good behavior

- Can be removed from office only if impeached and convicted by the House of Representatives and the Senate, a process that has resulted in only fifteen impeachments and eight convictions in more than 200 years

JUDICIAL DEMOGRAPHICS

Throughout most of the country's history, the courts have been demographically uniform—white, male, and predominantly Christian. President Jimmy Carter broke that trend, vowing to use his nominations to increase the diversity in the federal courts. President Bill Clinton renewed that commitment: nearly half of his appointees were women and minorities. Bush and especially Obama continued the trend. Without concerns about diversity

6.3: HOW PRESIDENTS COMPARE ON THE RACIAL AND ETHNIC DIVERSITY OF APPOINTED JUDGES

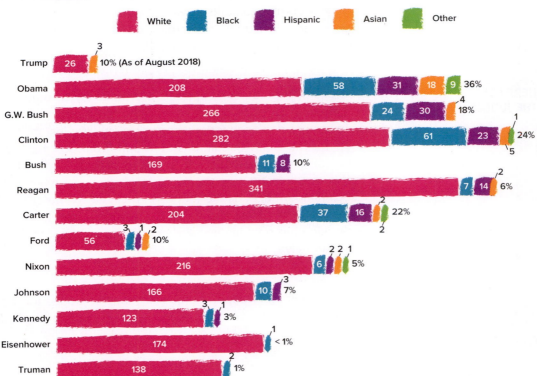

Source: Pew Research Center, "How Presidents Compare on the Racial and Ethnic Diversity of Appointed Judges," March 20, 2018, http://www.pewresearch.org/fact-tank/2018/03/20/trumps-appointed-judges-are-a-less-diverse-group-than-obamas/ft_18-03-13_judicialdiversity1/.

and without a Senate filibuster to block him, President Trump was quick to start filling empty slots with candidates who were primarily white and male.

JUDICIAL IDEOLOGY

These days, an increasingly important qualification for the job of federal judge is the ideological or policy positions of the appointee. In the 1970s, Richard Nixon ran for president on the idea that the courts were liberal policymaking institutions, soft on crime and in need of conservative correction. As presidents have taken advantage of the opportunity to shape the courts ideologically, the Senate confirmation process has become more rancorous. But the nomination process has been more important to conservatives than liberals. By the end of George W. Bush's second term,

56.2 percent of the authorized judicial positions had been filled by Republicans, tilting the federal bench in a solidly conservative direction. Barack Obama, focused on the diversity of his appointees, had come under criticism from liberals for not filling seats quickly enough, and thus for failing to build a liberal judicial legacy. But at the end of his second term the federal bench had a narrow Democratic majority.

PLAYING POLITICS WITH THE COURTS

This was despite the fact that the Republicans attempted to block votes on *all* Obama nominations, even moderate ones that would typically have enjoyed bipartisan support, in order to stall the Obama administration's efforts and to gain leverage for other things they wanted. Ironically, when those nominations eventually came to a vote, they passed with the support of many of the Republicans who had engaged in the filibuster to delay the vote in the first place. These delay tactics allowed the party to score short-term political victories, and many federal judgeships went unfilled as a consequence. Because of the ensuing backlog of cases in the courts, then–Senate majority leader Harry Reid eventually invoked what is known as the *nuclear option*, eliminating the filibuster on non–Supreme Court federal nominees (see Chapter 4).

When Trump took office, that slim Democratic majority on the courts was quickly undone. The Trump administration, urged on by Senate majority leader Mitch McConnell, has focused on filling the federal bench, something McConnell openly said was a great priority for him.

THE ROLE OF MERIT

The growing influence of politics in the selection of federal judges does not mean that merit—the actual qualifications that candidates for the judiciary possess—is unimportant. As the nation's largest legal professional association, the American Bar Association (ABA) has had the informal role since 1946 of evaluating the legal qualifications of potential nominees. While poorly rated candidates are occasionally nominated and confirmed, perhaps because of the pressure of a senator or a president, most federal judges receive the ABA's professional blessing.

The ABA's role has become more controversial in recent years, as Republicans are convinced that it has a liberal bias. The Bush administration announced in 2001 that it would no longer seek the ABA's ratings of its nominees, breaking a tradition that went back to Eisenhower. In March 2009, the Obama administration restored the ABA's traditional role in the nomination process. Trump has ignored the ABA in making his appointments, resulting in a higher percentage of "unqualified" (according to the ABA's ratings) nominees.

THE UPSHOT

Before the removal of the filibuster, the increasing politicization of the confirmation process meant that many of a president's nominees faced a grueling battle in the Senate, and even if they got through the Senate Judiciary Committee hearings, they were lucky to get as far as a vote on the floor. That is still the case if the president is of a different party than the Senate majority. A president with a Senate majority behind him can put a major stamp on the judiciary, however, as Trump seems likely to do.

In general, the Republicans have been more effective at shaping the bench. The Republican base has been more energized about the courts as a political issue because of concern about core issues like preserving gun rights, and overturning abortion, affirmative action, and gay-friendly legislation. The Democrats, by contrast, have not had that single-minded focus.

6.7 THE SUPREME COURT

THE BIG KAHUNA

The top player in the U.S. judiciary is the Supreme Court. The founders clearly intended for it to have a major role in government by the very fact that they mentioned it in the Constitution. Giving further support to that intention are Hamilton's words in *Federalist Paper #78*, when he addressed the principle of judicial review (which does not, however, appear in the Constitution).

The founders also clearly wanted the Court to be above politics. Giving Supreme Court justices lifetime tenure meant the founders wanted them to stand above the storms of public opinion, to be able to rule unswayed by political controversy. To maintain that illusion, members of the federal bench wear long black robes (attire usually reserved for priests, recent graduates, and wizards). They sit surrounded by velvet drapery in a building that looks like an ancient marble temple. No TV or other media are present in the room when the Court sits—watchers scurry out to phone in results as they occur, but we are not brought into the Court as we are the Congress or even the Oval Office.

Further, the nine members of the Court do not publish their notes while they are living. And the entire final stage of judicial appeal is shrouded with just enough mystery and secrecy to maintain the narrative that what the justices do is not soiled by earthly concerns of winning and losing and making deals.

BUT, STILL AND ALWAYS, A POLITICAL INSTITUTION

> But, of course, the Court remains a political institution.

It was sensible for the founders to want people to see the Court as above politics—that would give the justices' rulings more legitimacy and prestige. But in point of fact, the very reasons the founders could not be frank about their plans for the Court in the Constitution show just how politically volatile the whole institution was.

As we will see in this section, just like Congress and the presidency, the Court is up to its ears in politics. In fact, it is political in three key respects:

\# How the members are chosen

\# How those members make decisions

\# The impact of those decisions on the rest of us

THE POLITICS OF GETTING ON THE COURT

> Getting on the Supreme Court is not easy, but it is political—just ask Merrick Garland, whom President Barack Obama nominated to replace Justice Antonin Scalia after Scalia's sudden death in February 2016. Article II of the Constitution, establishing the executive branch, says that the president "shall nominate, and by and with the Advice and Consent of the Senate, shall appoint . . . Judges of the Supreme Court." But Senate majority leader Mitch McConnell saw an opportunity to hold on to the seat for a Republican president to fill, and he simply decided not to hold any hearings on Garland's nomination. McConnell's norm-busting gambit paid off when the Senate confirmed Neil Gorsuch shortly after Trump was inaugurated.

McConnell's move was undoubtedly political. Although he seriously bent the rules, it's not exactly clear that he broke them. There have certainly been ideological battles over justices before (notably over Robert Bork, Ronald Reagan's nominee who was defeated by Senate Democrats after rancorous hearings in 1987). More recently, Brett Kavanaugh's 2018 confirmation turned into a bitter and divisive partisan fight. But because Garland was denied even a hearing, a number of Democrats argue that an important norm was broken. It will be interesting to see what happens when a Democratic Senate majority next holds the fate of a Republican president's

TABLE IT!

6.7: WHO'S WHO ON THE SUPREME COURT?

Composition of the Supreme Court, as of September 2018

Justice	Year born	Year appointed	Political party	Appointing president	Home state	College/law school	Religion	Position when appointed
Clarence Thomas	1948	1991	Rep.	G. H. W. Bush	Georgia	Holy Cross/Yale	Catholic	U.S. Appeals Court Judge
Ruth Bader Ginsburg	1933	1993	Dem.	B. Clinton	New York	Cornell/Columbia	Jewish	U.S. Appeals Court Judge
Stephen G. Breyer	1938	1994	Dem.	B. Clinton	California	Stanford, Oxford/Harvard	Jewish	U.S. Appeals Court Judge
John G. Roberts Jr.	1955	2005	Rep.	G. W. Bush	Maryland	Harvard/Harvard	Catholic	U.S. Appeals Court Judge
Samuel A. Alito Jr.	1950	2006	Rep.	G. W. Bush	New Jersey	Princeton/Yale	Catholic	U.S. Appeals Court Judge
Sonia Sotomayor	1954	2009	Ind.	Obama	New York	Princeton/Yale	Catholic	U.S. Appeals Court Judge
Elena Kagan	1960	2010	Dem.	Obama	New York	Oxford/Harvard	Jewish	Solicitor General
Neil Gorsuch	1967	2017	Rep.	Trump	Colorado	Columbia/Harvard	Catholic/Episcopal*	U.S. Appeals Court Judge
Brett M. Kavanaugh	1965	2018	Rep.	Trump	Maryland	Yale/Yale	Catholic	U.S. Appeals Court Judge

*Gorsuch was raised Catholic but is currently a member of an Episcopal church

Source: Supreme Court of the United States, "The Justices of the Supreme Court," www.supremecourtus.gov/about/biographies.aspx.

nominee in its hands. But, more to the point, this anecdote debunks the myth that politics has no role in the selection of Supreme Court justices.

So how does one get on the Court? In many ways, the process is similar to the selection of judges for the federal bench, but with bigger stakes. Presidents (and senators) consider merit and demographics, but mostly they are fixated on ideology.

IDEOLOGY, IDEOLOGY, IDEOLOGY

We've discussed ideology at length in this book—in Chapter 1 we looked at the liberal and conservative social and economic ideas that define Americans' different views of the world. To think about what justices mean by ideology, you need to go back to Chapter 3, where we discussed the right to privacy. Recall that in *Griswold v. Connecticut*, a Court whose majority were **judicial interpretivists** ruled that the totality of the Constitution implied a right to privacy and that the founders had never intended to create an intrusive government that could interfere with people's right to use birth control. The opposing side, who were **strict constructionists**, believed that if people wanted a right to privacy they needed to amend the Constitution to create one because if the founders had wanted one, they would have said so. This echoed Hamilton's argument in *Federalist Paper #84* about why a bill of rights could prove to be dangerous.

This issue is a political hot button right now because, until Justice Scalia's death, a 5–4 majority were sufficiently committed to interpretivism that they supported the right to privacy and the case that was based on *Griswold*, *Roe v. Wade* (1973). *Roe* made it legal for a woman to make her own decision about whether or not to have an abortion in the first trimester of pregnancy. Social conservatives, who desperately want to overturn *Roe*, want a majority of strict constructionists on the Court, which they got with McConnell's gamesmanship over Gorsuch and Brett Kavanaugh's confirmation.

DIG DEEPER

For a classic movie about a case that found its way to the Supreme Court, and a look at the mechanics of judicial decision making, watch *Gideon's Trumpet*.

Go to **edge.sagepub.com/dig-deeper**

THE POLITICS OF MAKING A DECISION

> Once people are placed on the Court through such a political process, it would be surprising if they didn't carry those political concerns onto the Court with them. Of course they do. Kavanaugh's fury at what he say as a "democratic hit job" during his confirmation hearings made it clear. They need to choose which cases to hear, make their decisions, and write opinions, and politics enters at each of those points. This is a hazardous process for what one political scientist has described as "nine scorpions in a bottle." It's easiest to think of the process as a series of steps:

. . . .

judicial interpretivists: supporters of a judicial approach holding that the Constitution is a living document and that judges should interpret it according to changing times and values

strict constructionists: supporters of a judicial approach holding that the Constitution should be read literally, with the framers' intention uppermost in mind

SKIM IT!

6.4: THE SKIMMABLE SUPREME COURT DECISION-MAKING PROCESS

Step	What happens	What it means politically
1	# Petitions for **writs of certiorari** arrive at the Court. These are pleas from a party who lost in a lower court and who believes there is a procedural or legal problem with the verdict.	# Roughly 8,000 petitions arrive yearly – way too many for the Court to hear. They are reviewed by law clerks, young lawyers fresh out of school, who summarize all the positions for each petition in a two- to five-page memo.
2	# The memos are circulated to the justices' offices with the clerks' comments. # The list of cases the justices want to talk about at the Friday meetings is called the **Discuss List**, and is circulated among the justices so they can add to it.	# This gives a lot of power and discretion to people who have little experience in the legal world. # Keep in mind, getting on the discuss list is a huge deal, but it by no means guarantees a case will be heard.
3	# During the meeting it takes four justices to decide to hear a case. The Court calls this the **Rule of Four**. # If they decide to hear case they issue a writ of certiorari and the records are called up from the lower court.	# The Rule of Four gives some power to a minority of members on the Court to decide to hear a case, even though it takes five justices to actually make a decision. # The denial of certiorari does not necessarily mean the Court is endorsing a lower court's ruling; it simply means the case was not seen as important or special enough to be heard by the highest court.
4	# Concerned people and groups attempt to influence the Court by submitting **amicus curiae** ("friend of the court") **briefs**, and public relations campaigns are launched.	# It's hard to say if any of this has an impact on justices, who of course have their own views and opinions. # When the United States, under the representation of its lawyer, the **solicitor general**, is party to a case, the Court is much more likely to hear it. Between

writs of certiorari: formal requests by the U.S. Supreme Court to call up the lower court cases it decides to hear on appeal

amicus curiae briefs: "friend of the court" documents filed by interested parties to encourage the Court to grant or deny certiorari or to urge it to decide a case in a particular way

solicitor general: the legal officer who argues cases before the Supreme Court when the United States is a party to that case

Step	What happens	What it means politically
		70 and 80 percent of the appeals filed by the federal government are granted cert by the justices.
5	# The case is heard. Lawyers from each side submit written briefs and are given about an hour to make their oral case. They are often interrupted by the justices, who seek clarification or who want to make a point.	# The time lawyers are given to make their case is short, and they have to make it count. The interruptions can be really disruptive. # Because the solicitor general is experienced at appearing before the Court, he or she is more adept at dealing with the
6	# Justices deliberate on their own, in discussions with each other, and in conference. # Conference debates and discussions take place in private, although justices have often made revealing comments in their letters and memoirs that give insight into the dynamics of conference decision making.	# The goal of each justice is to form a majority around his or her views. For that they need four other votes. # Lots of adjustments are made and back and forth goes on as smart justices try to convince other smart justices that they are right. Arguing, debating, and deal-making are all political tools.
7	# A **majority opinion**, which requires at least five votes, is written. # Justices who agree with the opinion but for different or extra reasons can write **concurring opinions**. # Justices who disagree and want to be on record can write **dissenting opinions**.	# The opinion of the case is central—the ruling is what lives on and becomes precedent. # Opinions craft what are often political decisions in the sense that they change how lives are lived and who has power. # Dissenting opinions are important, too. Occasionally, when times change and a Court is prepared to overrule itself on an issue, it goes back to the original dissent for the reasons to do so.

majority opinion: the written decision of the Court that states the judgment of the majority

concurring opinions: documents written by justices expressing agreement with the majority ruling but describing different or additional reasons for the ruling

dissenting opinions: documents written by justices expressing disagreement with the majority ruling

THE UPSHOT

Although the process of making a Supreme Court decision is largely hidden from public view, we can tell that both external and internal influences help shape the outcomes. People with power (including the justices themselves) have an opportunity to put pressure on the Court. Social media campaigns, protests, and group membership all help amplify voices. Only sometimes can we tell whether they make a difference. Consider the changes in public opinion that happened between 1857, when the Court ruled 7–2 that Dred Scott, a former slave, could not bring a case before the Court, and 1954, when all nine justices signed Chief Justice Earl Warren's carefully crafted opinion that desegregated the schools.

THE POLITICAL IMPACT OF COURT DECISIONS

As the *Dred Scott v. Sanford* and *Brown v. Board of Education* cases we just referred to make clear, the Supreme Court wields enormous clout. Hamilton may have called the Court the least dangerous branch, but depending on where you are standing, it can exercise power over you that can change your world. Consider the cases we have reviewed in this book. Over the past 200-plus years, the Court has decided that

\#   It should be the ultimate decider of what is constitutional in the U.S. federal government and the states (*Marbury v. Madison,* 1803)

\#   Congress has the power to do anything "necessary and proper" to carry out its duties, rendering almost meaningless the Tenth Amendment, which says leftover powers go to the states (*McCulloch v. Maryland,* 1819)

\#   Segregation was legal (*Plessy v. Ferguson,* 1896)

\#   And then it was illegal (*Brown v. Board of Education,* 1954)

\#   States and national government could not regulate working hours (*Lochner v. New York,* 1905)

\#   States need to respect the rights in the Bill of Rights (multiple cases, including *Gideon v. Wainwright,* 1963)

\#   Americans are entitled to equal representation (one person, one vote; *Baker v. Carr,* 1962)

\#   We enjoy a variety of civil liberties, all of which have some limits on them (a variety of cases)

\#   People have the right to privacy (*Griswold v. Connecticut,* 1965)

\#   A woman has a right to make her own reproductive decisions and to have an abortion in the first trimester of pregnancy (*Roe v. Wade,* 1973)

The president is not above the law (*United States v. Richard Nixon*, 1974)

Corporations can give unlimited funds to political campaigns and causes (*Citizens United v. FEC*, 2010)

YOUR TURN This list goes on and on. Give it a Google. What other major policymaking Supreme Court cases would you include here?

Big Think

→ What are the goals of a criminal justice system? Does an adversarial system or an inquisitorial system seem better able to fulfill those goals?

→ Does the process of electing state judges seem just to you? If so, by what definition of justice?

→ What can be done to equalize the experiences that whites and blacks have with the criminal justice system?

→ Is there any way to minimize the politics in the Supreme Court? How large is the impact of the Court on our political lives?

Key Terms

CONCEPTS

adjudication (p. 188)

administrative laws (p. 185)

adversarial system (p. 187)

amicus curiae briefs (p. 208)

appeal (p. 182)

civil law tradition (p. 186)

civil laws (p. 184)

common law tradition (p. 186)

concurring opinions (p. 209)

constitutional laws (p. 185)

crime (p. 184)

criminal laws (p. 184)

dissenting opinions (p. 209)

executive orders (p. 185)

inquisitorial system (p. 187)

judiciary (p. 182)

jurisdiction (p. 196)

litigious system (p. 188)

majority opinion (p. 209)

precedent (p. 185)

procedural laws (p. 184)

racial profiling (p. 192)

rule of law (p. 183)

statutory laws (p. 185)

substantive laws (p. 184)

tort (p. 184)

writs of certiorari (p. 208)

IMPORTANT WORKS AND EVENTS •

KEY INDIVIDUALS AND GROUPS •

#7 PARTIES AND INTEREST GROUPS

In this chapter:

7.1 Introduction to PARTIES AND INTEREST GROUPS

TWO SIDES OF THE SAME COIN →

Political parties and interest groups are two sides of the same coin. Both are groups of people who are bound together by a shared interest, one that is different from the interest of the public as a whole, or the *public interest*. Even if these groups *think* their goals are in the public interest, some portion of the public disagrees. Both groups try to use the political system to realize their political goals.

IN A NUTSHELL

If these groups sound familiar, it's because you have met them before—these are the **factions** James Madison feared would be so destructive to democracy. In *Federalist Paper #10*, he wrote that the republic was so large that groups could not form or, if they did, would cancel each other out. But here we are, more than 200 years later, and factions are alive and well and powerful in the form of parties and interest groups.

WHERE WE GO IN THIS CHAPTER

By the time you finish reading this chapter, you will understand

- → What political parties and interest groups are, how they are similar, and how they differ
- → What role parties play in a democracy
- → How party organization and internal decision making work
- → How political parties operate today
- → The basics of interest groups (why they form, what kinds there are, and so on)
- → The role interest groups play in our political system
- → Whether Madison was right to be concerned about the role of factions in a democracy

DIG DEEPER

Refresh your memory about what Madison had to say.

Go to **edge.sagepub.com/ dig-deeper**

7.2 PARTIES AND INTEREST GROUPS DEFINED

SIMILAR, NOT SO SIMILAR

> Parties and interest groups may be two sides of the same political coin, but there is still plenty that makes them different. Though both kinds of groups use the political system to attain group goals that differ from what other people want, *the way they go about working the system to realize those goals is totally different.*

We'll get to the details shortly, but here are three essential points to start you off:

THREE KEY DISTINCTIONS TO REMEMBER

> \# **Political parties** are groups that are bound by a common interest or interests and that *seek to use the political system to attain their goals from inside the system by controlling government.* They do this by **electioneering** (nominating and electing candidates to office) and by **governing** (running the show) if they are successful. The two main parties in the United States are the Democrats and the Republicans.
>
> \# **Interest groups**, by contrast, are groups, including corporations, that are bound by a common interest and that *seek to use the political system to attain their policy goals from the outside, by persuading people in power to give them what they want.* The act of persuading officials is called lobbying—they can engage in direct lobbying by working with government actors, or indirect lobbying by encouraging the public to put pressure on government actors.

. . . .

factions: groups of citizens united by some common passion or interest and opposed to the rights of other citizens or to the interests of the whole community

political parties: groups that are bound by a common interest or interests and that seek to use the political system to attain their goals from inside the system by controlling government

electioneering: nominating and electing candidates to office

governing: activities directed toward controlling the distribution of political resources by providing executive and legislative leadership, enacting agendas, mobilizing support, and building coalitions

interest groups: groups, including corporations, that are bound by a common interest and that seek to use the political system to attain their policy goals from the outside, by persuading people in power to give them what they want

\# Very often, the people the interest groups are lobbying are party members who have won positions of power in the government. It is common for party representatives in government and interest group lobbyists outside the government to develop close working relationships in which their interests overlap. *This magnifies their power*. We will return to this point at the end of this chapter.

7.3 THE ROLE OF PARTIES IN A DEMOCRACY

WHAT'S INVOLVED IN BEING A POLITICAL PARTY?

A political party's job is to represent the interests of its members by gaining control of government. It does that by nominating and electing candidates for office and then running the government if it wins. This is a huge task that requires a multifaceted organization to manage it. The trouble is, as we will see, American political parties are not always organized in such a way that they can succeed at both activities.

Madison was wary of parties because he saw them as factions likely to pull apart the republic. Ironically, even he was a party member before his political career was over. Madison's distrust notwithstanding, parties are uniquely positioned to strengthen and facilitate democracy in some important ways. That doesn't mean they always *do* strengthen or facilitate it—it just means that they *can*.

DEMOCRACY STRENGTHENERS

\# **Connection.** Parties can provide a link between voters and the officials they elect. Knowing that parties stand for particular policies and ideals can help voters to identify with and support those who share their views. Identifying one's own interests with a party's is called **partisanship**. Candidates running under the party label promise to carry out the party's agenda, and if they fail to do so, voters hold them accountable by voting them out of office. **Accountability**—ensuring our elected officials do what they say they are going to do—is a key component of democracy.

\# **Cohesion.** Parties can make a fragmented political system (think federalism and separation of powers) feel more cohesive. Government may be divided into layers and branches, but the fact that there are

. . . .

partisanship: one's allegiance to one's party

accountability: ensuring elected officials do what they say they are going to do

Democrats and Republicans in all of those divisions gives continuity and structure to a complex system.

\# **Voice.** Parties provide an opposition voice to those who are not in government. Even though a party may not gain control of any branch of government, it doesn't disappear. Members continue to reformulate their ideas and articulate what they think is wrong with the current government in preparation to run again another day. This helps place a check on the party in power and gives voters an alternative.

Parties are better at performing all these democratic strengthening functions to the extent that they can conform to a set of ideals about how parties should operate. We call this the **responsible party model**. In a perfect world, the party system would provide a sorting mechanism for voters who have different values, views of government, and policy preferences. It should act as a useful guide for busy voters and as a mechanism of democratic accountability.

KEY POINT: WE DO NOT LIVE IN A PERFECT WORLD

Think of the responsible party model not as a description of reality in the United States but as a yardstick against which actual parties can be measured to see where they are making voters' jobs simpler and enhancing democratic accountability and where they are not. These are the conditions of the model:

CONDITIONS OF THE RESPONSIBLE PARTY MODEL

\# Each party promotes a distinct set of policies (called a **party platform**) based on its ideology. That platform should be clearly different from other parties' platforms and presented to voters in a way that voters can tell the difference.

\# Candidates in the party promise to follow the party's platform and enact it if elected.

\# Voters make their choices based on the policies the parties promote in their platforms and are willing to vote against their party's candidates if they fail to keep their promises.

\# If party officials fail to carry out the platforms they are pledged to, voters reject them at the polls and vote in someone else.

responsible party model: an ideal model of how parties might operate to maximize voter information and elected official accountability

party platform: a distinct set of policies set forth by a political party that is based on its ideology

WHERE TODAY'S PARTIES FIT THE MODEL AND WHERE THEY DON'T

Americans don't stick very closely to the responsible party model. That doesn't mean parties in the United States are "irresponsible" or "bad." It just means this model doesn't describe them very well. But we can learn a lot about the party system by looking at why that is.

American parties do create distinct party platforms, and they are clearly different from each other. Voters who argue that the two parties are the same are standing at an ideological point so far away from both parties that they appear closer to each other.

Candidates do in general promise to support their party's platform if elected. In that sense, parties have moved closer to the model than they were in the days when conservative southern Democrats voted more often with the Republican Party than with their own. Most of those conservative southerners have now become Republicans through a process we call **partisan sorting**—people identify with the party because it most closely stands for their own views and values and not for regional or other non-ideological reasons. Consequently, there are fewer conservative Democrats or liberal Republicans than there once were.

DIG DEEPER

Read this important article about hyperpartisanship by Thomas Mann and Norman Ornstein.

Go to **edge.sagepub.com/dig-deeper**

Over time, partisan sorting has been enforced by voters rather than by tight party regulations. Parties in the United States do not have rules that force conformity among members (although they do have rules that govern how they are organized and how decisions are made). To the extent that the parties have become more ideologically consistent, it is because the most active and ideological voters have punished moderate candidates.

The American party system also deviates from the responsible party model in that party members are increasingly not just partisan (that is, identifying with the team), but hyperpartisan. That means they will choose their team over the other team every time, even if it requires that they change their minds on policy priorities or values to do so.

THE CURSE OF HYPERPARTISANSHIP

Hyperpartisanship works against democratic accountability. When voters aren't willing to vote against their party when it lets them down *because they would rather deny their opponents a win*, they send a message to their party that it is okay that elected officials don't keep their promises.

partisan sorting: the process through which citizens align themselves ideologically with one of the two parties, leaving fewer citizens remaining in the center and increasing party polarization

hyperpartisanship: a commitment to party so strong that it can transcend other commitments, including that to the national interest

7.4 PARTY ORGANIZATION AND DECISION MAKING

THE WAY WE WERE: CHOOSING CANDIDATES IN SMOKE-FILLED ROOMS

Today's party organizational rules are a result of reforms that cleaned up the old-time **party machines** of the early twentieth century, where party leaders or "bosses" made the decisions and kept the loyalty of their voters by providing them with jobs, services, and support. Those old parties were effective at doing a lot of things, but they were also vulnerable to corruption because there were no checks on the party leaders' power. Reforms included bringing party decisions, like whom to nominate, out of the proverbial "smoke-filled rooms"—a reference to the back rooms filled with all-male, all-powerful leaders who made decisions without consulting the voters.

CHOOSING CANDIDATES TODAY IN THE SMOKE-FREE AIR OF DEMOCRATIC WRANGLING

Today, *electioneering,* one of the two defining jobs of a party we mentioned earlier, takes place through a series of recruiting efforts made by party officials inside and outside the government. Rather than in smoke-filled rooms, these decisions are now made by party members voting in **primaries** (preliminary party elections) or participating in **caucuses** (party gatherings where candidate choice is debated openly).

After each state holds its primary or caucus (or both), the parties meet in a nominating convention at the end of the summer and officially endorse their choice (see Chapter 8), almost certainly the person who won the most support during the primary process.

Although party officials still have a great deal of clout and resources, they are no longer "the boss." They do not always get their way about who should run or how a campaign should be conducted. Sometimes candidates decide to run without the party's blessing, and sometimes the voters choose someone the party leaders think is unelectable or inconsistent with the party's ideals.

DIG DEEPER

For a poignant, fictional look at the demise of the old-fashioned party machine, check out the 1958 film *The Last Hurrah.*

Go to **edge.sagepub.com/dig-deeper**

party machines: a system in which party leaders or "bosses" made decisions about policy and kept the loyalty of their voters by providing them with services and support

primaries: preliminary party elections

caucuses: party gatherings where candidate choice is debated openly

A FOUR-PART PARTY STRUCTURE

> Today's parties have four segments:

Party identifiers are people in the electorate who think of themselves as partisans (team members) and generally vote for the party. We will talk more about what causes people to identify more with one party or another in Chapter 8.

A subset of those identifiers are the **party activists**, or the party base. These are the most ideologically extreme of the party's voters (meaning, if they are Republicans, they are the most conservative, and if they are Democrats, they are the most liberal). They are also the most motivated to pay attention, engage online, campaign for candidates, and vote in primaries. *They thus have a disproportionate impact on who the party's candidates turn out to be.*

The party is run by the official **party organizations**—the Democratic National Committee and the Republican National Committee—which are filled with career party officials. These people are paid political operatives who are in charge of keeping the party infrastructure working.

Finally, there are the people who get elected—the **party-in-government**. At the very top, they have considerable say over who leads the party organization. Although the parties have not completely democratized, they are much more open and accountable than they used to be. The party-in-government, not surprisingly, is in charge of the key function of *governing*—filling key positions and making policy. The closer they govern in line with what they said they were going to do, the easier it is for voters to hold them accountable.

WHY DOES THE UNITED STATES HAVE ONLY TWO PARTIES WHEN SOME COUNTRIES HAVE LOTS?

> You might think that democracy in the United States would be enhanced if we had a multiparty system in which more interests could be represented, and you'd be right. Countries that have more than two parties are forced

party identifiers: people who associate themselves with a particular party because they share its values, culture, policy preferences, or social network

party activists: the most ideologically extreme of a party's voters, also called the "base"

party organizations: the Democratic National Committee and the Republican National Committee, both of which are staffed with officials who are paid political operatives in charge of keeping the party infrastructure working

party-in-government: elected officials who are in charge of the key function of governing—filling key positions and making policy

to pull together to form a workable government. India, for instance, has seven national parties, forty-nine state parties, and over a thousand unofficial parties. In these countries, coalitions of the parties winning the highest percentages of the votes have to form in order to create a functioning government. This means that partisanship generally has to bow to practicalities and compromise, or a party gets left out in the cold.

The United States, however, does not have such a system. There are many reasons, both structural and legal, for our two-party system. At this point, you might want to object, noting that there *are* more than just two parties in the United States—maybe you even voted for what we call a third-party candidate. At the state level, sometimes third parties can indeed thrive. But it's very difficult for third parties to get any traction at the national level. Even though independent candidates can win election to Congress, they generally decide to cooperate with one of the two major parties in order to have any power in the institution. Third-party candidates sometimes play the role of spoilers—pulling enough votes away from one candidate to ensure the election of her or his opponent—but winning is highly unlikely.

STRUCTURAL REASONS FOR THE TWO-PARTY SYSTEM

The major structural reason for our two-party system is that the United States does not have a system of proportional representation, often found in parliamentary governments. In that type of system, people cast their vote for a legislative party, not one specific person. The winning party then installs candidates in the legislature according to the proportion of the whole vote it gets. Voting for a party list means you are voting for a set of principles and policies, not a candidate, and it potentially allows a lot more parties into the mix.

In the United States, congressional districts are called **single member, first past the post** districts, which means that only one person is elected from each district—the person who gets the most votes. A party whose candidate comes in second gets nothing in such a district. (In a proportional system, by contrast, coming in second *can* bring a lot of power with it when the party and not a candidate is on the ballot. Of course, one party can win a majority, but the possibility of coalition building gives a party more pathways to power.)

LEGAL BARRIERS TO THIRD PARTIES

Third parties struggle in the United States for other reasons, too. In the past, campaign finance laws designed by the two major parties made federal

single member, first past the post: a system of representation in which only one person is elected from each congressional district—the person who gets the most votes

matching funds available to enhance the fundraising of their candidates in a presidential election if those candidates agreed to limit their spending. Laws made it difficult for third-party candidates to qualify for those funds.

Since 2008, when Barack Obama was able to raise seemingly limitless funds from small donors online (as well as from larger corporate donors), and so rejected the matching funds, that system has been pretty much defunct. That moment when mediated citizenship allowed citizens to make direct deposits from their bank accounts to the campaign funds of their preferred candidates was a game changer. When candidates could reach out directly to their supporters, they were no longer as dependent on the parties for their infrastructure. At the same time, as we came to learn in 2016, they became vulnerable to the effects of social media being manipulated and weaponized against them.

PARTIES STRUGGLING TO KEEP FINANCIAL CONTROL IN THE INTERNET AGE

With parties struggling to control the purse strings, there is much more opportunity for those not blessed by a major party's nomination to stage a campaign. Bernie Sanders, who competed for the Democratic nomination in 2016 without actually being a Democrat, and Donald Trump, who won the Republican nomination that same year against many well-funded establishment party members, perhaps foreshadow ways that mediated citizenship will diverge from traditional party politics.

Parties have another way to maintain their financial clout, however. Although donations to candidates are limited, unlimited corporate and interest group funds are available to parties, and those parties have spent them on efforts to help get out the votes for their candidates.

LOCAL TWO-PARTY CONTROL

Other barriers are created by the many laws governing how a party can qualify to compete in an election, and most of those laws were also designed and passed by the two major parties to reduce competition from upstarts. Thus, in most states (elections are controlled at the state level), a third-party candidate has to collect a certain number of signatures on a petition to get on the ballot. Even then, recognition by the media and other parties is tough to come by and inclusion in formative activities like televised debates depends on polling above a certain level.

What most often happens when a third party begins to gain traction and draw support from the major parties is that one of the parties will move to co-opt the winning issues. When Ross Perot made his unusual run for the presidency in 1992 based largely on the issue of the growing national deficit, Bill Clinton started talking about the deficit, too, taking some of the wind out of Perot's leaky sails.

The value of belonging to one of the two major parties when making a run, particularly on the national stage, is illustrated by Vermont independent senator Bernie Sanders's 2016 campaign for the Democratic nomination for the presidency. Although Sanders votes with the Democrats in the Senate for organizational purposes (choosing leaders and the like), he is not now and was not then a Democrat. He chose to run as one because it gave him built-in advantages and let him avoid many of the challenges that hinder third-party candidates.

THE UPSHOT

For voters in a system like ours, voting for a third party is essentially the same as throwing away your vote, unless the two-party candidates are unacceptable to you for some serious reason. In that case, voting for a third party might allow you to fulfill your patriotic duty while making a personal statement or solving a psychological or moral dilemma. What might motivate people to vote for a third party?

7.5 THE PARTIES TODAY

A (VERY) SHORT LOOK BACK

Although historically we've gone through extended periods in which one party has had control over the government, the current **party era** (period of party dominance or party instability) is characterized not by one-party control but by a trading of power back and forth. Sometimes switches from one party era are precipitated by a single **critical election**, like the one after the Great Depression that ushered in Franklin Roosevelt and Democratic control in the 1930s. More often, the **realignment** from one system of party dominance to the other is ushered in gradually. It is often hard to know if you are in a period of realignment until you have the advantage of hindsight to look back at where you have been. The concept of party eras seems to have been a more useful way to describe the power balance between the parties in the past.

party era: a period of party dominance or party instability

critical election: an election signaling a significant change in popular allegiance from one party to another

realignment: a substantial and long-term shift in party allegiance by individuals and groups, usually resulting in a change in policy direction

GEN GAP!

PARTY IDENTIFICATION AND POLICY PREFERENCES ACROSS THE GENERATIONS

The overall take so far in our GenGap features is that Millennials are more liberal than their elders, partly because they are so much more diverse. Remember from the GenGap box in Chapter 4 (p. 134) that they are far more likely to identify with the Democratic Party. As it turns out, that ideological leaning shows up in other issues beyond party preference as well.

FIGURE IT!

7.1: MILLENNIALS, INCLUDING MILLENNIAL REPUBLICANS, TEND TO BE MORE LIBERAL ON MANY ISSUES THAN OLDER GENERATIONS

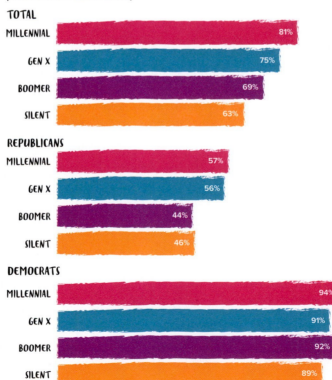

THERE'S A BROAD DIFFERENCE OF OPINION BEWTEEN DEMOCRATS AND REPUBLICANS OVER GLOBAL WARMING

% who say there **is** solid evidence of global warming caused by natural patterns and/or human activity

TOTAL

MILLENNIAL	81%
GEN X	75%
BOOMER	69%
SILENT	63%

REPUBLICANS

MILLENNIAL	57%
GEN X	56%
BOOMER	44%
SILENT	46%

DEMOCRATS

MILLENNIAL	94%
GEN X	91%
BOOMER	92%
SILENT	89%

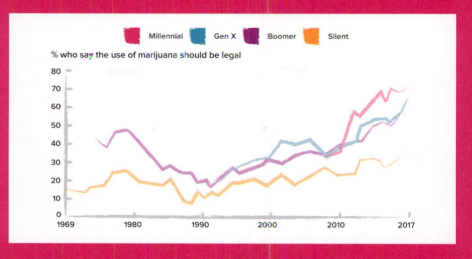

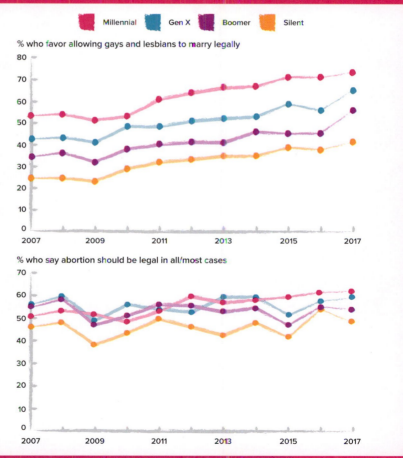

Source: Pew Research Center, The Generation Gap in American Politics, March 1, 2018, http://www.people-press.org/2018/03/01/4-race-immigration-same-sex-marriage-abortion-global-warming-gun-policy-marijuana-legalization/030118_4_7/, http://www.people-press.org/2018/03/01/4-race-immigration-same-sex-marriage-abortion-global-warming-gun-policy-marijuana-legalization/030118_4_9/, and http://www.people-press.org/2018/03/01/4-race-immigration-same-sex-marriage-abortion-global-warming-gun-policy-marijuana-legalization/030118_4_6/.

The charts here reflect the issues that many interest groups advocate for. You can see that Millennials tend to be more liberal on climate change (even among Republicans!), on the legalization of marijuana, on marriage equality, and, marginally, on reproductive rights.

TAKEAWAYS

→ **If Millennials, who are fast becoming the largest generation, stay with the political and policy positions they have now, the United States is likely to eventually become a much more left-of-center country for a generation**, after having been a right-of-center nation since the 1980s. What might be driving that change?

→ **Young people are far less likely to vote than older people, so even though Millennials have these more liberal tendencies, they may not show up until that generation has begun to marry, buy homes, and start families**—activities they are beginning later than ever, as we saw in Chapter 1. The 2018 midterms marked a change in that voting pattern. Why?

→ **Some issues, like fighting climate change, supporting marriage equality, and legalizing marijuana are becoming less partisan for Millennials**—they are favored by both young Democrats and young Republicans. How will that change the issues the parties stand for?

Today's back-and-forth era is notable precisely because no single party has been able to seize control of Congress for any length of time since 1994. This is less a reflection of a well-functioning responsible party model and more a result of the country's being narrowly divided ideologically. The current party system is highly polarized and hyperpartisan, although not yet to the same degree in both parties.

To understand what this means, we need to understand what the parties stand for and who supports them.

DEMOCRATS AND REPUBLICANS IN HISTORICAL PERSPECTIVE

The Democrats and the Republicans have not always stood for the things they stand for today. In fact, the two parties have not always been the Democrats and the Republicans. The United States has had parties called the Federalists, the Whigs, and even the Democratic-Republicans. But generally, there have been only two at a time, except during periods of transition between party eras.

Today, it's the Democrats and the Republicans, with a smattering of Greens and Libertarians. But mainly just the two.

BIG CHANGES AFTER THE CIVIL WAR

What the parties have stood for, though, has morphed a lot through time. Once the Republicans were the party of Abraham Lincoln and led the Union in the Civil War against slavery, while the Democrats were pro-slavery southerners. Fast-forward a hundred years and the parties had switched positions on race. Conservative southerners, still holding a grudge against the party of Lincoln, continued to be Democrats despite Roosevelt's leading the Democrats into the age of economic liberalism through the 1930s and 1940s. Democrats dominated the political scene for the next thirty years.

At that point the dividing lines were predominantly economic. Democrats stood for an activist government that believed it could and should solve economic and social problems at the national level. The Republican Party was a hands-off, antiregulatory business party. But there were more economically liberal conservatives in the northeastern part of the country and some economically conservative Democrats in the South. That left many people more or less in the middle as "moderates."

DIG DEEPER

Watch here to see how that has changed.

Go to **edge.sagepub.com/ dig-deeper**

What you are seeing in that video is the process of partisan sorting we talked about before. It is due in large part to what happened to the parties in the 1960s and 1970s.

NIXON'S "SOUTHERN STRATEGY"

A lot changed beginning in the mid-1960s. By that decade, the Democrats had a pretty solid hold on Congress with their coalition of southern Democrats, working-class white immigrants in the North, and farmers. Frustrated that the Republicans could not break the Democratic majority in Congress, Richard Nixon, then the Republican presidential candidate, has been credited with what has come to be called his "southern strategy." He used race as a wedge issue to break conservative southern Democrats away from the Democratic Party and give the Republicans a majority.

Those southern Democrats may have been happy with the economic policies of the FDR Democrats, but they were not happy with the civil rights policies of the Lyndon Johnson Democrats. As the Democrats became the defenders of racial equality, the parties flipped, with Lincoln's Republicans becoming the party of resistance.

THE "NEW" REPUBLICAN COALITION

To follow this discussion, it might help you to refer to the chart on American ideologies in Chapter 1 (see p. 15). The hands off the economy, limited government, pro-business Republicans had to make room in their party for new voters who were considerably more socially conservative than they were. Traditional southerners were far more hierarchical, authoritarian, and evangelical Christian than the average economic conservative Republican, who believed the government that governs best, governs least.

PROMISES UNMET

For decades after Nixon set his strategy in motion, the relationship between these two groups of Republicans led to considerable friction and broken promises. Republicans promised to support policies that favored traditional gender roles, prayer in school, and other Bible-based issues, and to vote against legislation that would extend civil rights, women's rights, affirmative action, gay rights, reproductive rights, and the legalization of marijuana.

The problem was that the economic conservatives went along with the social conservatives, but they were not themselves particularly worried about race, women's rights, or even sex, drugs, and rock and roll. For a time, they paid lip service to those concerns to keep the peace. But by 2008, abortion was still legal, women were going to college in greater numbers than men, gay rights were moving toward marriage equality, and there was a black family living in the White House. The degree to which the promises were unkept became suddenly, glaringly obvious. At the same time, demographic trends meant that whites were going to shortly (by 2044) lose their majority status and become just one of many minority groups in the United States.

TEA PARTY REBELLION

Interparty warfare started in the Republican Party when the base rebelled during the 2008 election. Party activists were not that enthusiastic about having John McCain, to them a conventional military hero, at the top of their ticket, but they adored the antiestablishment, self-proclaimed maverick governor from Alaska running for vice president. Sarah Palin articulated the years of pent-up grievance that many members of the Republican base felt from not being heard and being taken for granted.

More than once, the socially conservative base had helped put a Republican majority in Congress, only to find their policy preferences ignored or blocked by other Republicans. Palin spoke for them. After the McCain-Palin ticket lost to Barack Obama and Joe Biden, the conservative voice of what came to be called the Tea Party spoke even more loudly, demanding that they "take our country back." From what or from whom was rarely spelled out, but the rallying cry came to stand for a rejection of San Francisco liberals like Speaker of the House Nancy Pelosi, undocumented workers, people of color, and others who just were not what Palin called "real Americans."

In the 2010 midterm elections, these angry social conservatives got themselves on primary ballots in many states. The party base, more likely to vote in primaries, picked those candidates to run. Many Tea Party candidates eventually won office, allowing the Republican Party to take back the majority in Congress. The Tea Party, along with other social conservatives, were able to block Obama's agenda and to keep the new Republican Speaker of the House, John Boehner, from compromising on anything the Democrats wanted.

They could block Obama, but they could not stop him from taking executive actions. The economic recovery he oversaw was starting to pick up steam, but too many people felt left behind and angry despite their representation in Congress. That anger, combined with other factors, propelled Donald Trump, who channeled the same resentment and grievance that Palin had, to a narrow victory for the Republicans in 2016.

THE REPUBLICAN PARTY NOW

To understand where the parties stand today means understanding that context. The parties still have their economic left-right divisions. Republicans are pro–tax cuts and anti–government spending, although they have relaxed the objections to deficit spending they had when Obama was president (that is, they are now willing to go further into debt). They oppose what they think of as unnecessary government interference, and the Trump administration has been quietly undoing many of the regulations put in place during the Obama administration, as well as other economic and environmental rules that have been on the books for years, including those intended to control banks, create global trade alliances, and counteract climate change.

The social conservative dimension of Trump's coalition is an interesting one, as social conservatives seem to have set aside the traditional values that so motivated them in years past. Trump is not a natural fit for that base—he is not himself an evangelical, and he does not have a history of expressing conservative moral values and views. Although they stumble sometimes in their defense of his actions, what social conservatives essentially say is that they are willing to overlook the less attractive parts of Trump's personal history so long as he backs the policies they want. (Democrats, who have not historically advocated for traditional, religiously based policies, do not find themselves in similar conflict when Democratic politicians display personal behavior that is objectionable.)

Trump has embraced limiting legal immigration and rolling back protections for Dreamers—immigrants without legal status whose parents brought them to the United States when they were little. He has also advocated more restrictive voting laws and supported policies that protect the rights of Americans not to have to act in ways counter to their religious convictions—providing birth control for employees, for instance, or baking wedding cakes for gay couples.

With Trump's win came another twist in the party: what had been a law-and-order party turned against the Federal Bureau of Investigation; what had been an anti-Russia party suddenly saw Russian president Vladimir Putin as less of a threat; and what had been a pro-trade party advocated for tariffs on goods like steel. Social conservatives changed the Republican Party, but Trump, in his turn, changed the views of social conservatives.

THE DEMOCRATIC PARTY NOW

The Democrats are economically liberal, but since the 1990s they have blunted the edge of their liberalism as the country moved to the right after Republican president Ronald Reagan's two terms in office. In recent years, many left-leaning Democrats have grown increasingly irate with what they saw as President Obama's over-willingness to compromise with Republicans during his two terms in office, creating space for challengers far to the left of most of the Democratic Party in 2016. Bernie Sanders's campaign called for free college tuition and single-payer health care but was hazy on how these benefits were to be paid for. Many Sanders supporters were so convinced by him that Hillary Clinton was really a corporate shill that, when the general election came around, they voted for Green Party candidate Jill Stein, for Republican Donald Trump, or they stayed home.

This does not bode well for the Democratic Party. If the party undergoes the same kind of internal ideological purification process that the Republican Party experienced, the Democrats will endure the same kind of internal conflicts and contradictions that are currently plaguing the Republicans. Democrats tend to be solidly together on social issues—in favor of marriage equality, women's rights, immigration, environmental policy to combat climate change, and policies favoring greater diversity, but they disagree on how far right to go on the economic scale. The party has pretty much come together on the call for a single-payer health care system, but members disagree on the regulation of Wall Street, global trade, and whether solving the problem of economic inequality will solve all our social inequalities.

The 2018 midterm elections showed that while progressives had made inroads in Democratic ideology, establishment candidates did well. There is no clear party split as there was after 2010. The one visible bit of discord was over Nancy Pelosi's speakership. Republicans had so successfully demonized her during the election that several Democrats promised not to vote for her leadership if elected. For the most part she successfully navigated the challenge to her position, but there is no doubt that Democrats are ready to see younger leadership move in to control of the party.

Republicans are in a clear moment of tension between social and economic conservatives. Democrats are at the threshold of their own struggle between economic liberals and moderates, old and young leadership. We have seen the dynamics that cause this to happen.

KEY POINT

Historically, when the party bosses chose their candidates in smoke-filled rooms, they were concerned with one thing—electability. Their ultimate goal was to consolidate and continue their party's power. Party activists voting in primaries today, however, care far more about a candidate's ideological purity—their strict adherence to certain positions across the party platform. Their candidates have to sometimes take extreme positions to win the nomination. Taking extreme positions to win the primaries pulls the candidates farther apart. We can see the results in the parties today.

But elections are rarely won at the primary level (unless a district or a state is so clearly safe for one party or the other that the major battle is for the nomination). Most elections are won in a general electorate, where voters may be partisan, but they tend to be far more moderate than the activists.

7.1: THE SKIMMABLE PARTY PLATFORMS, 2016

Policy Position	Democrats	Republicans
Abortion	"[E]very woman should have access to quality reproductive services, including safe and legal abortion. . . ."	"[T]he unborn child has a fundamental right to life that cannot be infringed."
Health care	"[H]ealth care is a right, not a privilege. . . ."	"[I]mproving health care must begin with the repeal of the dishonestly named Affordable Care Act of 2010: Obamacare. . . ."
Gun rights	"[W]e will expand and strengthen background checks and close dangerous loopholes in our current laws . . . to keep weapons of war . . . off our streets.	"We uphold the rights of individuals to keep and bear arms."
Taxes	"[W]e believe the wealthiest Americans and largest corporations must pay their fair share of taxes."	"Wherever tax rates penalize thrift or discourage investment, they must be lowered. Wherever current provisions of the code are disincentives for economic growth, they must be changed."
Education	"[E]very student should be able to go to college debt-free, and working families should not have to pay any tuition to go to public colleges and universities."	"In order to bring down college costs and give students access to a multitude of financing options, private sector participation in student financing should be restored."
Immigration	"[W]e need to . . . create a path to citizenship for law-abiding families who are here. . . . We will work with Congress to end the forced and prolonged expulsion from the country that these immigrants endure when trying to adjust their status."	"[T]he interests of American workers must be protected over the claims of foreign nationals seeking the same jobs. . . . Illegal immigration endangers everyone, exploits the taxpayers, and insults all who aspire to enter America legally. We oppose any form of amnesty. . . ."

Until recently, candidates had to scramble back to the ideological middle to fight in the general election. Elections were a moderating force on the parties, like the decisions of party bosses had been. Electability in a general election meant the parties could not move too far away from each other.

DO THE OLD RULES HOLD IN AN AGE OF EXTREME POLARIZATION?

In the current age of polarization, with fewer votes to be found in the middle, parties and their candidates have taken to focusing less on pivoting to the ideological middle and more on turning out their bases on Election Day.

We saw the culmination of that strategy in 2016. While Democratic candidate Hillary Clinton played by the old rules, focusing on the more progressive parts of her policy program in the primaries and returning to the center in the general, Donald Trump played almost exclusively to his base all the way through and won the election. While he tried the same approach during the midterms and undoubtedly mobilized his base to turn out, liberals had learned their lesson and turned out in even greater numbers.

It's worth noting that although this approach netted Trump an Electoral College victory, he did not win the popular vote, and other forces at play in that election might have skewed the result. He also lost the midterms to a "blue wave." We don't have enough evidence to say for certain that presidential candidates no longer need to appeal to party moderates. But we do know that the old rules are in flux as the parties struggle with the passion of their activists to create ideological purity among their members.

7.6 INTEREST GROUP BASICS

INTEREST GROUPS DON'T NEED TO BE MODERATE—IN FACT, IT'S JUST THE OPPOSITE.

Interest groups don't have to worry about appealing to the broad public. They don't seek election, so they never need to moderate their positions. They don't govern, so they don't have to compromise. In fact, the more stalwart and uncompromising they stand on their positions, the better situated they are to attract members who share their particular views.

Interest groups, remember, are people drawn together for support of a common political interest (and this can include a single corporation or industry whose interest is making more money for itself), who seek to influence policy to their advantage from the outside—lobbying government officials to see things their way.

CONTRARY TO MADISON'S FEARS, INTEREST GROUPS CAN (BUT NOT NECESSARILY DO) BOLSTER DEMOCRACY.

Although Madison feared such groups, like parties they can play an important role in strengthening democracy. At their best, interest groups give citizens, who are limited by the Constitution from playing an expansive, direct role in government, additional ways of using the system to get their way. This was precisely what Madison didn't like about them, but they can strengthen citizen power in six ways:

Representation. The most important thing about you may not be where you live. It may be who you are, what you do, what you value— and yet the Constitution bases representation almost entirely on geography. Interest groups give people a way to get other interests they care about represented in the making of government policy.

Participation. Similarly, the Constitution limits citizens' ability to participate in the decisions that affect them, but psychologists report that people who participate feel more political efficacy— that is, more powerful to control their lives. Interest groups give people lots of participation opportunities that they would not normally have.

Amplifying the power of one. We all know the saying "there is strength in numbers." What one voice may not be able to achieve, a chorus of multitudes may do much more easily. Finding people who share your interests, solidifying them around your cause, and urging them to action you have charted out is a potent political weapon.

Education. Policymakers and citizens alike have limited time to become experts on everything they need to make decisions about. Interest groups provide information on their cause to policymakers by testifying in front of congressional committees or working with bureaucrats, or by communicating directly with their members. Enhancing the quality of information that informs decision making enhances democracy—*as long as people think critically about the information they receive.*

Agenda building. If Congress isn't thinking about a policy issue or defining something as a problem, it isn't going to take any action on it. By publicizing the things they care about to the public and to policymakers, interest groups can get issues onto Congress's radar screen.

Provision of program alternatives and program monitoring. When a group succeeds in getting its issues on the political agenda, it needs to keep pushing to be sure its preferred solutions are considered. Because interest groups are more likely than lawmakers to be

political efficacy: citizens' feelings of effectiveness in political affairs

experts, they can promote policy alternatives that might not otherwise be considered. And if policymakers do take action, interest groups are situated to evaluate the policies and to provide alternatives if the policies don't fulfill their goals.

SO, YOU SAY YOU WANT TO START AN INTEREST GROUP?

Interest groups organize to advance their political interests, but sometimes organizing people to solve a common problem can be difficult. A lot of the things that interest groups try to provide are what social scientists call collective goods. That is, they are benefits that, if the group is successful in obtaining them, can be enjoyed by everybody, whether they were members of the group and contributed to the effort or not.

To take just one example, think about environmental groups that work to improve air quality. If they manage to do so, all people will be breathing healthier air, not just the people who did all the work and spent all the money to make it happen.

THE PROBLEM OF COLLECTIVE ACTION

This can make it hard to convince people to join forces with you—even if they share your interests. Why should they? If they know you are going to do the hard work, the rational thing might be for them to sit back and wait for you to produce. This is called the free rider problem, and everyone who has ever done a group project knows that free riders can be a real drag on the team. The problem of collective action—how to get people to join a group effort if they will enjoy the benefit anyway—has teased many smart political scientists and economists.

MEMBERSHIP HAS ITS BENEFITS.

Look at almost any invitation to join or support a group and almost the first thing you see is the touting of benefits you get if you join. Sometimes it's material benefits—items of real monetary worth, like insurance discounts

collective goods: benefits that, if the group is successful in obtaining them, can be enjoyed by everybody, whether they were members of the group and contributed to the effort or not

free rider problem: the social dilemma faced when people can receive a collective good without having to put in any individual resources to earn it

material benefits: group member benefits that involve items of real monetary worth, like insurance discounts or professional paybacks or professional paybacks. Sometimes they offer **solidary benefits**, appeals to your desire to associate with other people who care about the same things you do. Or they offer **expressive benefits**, the opportunity to do work for something that matters deeply to you.

KEY POINT ❯ All of these are called **selective incentives**—benefits offered to induce people to join up—and depending on the kind of group, they may be necessary to combat the problem of collective action.

WAIT, THERE IS MORE THAN ONE KIND OF GROUP? ❯ Indeed, there is more than one kind of group. We can understand interest groups politics best if we think about the kinds of interests that bind their members together into different kinds of groups.

YES, THERE ARE FOUR. ❯ Some people join together because they have a common interest in what they do, some in who they are, others in what they think will make a better world for everyone, and still others, because of the state, local, or foreign government that they represent.

\# **Economic interest groups** are groups that seek to influence policy for the pocketbook issues of their members, that is, *what they do*. Labor unions, the Chamber of Commerce, professional groups like the American Medical Association, even major corporations whose focus is their own economic well-being fall into this group. Things they seek might include better regulations (or deregulations) of the workplace, lower taxes, or fewer environmental restrictions.

\# **Equal opportunity interest groups** seek to influence government on behalf of people who feel they are not represented on account of

solidary benefits: group member benefits derived from an individual's desire to associate with other people who care about the same things

expressive benefits: the opportunity to do work for something that matters deeply to you

selective incentives: benefits offered to induce people to join groups

economic interest groups: groups that seek to influence policy for the pocketbook issues of their members, that is, for what they do

equal opportunity interest groups: groups that seek to influence government on behalf of people who feel they are not represented on account of who they are

who they are. The people are members of demographic groups—women, African Americans, Latinos, the LGBTQ community, older people, or other groups that people are generally born into—that they feel have needs the government is not addressing, for instance, equal treatment, equal opportunity, or equal protection.

\# **Public interest groups** are groups that try to change policy in accordance with values that *they believe* are good for everyone. Other groups might disagree that the policy goal is good for them, but the clash of visions of the public good are part of what politics is about. Generally, the policies that public interest groups try to achieve are collective goods like clean air and water, world peace, or even more controversial goals like pro-life legislation, pro-choice laws, or the right to smoke marijuana. But because these groups try to achieve collective goods, they are more subject to the free rider problem and tend to struggle with membership issues unless they are able to use selective incentives effectively. The National Rifle Association would consider the absence of gun restrictions to be a policy that benefits everyone (remember—others can disagree), but they have created a culture of very strong solidaristic and expressive benefits that has generated an intense and loyal membership.

\# **Government interest groups** are slightly counterintuitive, but yes, governments hire people to lobby other governments—to get favorable trade policies or foreign aid packages, in the case of other nations, or to get federal assistance for disasters or other resources or to get exemptions from national policies, in the case of the states. Because people who have worked in the U.S. government know their way around and have lots of contacts, former U.S. officials are often hired to lobby the government in which they previously worked.

Officials hear from representatives of all these groups when they engage in policymaking. No wonder some people say making laws is like making sausage!

· ·

public interest groups: groups that try to change policy in accordance with values that *they believe* are good for everyone

government interest groups: groups hired by governments to lobby other governments

7.7 INTEREST GROUP POLITICS

WHAT DO YOU MEAN BY "INTEREST GROUP POLITICS"—ARE LOBBYISTS POLITICIANS?

Interest groups and their lobbyists are not "politicians" in the conventional sense of being elected officials, but they are political actors in that they can bring considerable power to bear on elected officials. What all interest groups want to do is work to influence the things government does that affect them. Sometimes that means persuading the government. Often that means fighting against each other.

KEY POINT

Power is relative among interest groups. On the one hand, interest groups' political clout is simply the strength-in-numbers principle put to work: it is easier to accomplish something with many voices rather than with just one. On the other hand, different interest groups have different resources they can bring to political battle, so the groups are not necessarily fighting on an even playing field. Groups plagued by the free rider problem are at a particular disadvantage. As we will see, those with more resources, as well as those with more voices, have a huge advantage.

LOBBYING: DIRECT AND INDIRECT

When interest group members try to persuade government officials to do something, the activity they engage in is called **lobbying**, something that is usually done by professionals called **lobbyists**. Lobbying can be directed toward any government official, from the president and the bureaucrats of the executive branch, to members of Congress, to the courts. Lobbying that impacts public officials directly is called, well, **direct lobbying**. Sometimes lobbyists will focus their efforts on getting the public to put pressure on elected officials. Not surprisingly, that is called **indirect lobbying**.

WHERE DO PROFESSIONAL LOBBYISTS COME FROM?

Lobbyists often come from the ranks of professional politicians. Since having access to the right people in government is going to be key to interest group efforts, the lobbyists they hire are likely to have been former government

lobbying: efforts by groups to persuade government officials to do something

lobbyists: professionals who are hired to persuade government officials to do something

direct lobbying: lobbying that impacts public officials directly

indirect lobbying: a type of lobbying focused on getting the public to put pressure on elected officials

officials themselves. In a practice called the **revolving door**, people move from the public sector to the private sector and then sometimes back to the public sector again. Interest groups hire former members of Congress and former administrators, but they also hire the family members of officials— anyone they think can give them access. Because conflicts of interest can obviously arise from this practice, some presidents have put limits on members of their administration going to work directly for lobbying firms.

DIRECT LOBBYING OF CONGRESS ❯ Lobbyists can target any part of government to influence its decisions and actions. Since members of Congress make the laws, naturally interest groups who want to influence the laws zero in on them. The members they focus on are the ones who are on the committees and subcommittees that deal with the policies they care about. Food producer groups, agricultural groups, and consumer groups will go straight to members of the Agriculture Committees. Although more than one committee might be relevant to their efforts, wining and dining the Intelligence Committee, for instance, would be a waste of time.

A HOW-TO GUIDE ❯ The techniques of lobbying Congress include the following:

\# **Face-to-face contact.** Creating personal relationships is a powerful way to influence someone. Lobbyists meet with legislators formally and informally, and often they become friends.

\# **Providing testimony and expertise.** Remember those committee and subcommittee hearings we talked about in Chapter 4? The people doing the testifying are the people who know the most about the laws being debated, and who knows better than groups who care the most? Interest groups conduct research and investigate policy options and bring their findings to members of Congress who themselves cannot become experts on every topic on which they pass laws.

\# **Giving money.** A major way to influence someone who regularly has to run an expensive campaign is to give them lots of money. The Federal Election Campaign Act of 1974 limited how much money a group can give to a candidate but allowed for the creation of **political action committees (PACs)** to raise money. A variety of loopholes and court rulings have limited many of the restrictions on political

revolving door: when people move from the public sector to the private sector and then sometimes back to the public sector again

political action committees (PACs): the fundraising arms of interest groups

expenditures by groups and corporations. Even when contributions to candidates are limited, PACs can run *issue advocacy ads*, encouraging voters to support an issue but not a specific candidate (more on those in Chapter 8). The strongest support for interest groups' ability to give money to campaigns came from the 2010 Supreme Court case *Citizens United v. Federal Election Commission*.

\# **Coalition building.** If there is strength in numbers of people, how much more strength is there in numbers of groups? One way for interest groups to increase their power is to form coalitions with other groups. For instance, by banding together, multiple groups involved in health care were able to magnify their influence on the Affordable Care Act leading up to its passage in 2010.

DIRECT LOBBYING OF THE EXECUTIVE ❯ Interest groups are just as interested in influencing the people who implement the laws as they are in influencing those who make them. Some of the same techniques that work with Congress work here: personal contact with

SKIM IT!

7.2: THE SKIMMABLE COURT WATCHER: *CITIZENS UNITED V. FEC* (2010)

Before	The Case	The Ruling	The Impact
Citizens and corporations could give unlimited amounts of money to nonprofits and 527 groups (formed under a campaign law loophole), but those organizations could not advocate directly for a candidate and corporations could not spend money on political ads.	Citizens United (a conservative nonprofit group) argued that political spending is a form of free speech (an argument the Court had previously accepted for individuals) and that restrictions on the political spending of corporations amounted to a violation of the First Amendment.	Vote: 5–4 \# The majority: corporations can engage in independent political spending directly advocating for the election or defeat of a candidate. \# The dissent: unlimited corporate spending can "drown out the voices of real people."	Through Super PACs, corporations can now spend as much as they want to try to influence the outcome of an election. \# A number of wealthy individuals and families as well as corporations have formed groups whose members are undisclosed but that can spend as much money as they want in an effort to get the election result they prefer.

the president, the administrative staff, and the bureaucrats who enforce the laws, and campaign contributions to the president.

IRON TRIANGLES— THE PUBLIC GETS SHUT OUT OF THE POLICYMAKING PROCESS. One of the focal points for lobbyists is the regulatory boards that write the rules that govern the industries or professions they represent. Often, lobbyists, bureaucrats, and members of Congress end up working together so closely on laws affecting a particular sector that they come to identify with each other's interests. Instead of laws being made for the public good, we get laws made for the good of those who are directly affected by the laws. When, for instance, dietary guidelines protect the food industry at the expense of public health, the public good is not being served. We call these close policymaking relationships among legislators, regulators, and the groups being regulated **iron triangles** (see Chapter 5): "triangles" for obvious reasons and "iron" because they are not easily permeated by representatives of the public (who are almost always public interest groups and who suffer from all the problems of free ridership).

DIRECT LOBBYING OF THE COURTS We don't usually think of the courts as institutions that can be lobbied because we are socialized to think of them as above politics. But, as we saw in Chapter 6, they are very political in multiple ways.

State judges are often elected and willing to take campaign contributions— one of the very reasons critics argue that judicial elections are corrupt. In addition, even the Supreme Court can be lobbied by the *amicus curiae* briefs that groups with an interest in a case can write. And, although we don't always think of it this way, the very act of challenging a law in court is a way of lobbying the court to change the law. Major changes in U.S. policy have been created by lobbying the courts: desegregation, reproductive rights, and marriage equality come to mind. Often an interest group whose goal is too divisive or controversial for Congress to be able to give it what it wants will target the courts in the hope of getting a ruling from those less dependent on public opinion than elected officials.

. . . .

iron triangles: close policymaking relationships among legislators, regulators, and the groups being regulated that tend to exclude the public

INDIRECT LOBBYING

> Direct lobbying involves interest group–to–government contact. Sometimes groups find it more effective to keep their fingerprints off the lobbying effort by staying concealed behind an ostensible social movement. In those cases, they try to persuade the public (that's us!) to put pressure on our representatives. The theory is that if the people we elect think we won't reelect them if we don't get what we want, they'll give in to us even if they might not have yielded to a professional lobbyist.

FOR REAL

> Popular movements can arise spontaneously from a group that finds itself with a common cause—the Tea Party after the passage of the Affordable Care Act, for instance, or Black Lives Matter in the wake of continued unpunished shootings of African Americans by the police. Those groups, especially the ones rising from social protest movements, are genuinely grassroots lobbying efforts. Elected officials see the emotion and passion in a crowd and move to "get ahead of the parade," so to speak. After the #MeToo movement began to catch fire in 2016, legislators in the Democratic Party forced Senator Al Franken of Minnesota to resign as a way to preemptively respond to anticipated constituency demands.

FOR FAKE

> At other times, what looks like a spontaneous, grassroots uprising is really an orchestrated effort by an established interest group dressed up to look like a genuine popular movement. We call this more cynical use of the public astroturf lobbying, the name indicating that what appears to be coming from the grassroots is fake. The name notwithstanding, these efforts are not always completely fake—there may be genuine sentiment in the public that is simply not organized.

> Astroturf lobbying is not new, but it is made infinitely easier by Supreme Court rulings that say that spending money by individuals, groups, or corporations is a form of protected free speech. This allows a flood of issue advocacy ads on traditional and social media. In fact, the spread of social media information and advertising has made it much easier to disguise who is really behind a message. The revelation that Russian trolls disguised themselves as Americans to convince voters to reject Hillary Clinton and support

- -

grassroots lobbying: indirect lobbying efforts that spring from widespread public concern

astroturf lobbying: indirect lobbying efforts that manipulate or create public sentiment, "astroturf" being artificial grassroots

Bernie Sanders and Donald Trump in 2016 shows that even a foreign government can try to obtain policy outcomes they want by pressuring voters to choose certain leaders.

7.8   WAS MADISON RIGHT TO WORRY?

BACK WHERE WE STARTED

So these are the factions—these political parties and interest groups—that James Madison was worried about. He feared that, having a particular interest different from the public interest, they would corrupt or damage the government they were petitioning for change.

Madison had the now-quaint-seeming idea that a large republic would save us from the effects of factions by making it hard for groups to organize. Certainly technological advances he could not have foreseen mean that groups can organize around the world in an instant. And the multiplicity of groups that he thought would cancel each other out just seems to magnify the noise in the system.

What we have learned is that Madison's fears are not unwarranted, but they do oversimplify the roles these groups play.

THE UPSHOT

Political parties and interest groups do a lot to enhance and strengthen democracy. Since Madison was not a huge fan of pure democracy (remember, he preferred republics), perhaps that benefit would not have offset what he thought were the dangers. That groups organize and magnify their voices seems consistent with democracy to us, if not to him.

But to see these groups simply as enhanced majority rule is to miss the ways in which they might damage the system the founders so carefully checked and balanced. For instance, parties and interest groups don't just collect the numbers of people who agree on an issue and carry that view into government policy. They also magnify the power of those who feel intensely—the party base, for instance, or those interest groups who vote consistently on only one issue—gun rights or immigration, let's say. Should people who feel more intensely have more political power than those who do not?

And what about the impact of money? Groups that have corporate backers or deep pockets of their own have way more power than groups, especially some public interest groups, that may have lots of members but many free riders too. Should money carry extra weight in the democratic process?

Since Madison was concerned about maintaining both political stability and individual freedom from a repressive government, would he have seen these modern twists as pluses or minuses? How would you assess the threat posed by factions in modern American government?

Big Think

→ Do you think it is worthwhile to cast a third-party vote in the United States? Why or why not?

→ How would a multiparty structure change American politics, and how would American politics have to change to accommodate multiple parties?

→ On balance, do interest groups enhance democracy or damage it?

→ How would *you* assess the threat posed by factions in modern American government?

Key Terms

CONCEPTS

accountability (p. 216)

astroturf lobbying (p. 242)

caucuses (p. 219)

collective goods (p. 235)

critical election (p. 223)

direct lobbying (p. 238)

electioneering (p. 215)

expressive benefits (p. 236)

free rider problem (p. 235)

governing (p. 215)

grassroots lobbying (p. 242)

hyperpartisanship (p. 218)

indirect lobbying (p. 238)

iron triangles (p. 241)

lobbying (p. 238)

material benefits (p. 235)

partisan sorting (p. 218)

partisanship (p. 216)

party era (p. 223)

party-in-government (p. 220)

party machines (p. 219)

party organizations (p. 220)

party platform (p. 217)

political efficacy (p. 234)

primaries (p. 219)

realignment (p. 223)

responsible party model (p. 217)

revolving door (p. 239)

selective incentives (p. 236)

single member, first past the post (p. 221)

solidary benefits (p. 236)

KEY INDIVIDUALS AND GROUPS

#8 PUBLIC OPINION, CAMPAIGNS, AND ELECTIONS

In this chapter:

8.1 Introduction to PUBLIC OPINION, CAMPAIGNS, AND ELECTIONS

WHO CARES WHAT THE PUBLIC THINKS? → In a democracy, what the public thinks matters. You can debate (and people do) just how much **public opinion** *does* matter or how much it *should* matter, but if it doesn't matter at all, you don't have a democracy. The late, great political scientist V. O. Key, Jr., once said, "Unless mass views have some place in the shaping of policy, all talk about democracy is nonsense." Nonsense or democracy—that's how important public opinion is.

There are two main ways of finding out what the public thinks:

→ We can measure public opinion through the science and technology of **polling** and the analysis of social media data.

→ We also have a more old-fashioned way—asking people to go to the **polls** in person and vote in an **election**.

THREE WAYS POLLING IS DIFFERENT FROM "GOING TO THE POLLS" Note that the word *poll* appears in both those ways of measuring public opinion. *Poll* actually just means head—conducting a poll is taking a head count and going to the polls is also taking a head count—it's just the method of sampling, timing, and import that differ.

SAMPLING → In a public opinion poll, as we will see, we try to *sample* respondents to get a group as representative of the voting public as we can. In elections, we let the voters self-select—those who cast a ballot are people who are legally qualified, who are not prevented by some legal barrier, and who feel motivated to weigh in. That is, in polling, the sample is chosen by pollsters to look like the pool of citizens, and in voting the sample is chosen by voters themselves, within certain constraints. The first, polling, is a scientifically estimated model of the second, voting.

TIMING → Of course, the timing of polls and elections also differ. Polls can be conducted whenever some educational institution, marketing company, or media outlet has the time, money, and inclination to conduct it. Elections are conducted when local, state, and federal laws and constitutions say so.

IMPORT → Oh, and one final difference. Polls can give us information about what the public wants, motivate candidates to take particular stands, and inform our officials of what their employers (that's us) think is important. But polls are not binding on anyone—they can be paid attention to or ignored. Elections choose governments. And no one can ignore that.

IN A NUTSHELL

Public opinion polling and elections are essentially two ways of doing the same thing—finding out what the public thinks. In the first case, the results can be used for a variety of purposes. In the second case, public opinion—in the snapshot taken by an election—determines who will govern us and how.

By the time you finish reading this chapter, you will understand

WHERE WE GO IN THIS CHAPTER

→ The quality of public opinion

→ Ways we measure public opinion through polling

→ How opinions are formed and how we pass them from generation to generation to keep regimes stable

→ The act of voting

→ Presidential elections in the United States

→ How the Electoral College works

8.2 THE QUALITY OF PUBLIC OPINION

HOW SMART IS PUBLIC OPINION?

Public opinion is not a mysterious thing—it is the collected opinions of individuals on a given topic. The quality of that opinion—whether it reflects informed, well-thought-out ideas and preferences or ill-conceived ignorance—is only as good as the citizenry who answer the polls.

public opinion: the collective attitudes and beliefs of individuals on one or more issues

polling: the use of scientific methods and technology to measure public opinion

polls: the instrument though which public opinion is measured, or the place where one goes to cast a vote

election: the formal process of voting candidates into office

IN AN IDEAL WORLD . . .

> In Chapter 1, we talked about different visions of citizenship—one that focuses on the public good and one that focuses on the individual citizen's good. In the classic view of democratic theory, citizens are

Well informed about government, rules, and political actors

Tolerant of ideas other than their own

Willing to compromise to further the collective interest

Happy to participate at a variety of levels and to engage in civic activities

That's the theory, anyway.

AND IN THE WORLD THAT ACTUALLY EXISTS . . .

> In reality, Americans don't measure up well to the ideal. Most are not very well informed, as indicated by multiple public opinion polls that show they are not sure how the government works or whom to hold accountable for its actions. Americans are tolerant in theory but less so in practice. They uphold the right of hypothetical groups to speak their minds, but when actual unpopular groups speak out, tolerance drops. Increasingly, some groups see compromise as a fundamental betrayal of values rather than as the grease that keeps the wheels of democratic governance turning. National, presidential elections elicit very low voter turnout rates. Midterm, state, and local races are even worse.

WHOSE VIEWS SHOULD COUNT?

> If citizen engagement is so far from the democratic ideal, is it really such a good idea to have public opinion reflected in public policy? Occasionally, politicians have suggested that participation should be restricted to those who are informed and engaged. But one of the democratic ideals is *tolerance*, and those who are committed to democracy need to accept that the people who participate are not necessarily the ones they would prefer to participate. That is, democracy means letting everyone be heard—the voters whose preparation and intelligence you approve of and those who seem ignorant and ill informed.

WHO ARE YOU CALLING IGNORANT?

> Besides, being an ideal democratic citizen is a full-time job, and most of us already have a job, or go to school, or raise our kids, or maybe all three. Choosing not to be informed about politics may actually make sense—that is, those folks may be reflecting **rational ignorance**. If the payoff from

- -

rational ignorance: the state of not engaging in politics because the payoff seems remote or insignificant

participating feels remote, or the difference it makes feels insignificant, then *not* investing a lot of time and effort in politics might make sense.

But where does that leave democracy?

SHORTCUTS THAT MAY SAVE THE COUNTRY FROM AN ILL-INFORMED POPULACE

It's not a perfect solution, but social scientists have found that Americans use political cues and shortcuts to help offset the fact that they fall so far short of the ideal:

- **WE PROBABLY AREN'T AS IGNORANT AS WE SOUND.**

- **AND IF WE ARE, WE ARE LIKELY TO FIND SOMEONE TO GIVE US A CLUE.**

\# **Online processing.** Online processing has nothing to do with the Internet, at least not directly. It refers to the phenomenon of having ended a busy day with a head full of opinions picked up on the fly with no very clear idea of how one arrived at them.

That's not to say those opinions are irrational—they may have made a lot of sense as one listened to the car radio, caught a news clip at the doctor's office, and finished the day zipping through social media feeds. But many people have a hard time tracing them back to their source. Ask them why they think something, and they sound like that person late-night comedians like to discover who doesn't know where the West Coast is located. But in fact people often have pretty good reasons for holding their views. They just processed them too quickly for the source to have sunk into their memory banks.

\# **The two-step flow of information.** If online processing is not about the Internet, the two-step flow of information is not a country dance. Rather, it is the psychological process by which opinion followers (the vast majority of citizens) look to opinion leaders (people who are well informed and involved in civic activity) for cues on how to vote. Because opinion followers tend to pick out opinion leaders who share their values, background, and interests, they often end up making the same decision they would have made if they had done the careful research to decide on their own.

online processing: the experience of picking up various decision-making cues throughout the day that help you arrive at a rational conclusion even though you might not be able to re-create the process of getting there

two-step flow of information: a psychological process by which opinion followers look to opinion leaders for cues on how to vote

opinion followers: the vast majority of citizens who take their cues about what to think from opinion leaders

opinion leaders: the subset of the population who are well informed about politics and involved in civic activity

Not to put too much pressure on you, but many of us who get some higher education will become opinion leaders ourselves, providing cues and guidance to family members, friends, and members of groups we belong to about what to think about politics. So up your game!

\#   **Political parties and interest groups.** And, of course, we have already seen that many people cut short the steps to political decision making by following the lead of a party or group (perhaps a religious institution or a group that shares a particular interest of ours). This is akin to the two-step flow except that the opinion leader is a group, not an individual, and it allows us to engage in more sheep-like behavior because the party or group has a position on most issues.

A WORD OF WARNING! THESE SHORTCUTS ARE NOT FOOLPROOF. DON'T BE A FOOL!

> All of these mechanisms enable a citizenry who spend less time becoming informed (perhaps for good reason) to make decisions that seem informed and are consistent with their interests. A warning, however. There is no guarantee that these shortcuts will lead to decision making that is in fact informed and smart. The best way to ensure our interests are represented is by doing the hard work needed to be part of the educated electorate. Congratulations! Taking this course is a key piece of that work!

8.3 HOW DO WE KNOW WHAT AMERICANS THINK?

DO THOSE POLLSTERS USE A CRYSTAL BALL, OR WHAT?

> When we talk about public opinion, we are not just making guesses about what Americans think. Crystal balls would be nice, but they don't work as well as we would like. There is nothing magical about reading the public's mind. The science of public opinion polling has come a long way since the days when magazines would ask readers to mail in a card with their vote preference and make predictions based on the result. We now know that is a really bad way to measure public opinion.

MAJOR ELEMENTS IN THE SCIENCE OF POLLING

> Here is what else we know:

\#   Statisticians have determined that a **random sample** of only 1,000 to 2,000 people can be very representative of the more than 300 million residents of the United States.

random sample: samples chosen in such a way that any member of the population being polled has an equal chance of being selected

\#   A random sample means that everyone has an equal chance of being chosen and that no one group is over-represented, so that the results can be generalized to the whole. Otherwise, we say that a poll suffers from **sample bias** (giving disproportionate weight to one part of the population).

\#   One of the toughest parts of polling these days is getting people to respond. Since most people screen their calls or refuse to talk to strangers about their views, polls can also suffer from **nonresponse bias**. The job of the polling scientist is to figure out what groups are least likely to respond and to use statistical **weighting** of the results to compensate. Polling is an imprecise science, and even the experts can get it wrong.

\#   No poll will be perfect (in fact, as we will see, even elections can yield different results depending on whether you measure the popular or Electoral College vote). Consequently, polls are reported along with their **sampling error**, the +/− number you see after a percentage. If a poll reports that 43 percent of the people approve of the president, +/− 3, that means the margin of error is a total of six points. The true result could be as high as 46 percent or as low as 40 percent (a six-point spread).

\#   **Likely voter polls** are particularly worrisome to pollsters because they have to figure out who is actually going to vote. Until they get close to an election, pollsters only ask if their respondents are registered to vote. But to predict how an actual election is going to turn out, you need to know who is going to vote. Asking doesn't help, as often people mean to vote and don't, or they flat out lie about their intentions.

   Pollsters use **likely voter screens** to try to weed out the nonvoters—asking them if they voted in the last election, if they know where their

- -

sample bias: the effect of having a sample that does not represent all segments of the population

nonresponse bias: a skewing of data that occurs when there is a difference in opinion between those who choose to participate and those who do not

weighting: adjustments to surveys during analysis so that selected demographic groups reflect their values in the population, usually as measured by the census

sampling error: a number that indicates within what range the results of a poll are accurate

likely voter polls: polls of respondents who pollsters have determined are likely to vote by asking questions about prior voting behavior

likely voter screens: the questions that different pollsters use to decide how likely they think a respondent is to vote

polling place is, and a variety of other questions designed to evaluate the probability that the respondent will go to the polls. Because different polling operations use different screens, their results can vary dramatically. And they generally miss first time voters who are in fact *unlikely* voters until they actually vote.

\# In fact, because their samples and thus their margins of error are different, all polls vary at least a little. The best way to interpret them is by averaging their results together, as **polling aggregators** do, rather than following a single pollster. That also helps to eliminate **house effects**—a term that describes the way a particular pollster's results tend to favor Democrats or Republicans—perhaps because of the way they gather their sample, the way they word their questions, or the time of day they do their polling. Polls can reflect differences in all those things.

\# Polling hit its heyday when enough Americans owned telephones to make **random digit dialing** a good way to draw a random sample. Before people could screen their calls, they tended to answer the phone when it rang, and pollsters had a good chance of getting the person who answered to respond to polling questions.

Caller ID, cell phones, and voice mail have made telephone polling a challenge. People don't answer calls from unfamiliar numbers, Millennials and post-Millennials tend not to have landlines, and many people are suspicious of giving out information over the phone. Consequently, some pollsters increasingly rely on Internet polls using randomly selected samples of people who have enrolled and provided demographic data so that the data bank can produce random samples who will actually respond.

ARE ALL POLLS THE SAME?

Public opinion polling can take different forms. Here are the ones you are most likely to encounter:

\# National polls that measure where a majority of Americans stand on particular issues are released periodically by major media organizations that can afford the expense of assembling and fielding a large poll. They can be on any issue or official.

polling aggregators: analysts who combine polls by averaging or other techniques in order to minimize sampling error and make the polls more accurate

house effects: the way a particular pollster's results tend to favor Democrats or Republicans

random digit dialing: the process of choosing respondents for a poll by letting a computer pick phone numbers without bias

\# **Tracking polls** are polls that keep track of data over time to detect changes in support for people or issues. The Gallup organization used to track presidential approval every day with a rolling three-day average (that means every day they would add new responses to the sample and drop off the oldest, which would be three days old).

Tracking polls can be particularly helpful to people running for office so that they can see how they are doing compared with their opponents. Many candidates, especially at the presidential and senatorial levels, commission their own polls. As Election Day nears, media organizations start releasing their polls more frequently, although few do it daily. As with all polls, it's best to watch the polling averages, not a single poll.

\# **Exit polls** are polls taken as people leave their polling places immediately after voting (which kind of makes them poll polls). Exit polls are paid for by major media outlets that want to use the data to help them predict winners and call elections before all the returns are in. Exit polls can be riddled with errors, however. Relatively few people are willing to respond, and the raw data are not useful until they have been weighted by information drawn from actual voting.

Nonetheless, the raw data are often leaked early, creating inaccurate expectations of who might win. In 2000, faulty exit polls in Florida led TV networks to call the election for Democrat Al Gore, then to retract that call and call the election for George W. Bush. In fact the election was always too close to call. The premature call for Bush made him the presumptive winner. Gore's efforts to contest the

DIG DEEPER

Gallup has a fun interactive site that allows you to compare the approval trends of up to four presidents at a time going back to Harry Truman.

Make your voice heard. Sign up for an online polling panel at Civiqs and YouGov.

Go to **edge.sagepub.com/dig-deeper**

tracking polls: polls that keep track of data over time to detect changes in support for people or issues

exit polls: polls that are taken as people leave their polling places immediately after voting

race became an uphill battle, even though he won the popular vote nationwide and by some counts would have won Florida's electoral votes as well.

\# **Fake polls** also abound. TV polls that ask you to text a response to a question or Internet polls that want you to click on a preference are not really measuring anything useful because they have serious sampling problems. They can only tell you what the group of TV viewers or people visiting a site who also have the energy to bother to respond think. It is a way for media figures to engage their audience and to encourage them to think that many people agree with them, but they are not real polls and tell us nothing about the real world.

THE UPSHOT

Polls in general are quite good if they are conducted scientifically, but any individual poll can suffer from sampling error. The best thing to do to find out where the public really stands on an issue or candidate is to find a site that aggregates the polls.

8.4 HOW DO WE FORM OUR OPINIONS?

WHERE DO OUR OPINIONS COME FROM?

> The process of learning civic values and ethics is called **political socialization**—a transfer of political attitudes, narratives, and beliefs from generation to generation. Political socialization is essential for any government because it helps create a stable, loyal citizenry who buy into the foundational values of the system. In other words, it creates a basis of political legitimacy among people who start accepting the authority of the government from a very young age.

POLITICAL SOCIALIZATION CAN HELP BRING US TOGETHER AROUND COMMON VALUES.

> The agents of socialization are families, schools, religious institutions, peer groups, and the media. As we saw in Chapter 1, many of our relationships and all of the information we consume are increasingly *mediated* (coming through a social media channel), so the media piece of socialization becomes more important than ever.

fake polls: polls that are conducted to sway or manipulate public opinion, not to measure it

political socialization: the process of picking up values and commitments to a regime through various social agents like family, schools, religious institutions, peer groups, and the media

On the one hand, the process of socialization generally instills in us an affection for and allegiance to the political system (although if we are an out group that has been excluded from the benefits of the system, our trust in it may be lower than those whom the rules have favored). We call that shared loyalty to our country and its institutions **patriotism**.

BUT SOME AGENTS SOCIALIZE US TO BREAK INTO SEPARATE GROUPS.

The agents of socialization are personal—they are our families, our schools in our neighborhoods, our houses of worship, our friends. More and more, the information we consume via the media reinforces the views we learn from these personal sources because we choose our media outlets to fit our comfort zone. These sources of socialization commit us to a set of interests and values that we share with other citizens (in terms of allegiance to the system and to the political culture), but they also divide us according to the *ideologies* we talked about in Chapter 1.

Influencing our particular political views, the opinions we express, and the votes we cast are party, issues, and the candidates themselves.

LIKE, PARTY!

The biggest influence on the opinions we hold and the votes we cast is the political party with which we identify. We discussed party identifiers in Chapter 7—people who say they identify with or lean toward one party or the other. Not only is **party identification** (or party ID) the major shaper of our opinions, but if the party shifts to policy positions we did not previously favor, many people are more inclined to shift with the party than to leave it. An example is how quickly Republicans shifted to favor Donald Trump's nontraditional (from the Republican point of view) positions on trade, immigration, and the FBI. Some people did leave the party because of Trump, but the majority stayed.

But party ID is not assigned randomly. It correlates highly with characteristics like race, gender, education, where you live, and the generation to which you belong.

WHAT DO THE DATA TELL US?

The data on party ID change frequently—what you read today may change in weeks or months—but if we step back, we can discern certain trends over time. Consider the following figure:

patriotism: shared loyalty to our country and its institutions

party identification: the tendency of members of the public to associate themselves with a particular party because they share its values, culture, policy preferences, or social network

FIGURE IT!

8.1: DEMOGRAPHIC VARIATIONS IN PARTY IDENTIFICATIONS

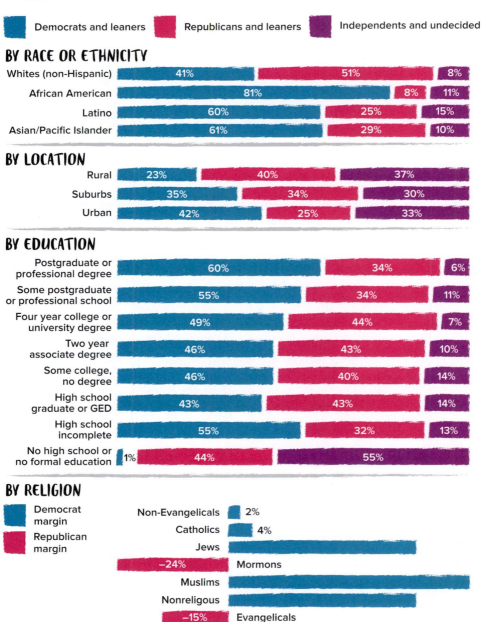

■ Democrats and leaners   ■ Republicans and leaners   ■ Independents and undecided

BY RACE OR ETHNICITY

	Democrats	Republicans	Independents
Whites (non-Hispanic)	41%	51%	8%
African American	81%	8%	11%
Latino	60%	25%	15%
Asian/Pacific Islander	61%	29%	10%

BY LOCATION

	Democrats	Republicans	Independents
Rural	23%	40%	37%
Suburbs	35%	34%	30%
Urban	42%	25%	33%

BY EDUCATION

	Democrats	Republicans	Independents
Postgraduate or professional degree	60%	34%	6%
Some postgraduate or professional school	55%	34%	11%
Four year college or university degree	49%	44%	7%
Two year associate degree	46%	43%	10%
Some college, no degree	46%	40%	14%
High school graduate or GED	43%	43%	14%
High school incomplete	55%	32%	13%
No high school or no formal education	1%	44%	55%

BY RELIGION

■ Democrat margin
■ Republican margin

Non-Evangelicals	2%
Catholics	4%
Jews	
Mormons	−24%
Muslims	
Nonreligous	
Evangelicals	−15%

Sources: Data for race and ethnicity, religion, education, and location are from Pew Research Center polls from January and April 2016, and January, February, and April 2017 (*N* = 8,523). Data for gender are from CBS News/*New York Times* surveys, 1977–2017. Created by author.

From the data in the figure, this is what we know:

Race and ethnicity. Over time the Republican Party has become whiter. About half of white voters currently identify themselves as Republicans and only 43 percent identify as Democrats. But African Americans are far more likely to be Democrats (ten Democrats for every one Republican), as are Latinos and Asian Americans (both by a two-to-one margin).

Gender. Since the 1960s, there has been a discernable gender gap in American politics: women are more likely to be Democrats than are men, who are more likely to be Republicans. That is more true for Millennials than for previous generations by a large margin, and, from the limited data we have so far, it looks to be true for post-Millennials as well.

Religion. White, evangelical Protestants are much more likely to be Republicans. For white mainline Protestants, the party split is much closer, and black Christians are overwhelmingly Democratic. Catholics split along ethnic lines: white Catholics are very slightly likely to be Republicans; Hispanic Catholics are much more likely to identify as Democrats. Democrats have a huge advantage among Jews, as Republicans do among Mormons. The religiously unaffiliated are predominantly Democrats.

Education. Education has long had a predictable effect on political attitudes. The more education one has, the more one knows about politics, the more tolerant of other views one is, and the more likely one is to participate. But recently, education has begun to form a significant division between the parties, with more educated voters moving toward the Democrats.

Where you live. If you think about the demographic profile of the two parties that is emerging, it won't surprise you to know that Democrats tend to cluster in urban and, increasingly, suburban areas and Republicans tend to live in outer suburban and rural areas. This is reflected in the commonly seen electoral map that is colored intensely blue in small, densely populated dots, with red swaths across vast less-inhabited areas of the country.

Generation. Get ready for this. Just as the demographic trends we have seen so far foreshadow geographic partisan divisions, they also

· ·

gender gap: the tendency of men and women to differ in their political views on some issues

foretell differences among the generations. All the trends we have discussed become increasingly strong as the voter pool gets younger. We have been watching generational movements throughout this book in our Generation Gap boxes, and they should give you a pretty good idea of just how your birth year influences your political views.

TRENDS IN PARTY ID

What the data tell us overall is that Americans are sharply divided but that the Democrats are what journalist and data analyst Ronald Brownstein calls the *coalition of the ascendant*—that is, of the racial and ethnic groups that are getting bigger, quickly. Republicans are a smaller group that is aging out, what Brownstein calls the *coalition of restoration*—the group composed of older, blue-collar, evangelical, rural whites who are least equipped to ride out the social and economic upheavals of the future and who want to "restore" the social order of the last century, in which they knew the rules and had a sense of belonging. The fact that the past was also a place where women and minorities had fewer rights and opportunities than they do today only heightens the division between the two coalitions.

There is nothing written in stone about these trends, however: Democrats could easily take their voters for granted (as some accuse them of doing already) and stop proposing policies in line with their interests and needs, or Republicans could reach out to them as many members of the party have suggested. But Brownstein's research suggests that without a change in the current trends, the gulf between the parties will only widen when the post-Millennials start to come of age in the next couple of years.

DIG DEEPER

Read Ronald Brownstein's essay here.

Go to **edge.sagepub.com/ dig-deeper**

Clearly, party ID is a powerful influence on us. Even so-called independent voters usually lean one way or the other if pushed by an interviewer. People identify with a party originally because it takes policy positions that they agree with, but eventually the party becomes a kind of information shorthand for them. If voters trust the party, and it takes a particular position, they generally assume that position is what works for them, too—a variation of the two-step flow of information we talked about earlier. Especially now that the parties are becoming demographically distinct, chances are that when voters see a party be responsive to people who are similar to them, they assume their needs will be met as well. Consequently, many of us use party ID as a way of making up our minds on what we think about an issue or on how to vote.

US VS. THEM

Party is a stand-in for many other influences. As Americans become more polarized, voters are less likely to leave the comfort zone of their party to vote with the other side. In fact, some political scientists have discovered that, in times of extreme polarization, the dislike of the other party is as much a motivation for our views as is affection for the party with which we identify.

IF PARTY IS SO IMPORTANT IN SHAPING OPINIONS, DO ISSUES EVEN MATTER?

Because Americans have so thoroughly sorted themselves into parties that they agree with ideologically and that fit the same demographic profile, that doesn't leave a lot of room for issues to have a role of their own in shaping opinions. Still, there are some voters for whom a particular issue can be a deal breaker. So-called **single-issue voters** will not consider voting for a candidate who doesn't share their views on an issue that they consider to be fundamental, regardless of party. For instance, those who refuse to entertain any regulation of the right to own guns will use that as a litmus test—regardless of party, they will reject any candidate whom they see as weak on their central issue. For other voters, reproductive rights (pro and con) are the deal breaker. A Democratic candidate running in a conservative part of the country will probably have to have a pro-gun record or risk losing even the votes of Democrats, and a Republican running in a more liberal part of the nation will likely take a pro-choice position (or say that he or she is personally against abortion but doesn't believe that the state should be involved in the decision) or risk losing moderate Republican voters.

HOW ABOUT THE CANDIDATES THEMSELVES?

And then there is the image and personality of the candidates themselves. People are certainly guided by party as they shape their opinions of whom to vote for, but even given party preferences, candidate image can make a big difference.

Probably no one, including Donald Trump, thought that he would win the Republican nomination for president in 2016. But despite unorthodox, norm-breaking behavior and multiple scandals, Trump's bow-before-no-one, larger-than-life persona convinced many Americans that he was the person to represent them and make their lives better. His message of returning America to a time when it had been better for his voters caused them to overlook behaviors and gaffes that would have sunk another candidate. Similarly, the hard shell Hillary Clinton had developed to deflect political attacks over the years caused even some Democrats to find her unlikable enough that they defected and voted for Trump, for a third party, or for no one at all.

single-issue voters: voters who make electoral choices based on a particular issue

THE UPSHOT | Party cues are hugely important in shaping our political opinions, but whether we choose to act on them can depend on a particular candidate's ability to motivate us to vote.

8.5   THE ULTIMATE POLL—VOTING IN U.S. ELECTIONS

THE UNITED STATES DOES A BAD JOB OF BEING THE WORLD'S GREATEST DEMOCRACY.

Voting is a precious right in a democracy—it is the ultimate way in which citizens can participate in a poll that counts. And many Americans believe that we live in the greatest democracy in history. So, naturally, all Americans take advantage of this right. Right?

Actually, wrong. The United States has one of the lowest voter participation rates among industrialized democratic nations. In 2016, the last presidential election, only 55.7 percent of eligible voters cast a vote, and those elections tend to get higher **voter turnout** than elections held in the off years.

WHY DON'T ALL THE PEOPLE VOTE?

People don't vote for a variety of reasons—ranging from disinterest to being prevented by legal barriers. Efforts to legally limit who can vote are a way of **regulating the electorate**, and they are often politically motivated—one party is trying to prevent members of another party from voting. Efforts to get more people to vote are met with arguments that, given the quality of public opinion, maybe we don't want to make it too easy to vote. It's a complicated issue with a complicated history. Let's break it down.

WHAT IF ONLY THE SMARTEST, MOST INFORMED PEOPLE WERE ALLOWED VOTE?

If Americans were only interested in the votes of ideal democratic citizens, we would be letting precious few people vote and we would not really be interested in a democracy. In fact, we would be supporting a form of elite rule that is at odds with what democracy is all about. If the electorate is regulated so that only more advantaged and educated voters who can afford the resources to learn about the issues and the time to cast an informed vote go to the polls, then the vote won't represent what the majority of Americans want. It would be skewed to the interests of those higher on the socioeconomic scale, not everyday Americans.

voter turnout: the percentage of the eligible population who turn out to vote in an election

regulating the electorate: the practice of trying to limit the number of eligible voters by law or custom in order to maximize one's party's fortunes

8.2: VOTER TURNOUT IN THE UNITED STATES AND OTHER DEVELOPED DEMOCRACIES

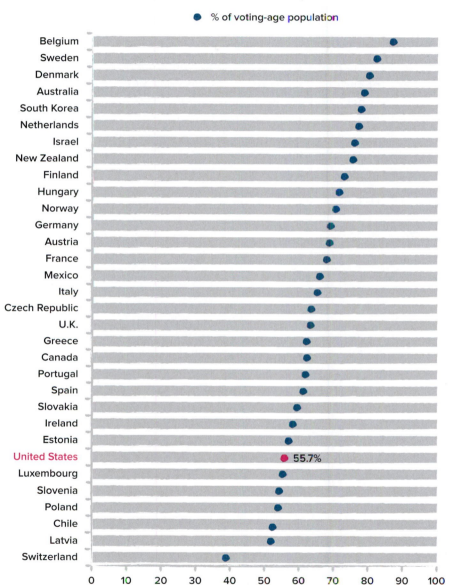

● % of voting-age population

Belgium	
Sweden	
Denmark	
Australia	
South Korea	
Netherlands	
Israel	
New Zealand	
Finland	
Hungary	
Norway	
Germany	
Austria	
France	
Mexico	
Italy	
Czech Republic	
U.K.	
Greece	
Canada	
Portugal	
Spain	
Slovakia	
Ireland	
Estonia	
United States	55.7%
Luxembourg	
Slovenia	
Poland	
Chile	
Latvia	
Switzerland	

0 10 20 30 40 50 60 70 80 90 100

Source: From Drew DeSilver, "U.S. Trails Most Developed Countries in Voter Turnout," Pew Research Center, May 21, 2018, http://www.pewresearch.org/fact-tank/2017/05/15/u-s-voter-turnout-trails-most-developed-countries/.

THE FOUNDERS WEIGH IN . . .

It's true that the founders were leery of direct democracy, which is why, for instance, the Electoral College was created (as we will see shortly). But those elite signers of the Constitution wanted all the citizens (at the time, white males) to vote for those positions that were open to popular election. Since their day, the category of legal voter has been expanded by constitutional amendment to include African Americans, women, and eighteen-year-olds.

In Chapter 3, we saw the fight of different groups to be included in the class of citizens who were entitled to vote. We saw the battle for the constitutional amendments that opened the door to excluded groups, and we saw that Congress and the Supreme Court repeatedly struck down efforts by white southerners to regulate who could vote through barriers like literacy tests and poll taxes.

SO, IT'S EASY FOR EVERYONE TO VOTE NOW, RIGHT?

Unfortunately, it's still not easy for everyone to vote. Efforts at regulating the electorate are still alive and well. If we wanted everyone to vote, we would make it as easy as possible—allowing same-day voter registration, allowing voting by mail, encouraging early voting, and extending the voting period or at least making Election Day a weekend or a national holiday so that people don't have to juggle working and voting. There are lots of ways we could regulate the electorate to make it *easier* for people to vote and that would no doubt raise voter participation.

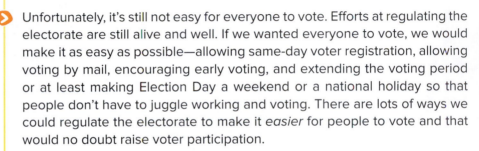

But a political issue lies behind the debate over how easy the voting process should be. The voters who tend to vote reliably are older, whiter, wealthier, and more educated Americans. In fact, although the voting population includes many Democrats, it really fits the profile of the Republican Party. Younger voters, newer voters, people of color, single moms, and people lower on the socioeconomic scale are less likely to vote, and if they do, they are more likely to vote for Democrats.

YOU SEE THE POLITICAL PROBLEM?

The stumbling block to making voting easier should be obvious here—it's a political one. Both Republicans and Democrats think that making it easier for people to vote will bring in more of the less reliably voting public who are more likely to cast their votes for Democrats. So Republicans want to make voting more difficult, and Democrats want to make it easier.

Of course, those are not the terms in which they couch the debate. Republicans say they are worried about voter fraud—specifically, people who are not legal voters casting votes—so they want to tighten regulations. This, even though no evidence of significant voter fraud has been found, despite presidential commissions designed to look for it. They do this in places where they control the state governments (the Constitution leaves it to the states to determine the time and manner of elections) by, for instance, requiring fewer polling places in areas where Democrats are likely to live (college campuses, low-income areas), a government-issued photo ID, perhaps matching one's address to one's voting precinct, requiring registration well before Election Day, and limiting voting hours. Democrats protest all these measures, claiming that they limit the ability of young people (whose driver's licenses may be issued in their home states but who want to vote where they go to college), poor people (who don't own cars and have less need for a government-issued ID), people who cannot afford to take time off work to wait for hours in line, and so on.

THE POLITICAL STAKES IN REGULATING THE ELECTORATE

In other words, the battle over regulating the electorate is really a political battle about which party should have the advantage. Democrats (and some Republicans) say that if Republicans want to win, they should reach out to the groups who tend to vote against them. At least recently—especially since the midterm elections in 2010 that gave Republicans control of many state governments and a Supreme Court ruling that reduced judicial scrutiny of voting practices in the Deep South—Republicans have found it easier simply to regulate those folks out of the electorate.

SO, IF AMERICANS STOPPED REGULATING THE ELECTORATE, WOULD U.S. VOTER TURNOUT RATES INCREASE?

Based on the experience of states that have made it easier for people to vote, studies show that voter turnout rates would probably increase if Americans decided to reduce the legal barriers to voting. Studies also show that voter fraud is not the problem that Republicans tell themselves it is in order to justify tighter voting rules. President Trump's own commission to investigate the fraud he claimed occurred during the 2016 election found nothing.

But if you waved a magic wand and made it possible for people to register at the same time that they voted, without a picture ID and with lots of polling places open to them, and even gave them extensive early voting opportunities and a day off work to do it, we still would not have 100 percent turnout rates in the United States.

PERSONAL REASONS FOR NOT VOTING

Regulations are not the only reason people fail to vote. People don't vote for personal reasons, too. For instance,

\# They don't have time in their busy schedules to become informed enough to care about the issues they are voting on.

\# They don't think their votes make a difference.

\# They don't feel engaged in or connected to American society.

\# They don't feel like they are offered meaningful choices, or they feel that all their choices are corrupt.

\# Their parties don't engage in voter mobilization, making an effort to get out the vote of the people who they know support them. Sometimes being asked to vote is enough to move someone to do it.

Unfortunately for the Democrats, the people who are most affected by these reasons are likely to be potential Democratic voters—young people who think politics is irrelevant to their lives or who are cynical about politics, minorities who feel the political system does not welcome them, and people with lower incomes juggling multiple jobs with family obligations. Looser voting regulations might alleviate some of these reasons for not voting, but tighter voting regulations are likely to hit these same populations disproportionately.

WHAT DIFFERENCE DOES IT MAKE IF PEOPLE DON'T VOTE?

It turns out that Democrats are more likely than Republicans to decide not to vote—or to be prevented from exercising their rights. So, even though more people might actually identify as Democrats, that doesn't always help the party. If you are a Republican, that is probably good. If you are a Democrat, it's not so good. In elections as close as the 2016 election, votes really do matter.

Another consequence of not voting—and one that is equally important for both parties—is that it can reduce the legitimacy of the elected government. If half the voting population sits out the election, and a candidate wins with half the vote, how much of an **electoral mandate** or endorsement to govern can the winner claim?

THE UPSHOT

Finally, voting is important so that everyone's policy preferences get represented and people feel invested in their government's actions. Who wins can also make a decisive difference in the lives of voters and nonvoters alike. We don't know how long democracy can survive the absence of democratic citizens.

. . . .

electoral mandate: the perception that an election victory signals broad support for the winner's proposed policies

GEN GAP!

HOW YOUNGER VOTERS FEEL ABOUT VOTING

Different issues turn different people "cn" at election time, but there are real generational differences, as the figures below make clear. In fact, the most important characteristic that excites young voters is a candidate than speaks to them. Most candidates do not speak to the issues young voters care about because they assume they will not vote, and can safely be ignored. The 2108 Midterms show that that may no longer be a safe assumption—Millennials are eager to grasp the reins of power.

FIGURE IT!

8.3: HOW EXCITED ARE YOU ABOUT A CANDIDATE THAT . . . ?

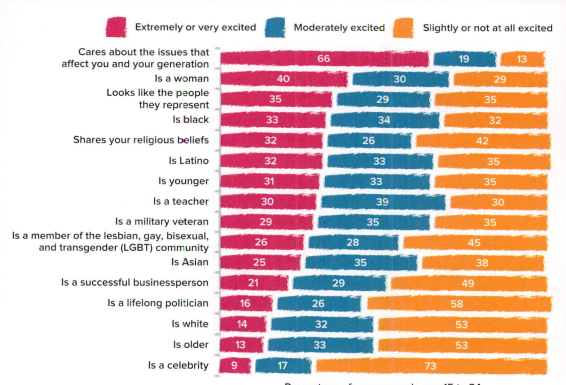

	Extremely or very excited	Moderately excited	Slightly or not at all excited
Cares about the issues that affect you and your generation	66	19	13
Is a woman	40	30	29
Looks like the people they represent	35	29	35
Is black	33	34	32
Shares your religious beliefs	32	26	42
Is Latino	32	33	35
Is younger	31	33	35
Is a teacher	30	39	30
Is a military veteran	29	35	35
Is a member of the lesbian, gay, bisexual, and transgender (LGBT) community	26	28	45
Is Asian	25	35	38
Is a successful businessperson	21	29	49
Is a lifelong politician	16	26	58
Is white	14	32	53
Is older	13	33	53
Is a celebrity	9	17	73

Percentage of young people age 15 to 34

Source: AP/NORC, "MTV/AP-NORC: Young Americans and the Midterm Election," http://www.apnorc.org/projects/Pages/HTML%20Reports/youth-midterm-election.aspx.

8.4: WHO DO YOU THINK WOULD DO A BETTER JOB RUNNING THE COUNTRY?

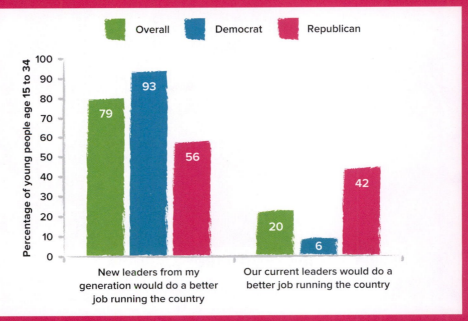

Source: AP/NORC, "MTV/AP-NORC: Young Americans and the Midterm Election," http://www.apnorc.org/projects/Pages/HTML%20Reports/youth-midterm-election.aspx.

8.5: HOW IMPORTANT IS . . . ? ("EXTREMELY IMPORTANT" OR "VERY IMPORTANT")

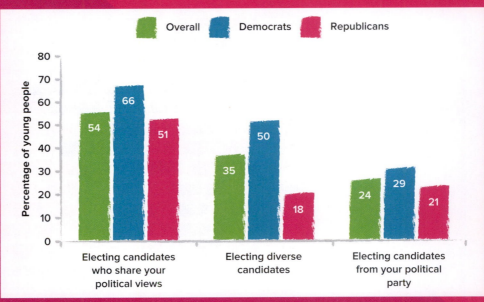

Source: AP/NORC, "MTV/AP-NORC: Young Americans and the Midterm Election," http://www.apnorc.org/projects/Pages/HTML%20Reports/youth-midterm-election.aspx.

8.6: WHAT ISSUES MATTER MOST TO YOU IN THE MIDTERMS? (2018)

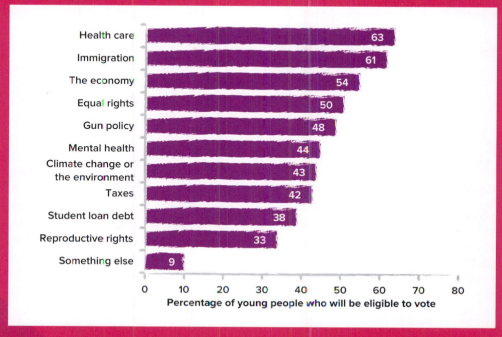

Issue	Percentage
Health care	63
Immigration	61
The economy	54
Equal rights	50
Gun policy	48
Mental health	44
Climate change or the environment	43
Taxes	42
Student loan debt	38
Reproductive rights	33
Something else	9

Percentage of young people who will be eligible to vote

Source: AP/NORC, "MTV/AP-NORC: Young Americans and the Midterm Election," http://www.apnorc.org/projects/Pages/HTML%20Reports/youth-midterm-election.aspx.

TAKEAWAYS

→ Young people are conscious of the diversity of the candidates they vote for, but **they care far more about the issues**. What issues energize them?

→ **Health care, immigration, the economy, and equal rights are the top issues on their list**. Why would that be so?

→ They seem to be **far less partisan than previous generations.** What might account for that shift?

→ **Young people are ready to take control of American politics.** Assuming you all don't change your minds as you get older, what would a country run by your generation look like?

8.6 PRESIDENTIAL ELECTIONS

WHAT ARE WE VOTING FOR?

> Americans have lots of elections. We elect members of Congress every two years; senators every six; and governors, state legislators, mayors, and local officials ranging from judges to school boards at all sorts of intervals. Usually the election that gets the attention is the general election held every four years in which the president, every member of Congress, one third of the Senate, and various state and local offices are on the ballot. The draw of the general election, of course, is the ability to choose the president of the United States. Voter turnout is always highest for the general election.

SO YOU WANT TO RUN FOR PRESIDENT? WHERE DO YOU BEGIN? THREE KEY STEPS OF THE ELECTION PROCESS

> Presidential elections happen every four years, but somehow it seems like they are almost always in progress. That is because the earliest stages of the next election happen almost as soon as the current president is elected. Presidential candidates go through multiple election cycles: an invisible one that takes place largely out of public view and can start before the current president gives his first State of the Union address; the primary season that begins the year before the election year, during which they run for their party's nomination; and then the general election itself, which technically doesn't begin until Labor Day of election year. Let's look at each.

STEP ONE (BEHIND THE SCENES)

> \# **The invisible primary.** Running for president is hard work. Candidates go through a lot of testing of the waters before they decide to run. If they can't get commitments of support and promises of big money, they know they can't launch a viable campaign. Some candidates might launch a campaign anyway, if their goal is not so much to win as to draw attention to a favorite issue or to gain name recognition for a future run. But a serious campaign needs serious resources, and if they aren't forthcoming, there is not much point in running. This water-testing process is called the **invisible primary**. If it is successful and a candidate is encouraged to continue, he or she sets up an exploratory committee, so that the important business of money-raising can begin, and plans a splashy announcement event with lots of media attention. Donald Trump's announcement following an escalator descent in Trump Tower was more dramatic than most, but his speech was full of messages that were designed to appeal to his base and got lots of media coverage.

invisible primary: the period of time before primaries begin when candidates are sounding out support, testing the waters, and trying to decide whether to run

STEP TWO (GETTING THE NOMINATION)

 # Party primaries and **party caucuses**. As we touched on in Chapter 7, parties choose their nominees through a combination of **party primaries**, or statewide elections between members of the same party, and **party caucuses**, which are meetings at which the merits of the candidates are debated and delegates decide for whom to stand. The point of both is to get more delegates than your opponents, because the candidate with the most delegates by the party's national convention in the summer wins. Primary season also includes a series of debates between members of the same party. As the season progresses, some candidates drop out for lack of money or support in the polls.

Primaries and caucuses are held in every state (and Washington, D.C., and Puerto Rico for the Democrats). States choose to have one or the other or sometimes both. The one thing for sure is that the first primary is in New Hampshire and the first caucus is in Iowa. The first contests get lots of candidate and media attention, so naturally everyone wants to go first, but New Hampshire and Iowa have made it their business to stay first in line. If the others try to move earlier, which they do on occasion in a process called **front loading**, Iowa and New Hampshire simply move up their dates. The parties actively discourage front loading because it prevents late-blooming candidates from having a chance. It is bad for democracy, too, because only the most fervent of party activists are paying attention to politics that early in the season. Without limits on front loading, the candidates would be chosen before most of the country woke up to the fact that an election was going on.

The goal through the primary season is to be seen as the **front runner** (the leader of the pack) and to hold on to that position. The best way to do that is to create the impression that you have **momentum**, which means winning debates and keeping an

---

party primaries: elections in which candidates from each party are chosen to run in the general election

party caucuses: a local gathering of party members to choose convention delegates

front loading: the process of scheduling presidential primaries early in the primary season

front runner: the candidate who appears to be the likeliest to win the election at a given point in time

momentum: a sense of forward movement and enthusiasm that candidates can get from primary wins or other positive events

advantage in the early contests. But momentum is as much a matter of narrative as it is actually winning. It is a perception that is fed by careful tending of a media story so that you are treated as the presumptive winner. Front-runner status can backfire, however. If for some reason you do not perform as well as you have led the media to expect, you can look like a loser, even with a relatively solid performance. Managing expectations is an important part of the early run for the presidency.

STEP THREE (RALLYING THE PARTY)

\> \# **The national conventions**. At the end of the summer or very early fall before the election, the parties hold their national nominating conventions. Traditionally the incumbent president's party goes last because candidates tend to get a little polling bounce out of their conventions (if they go well), and so the incumbent party gets the advantage of having the bounce going into the general election campaign.

National conventions used to be events where serious decisions were made about the nomination. Today, that decision has largely been made by the primaries and caucuses, long before the convention starts. Consequently, conventions are party mending, strengthening, and rallying events that the media have little interest in covering. The party's challenge is to plan enough speeches and events to keep the media's interest. Still, without cable news, much of the conventions would go unrecorded. The convention ends with the candidate's official acceptance of the nomination, and then it is on to the general election.

THE UPSHOT

Obviously, just getting to the starting line of the general election with your party behind you is an arduous process. Most voters will not even be paying attention until the summer ends in a presidential election year. That means that all the early decisions, from the invisible primary through the nominating season to the convention, are made by the party elite and the party faithful—people who are essential to a party's success but are not representative of the electorate as a whole. Those folks start to tune in when Labor Day rolls around, only to find that the menu of their choices has been written by the party faithful and may not reflect their preferences.

national nominating convention: a formal party gathering at which candidates for the general election are chosen

8.7 THE GENERAL ELECTION AND THE ELECTORAL COLLEGE

FINALLY! THE ELECTION

> The general election campaign opens on Labor Day, even though it may feel like it has been happening forever by then. Officially, it lasts about three months, although in reality it may have begun behind the scenes several years earlier.

THE ULTIMATE PRIZE—MORE VALUABLE EVEN THAN THE POPULAR VOTE!

> When it comes to presidential elections, the prize is the **Electoral College**. As both Hillary Clinton (2016) and Al Gore (2000) can tell you, winning the popular vote is not enough. Donald Trump and George W. Bush both won the presidency while getting a minority of the popular votes. It can be hard to wrap your mind around that idea when you live in a country you call a democracy, but the American founders were too leery of what they feared might be a mob mentality if people voted for the president directly. They didn't want Congress to choose the president, either, the way parliaments choose their executives in countries like England. So their solution was to create a separate institution that exists only for the purpose of choosing the president, and then disappears for the next four years.

When you cast your vote for a presidential candidate, you are really voting for a delegate (or an "elector") to the Electoral College who will go on to vote for your candidate on behalf of your state. The founders thought that if the people made a poor choice, the electors could step in and cooler heads would prevail. In fact, almost every elector votes for the candidate he or she is pledged to support. Electors are active party members, and if they go against the party to support the opposing candidate, their political future will be bleak.

HOW THE ELECTORAL COLLEGE WORKS

> Electoral votes are distributed by state—each state has a number of electors equal to its total number of members of Congress including senators. That means that small, less populated states get an advantage because, although their population might warrant only one electoral vote, they get at least three. A candidate needs 270 votes to win.

All of the states except two—Maine and Nebraska—give all their votes to the plurality winner in their state. That is called winner-take-all. No matter

. . . .

Electoral College: an intermediary body that elects the president

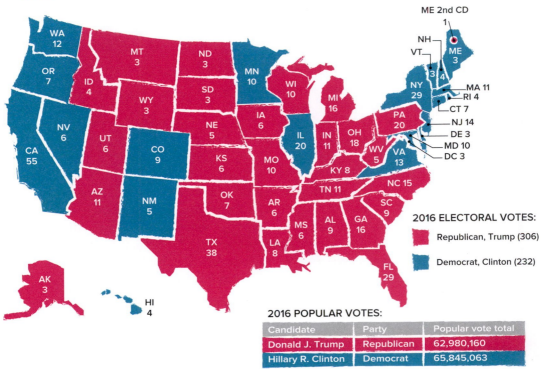

2016 ELECTORAL VOTES:

Republican, Trump (306)

Democrat, Clinton (232)

2016 POPULAR VOTES:

Candidate	Party	Popular vote total
Donald J. Trump	Republican	62,980,160
Hillary R. Clinton	Democrat	65,845,063

Source: U.S. National Archives and Records Administration, https://www.archives.gov/federal-register/electoral-college/2016/election-results.html

how small the margin of victory, the winner gets the entire haul of votes—quite significant in states like California (fifty-five electoral votes) or Texas (thirty-eight). Maine and Nebraska employ a somewhat complicated formula that allocates their small number of votes partly by congressional district and partly by who wins the state.

Any state can change its mind about how to allocate its votes—the Constitution gives them that power. States could distribute their electoral votes by congressional district, or they could allocate their electoral votes proportionally, putting the Electoral College vote more in sync with the popular vote. Hoping to prevent the kind of result that our system produced in 2000 and 2016, when the popular vote winner lost the election, some states have entered into an agreement to cast their votes for the popular vote winner, rather than the winner of their state, if it looks like the popular vote winner could lose. Called the National Popular Vote Interstate Compact, it kicks in if states accounting for 270 electoral votes enter the agreement. Currently twelve states and the District of Columbia have signed on, providing nearly two thirds of the necessary votes.

KEY POINT ❯ The way the states distribute their electoral votes is not fixed in the Constitution and can be changed at any time by the states. Different methods of allocation will produce different winners and losers. If all the states had used the Maine/Nebraska method in 2012, Mitt Romney would have beaten President Obama, despite Obama's five million more popular votes. If all the states distributed their votes proportionality in 2016, Hillary Clinton would have won. Rules matter!!

This is complicated, so let's review . . .

8.1: THE SKIMMABLE ELECTORAL COLLEGE

Why do we have it?	The founders didn't entirely trust the people or Congress with the task of choosing the president.
Where is the power?	Basically in the states. # Each state is allocated a number of votes equal to the total representatives it has in Congress: two for its senators plus one for each of its House representatives (determined by population).
How do you win?	There are a total of 538 possible electoral votes—it takes 270 to win. # The candidate's goal is to win the popular vote in enough states that the total allocated to him or her by the states will exceed 269.
How does each state allocate its votes?	Popular elections are held in each state, and delegates to the Electoral College are chosen who are committed to vote for a particular candidate. # State law determines how many delegates each candidate gets. All states but Maine and Nebraska give ALL of their electoral votes to the popular vote winner. # Any state could change that method of allocation and use the actual vote or winners in each congressional district or some other formula.
How can a candidate like George W. Bush or Donald Trump win the presidency despite losing the popular vote in the nation?	Because so many states are winner-take-all, the person who wins California, even by one vote, gets all fifty-five electoral votes. # So the votes don't necessarily reflect the popular vote at all. # Conversely, you could win ALL the votes in California and still "only" get fifty-five electoral votes while your opponent wins a lot of sparsely populated rural states that are guaranteed at least three votes, even if their population doesn't warrant it. # There are multiple ways to add up an Electoral College win that runs counter to the popular vote.
So, why do we keep this system?	There have been calls to change it, but the truth is, some people are winners under this system. Small states get more votes than they might otherwise, and large states get a lot of attention.

HOW THE ELECTORAL COLLEGE INFLUENCES THE WAY CANDIDATES CAMPAIGN

> Now that you understand how the Electoral College works, you can imagine that it shapes the way candidates campaign. Some states have much higher payoffs than others, but some states are not really in contention. California almost always votes Democratic, so despite its fifty-five electoral votes, there is no real payoff for either Democrats or Republicans to campaign there. Similarly, although its population is changing, Texas's thirty-eight votes are still a sure win for the Republican candidate, so neither party spends many resources there either.

THE POLITICAL COLORING BOOK: RED, BLUE, AND PURPLE

> During election night media coverage, when a news network or organization decides that a candidate has received enough votes to claim a state, the graphic artists who give us large brightly colored maps turn the state red if a Republican wins it and blue if a Democrat wins. That has led us to refer to mostly Republican states like Texas, Alabama, and Mississippi as red states; mostly Democratic states like California, Connecticut, and New York as blue states; and those that can go either way (for example, Wisconsin, Michigan, and Iowa) as purple states. It is worth remembering, though, that those colors don't have any significance in and of themselves—they are just a media convention that has become tradition.

Some states are predictably red or blue because most voters who identify with one party or another are not up for grabs in a presidential election, and increasingly people live near people who are like them. That is not to say there are not blue pockets in red states and vice versa, but overall Texas tends to be conservative and California tends to be liberal.

IT DON'T MEAN A THING, IF YOU DON'T WIN THE SWING.

> It is swing voters, who might vote Republican one election, Democratic another, who are wooed and targeted by candidates, and those swing voters who really count live in swing states—ones that are not reliably blue or red, even though they might trend one way or the other.

These states: Colorado, Florida, Iowa, Michigan, Ohio, Pennsylvania, Wisconsin—and perhaps Arizona, Nevada, New Hampshire, North Carolina, Virginia, and Minnesota—have become the battleground on which much of the election is contested, leaving many states to feel left on the fringes of the action.

swing voters: the approximately one third of the electorate who are undecided at the start of a campaign

swing states: states in which the outcome of a general election is not easy to predict in advance

WHAT GOES INTO A WINNING CAMPAIGN?

> The race to win over undecided voters and to turn out the voters who are already inclined to vote your way requires a huge amount of resources: campaign talent, a strong message, media attention, money, and voter mobilization. Let's take a look at each of these "ingredients" of a successful campaign.

A SMART TEAM

> \# **Talent.** These days campaigns are professional organizations. The campaign managers, communications directors, political strategists, and data analysts are people who have come up through the ranks and proved themselves in previous campaigns. A good team can *help* you win, but it can't do it for you. In 2016, Hillary Clinton had the kind of political organization that candidates dream of; with the assumption that she would win, many skilled Democratic operatives wanted to be part of the team. Donald Trump, by contrast, was flying by the seat of his pants a good deal of the time without most of the typical talent that a campaign requires. In retrospect, we know that there were multiple external forces—from the use of data provided by Cambridge Analytica that helped them target ads to specific audiences, to disinformation campaigns by Russian bots—that helped Trump's campaign and made the election an atypical one. Generally, the campaign with the most money, expertise, and data-gathering operations is going to be able to out-strategize and out-perform one that is less adept.

A SHARP AND MEMORABLE MESSAGE

> \# **Message.** Even though hard-core partisans will vote for their party's nominee no matter what, most swing voters want to know what a candidate stands for before making a decision. Generally, candidates support their party's platform and the issue positions that are important to their party's voters. Sometimes a candidate can find a **wedge issue** that he or she can use as a lever to divide an opponent's voting coalition. Recall that this was what Republican Richard Nixon did with the issue of race after the Democrats' support of civil rights alienated the conservative, southern members of the party in the 1960s.

> Beyond standing up for the party's platform, a candidate needs to be able to explain why he or she is running for office. Donald Trump's message was clear to all: *Make America Great Again* was on the red cap he wore to most campaign events. It was a message that resonated with voters who felt that America's best days were behind

wedge issue: a controversial issue that one party uses to split the voters in the other party

it. Hillary Clinton's message, *Stronger Together*, was not universally recognized as a message by media commentators, who were more accustomed to the strong action verbs around which messages are usually built. As more women become candidates for the highest office, either they will adapt to the leadership standards established by male candidates or the process will come to be less gendered and nontraditional messages will be recognized as messages nonetheless.

FREE MEDIA!   ❯ #   **Media attention.** Paid media coverage is incredibly costly for any campaign but especially for a national campaign that has to advertise in expensive markets. The first goal of any campaign is to maximize the unpaid coverage by staging events and making appearances that the media want to cover.

In 2016, everyone was left in Donald Trump's dust when it came to garnering free media coverage—none of the Republicans running against him could compete, and neither could Hillary Clinton. While other candidates fought to get a sliver of free air time, Trump's rallies, at which he could be counted on to say something outrageous or controversial, were aired from start to finish by cable news. When the media's attention drifted away from him, he was expert at calling it back with a well-timed tweet that would have everyone talking about him again. An experienced showman, he exposed the mainstream media as the ratings-hungry monster it is, by occupying a disproportionate amount of time not just on conservative Fox or more neutral CNN but even on the liberal MSNBC. Trump was ratings gold, and he knew it.

In more conventional years, the candidates tend to be more evenly matched and they fight for media attention on a more even playing field. Presidential debates give candidates an opportunity to demonstrate not just expertise but a sense of humor and humanity and presidential stature. A worry for candidates running against an incumbent president is whether they will be able to match the president's stature.

For candidates, a good commercial that goes viral and is seen multiple times on cable news and the Internet without having to be paid for is golden. Campaign commercials can be positive—saying good things about the candidate—or they can constitute **negative advertising**, in which they criticize the candidate's opponent without

negative advertising: campaign advertising that emphasizes the negative characteristics of opponents rather than one's own strengths

even mentioning the candidate's name. Negative advertising is a bit of a gamble—it can do a good job of tarnishing one's opponent, but it runs the risk of turning off all voters and keeping them from showing up to vote.

$$$$$$$

\# **Money.** All advertising requires money, and money is a resource that candidates spend a great deal of their time chasing. Long gone are the pre-Obama days when candidates limited themselves to raising a set amount of money and then having that matched by federal funds. Obama showed that a candidate could turn the Internet into a steady stream of financial support via small donations, even as he raised larger sums from big donors. Realizing he could raise more money without federal funds and not have his spending limited, he turned down the federal funds and created an environment in which no candidate would have the incentive to accept those funds and limit his or her spending again.

Campaign finance law limits how much **hard money**—the money that goes directly to a candidate—an individual can donate. That limit is currently $2,700 per election (primaries and generals are counted as separate elections). Fundraisers can bundle donations from many individuals and present it to a campaign as a huge lump sum, which might gain *bundlers* prestige and access to the candidate, but those individuals are limited in what they can give.

By contrast, **soft money**—donations to parties and other groups that can spend it on a candidate's behalf—can be raised in unlimited amounts. There are some restrictions, however. Soft money cannot be given to the candidate, the candidate cannot control how it is spent or coordinate with the group doing the spending, and it cannot be used to urge people to vote for the candidate. It can, however, be used to mobilize voters, to advertise against opponents, and to pay for **issue advocacy ads** that help a candidate by promoting his or her issues or criticizing the opponent's stand.

The 2010 Supreme Court case *Citizens United v. Federal Election Commission* made it clear that the Court considers such spending

. . . .

hard money: campaign funds donated directly to candidates; amounts are limited by federal election laws

soft money: unregulated campaign contributions by individuals, groups, or parties that promote general election activities but do not directly support individual candidates

issue advocacy ads: advertisements paid for by soft money, and thus not regulated, that promote certain issue positions but do not endorse specific candidates

to be protected under the First Amendment and that such rights are possessed not only by individuals but also by corporations. *Citizens United* changed the financial playing field of elections in dramatic ways by allowing groups or individuals to spend without limit and without identifying themselves. This so-called **dark money** can give very wealthy individuals a disproportionate influence on elections. Examples are the Koch brothers and the Mercer family on the Republican side and George Soros and Tom Steyer on the Democratic side.

GOTV!

\# **Voter mobilization.** Convincing all the voters in the world that you are a great candidate does you no good if they stay home on Election Day. We have already seen that there are lots of reasons why people might choose not to vote or might want to vote but encounter barriers that prevent them from doing so. It is up to candidates and their parties to engage in voter mobilization, or **get-out-the-vote (GOTV)** efforts, a burden that weighs more heavily on Democrats. Left to their own devices, Republicans are more reliable voters. That is, they are more likely to turn out without a push from the party.

But there are members of both parties who need a nudge or a reminder, or a ride to the polls. Knowing where your voters are, which ones have voted, and which ones need that extra assist is an increasingly sophisticated part of campaigns. The Obama campaign in both 2008 and 2012 was groundbreaking in its use of technology to map the areas where Obama voters lived, check whether they had voted, and dispatch someone to make a call or knock on doors if they hadn't.

THE UPSHOT

Elections are big business. The stakes are huge, and stakeholders who have the means to contribute can do so in a big way. But all of us are stakeholders in an election, and even if we don't end up with the president's private number, several recent elections have made it clear that every citizen's vote counts. Ultimately, we all have a great deal at stake in how our elections turn out.

. . . .

dark money: campaign money that goes to nonprofits (including political groups like unions and trade groups) that can be spent to influence elections and whose donors do not need to be revealed

voter mobilization: a party's efforts to inform potential voters about issues and candidates and to persuade them to vote

get-out-the-vote (GOTV): efforts by political parties, interest groups, and the candidate's staff to maximize voter turnout among supporters

Big Think

→ How close are you to the ideal democratic citizen? Should your views count?

→ Do Americans have too many elections?

→ Who should choose the president of the United States—citizens or states?

Key Terms

CONCEPTS

dark money (p. 280)

election (p. 248)

Electoral College (p. 273)

electoral mandate (p. 266)

exit polls (p. 255)

fake polls (p. 256)

front loading (p. 271)

gender gap (p. 259)

get-out-the-vote (GOTV) (p. 280)

hard money (p. 279)

house effects (p. 254)

invisible primary (p. 270)

issue advocacy ads (p. 279)

likely voter polls (p. 253)

likely voter screens (p. 253)

momentum (p. 271)

negative advertising (p. 278)

nonresponse bias (p. 253)

online processing (p. 251)

party identification (p. 257)

patriotism (p. 257)

political socialization (p. 256)

polling (p. 248)

polling aggregators (p. 254)

polls (p. 248)

public opinion (p. 248)

random digit dialing (p. 254)

random sample (p. 252)

rational ignorance (p. 250)

regulating the electorate (p. 262)

sample bias (p. 253)

sampling error (p. 253)

soft money (p. 279)

swing states (p. 276)

tracking polls (p. 261)

two-step flow of information (p. 251)

voter mobilization (p. 280)

voter turnout (p. 262)

wedge issue (p. 277)

weighting (p. 253)

IMPORTANT WORKS AND EVENTS

national nominating convention (p. 272)

party caucuses (p. 271)

party primaries (p. 271)

KEY INDIVIDUALS AND GROUPS

#9 MEDIA AND POLITICAL COMMUNICATION

In this chapter:

MEDIA BABIES

When we introduced you to American politics in Chapter 1, we discussed the context in which most of us experience it these days—through some form of **media**. The media may be "old-fashioned" like television and radio, or we may get curated news feeds on our smartphones. But the truth is, none of us really goes out and does our own reporting. We are all dependent on the channels of communication that have been established for transmitting news and entertainment, and that we now use for everything else, including shopping, reading, and even conducting relationships.

That makes us media babies in ways we have never been before. First-year students entering college now are part of the first generation that has never *not* had the potential to communicate, play, or interact through a screen. The reality that many of us experience is filtered through the technology that makes the constant flow of information, communication, and transaction possible. That powerful complex of media technology not only carries information *to* us but also collects information *about* us. It has the ability to gather information on where we have been, who we have talked to, and what we have bought. The degree to which we have "shared" (intentionally and unintentionally) just about everything there is to know about ourselves makes the privacy issues we discussed in Chapter 3 almost naive.

Throughout this book, we have seen that a major component of power is control of information, or the way information is assembled into narratives. And we have come to recognize a truth that is right under all of our noses—information is no longer a scarce resource. It is now an abundant resource, and the clamour of the information marketplace is the sound of many people seeking to tell and sell their narratives at increasing volume. The phenomenal increase in the number of channels through which information can flow for the mediated citizen—that is, the explosion of the media in the past century but especially in the digital age—has made understanding the relationships among power, narratives, and political communication all the more central. Indeed, as citizens and scholars, we ignore it at our peril.

IN A NUTSHELL

This describes the media today: all encompassing, enormously powerful, and invasive. Yet they are also more porous and open to our own influence than ever before.

By the time you finish reading this chapter, you will understand

→ Where we get our information

→ How media ownership and government regulation impact the information we get

→ What journalists do

→ How the media shape and perpetuate narratives

→ How politicians try to control the narratives themselves

→ What citizens can do to identify "real news," build narratives, and be critical consumers of the media

9.2 WHERE WE GET OUR INFORMATION

HOW DO WE KNOW WHAT WE KNOW?

When information is as pervasive and as controversial as it is today, it can be hard to trace it back to its roots. The origins of what we think we know can be hazy, especially in an age of **media aggregators** like *BuzzFeed, Drudge Report,* or *Huffington Post,* which simply pick and choose from the reporting of others. And then there are the sources that provide you with what you'd like to read based on algorithms (but that don't do the reporting themselves), like Facebook and Reddit.

Reporting is, or should be, the heart of the news industry. It involves professional **journalists** tracking down facts, checking them, asking hard questions, not settling for easy answers, and pushing until they have found the truth. What serious reporters produce is the most accurate version of events they can discover. If they make an error, they correct it immediately. That is the tradition of journalism and reporting in America in most of the past century.

media: channels of communication

media aggregators: web sites, applications, and software that cull content from other digital sources

reporting: the action of seeking out facts to tell a complete story about a public event or individual

journalists: professional communicators who focus on news sharing and narrative building

WHO ARE YOU CALLING FAKE?

> The truth is not relative—it is verifiable with empirical (real-world) evidence. The habit some of us have gotten into of labeling "fake news" any information we don't like is dangerous for democracy . . . and also silly. You don't make the truth go away by denying it exists.

A classic example of professional reporting is the way Bob Woodward and Carl Bernstein uncovered the Watergate scandal involving President Richard Nixon in the early 1970s. There is still a lot of excellent reporting out there (some of it done by Woodward and Bernstein, as a matter of fact!). But fielding reporters in locations around the country and the world is expensive. That is why more and more news sites rely on the reporting of others, including the wires services like the Associated Press.

If you remember the childhood game of telephone, where you sit in a circle and whisper something to the person next to you, who whispers to the person next to him or her, you recall that the message may be barely recognizable by the time it returns to you. Much so-called reporting can be like that today, when news sites rely primarily on the work of others.

KEY POINT

> As the American founders knew, the survival of democracy is closely tied to the free flow of information. That means our system would be in serious trouble without the reporting of skilled and persistent journalists. The integrity of those sources is key to the quality of the news we get. A hallmark of authoritarian systems is the state's effort to control the narrative by controlling the press.

THE MEDIA MENU

> Consider the ways you can get information—the kinds of media channels you rely on for news and other data. In Chapter 1, we reminded ourselves that media are channels—much like the channel of communication a medium claims to have to another world. Our media channels range from

- \# Word of mouth (dinner table conversation, water cooler gossip)
- \# Print (newspapers, magazines)
- \# Broadcast (radio, TV)
- \# Electronic (a rapidly growing number of online and mobile outlets)

People will always talk, but the other forms of media are not in equally good shape. The print media are in decline, still struggling to figure out their role in an electronic world. TV news, especially local news, remains a draw among older generations, but its audience is dwindling. The cable news networks vie for viewership by being right wing (Fox), middle of the road

(CNN), or left wing (MSNBC). Talk radio has its devoted audiences, but they are comparatively small. It is the Internet that is rapidly becoming the go-to place for people, especially young people, to seek information. Most of us get our news from a lot of sources, what scholars call **media convergence**.

TABLE IT!

9.1: WHERE AMERICANS GET THEIR NEWS

Americans say they . . .	Percentage of Americans saying that	The major players
Often get news from newspapers	18	*Wall Street Journal, New York Times, Chicago Tribune*
Often get news from radio	25	**Fox News Radio, NPR**
Often get news from major broadcast networks	26	**ABC, NBC, CBS**
Often get news from cable TV	28	**FOX News Channel, CNN, MSNBC**
Often get news from local TV	37	**The Sinclair Group, Gannett**
Often get news from news apps and web sites	33	**Apple News, Google News,** *New York Times,* ***BuzzFeed,*** **Reddit**
Access news from smartphones or other mobile devices	80	**Apple, Samsung, Lenovo, LG, Sony**
Have a customizable news feed	37	**Twitter, Digg, Reddit, Feedly**
Communicate with others online about the news	37	**Reddit, Facebook**
Get some news on social media	67	**Twitter, Facebook, Instagram**

media convergence: the merging of traditional media with digital communication technologies such as telecommunications and the Internet

> Remember that we use these channels not just to get information. We also use media, especially electronic media, to shop, to form or maintain relationships, to organize politically, to manage our travel plans, and even, for many of us, to earn a living. The media not only provide channels through which we gain information but also establish the lines of communication though which we live much of our lives, including our political lives. That makes us **mediated citizens**, which means . . .

**We can pop the bubble.** External forces that feed us information supporting a particular narrative might enable us to live in an **information bubble**. We can limit the channels of communication we use to keep ourselves in our comfort zones. We have the opportunity to launch our own channels and to create our own narratives, but we also can stay where we are less anxious—listening to the news, curating our social media, and meeting new people who reinforce the ideas we already have.

Our decision not to challenge that information bubble is what keeps us in it. Popping the bubble should be a fundamental goal of an educated person.

**We are vulnerable to manipulation.** Being a mediated citizen also leaves us vulnerable to being manipulated by others who control the channels of communication through which we live our lives. Anyone who has searched for something on the Internet and then seen ads for that product repeatedly on other web sites until they have broken down and purchased it knows exactly how that manipulation works. More serious examples involve Russian bots targeting audiences with disruptive and often false news in order to divide people socially and politically. If algorithms can pick up on what we are shopping for, they can also figure out what kind of music or restaurants or airlines we like. And they can certainly detect the news stories we search for. If we reinforce these algorithm-based sites by clicking on those items, gradually we cease to see stories that we don't agree with, and we are in the information bubble we just talked about.

. . . .

mediated citizens: people who are constantly receiving information through multiple channels that can and do shape their political views but who also have the ability to use those channels to create their own narratives

information bubble: a closed cycle in which all the information we get reinforces the information we already have, solidifying our beliefs without reference to outside reality checks

GEN GAP!

MEDIATED CITIZENSHIP ACROSS THE GENERATIONS

As you might guess, Millennials and Gen Xers lead the way on technology use and social media involvement. iGen will presumably be right behind. This only reinforces the notion of the mediated citizen—most of us have multiple ways to stay in touch and get news. Older generations are catching up as well, although they tend to prefer different platforms.

FIGURE IT!

9.1: ALL GENERATIONS ARE USING TECHNOLOGY, BUT MILLENNIALS AND GEN XERS ARE LEADING THE CHARGE

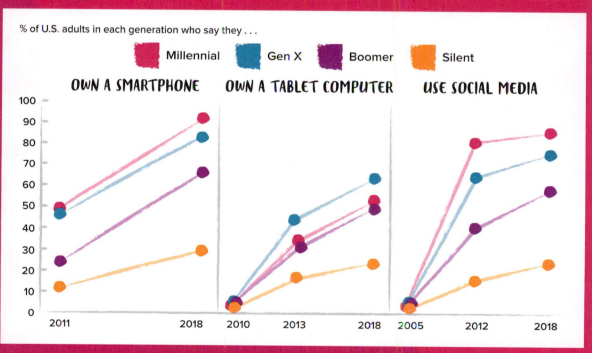

% of U.S. adults in each generation who say they . . .

Millennial · Gen X · Boomer · Silent

OWN A SMARTPHONE · OWN A TABLET COMPUTER · USE SOCIAL MEDIA

Source: JingJing Jiang, "Millennials Stand Out for Their Technology Use, but Older Generations Also Embrace Digital Life," Pew Research Center, May 2, 108, http://www.pewresearch.org/fact-tank/2018/05/02/millennials-stand-out-for-their-technology-use-but-older-generations-also-embrace-digital-life/.

9.2: FACEBOOK AND YOUTUBE ARE THE TOP SOCIAL MEDIA SITES

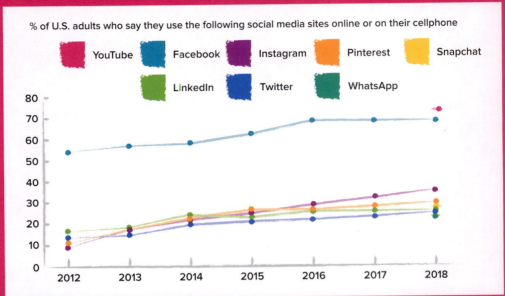

% of U.S. adults who say they use the following social media sites online or on their cellphone

Legend: YouTube, Facebook, Instagram, Pinterest, Snapchat, LinkedIn, Twitter, WhatsApp

Source: Aaron Smith and Monica Anderson, *Social Media Use in 2018*, Pew Research Center, March 1, 2018, http://www.pewinternet.org/2018/03/01/social-media-use-in-2018/.

Note: Pre-2018 telephone poll data is not available for YouTube, Snapchat, or WhatsApp.

9.3: YOUNG PEOPLE PREFER SNAPCHAT AND INSTAGRAM TO OTHER SOCIAL MEDIA SITES

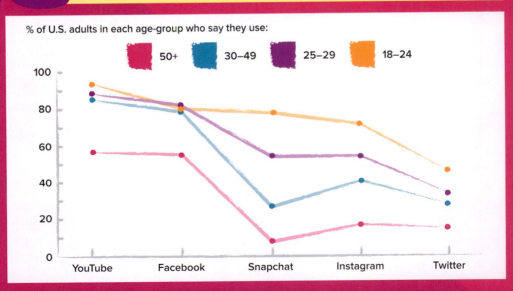

% of U.S. adults in each age-group who say they use:

Legend: 50+, 30–49, 25–29, 18–24

Source: Aaron Smith and Monica Anderson, *Social Media Use in 2018*, Pew Research Center, March 1, 2018, http://www.pewinternet.org/2018/03/01/social-media-use-in-2018/.

9.4: MOST SOCIAL MEDIA USERS USE MORE THAN ONE PLATFORM

Substantial "reciprocity" across major social media platforms

% of __ users who also...	Use Twitter	Use Instagram	Use Facebook	Use Snapchat	Use YouTube	Use WhatsApp	Use Pinterest	Use LinkedIn
TWITTER	—	73%	90%	54%	95%	35%	49%	50%
INSTAGRAM	50%	—	91%	60%	95%	35%	47%	41%
FACEBOOK	32%	47%	—	35%	87%	27%	37%	33%
SNAPCHAT	48%	77%	89%	—	95%	33%	44%	37%
YOUTUBE	31%	45%	81%	35%	—	28%	36%	32%
WHATSAPP	38%	55%	85%	40%	92%	—	33%	40%
PINTEREST	41%	56%	89%	41%	92%	25%	—	42%
LINKEDIN	47%	57%	90%	40%	94%	35%	49%	—

Source: Aaron Smith and Monica Anderson, *Social Media Use in 2018*, Pew Research Center, March 1, 2018, http://www.pewinternet.org/2018/03/01/social-media-use-in-2018/.

TAKEAWAYS

→ **Younger generations prefer photo-based social media that they can control more than Facebook and that help them keep track of friends.** Does that affect the way political information is shared?

→ **Facebook is flatlining.** If you've been following the news, what do you think might be behind that trend? What, if anything, could Facebook do to reverse the trend?

→ **Everyone loves YouTube.** Why?

9.3 MEDIA OWNERSHIP AND GOVERNMENT REGULATION

WHO OWNS THE MEDIA? AREN'T AIRWAVES AND CYBERSPACE FREE?

Airwaves, and cyberspace, may be considered "public goods" belonging to everyone, but that doesn't make them free. The government sells licenses to radio and TV stations and is now questioning the role social media play in national security.

Even though we are so immersed in the media world that it seems as though it must be free, the truth is, it is not. The media are big business globally. In the United States alone, six corporations own most of the major national newspapers, the leading news magazines, the national television networks including CNN and other cable stations, as well as publishing houses, movie studios, telephone companies, entertainment firms, and other multimedia operations. Big tech companies have added to the media wealth: Facebook, Apple, Amazon, Netflix, and Google (Alphabet) alone have a value of more than $3.25 trillion. And since the demise of net neutrality (more on that later), companies can charge different rates for different content from different providers.

WHAT DIFFERENCE DOES IT MAKE WHO OWNS WHAT?

The people who control the news we get are essentially gatekeepers—they are in charge of what information gets to us. We have seen that the gatekeeping structure of the American media has changed radically since the days of the nation's founding. Back then, newspapers were partisan instruments dependent on government for their very existence. But today, as we have just seen, most news comes from—or at least through—massive, corporate-owned sources—whether they are conventional news sources like the *New York Times* and CBS or through new platforms like Facebook and Google.

BIAS IN THE MEDIA . . . AND NOT THE KIND YOU THINK

What does the concentrated corporate ownership of the traditional mass media mean to us as consumers of the news? We should be aware of at least five major consequences:

\# There is a commercial bias in the media today toward what will increase advertiser revenue and audience share. Journalistic

gatekeepers: journalists and media elite who determine which news stories are covered and which are not

commercial bias: the tendency of the media to make coverage and programming decisions based on what will attract a large audience and maximize profits

9.2: THE SKIMMABLE GUIDE TO MEDIA OWNERSHIP

Verizon	Alphabet	Comcast	Disney	Facebook	Time Warner	CBS	Viacom	Hearst	21st Century Fox	News Corp	Advance Publications	Twitter
$126B	$110.8B	$84.5B	$55.1B	$40.7B	$31.3B	$14.1B	$13.8B	$10.8B	$8.6B	$8.6B	$2.4B	$664M
AOL; Flickr; Huffington Post; Tech Crunch; Tumblr; Yahoo	Google; YouTube; Blogger Zagat	NBC Universal; CNBC; Universal Pictures; DreamWorks; SYFY; E!; Bravo; NBC Sports; MSNBC; Telemundo; Focus Features; USA; Hulu	ABC; Pixar; ESPN; ESPN Radio; ESPN Magazine; Lucasfilm; Marvel Studios; Marvel Comics; A & E; Lifetime; History; Hulu	Instagram; Messenger; WhatsApp	CW; CNN; DC Comics; Cartoon Network; HBO; Warner Bros; New Line Cinema; TBS; Hulu	CW; CBS Radio; CNET; Smithsonian Channel; Simon & Schuster; Showtime	Paramount Pictures; Nickelodeon; CMT; MTV; BET; Comedy Central	Cosmo; Esquire; Car & Driver; ESPN Magazine; A & E	Fox; Fox News; Fox Sports; FX; 20th Century Fox; Hulu	Harper Collins; New York Post; Wall Street Journal	Conde Nast; GQ; New Yorker; Reddit; Vogue; Wired	Periscope

judgment and ethics are often at odds with the imperative to turn a profit.

\# The effort to get and keep large audiences, and to make way for increased advertising, means a reduced emphasis on political news. This is especially true at the local television level, where older Americans, in particular, tend to get their information.

\# The content of the news we get is lightened up, dramatized, and turned into **infotainment** to keep audiences tuned in. Some web sites, like *BuzzFeed,* specialize in **clickbait** pieces—sensational headlines that tease you into clicking a link to find some intriguing-sounding information. Other news web sites tell you in advance how many minutes it will take to read an article so that you know what you are committing to before you start.

\# The corporate ownership of today's media means that the media outlets frequently face conflicts of interest in deciding what news to cover or how to cover it.

infotainment: when the news is presented in a deliberately entertaining way in order to keep audiences interested

clickbait: sensational headlines designed to tempt Internet users to click through to a specific web site

\# Breaking a news story has always been a point of pride for editors and journalists. (It is the *Washington Post* that gets kudos for breaking the Watergate scandal—nobody remembers the second newspaper to chime in.) In the rush to avoid getting "scooped" by another station or newspaper, reporters and editors alike have sometimes jumped the gun, disseminating incorrect information or flat-out lies without taking the time to fact-check or analyze them.

DO WE HAVE A CHOICE?

You'd think with all these massive media voices, smaller outlets would find a niche among those who follow a different drummer. And they do. The late, lamented New York City–based *Village Voice* stayed small and local for more than sixty years, until it ceased production in 2018. Indeed, today anyone can start a blog or a web site or a podcast or a YouTube Channel and start publishing his or her independent views.

FROM STARTUP TO STAR POWER

The trouble tends to be that, if a smaller operation looks like it will be profitable, an enterprising corporation has an incentive to scoop it up. Even Facebook was once a small startup. Most of the media giants we see in the *Skimmable Guide to Media Ownership* started out as small alternatives to the mainstream media until they grew and grew.

Today there are some outlets that look like alternative media, but they have the funding of giants behind them. Sometimes they were small shops that proved profitable and got gobbled up by a corporation. FiveThirtyEight .com, for instance, started off as a solo reporter, Nate Silver, posting election predictions under a pseudonym (Poblano) on the lefty blog the Daily Kos, before he went independent, got picked up by the *New York Times,* and then by ESPN. FiveThirtyEight is currently owned by ABC, which as you can see in the *Skimmable Guide* is part of Disney. In today's media world, successful alternatives tend to get bought up and become part of the corporate world.

MEDIA FUNDED BY NONPROFITS

A small independent press continues to thrive outside the for-profit world, but these outlets have an ideological reason for maintaining independence. They'd lose their identity if they went corporate. A few investigative magazines—like *Mother Jones* (published by the Foundation for National Progress) and *Consumer Reports* (published by Consumers Union)—and web sites like FactCheck.org (University of Pennsylvania) and ProPublica rely on funding from subscribers and members of their nonprofit parent organizations. However, unless they are completely free of advertising (as is *Consumer Reports*), even these independent publications are not entirely free from corporate influence.

Government-supported media—like the Public Broadcasting System (PBS) and National Public Radio (NPR), for example—can provide an alternative to for-profit media, but their limited public funding, through the nonprofit Corporation for Public Broadcasting, has become politically controversial. These media are largely supported by member stations and audience donations. Various corporations support them, too, and although they take steps to stay clear of outside influence, no media outlet achieves that completely.

THE UPSHOT

Unless a media outlet is completely free of all corporate influence, and almost none are, they are subject to all of the corporate biases and pressures we discussed earlier. It doesn't mean we shouldn't trust them, but it does mean we should bring a critical understanding to what we read, hear, and see.

DOES A FREE PRESS MEAN THERE ARE NO CONSTRAINTS ON THE MEDIA?

The media in America are almost entirely privately owned, but they do not operate without some public control. Although the constitutional principle of freedom of the press keeps the print media nearly free of restriction, the broadcast media have been treated differently and control of the Internet has become controversial and complex.

The Federal Communications Commission (FCC) was founded in 1934 to ensure that radio and television represented a variety of viewpoints, but that was back when access to the airwaves was scarce and there were few channels. In today's abundance of TV stations, radio (public and paid), and Internet outlets, scarcity isn't the problem it once was, and the reasons for the regulations (and the regulations themselves) are long gone. With fewer limitations on how many stations an owner can possess, the potential for media monopoly has become enormous.

Although traditional media have been shedding their regulations, the Internet is still relatively new terrain and Congress has not decided how to handle it. Since the mid-2000s, regulators began pursuing a policy of **net neutrality**, which meant that service providers could not charge a premium for some kinds of content to advantage it over others. Supporters of net neutrality have a sort of Wild West attitude about the Internet—that it should be an open-access forum for innovation. We have yet to see how the Trump administration's overturning of the policy will play out.

HOW FREE SHOULD THE INTERNET BE? AND ARE WE PREPARED IF IT TURNS AGAINST US?

Since finding out that the Russians were able to hack into private email accounts and manipulate social media like Facebook and Twitter to sow

net neutrality: the principle that Internet service providers cannot speed up or slow down access for customers or make decisions about the content they see or the apps they download

discord and try to delegitimize the 2016 presidential election, members of Congress have begun to hold hearings to investigate how that could have happened. Unfortunately, a lot of them are not among the generations that are Internet savvy, and they often don't seem to know what they are looking for. The tech geniuses who invented the platforms haven't got the experience or training needed to grapple with the democratic import of the sites they dreamed up in their doom rooms. Many of them promise accountability but there are costs to transparency that they don't want to pay. We are just beginning to glimpse the implications of the mediated world we have created.

9.4   WHAT DO JOURNALISTS DO?

CHASING THE NEWS

 That's what many journalists do. We mentioned earlier that the profession of journalism involves reporting, although, as we will see, there are other journalistic roles.

Reporting means digging out nuggets of truth where you can find them and stitching them together into a coherent story that informs the public of what is happening in their world, particularly their political world. Sometimes the whole story doesn't come out at once. Think about the revelations about producer Harvey Weinstein that launched the #MeToo movement. We didn't get that story all at once—it began with information dripping out in bits and pieces until reporter Ronan Farrow was able to bring them together in a long feature in the *New Yorker*. That wasn't the end of it, either—new revelations continue to come out and tell more and more of the narrative.

DIG DEEPER

Read about how Farrow landed his big story about Weinstein.

Go to **edge.sagepub.com/ dig-deeper**

A story like Farrow's is especially tricky because reporters need to verify their facts, and in the kind of claims that Weinstein's accusers were making there was a he said/she said quality. Whose word do you believe? Farrow's kind of reporting meant that he looked for contemporaneous accounts. Did women who accused Weinstein of assault tell anyone else at the time? Did they write it in a journal? That kind of documentation helps establish that people are telling the truth. Because of Weinstein's influence, Farrow's former employers at NBC killed the story, so Farrow eventually took it to the *New Yorker*, where he became part of a team that won the Pulitzer Prize for their work. Weinstein ultimately lost his job, and a movement was born with powerful political implications in that it encouraged many women to run for political office.

What Farrow does is reporting. What Bob Woodward and Carl Bernstein did in the 1970s to uncover the Watergate scandal was reporting. (And they're still doing it in their coverage of the Trump administration, with Woodward as a book author and Bernstein at CNN.) That kind of special reporting brought down the powerful, but solid, everyday reporting can also just keep citizens informed of the facts so that they can make informed decisions.

Reporting is key to the lifeblood of a democracy—if we can't dig into and verify the narratives told by our leaders and tell truth to power, democracy will not long survive. But there are other journalistic roles that are important (and some that are not so important). Just because someone calls himself or herself a journalist is not the measure of what he or she does—we need to keep a keen eye on whether journalists contribute valuable, factual information to the public debate.

FOUR KEY JOURNALISTIC ROLES

Gatekeepers. We already mentioned the important role journalists play in helping us understand what is important and why. Not all journalists perform this role—it belongs to editors and major reporters who decide what should be covered and what should not.

Disseminators. Disseminators are reporters who just focus on getting out facts. Sometimes they are criticized for not providing the public with enough context in which to interpret the facts, but they believe that providing such context goes beyond the scope of their job.

Investigators/analysts. These journalists (like Farrow and others), responding to the criticism that they need to provide context, dig for information and interpret its significance. It is difficult to do this without letting one's own values creep in, but the best are experts at compartmentalizing their personal views.

Public mobilizers. These journalists go beyond the reporting of objective analysis of facts. They have an agenda, and they consider it to be part of their job to make citizens aware of what is going on around them and to encourage them to take action. In the age of Twitter, it is a lot easier to discern the personal views even of journalists who try to stay objective on the job, but it is also easier to challenge and interact with those who urge a political agenda.

DIG DEEPER

Watch the movie *The Post*, which dramatizes the newspaper's decision to publish the *Pentagon Papers* and bring the Watergate scandal to light.

Go to **edge.sagepub.com/ dig-deeper**

THREATS TO PROFESSIONAL JOURNALISM

> Journalists are an endangered species. WHY?

 # It is too easy to make money off their work without paying them for it. The lines between "sharing" and "promoting" and "stealing" are extremely blurry. You don't have to be Ronan Farrow, or spend the time and resources of a Ronan Farrow, to link to his work. News aggregators provide readers with curated (that means carefully selected) collections of blurbs about articles reported and written by other people. They don't do the work of reporting, but they make money from it. It's not copyright infringement—the reporting is still on the original site, but the traffic that aggregators get for their short description attracts advertisers' dollars.

News aggregators pose a threat to journalism because good reporting costs money, lots of money. In their heyday, multiple newspapers and networks kept bureaus in the world's major cities to report the news as it happened. Now they are more likely to rely on a pared-down staff, a diminishing number of local journalists, or wire services like the Associated Press that sell their reporting to many subscribers. That means less reporting is happening and more of the same stories are being circulated over and over.

 # People have equated journalism with print journalism. Print journalism has been on the decline, although it has experienced a brief renaissance recently. People don't buy or subscribe to print outlets like they used to, and they object to paying for content online, even though the online reporting is at least as expensive as print. Ask yourself why people think the hard labor of others should be free when few of us would be willing to do a long day's work for nothing. As a result of the widespread belief that Internet content should be free, as well as the collapse of the classified ad business from competitors such as Craigslist, it has taken traditionally print media a long time to come up with models that require users to pay.

 # Belated appreciation of the possibilities of electronic media. As was the case with book publishers, it has taken the media business a long time to figure out what to do with this strange new technology suddenly at their disposal. For a long time, the electronic *New York Times* was just the *New York Times*, updated in real time but more or less what you would find at the newsstand. Now the *Times* has become incredibly creative in coming up with interactive graphics and other ways of conveying information that could not possibly translate to print. Just recently the analytics division, the Upshot, has begun conducting polls in real time so that you can see polling results change as new data are added in real time. Beyond the clever portrayal of data, we also have seen the creation of podcasts, news summary services with links to go deeper, like Axios, and other ways of delivering information to busy people who don't have the leisure to sit down and peruse every page of the *Times*. Something may be lost by that for sure, but other exciting things are being gained.

Public distrust of the media in general. With so many outlets putting out so many conflicting narratives, the public gets confused and unsure about what sources to trust. Our tendencies to live in information bubbles, coupled with the current president's particularly vehement war against any media outlet that is critical of him, doesn't add to public confidence. When the leader of the nation labels a story by a reputable news outlet "fake news," what are people supposed to think?

DIG DEEPER

Check out these interactive features at the *New York Times* and hear the podcast at *Pod Save America*.

Go to **edge.sagepub.com/dig-deeper**

GOOD JOURNALISTS DON'T WRITE FAKE NEWS.

Let's be clear. "Fake news" is an oxymoron. When people use that phrase, for the most part what they are trying to do is to control the narrative—an issue we discuss throughout this book. In reality, news is either fact based, in which case it is true, or it isn't news. What is distinctive about good journalism is reporters' commitment to accuracy, objectivity, and detail in telling their stories. Listening to a panel of journalists (the people who do the work), as opposed to commentators (the people who have opinions about the things that were written by the people who do the work), you can see how meticulous and precise reporters try to be in verifying their facts. That is not to say there are no bad journalists out there. There are some lazy, superficial, and sloppy people in the news business. But, as we said before, journalism is experiencing a renaissance, thanks to some very, very good journalists.

DIG DEEPER

Check out some sound advice about the "fake news fix" from the owners of Axios.

Go to **edge.sagepub.com/dig-deeper**

THE TRUMP EFFECT?

Given President Trump's near constant accusations of "fake news" and assertions that many media outlets are "failing," it is ironic that journalism is experiencing something of a rebirth precisely because of Trump. He is such a constant producer of attention-getting behavior that the media disseminate. A president like Trump could not survive without the media to publicize and talk about every tweet and unconventional thing he says.[1]

IS JOURNALISM DYING? CAN WE AFFORD TO LET IT?

Until recently, the demise of so many print outlets led to numerous stories about whether journalism was dead. Many cities have gone from two daily newspapers to one or none. But newspapers are not the same as journalism. Papers, at least the print versions, could die out altogether, and journalism would still thrive as long as we remain a culture willing to pay for quality reporting. (That means when you run into a paywall on the *Wall Street Journal* or the *New Yorker* or the *Guardian* or *Mother Jones* asking for a contribution, think seriously about the role good journalism plays in keeping democracies strong and whether it's worth a little beer money to help keep it alive.)

9.5 HOW THOSE IN THE MEDIA CAN SHAPE POLITICAL NARRATIVES

TELL ME A STORY.

The primary purpose of the news media (if not all the other interactive channels that shape our life choices) is to tell a convincing story. We know that politics is about creating a narrative and convincing others to believe it, and we rely on the media—the myriad channels of communication we have created—to convey those narratives. Ideally, in the news business, those are fact-based narratives. But in the political world there are plenty of people who want you to believe something that is not fact based or that represents only one part of the truth—either to get you to reject the facts altogether, or to put them in a light that benefits the storyteller. The essential goal of these political narratives is to legitimize or delegitimize the claims to political power. That means that storytelling shapes those narratives on which the health of democracy depends, but also the narratives that threaten its health.

EXACTLY WHO ARE THE STORYTELLERS?

We've talked about journalists. At the pinnacle of political reporting is the Washington press corps, the elite cadre of writers and broadcasters who have worked their way up the ladder of power in Washington. Some of

---

[1] According to Axios, print news, cable TV, books, and social media are all experiencing a "Trump bubble" (https://www.axios.com/newsletters/axios-am-c85d5c8e-ad0e-473d-bc9a-a8dcc8b6bc66.html).

these folks wield almost as much power as politicians themselves. In fact, some of them have *been* politicians, or at least members of the political world. ABC's George Stephanopoulos was communications director for Bill Clinton; MSNBC's Nicolle Wallace worked for the Bushes and John McCain; Karl Rove, a Fox commentator, was George W. Bush's campaign strategist and policy director; and Diane Sawyer, once ABC's nightly anchor, worked for Richard Nixon.

We call this practice of moving from the political sector to the public sector the **revolving door**. Some even go the other way or make a round trip. Journalist David Axelrod became communications director and senior adviser to President Obama and now runs an institute on politics at the University of Chicago, where he hosts a podcast and interviews politicians as a journalist.

AROUND AND AROUND

The revolving door can have some real advantages, because who knows more about what happens in inner circles than people who have inhabited them. The insights they can provide can be super useful. At the same time, even though some are stellar journalists, others' loyalty may lie more toward their political allies than to the public. It takes a critical thinker to know whether you are getting the straight story or political **spin**.

Spin doesn't have anything to do with revolving doors, although it sounds like it does. It is the use of selective pieces of information and intentional interpretation to make something sound like something else. After political debates, political staffers all pour out into "the spin room" to try to sell a narrative in which their candidate won, even if that is far from the truth.

Many of those who have been through the revolving door return in the role of **pundit**, which implies wisdom and experience but sometimes just means the person is a bloviator. Pundits can sometimes fall into the "analyst" category of journalists and their analysis can be piercing and on point, but others can be lazy and biased. Again, critical thinking is your only way to know for sure. Don't accept what "talking heads" say without finding out who they are, who they work for, who they have worked for in the past, and whether they are working from a basis of facts. Wikipedia can be your friend here—use it.

. . . .

revolving door: when people move from the public sector to the private sector and then sometimes back to the public sector again

spin: an interpretation of a politician's words or actions, designed to present a favorable image

pundit: a professional observer and commentator on politics reporting

**TOOLS OF THE
TRADE—HOW
JOURNALISTS CAN
SPIN A TALE AND
HOW YOU CAN
STAY UNSPUN**

Journalists—especially well-placed ones—have a lot of power at their disposal. Even if they are well meaning, objective, and committed to the facts, as so many are, some of the tools they use to create their stories inevitably have an effect on it:

Agenda setting. Agenda setting goes back to the gatekeeper role. What a journalist, editor, or producer decides is important becomes news and ends up on the political agenda. Every day, all kinds of interesting stories don't make the cut, and we rarely know what we don't know.

Framing. Like a frame on a picture, framing helps shape how you see it. By telling you what is important and what to pay attention to, journalists frame the story they tell. That doesn't make it wrong, and a well-framed story can communicate more than mere words, but it is worth paying attention to.

Reliance on professional communicators. Journalists often don't have time to become experts on everything they talk about, so they rely on the professionals who may be newly arrived through the revolving door. These folks may have solid credentials, or they may be wannabes with a good agent. Always, always check the source's pedigree.

Sticking to an easy, existing narrative. We saw when we talked about Ronan Farrow that good journalism can be excruciatingly hard work. Not every journalist wants to or does work that hard. Sometimes it's easy to fall back into a preexisting narrative—the parties don't get along, Congress is dysfunctional, the candidate is corrupt—without doing the hard work necessary to verify the narrative and, if it's true, find out why.

The feeding frenzy. Most Americans have gotten a little blasé about political scandal lately—there are so many, it's hard to focus on one before another pushes it off the front pages. This growing numbness to each new bit of outrageous news has actually been a bit of a relief, because journalism, especially the 24-hour cable news cycle, thrives

---

agenda setting: the process through which issues attain the status of being seriously debated by politically relevant actors

framing: the process through which the media emphasize particular aspects of a news story, thereby influencing the public's perception of the story

on scandal. In a "**feeding frenzy**," a term coined by political scientist Larry Sabato, scandal can turn perfectly normal journalists into human sharks, all circling their prey and waiting for the next tidbit of news to drop. What's true about this is that (1) in the long run the scandals are rarely important and (2) if they are, they need much more serious reporting than they get when they are the subject of journalistic one-upmanship. Not that competition for scoops can't be helpful, but it shouldn't become the point of the exercise.

\# **Horse race journalism.** As we saw in Chapter 8, there are so many pollsters out there that the results of the polls often become the news rather than the issues and candidates' ideas. **Horse race journalism** refers to elections reporting that focuses on who is ahead, who is losing support, and who is a surprise longshot, and not on the substance of what the election is about. It can be exciting, but ultimately, it is devoid of content.

\# **Soundbites**. Nothing is more annoying than to have listened to a great speech and then have media commentators or the Twitterati reduce it to a single line. That is what a **soundbite** is—a short and snappy memorable line that commentators can repeat over and over. Often it is taken out of context and the narrative it is used to support is on very thin ice. Some politicians, knowing that what they say will be reduced to a single juicy line, have taken to speaking in sound bites. They might not be as shallow as they sound, but they don't give you a lot of evidence otherwise.

THE UPSHOT

Journalism is an honorable, essential profession whose ability to freely dig for truth is the main safeguard of democracy. That doesn't mean it exists in a pure environment or cannot be abused. Cable news, the 24-hour news cycle, Twitter, YouTube, and all the other social media available to us have given poor journalists the ability to masquerade as good ones. Smart citizens learn to tell them apart.

- -

feeding frenzy: excessive press coverage of an embarrassing or scandalous subject

horse race journalism: the media's focus on the competitive aspects of politics rather than on actual policy proposals and political decisions

soundbites: a brief, snappy excerpt from a public figure's speech that is easy to repeat on the news

9.6   THE STAKEHOLDERS STRIKE BACK

SAYS WHO?

> Between the mainstream media and the hundreds of new media outlets that have emerged in the Internet era, it is easy to get swamped in a morass of stories and counter-stories. Not only do different media channels have their own agendas—whether it is conveying facts or spinning a specific political narrative—but politicians do not sit silently by and let the media define reality. Politicians find themselves at loggerheads with the media because they want to sell a particular narrative to the public and at least some portion of the media wants to counter with reporting and facts. That's why accusations of "fake news" are so prevalent in our current political era. If politicians can discredit the news media, they can keep citizens confused about what to believe and what is really true.

POLITICIANS FIGHT BACK.

> In fact, in the past fifty years, politicians have gotten increasingly adept at managing the message they want the media to disseminate, or in creating their own media channels that promote their own version of events. From Franklin Roosevelt to Richard Nixon to Donald Trump, technology has allowed politicians to try to create the bubble of information they want their supporters to live in by perfecting the art of political communication.

THIS IS YOUR PRESIDENT SPEAKING.

> FDR, of course, broke the mold, simply by using the new-fangled contraption called the radio. Families would sit around the box—no screen to watch—and listen to their president's weekly "fireside chat" as he talked them through the Depression, recovery, and war. The creation of "the living room president" brought this remote and august presence into everyone's homes. Newer technology has brought the president into everyone's pocket, or at least their computer. The ability to speak regularly to citizens has given politicians a powerful weapon in their perennial battle with the news media. In fact, some scholars have noted that in their effort to continually spin events and their actions to support their narratives, politicians have entered an era of the **permanent campaign**, where they never really stop selling citizens on their story.

. . . .

permanent campaign: the idea that governing requires a continual effort to convince the public to sign on to the program, requiring a reliance on consultants and an emphasis on politics over policy

TRADITIONAL NEWS MANAGEMENT AS CRAFTED BY NIXON

The permanent campaign works through something called **news management**. Political staffs have their hands full managing their boss's message and attempting to control what the media are talking about. These are the techniques of news management, many of which were developed during the Nixon administration:

Tight control of information. Staffers pick a "line of the day"— for instance, health care—and orchestrate all messages from the administration around that theme. This strategy frustrates journalists who are trying to follow independent stories. But it recognizes that the staff must "feed the beast" by giving the press something to cover, or they may find the press rebelling and covering stories they don't want covered at all.

Tight control of access to the politician. If the politician is available to the press for only a short period of time and makes only a brief statement, the press corps is forced to report the appearance as the only available news. Historically, this kind of practice has been standard operating procedure and remains true for most politicians. But today, Trump's frequent tweets, while bypassing the press, continually give the media new material to comment on.

Elaborate communications bureaucracy. The Nixon White House had four offices handling communications. Other administrations have followed suit, having multiple positions such as a communications director, a White House press secretary, an Office of Public Liaison, and a speechwriting office.

A concerted effort to bypass the White House press corps. During Nixon's years, this meant going to regional papers that were more easily manipulated. Today, when many regional papers are consolidated, it means television talk shows and late-night television, town hall meetings, and digital opportunities to reach the public through outlets like Facebook, Reddit, YouTube, and, of course, Twitter.

Prepackaging the news in sound bites. If the media are going to allow the public only a brief snippet of political language, the reasoning goes, let the politician's staff decide what it will be. In line with this, the press office will repeat a message often, to be sure the press and the public pick up on it, and it will work on phrasing that is catchy and memorable. Not incidentally, almost every serious

news management: the efforts of a politician's staff to control news about the politician

politician, including the president, now has a Twitter account that he, she, or the staff uses regularly.

 # Leaks. A final and effective way that politicians attempt to control the news is with the use of leaks, secretly revealing confidential information to the press. Leaks can serve a variety of purposes. For instance, a leak can be a trial balloon, in which an official leaks a policy or plan in order to gauge public reaction to it. If the reaction is negative, the official denies he or she ever mentioned it, and if it is positive, the policy can go ahead without risk. Sometimes leaks signal genuine dissatisfaction, animosity, or disloyalty in an administration, so it can be difficult to sort out communications strategy from politics.

HOW OTHER ADMINISTRATIONS HAVE "FED THE BEAST" OF THE WASHINGTON PRESS CORPS

Different administrations handle news management differently. Ronald Reagan, with an actor's instinct for an audience, ran a smooth public relations shop. Bill Clinton did not, until his second administration. Handling the Washington press corps is not the same as dealing with the media in Arkansas, and both Bill and Hillary had a steep learning curve. George W. Bush's communications office was smooth and professional and did an excellent job of keeping the press's attention where they wanted it. The Obama pressroom too was tightly controlled and frustrating for reporters; leaks and backbiting were nearly unheard of and when they did occur, they were squashed quickly. The Obama press office was really the first to bypass the traditional media, especially with its expert but unusual use of public appearances, as when Obama sang in public or was caught surfing or hanging with his kids.

THE "TRUMP RULES"

It's hard to characterize Donald Trump's press strategy. The press corps doesn't trust Trump's current press secretary, Sarah Huckabee Sanders, because of her habit of not telling the truth. There may be a new press secretary before you read this, but the truth problem is likely to remain since it is a White House strategy. When the communications office does settle on a message, the president often steps on it himself with an unexpected tweet that becomes the news of the day rather than the message his office had planned. Leaks in the Trump White House are legion and have made several book authors extremely rich (Bob Woodward's *Fear* sold 750,000

leaks: confidential information secretly revealed to the press

trial balloon: an official leak of a proposal to determine public reaction to it without risk

copies on the day it was released). Those leaks do not seem to be meant to advance the administration's message. Instead, they reflect a distrustful and suspicious staff that is convinced they need to protect themselves by leaking information that ultimately could be used against them.

In many ways, and for the first time in history, the president essentially runs the White House Communications Office himself. Several extraordinarily well-informed reporters who have connections in the administration (who regularly leak to them) characterize the "Trump Rules" this way:[2]

Deliberately make some people hate you. Polarization energizes his base and gives him a foil to rail against.

Exploit crises or even create them. Trump is comfortable in that high-adrenalin atmosphere and most people are not, which gives him an advantage.

Keep repeating your narrative, and people will believe it whether it is true or not.

Keep the people who work for you afraid and competitive for your favor.

Go for loyalty over skill.

Don't ever admit that you are wrong.

These reporters' observations of the Trump White House communications strategy show that much of what Trump does—while running counter to the methods of his more traditional predecessors—appears to be intentional. It is a strategy that has worked for him in the past, creating a brash persona that appeals to some of his strongest supporters.

THE UPSHOT

Most presidents closely control their message in order to control their political fortunes. Unlike other presidents who avoided scandal and chaos, Trump seems to understand how to use it politically and is confident of his ability to control the consequences, even though the evidence doesn't always bear that out.

The cost of Trump's approach is hard to measure—it is so unorthodox that most journalists don't know how to report on it, and most of the public is either outraged by it, pleased by it, or just numb to his behavior. In that sense, one thing is clear: it has sharpened partisan divisions.

---

[2]https://www.axios.com/donald-trump-rules-commandments-business-presidency-ecca0771-d27c-4b2f-b19e-536f6ee2747d.html

9.7 IMAGINE: HOW CITIZENS CAN RECLAIM THE NARRATIVE

TIME, FLYING

Fifty years ago, we never would have guessed we'd now be carrying all the available political information we needed to make good decisions in our pocket. There were only three TV stations and the giant boxes that were our televisions would not have fit in the Jolly Green Giant's pocket, if he had one. News was big, in many ways, and the narratives were few. Now the news is narrowly targeted, excessively abundant, portable, competitive, sometimes brilliant, often misleading, and requires a strength of civic will to interpret what is going on.

It would have been impossible for most people alive fifty years ago to imagine the potential of a smartphone. Computers themselves were lumbering machines that occupied entire buildings and had less capacity than your phone.

Today's media world, as we have said several times, leaves us extremely vulnerable to manipulation, and it's no coincidence that populist, nationalist movements across the globe are ginning up anger and resentment through the possibilities of the Internet.

But as we have also said multiple times, the potential of the Internet gives all of us a voice if we choose to use it—from the kids who fought back against guns in schools after the shootings in Parkland, Florida, to the young communications staff in the Obama administration who started the podcast series *Pod Save America* and its offshoots, to *Breitbart News* and the *Drudge Report,* which created an entire right-wing media universe.

Facebook. Amazon. Apple. Netflix. Alphabet. They go by the acronym FAANG (from when alphabet was still google.) These giants control a huge part of the world we live in. We have barely begun to tap the opportunities that the mediated world offers us. Our technological abilities have outrun our ability to think through the ethical implications of what is possible. They are equally likely to be our salvation or our destruction.

Thought experiment: Imagine fifty years from *now.* How will we have dealt with the challenges we now grapple with, and what new challenges will technology have generated for us to deal with?

The American founders never imagined any of this world we live in. The system they designed is strong enough to handle the challenges if enough citizens step forward to pick up the torch and continue to think through what the democratic experiment entails. Will they? Will you? What will you see when you look around fifty years from now? What will be in *your* pocket?

Big Think

→ How would the founders cope with the challenges of the media world today?

→ Having lived only as a mediated citizen, how would you write the rules for human interaction if it were up to you?

→ How can we deal with the media's eternal dilemma between reporting news and making a profit?

Key Terms

CONCEPTS

agenda setting (p. 302)

clickbait (p. 293)

commercial bias (p. 292)

feeding frenzy (p. 303)

framing (p. 302)

horse race journalism (p. 303)

information bubble (p. 288)

infotainment (p. 293)

leaks (p. 306)

media (p. 284)

media aggregators (p. 285)

media convergence (p. 287)

net neutrality (p. 295)

news management (p. 305)

permanent campaign (p. 304)

reporting (p. 285)

revolving door (p. 301)

soundbites (p. 303)

spin (p. 301)

trial balloon (p. 306)

KEY INDIVIDUALS AND GROUPS

gatekeepers (p. 292)

journalists (p. 285)

mediated citizens (p. 288)

pundit (p. 301)

#10 DOMESTIC AND FOREIGN POLICY

In this chapter:

10.1 Introduction to POLICY

YOU CAN RUN, BUT YOU CAN'T HIDE.

Our lives are ruled—limited and enhanced—by policies, both public and private. Just try to escape them. (*Hint:* Don't bother, you can't.)

Because policies are all around us, we use the word constantly but rarely stop to think about what it means. So we'll help you out. A **policy** is a pre-scribed course of action, a way of accomplishing a goal, or a set of opera-tional principles. Policies can be private or public depending not on whom they affect but on *who makes them*.

Many stores, for instance, have a no-return *policy* on sales merchandise. Restaurant owners alert customers to their *policy* toward underdressed din-ers with the sign "No shirt, no shoes, no service." A hotel may withhold the cost of a first night's stay if you cancel your reservation past a certain time. Those are all private policies.

Governments produce even more policies because that is partly, even mostly, what governments exist to do. Policies made by government are called public policies. Public policies include policy about taxes and immi-gration and drinking ages and pensions.

One of the big divisions in American politics, as we have seen, is that Americans don't really agree on the appropriate areas for government action (i.e., **policymaking**). Democrats think there should be health care policy and higher taxes to pay for it; Republicans think there should be no health care policy and lower taxes. Democrats think reproductive choices are none of government's business; Republicans want policies that limit them.

The parties are responding to their ideologies when they propose or make policies, but they also respond to their constituents. In some policy areas, such as social welfare reform and crime policy, politicians have responded to public opinion by limiting welfare and getting tougher on criminals. In other areas, notably Social Security and health care, politicians have responded to the powerful demands of organized interest groups by resist-ing changes to the programs.

In still other policy areas, primarily economic policy, some of the political decisions have been taken out of the hands of elected officials precisely because these individuals tend to respond to what voters and interest groups want, or what they imagine they want.

Public policy is a government plan of action to solve a problem that people share collectively or that they cannot solve on their own. That is not to say that the intended problem is always solved, or that the plan might not create more and even worse problems. Sometimes government's plan of action is to do nothing. That is, it may be a plan of *in*action, with the expectation (or hope) that the problem will go away on its own, or in the belief that it is not or should not be government's business to solve it. Some issues may be so controversial that policymakers would rather leave them alone, confining the scope of a policy debate to relatively "safe" issues.

IN A NUTSHELL

By and large, we can understand public policy as a purposeful course of action intended by public officials to solve a public problem. When that problem occurs here in the United States, we say that the government response is domestic policy; when it concerns our relations with other nations, we call it foreign policy.

WHERE WE GO IN THIS CHAPTER

By the time you finish reading this chapter, you will understand

→ How public policy is made

→ What is involved in social policy

→ The ins and outs of economic policy

→ The often hard-to-understand issues of foreign policy

10.2 MAKING PUBLIC POLICY

WHO DOES IT? 〉 All the political actors we have studied in this book have a hand in the policymaking process. Government actors inside the system—members of Congress, the president, bureaucrats, and the courts—are involved. In fact, national policies are best thought of as packages made by several actors.

policy: a prescribed course of action, a way of accomplishing a goal, or a set of operational principles

policymaking: the process of formulating policies

public policy: a government plan of action to solve a problem that people share collectively or that they cannot solve on their own

\# **Congress.** Policies are usually created by members of Congress in the form of one or more new laws. The role of Congress in creating and legitimating policy through its laws is critically important to understanding national public policy. As we just suggested, members of Congress follow their own values and consciences when making difficult political decisions but are more often most attentive to what their constituencies and the interest groups that support their campaigns want.

\# **The president.** Presidents may also create policy, perhaps by putting an issue on the public agenda, by including it (or not) in their budget proposal, by vetoing a law made by Congress, or by issuing an executive order that establishes a new policy or augments an existing one.

\# **Government bureaucracies at the federal, state, or local level** may create or enhance policy through their power to regulate. Administrative agencies are crucial to the policymaking process, helping to propose laws, lobbying for their passage, making laws of their own under authority delegated from Congress, and implementing laws. Moreover, agencies have enormous control over policy simply by how they enforce it.

\# **Courts.** Finally, the courts are policymakers as well. We have seen that the Supreme Court has been responsible for some of the major changes in policy direction in this country with respect to business regulation, civil rights, and civil liberties, to name just a few. When the courts rule on what the government can or should do (or not do), they are clearly taking an active policymaking role. In addition, they are often asked to rule on the implementation of policy decisions made elsewhere in the government—on affirmative action, for example, or welfare policy, or education.

SO, WHAT COULD GO WRONG?

It sounds like the process is smooth and efficient, but all kinds of things can get in the way of solving the nation's problems:

\# **People have different narratives about what constitutes a problem in the first place.** You can't look up the definition of a public problem in a book. It is the product of the values and beliefs of political actors and, consequently, is frequently the subject of passionate debate. Even something that seems to be as obviously problematic as poverty can be controversial. To people who believe that poverty is an inevitable though unfortunate part of life, or to those who feel that poor people should take responsibility for themselves, poverty may not be a problem requiring a public solution.

SKIM IT!

10.1: THE SKIMMABLE FEEDBACK LOOP OF POLICYMAKING

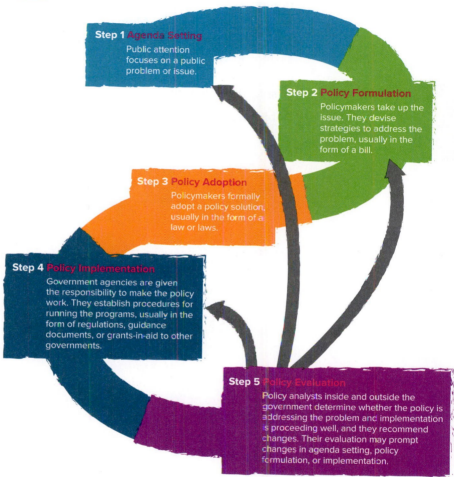

Step 1 Agenda Setting
Public attention focuses on a public problem or issue.

Step 2 Policy Formulation
Policymakers take up the issue. They devise strategies to address the problem, usually in the form of a bill.

Step 3 Policy Adoption
Policymakers formally adopt a policy solution, usually in the form of a law or laws.

Step 4 Policy Implementation
Government agencies are given the responsibility to make the policy work. They establish procedures for running the programs, usually in the form of regulations, guidance documents, or grants-in-aid to other governments.

Step 5 Policy Evaluation
Policy analysts inside and outside the government determine whether the policy is addressing the problem and implementation is proceeding well, and they recommend changes. Their evaluation may prompt changes in agenda setting, policy formulation, or implementation.

agenda setting: the process through which issues attain the status of being seriously debated by politically relevant actors

policy formulation: a phase of the policymaking process in which policies are developed to address specific problems that have been placed on the national agenda

policy adoption: a phase of the policymaking process in which policies are adopted by government bodies for future implementation

policy implementation: a phase of the policymaking process in which government executes an adopted policy as specified by legislation or policy action

policy evaluation: a phase of the policymaking process in which policymakers attempt to assess the merit, worth, and utility of a policy

\# **Solutions cost money**—often a lot of money. Finding the money to address a new problem usually requires shifting it out of existing programs or raising taxes. With an eye toward the next election, politicians are reluctant to spend tax dollars to support new initiatives.

\# **Public problems can be difficult to solve because their solutions often generate new problems.** Policies having to do with getting tough on crime can jam up the courts and slow the criminal justice system. Environmental policies can impair a business's ability to compete. Often the problems caused by a policy require new policies to solve them in turn.

\# **Public problems are complex.** Seldom are there easy answers to any public dilemma. Even when policymakers can agree on a goal, they often lack sufficient knowledge about how to get there. Policymaking in the American context is made even more complex by the federal system. Whose responsibility is it to solve a given problem—the federal, state, or local government's?

ARE ALL POLICIES THE SAME? ❯ Not all policies are the same—scholars have come up with a typology of domestic problems that require different kinds of policies to solve them. By different kinds of policies, we mean differences in who pays and who benefits.

THE POLITICS BEHIND THE POLICIES ❯ Clearly the politics behind each of these kinds of policies are different.

\# **Redistributive policies** are generally politically difficult to put in place because they take resources away from the affluent segments of society who are most likely to be politically active, to vote regularly, and to contribute to political campaigns or interest groups, and the benefits are received by those who are less likely to participate.

\# **Distributive policies**, by contrast, are much easier to make, because the costs are not perceived to be borne by any particular segment of the population. Instead, they are borne by the entire population. This means people don't necessarily notice or resent the groups who are gaining at their expense.

redistributive policies: policies that shift resources from more affluent segments of society to those who are less affluent and less likely to participate politically

distributive policies: policies funded by the whole taxpayer base that address the needs of particular groups

**Regulatory policies** don't distribute resources as much as they control behavior. Since the groups being regulated generally don't like it and since they frequently have greater resources at their disposal than the groups seeking the regulation (often public interest groups), the battle to regulate business can be lopsided.

THE UPSHOT

As we look at different policy areas—social, economic, and foreign—we will see most of these political dynamics at play depending on the type of policy involved.

SKIM IT!

10.2: THE SKIMMABLE POLICY TYPOLOGY

Type of policy	Policy goal	Who promotes this policy	Who benefits?	Who pays?	Examples
Redistributive	Helping the disadvantaged	Public interest groups, politicians motivated by compassion	Disadvantaged citizens	Middle-class and wealthy citizens	Medicaid, food security policy, health care
Distributive	Meeting the needs of specific groups	Legislators and interest groups	Members of targeted groups	All taxpayers	Veterans, farmers, middle-class mortgage holders
Regulatory	Limiting or controlling the actions of individuals or groups	Public interest groups, public demand	The public	Targeted groups	Environmental policy, food and drug regulation, automobile safety

regulatory policies: policies designed to restrict or change the behavior of certain groups or individuals

10.3 SOCIAL POLICY

NO, THIS IS NOT ABOUT YOUR SOCIAL LIFE.

> **Social policy** is serious business to many Americans, who depend on it to improve the quality of their lives. Since social policies are primarily distributive or redistributive, a good deal of political controversy usually surrounds them.
>
> Here are the key social policies in the United States: social welfare, welfare for the well-to-do, social insurance, and health care.

POLICIES THAT PROVIDE A MINIMUM QUALITY OF LIFE

> What you need to know about **social welfare policies**:
>
> These are government programs that provide for the needs of those who cannot, or sometimes will not, provide for themselves—needs for shelter, food and clothing, jobs, education, old age care, and medical assistance. Most social welfare policies are redistributive; they transfer resources, in the form of financial assistance or essential services, from those with resources to those without.

PROVING YOU ARE POOR

> These policies are usually **means-tested programs**; that is, beneficiaries must prove that they lack the necessary income or resources (means) to provide for themselves, according to the government's definitions of eligibility. Being on government support can carry a social stigma that keeps some qualified people from applying and makes others look down on recipients.

HISTORY OF "WELFARE"

> What we think of as "welfare" (as opposed to private charitable efforts to care for the poor) began with a New Deal policy called **Aid to Families with Dependent Children (AFDC)**, a policy designed to ensure that poor families could take care of their kids. It was means tested and the focus was on families with children—it did not provide assistance to childless adults.

social policy: distributive and redistributive policies that seek to improve the quality of citizens' lives

social welfare policies: government programs that provide for the needs of those who cannot, or sometimes will not, provide for themselves

means-tested programs: programs that require beneficiaries to prove that they lack the necessary income or resources (means) to provide for themselves, according to the government's definitions of eligibility

Aid to Families with Dependent Children (AFDC): a New Deal–era policy designed to ensure that poor families could take care of their kids

CRITICS

> AFDC was criticized because

- It contained no work requirements.
- It set no time limits for remaining on welfare.
- It seemed to transfer money from a hard-working segment of the population to one that did nothing to earn it.
- Many Americans believed that welfare recipients were unwilling to work, living off the generosity of hard-working taxpayers.
- It created disincentives for recipients to become productive members of society.

THE END OF WELFARE "AS WE KNOW IT"

> Since lower income people are less likely to organize for political purposes, welfare recipients put up no coordinated defense of their benefits. On August 22, 1996, President Bill Clinton signed the Personal Responsibility and Work Opportunity Reconciliation Act, fulfilling his promise to "end welfare as we know it."

TANF—WELFARE AS WE KNOW IT NOW

> With Clinton's signature, AFDC was replaced by **Temporary Assistance to Needy Families (TANF)**, which

- Provides block grants to state governments, giving states greater control over how they spend their money
- Caps the amount the federal government will pay for welfare
- Requires work in exchange for time-limited benefits
- Requires recipients to find a job within two years of going on welfare
- Removes recipients from the welfare rolls after a total of five years altogether or less, depending on the state

The reforms have successfully reduced the welfare rolls. The Department of Health and Human Services reports that, from August 1996 to December 2017, the number of welfare recipients fell from 12.2 million to 3.2 million. Most states met their 2004 goals in putting 50 percent of single parents to work for thirty hours per week and 90 percent of two-parent families to work for thirty-five hours per week.

. . . .

Temporary Assistance to Needy Families (TANF): a welfare program of block grants to states that encourages recipients to work in exchange for time-limited benefits

SNAP—FOOD STAMPS BY ANOTHER NAME

TANF is not the only policy designed to solve the problem of poverty in the United States. The largest food assistance program is the **Supplemental Nutrition Assistance Program (SNAP)**, previously called the Food Stamp program. SNAP provides low-income families with vouchers to purchase food (typically dispensed via an electronic system using a plastic card similar to a bank card). SNAP is part of the Farm Bill that has to be renewed every five years, though, which makes it a popular target for budget cuts.

THE UPSHOT

Though many Americans are unaware of it, the policy we have referred to for years as "welfare" is mostly gone. That doesn't stop us from arguing over who the government should help and who should take care of themselves. Since TANF is a block grant, it is relatively easy for politicians to cut if they are trying to save money, making it a convenient battleground.

POLICIES THAT PROVIDE WELFARE FOR THE WELL-TO-DO

What you need to know about **middle-class and corporate welfare**:

Social policies include programs that increase the quality of life for the middle class and those that benefit U.S. corporations. Such distributive policies give these group **subsidies**, which are financial incentives intended to encourage certain activities or behaviors. Even though these subsidies are designed to achieve government's ends, they have long since fallen into the category of benefits to which groups feel entitled.

FOR INDIVIDUALS

Workers, middle-class homeowners, students, and members of the military may receive tax deductions or cash grants to encourage home ownership or college attendance, for example. You do not need to prove that you are poor to receive these benefits, although some student aid is means tested. Churches don't pay property taxes, which makes them available to individuals for worship in areas they might not otherwise be able to afford.

Supplemental Nutrition Assistance Program (SNAP): a federal program that provides vouchers to the poor to help them buy food

middle-class and corporate welfare: a set of distributive policies that benefit the middle class and corporations

subsidies: financial incentives given by the government to individuals, corporations, or other government jurisdictions or institutions usually to encourage certain activities or behaviors

FOR CORPORATIONS

Corporations or other governments may receive price supports or tax breaks. According to some analysts, an estimated $170 billion is funneled to U.S. corporations through direct federal subsidies and tax breaks each year. Many corporate subsidies are linked to efforts to create jobs. However, there is little oversight for many of these programs, and in many instances subsidies have gone to companies that are downsizing or—in the case of many high-tech companies—moving jobs overseas. Business leaders also claim that subsidies for research and development are needed to keep American companies afloat in the global marketplace. The biggest winners are agribusiness, the oil industry, and energy plants.

DIG DEEPER

Watch *Park Avenue*, the PBS documentary by Alex Gibney about the gap between the rich and the poor in the United States.

Go to **edge.sagepub.com/dig-deeper**

POLICIES THAT PROVIDE SOCIAL INSURANCE

What you need to know about **social insurance policies**:

Whereas social *welfare* policies are usually designed to be temporary solutions for helping the poor, social *insurance* programs cover longer range needs. Social insurance programs are distributive because everyone pays, but only a certain segment of the population—in the case of Social Security, the elderly—receives benefits.

HISTORY OF SOCIAL SECURITY

Social Security was born in the midst of the Great Depression, when many older Americans found themselves facing an impoverished retirement. Lyndon Johnson's amendment to the act added health care benefits for the elderly in the form of Medicare (described later in this section). These two programs have brought financial security to many retired people, but they are costly programs, especially with the Baby Boomer generation reaching retirement age.

HOW DOES SOCIAL SECURITY WORK?

People contribute to Social Security during their working lives in order to receive benefits when they retire. Recipients contribute a portion of their income, matched by their employers, directly into a fund for Social Security. Contributions appear on workers' paychecks as a

social insurance policies: programs that offer benefits in exchange for contributions

Social Security: a social insurance program under which individuals make contributions during working years and collect benefits in retirement

withholding called FICA (Federal Insurance Contributions Act). Current workers pay the Social Security of current retirees, with any leftover money going into the Social Security trust fund. When workers retire, they receive monthly checks from the Social Security Administration, based on how much money they have paid into the system.

INSURANCE, OR WELFARE?

Most people, at least old ones, see Social Security in a positive light—as if they are receiving something they have earned and to which they are entitled, not a government handout. Even though Social Security is considered a social insurance program, it operates quite differently from traditional insurance. Lots of folks may pay into an insurance plan—say, one that protects your house from fire—but few people's houses actually burn down, so few claims are made. By contrast, most people who contribute to Social Security do end up collecting benefits, and, with longer life spans, most people end up getting much more back from Social Security and Medicare than they contribute. That puts an element of "welfare" into the program as well, one that its recipients generally refuse to see because of the stigma the word carries.

TROUBLE IN PARADISE?

Since there is no means test for Social Security, not only poor recipients but also billionaires can continue to collect this direct subsidy from taxpayers. So far this system has worked because the number of people in the workforce has been able to cover the retirement expenses of those leaving it, but that will change by 2034 as the number of retirees grows and the fund is tapped to pay their benefits.

AN ENTITLEMENT IS PAID NO MATTER WHAT

Unless the law changes that promise, the government will have to pay benefits whether or not the money is there. This is because Social Security is an **entitlement program**, which means that benefits must be paid to people who are entitled to receive them. Entitlements comprise an increasing share of the federal budget.

KEY POINT

Social Security could be made sustainable, but the remedies—means-testing benefits, cutting benefit levels, increasing taxes, or raising the retirement age—are politically unpalatable and vigorously opposed by groups like AARP (formerly known as the American Association of Retired People). If these changes were enacted, people would have to pay more, get less, or both, and those are unpopular options. This poses a problem politicians have not yet had the genius or the courage to solve.

entitlement program: a federal program that guarantees benefits to qualified recipients

POLICIES THAT PROVIDE HEALTH INSURANCE

What you need to know about **health care policy**:

The United States stands out among industrialized nations as the only one that doesn't have a universal health care system guaranteeing minimum basic care to all.

HEALTH CARE IN AMERICA PRE-2010: MEDICARE (COVERING OLD PEOPLE) AND MEDICAID (COVERING THE POOREST PEOPLE) AND LOTS OF UNINSURED PEOPLE WHO FALL THROUGH THE CRACKS

Before Congress passed and President Barack Obama signed the **Patient Protection and Affordable Care Act** (aka Obamacare or the ACA) in 2010, the federal government's only role in health care was confined to the provision of Medicare and Medicaid. Like Social Security, **Medicare** is a social insurance program designed to help the elderly pay their medical costs. Like TANF, **Medicaid** is a means-tested welfare program to assist the poor—especially children—with their medical costs. Between these two programs, many Americans were left uninsured, either unable to provide insurance for themselves, or willing to gamble that they would not need it. Indeed, an estimated 49.9 million Americans, or 16.3 percent of the population, were without coverage in 2010.

As the population ages and lives longer, and as medical costs skyrocket, Medicare has become an extraordinarily expensive program. Medicare is the nation's fourth largest expenditure, and the trustees for the Medicare trust fund estimate that full benefit payments can be made only until 2027, seven years before the Social Security trust fund is expected to experience a shortfall. Because of this, many people argue that policymakers need to deal urgently with Medicare as well as Social Security.

AND THEN CAME OBAMACARE.

The Affordable Care Act was intended to make access to health insurance more available and affordable for most Americans by 2014. But the politics of passing the bill were difficult. Republicans refused to support it at all, and the policy has been weakened considerably by lack of cooperation among some states and by executive action by President Trump.

health care policy: a country's decisions, plans, and actions designed to promote specific health care objectives

Patient Protection and Affordable Care Act: health care legislation passed during the Obama administration designed to make health care more affordable to more people

Medicare: the federal government's health insurance program for the elderly and disabled

Medicaid: a federally sponsored program that provides medical care to the poor

WHAT IS/WAS IN THE ACA?

When the ACA was signed into law in March 2010, it included

- The requirement that employers with fifty or more employees provide health care coverage

- A universal mandate that people without employer-sponsored coverage obtain insurance for themselves

- A regulation of private insurance companies so that they had to offer, through state exchanges, plans that could not deny coverage because of preexisting coverage, could not kick people off their coverage when they became sick, and could not cap benefits

- An expansion of Medicaid to states to subsidize the insurance premiums of those who could not afford them

- The provision of tax subsidies to small corporations

- An allowance that let children stay on their parents' insurance until they were twenty-six years of age

IMPLICATIONS OF THE 2010 MIDTERM LOSS FOR HEALTH CARE

After the grueling battle to pass the ACA, the public was frustrated with the partisan debate and still suffering from a demolished economy. They voted heavily against the Democrats in the 2010 midterm elections, in many places costing the Democrats control at the state level, a factor that would have eased implementation of the health care plan.

CRITICAL SCOTUS DECISIONS

The policy eventually ended up before the U.S. Supreme Court, at two different times. The Court upheld the policy but weakened the law's requirement that states participate in the Medicaid portion of the law. By October 2018, thirty-three states and the District of Columbia agreed to participate and expand Medicaid coverage. Another three states were considering expansion and fourteen had decided against it. The percentage of adults who were uninsured for at least part of the previous year plummeted from 51 million in 2010 to 33.2 million in the first nine months of 2017.

ATTEMPTS TO REPEAL, REFORM, AND REPLACE

The Republicans continued to rail against the plan, however, and held multiple votes in the House to repeal it. With Donald Trump's assumption of office in 2017, Republicans believed their opportunity to overturn the law had arrived. A repeal bill was introduced that put in place various provisions attractive to Republicans, such as giving states more flexibility in establishing essential health benefits and ending various ACA taxes and fees. The House finally passed the bill in May on a 217–213 vote, with twenty

Republicans—most of them moderates from districts that voted for Hillary Clinton in 2016—joining all of the House's Democrats in opposition.

The focus shifted to the Senate, where Republican leaders drafted their own version of the repeal bill behind closed doors. For the final vote, they lost three of their own party members' votes. Decrying the lack of bipartisanship (see pp. 136–137), Senator John McCain voted against the bill, along with Susan Collins and Lisa Murkowski, and all of the Senate's Democrats.

WHERE THE ACA STANDS TODAY ❯ Despite their failure to overturn the ACA, Republicans did succeed in 2017 in passing, as part of their tax overhaul bill, a repeal of the "individual mandate" requirement that most Americans have insurance or pay a fine. The nonpartisan Congressional Budget Office estimated that, in 2019, the move would raise insurance premiums in the individual market by 10 percent. Then, in February 2018, the Trump administration called for expanding short-term health insurance plans. Those plans are intended as temporary insurance coverage, generally to help people manage transitions between different sources of coverage. The administration's rule called for expanding the plans' duration, making them a long-term source of coverage. The ACA's supporters criticized the move as another way to drive up premiums in the individual insurance market and thus weaken the law.

THE UPSHOT Currently, the law has lived up to most of its supporters' expectations, but we have yet to see how the Republican changes and Trump's new policies will affect it.

10.4 ECONOMIC POLICY

MONEY MAKES THE WORLD GO AROUND. ❯ **Economic policy** addresses the problem of economic security, not for a particular group or segment of society, but for society itself. The U.S. economy is a regulated market system in which the government intervenes to protect rights and make procedural guarantees.

. . . .

economic policy: all the different strategies that government officials employ to solve economic problems

10.3: THE SKIMMABLE GUIDE TO ECONOMIC POLICY

Kind of economic policy	What is it?	Type of policy	What kind of problems does it solve?	Tools policymakers can use
Fiscal policy	The government's power to tax and spend to stabilize the economy	Redistributive	Stimulates a lagging economy by government spending, which helps create jobs, or by cutting taxes, which gives people money to spend; or cools off an inflationary economy by raising taxes and decreasing the ability to spend.	Politicians' decision to tax or hold off on spending may create **surpluses** (saved money); the decision to cut taxes or to spend may result in **deficits**. When the economy stabilizes, the budget can be balanced.
Monetary policy	The government's power to control the money supply by manipulating **interest rates**	Regulatory	When there is a lot of money, people can borrow it cheaply—that is, at low interest rates—and they are more likely to spend it, raising aggregate demand. # By raising and lowering interest rates, government can regulate the cycles of the market economy just as it does by taxing and spending. # When	The determination of interest rates is not a political decision since it would be heavily subject to lobbying by politicians. Instead the power to set rates lies with the **Federal Reserve System** (the Fed). The Fed is a system of 12 banks run by a board of governors whose chair is appointed by the president.

fiscal policy: the government's power to tax and spend to stabilize the economy

surpluses: the extra funds available because government's revenues are greater than its expenditures

deficits: shortfalls in the budget due to the government's spending more in a year than it takes in

monetary policy: the government's power to control the money supply by manipulating interest rates

interest rates: the cost of borrowing money, calculated as a percentage of the money borrowed

Federal Reserve System: the independent commission that controls the money supply through a system of twelve federal banks

Kind of economic policy	What is it?	Type of policy	What kind of problems does it solve?	Tools policymakers can use
			interest rates are high, people borrow less because it costs more; thus they spend less and cool down the economy.	
Tax policy	The government's power to require that individuals and businesses contribute to collective costs	Redistributive	Taxing is how we pay for things. # We tax as part of fiscal policy but also to pay for public projects and to pay off debt. # We cut taxes as part of fiscal policy and because Americans don't like to pay them and put a lot of pressure on politicians to cut them.	# **Progressive income taxes**: taxing people with more money at a higher rate. # **Regressive taxes**: flat taxes that consume a higher percentage of a poorer person's money, like sales taxes or **value-added taxes (VATs)** or some proposals for a flat income tax. # **Capital gains taxes**: taxes levied on the return from capital investments.
Regulatory policy	Government intervention to alter the market by controlling it or yielding control (**deregulation**)	Regulatory	Designed to correct present problems or prevent future ones: consumer protection, creation of a stable housing market, environmental protection, levels of risk financial institutions can take on.	Regulatory tools are political and bureaucratic. # Politicians are highly vulnerable to the pressure of interests that do not want to be regulated and bureaucratic agencies may be as well.

tax policy: the government's power to require that individuals and businesses contribute to collective costs

progressive income taxes: taxing people who have more money at a higher rate

regressive taxes: flat taxes, like sales taxes, that consume a higher percentage of a poorer person's money

value-added taxes (VATs): taxes levied at each stage of production, based on the value added to the product at that stage

capital gains taxes: a tax levied on the return from capital investments

deregulation: the elimination of regulations in order to improve economic efficiency

All the different strategies that government officials, both elected and appointed, employ today to solve economic problems, to protect economic rights, and to provide procedural guarantees to help the market run smoothly are called economic policy.

THE CONSEQUENCES OF AN UNREGULATED MARKET

For much of our history, policymakers have felt that government should pursue a hands-off economic policy, in effect letting the market take care of itself, guided only by the laws of supply and demand. This attitude was in keeping with a basic tenet of capitalism, which holds that the economy is already regulated by millions of individual decisions made each day by consumers and producers in the market. The Great Depression of the 1930s, however, changed the way government policymakers viewed the economy. Since that economic disaster, the goal of economic policymakers has been to even out the dramatic cycles of inflation and recession without undermining the vitality and productivity of a market-driven economy.

When we talk about economic policy, we are focusing on several different ways of solving economic problems: fiscal policy, monetary policy, tax policy, and regulatory policy.

Today policymakers use a combination of fiscal and monetary policy to achieve economic goals, and the highs and lows of boom and bust have been tempered greatly. Still financial crises like the crash of 2008 happen, often as a result of failed regulation or other political pressure on economic forces.

ECONOMIC POLICY AT WORK: AN EXAMPLE (NOT SHORT, NOT SIMPLE, BUT STICK WITH US AND SEE HOW IT WORKS)

Let's look at an example of economic policy making as it unfolded:

In response to the 2008 financial disaster, the new president, Barack Obama, pushed through a stimulus bill (using the government's tools of fiscal policy), but he was limited by a Congress that didn't give him as big a stimulus as he wanted. The results were predictable: a sluggish recovery.

With the 2010 deficit projected to be $1.3 trillion (just below the record $1.42 trillion of 2009), the issues of spending and taxing were back at the heart of partisan battles as the midterm elections approached. Republicans declared the stimulus bill a failure because it hadn't created enough jobs to pump up the economy, saying further that a recession was no time for government to spend money. They deplored the recklessness of running up the deficit by spending, while insisting that the Bush tax cuts, scheduled to lapse in 2010, be made permanent. The Democrats, by contrast, argued that a recession was the very time that government should spend money and demanded an end to the Bush tax cuts for the top 2 percent of the population.

The 2010 midterm elections were a disaster for Democrats. Republicans, many of them allied with the low-tax, limited-government Tea Party movement, regained control of the House of Representatives while picking up seats in the Senate. They vowed to balance the budget by reining in spending without raising taxes. House Budget Committee chair Paul Ryan, R-Wis., proposed a controversial long-term budget that called for overhauling Medicare for all those Americans currently under age fifty-five, turning Medicaid into a series of block grants to states, and switching the Social Security system to guaranteed private accounts. Even though the bill had no chance of passing in the Democratic-led Senate, the House adopted the Ryan plan in 2011 with only four Republican "no" votes and over unanimous Democratic opposition.

That action set the stage for one of the most politically volatile debates of recent years. During the summer of 2011, President Obama and congressional Democrats engaged in a fierce battle with Republicans over raising the federal debt limit, a measure necessary to allow the government to pay off debts it had already incurred. Between 1960 and August 2011, Congress had voted to raise the debt ceiling seventy-eight times as a way to make government borrowing easier.

But Republicans in the House openly called for the government to default on its debts as a way of forcing lawmakers to become serious about addressing longer term budget problems. They thwarted an attempt by President Obama to forge a "grand bargain" with House Speaker John Boehner, R-Ohio, when it became clear that such a deal might include tax increases, something most House Republicans opposed unconditionally. Eventually an agreement was struck to raise the debt limit, but the chaotic process took a heavy toll on the

DIG DEEPER

Check out the movie *The Big Short,* which dramatizes the causes of the 2008 financial collapse.

Go to **edge.sagepub.com/ dig-deeper**

federal government's credibility. The bond rating house Standard & Poor's downgraded the U.S. credit rating for the first time in history, and a *New York Times* poll showed the highest disapproval ratings for Congress since the newspaper began recording them. Veteran political scientists Norman Ornstein and Thomas Mann said the incident exemplified Congress's deep dysfunction and led them to call their 2012 book about Capitol Hill *It's Even Worse Than It Looks*.

THE UPSHOT

This is just one recent example of how political forces and economic forces can clash. The parties have different views on the value of fiscal policy—Democrats want to spend to stimulate the economy; Republicans want to cut taxes. The dissent within the Republican Party made the deal making even more complicated. Steady but slow economic growth eliminated the need for more stimulus but did not stop the demand for tax cuts, which were passed almost as soon as Donald Trump became president.

10.5 FOREIGN POLICY

POLICY ACROSS THE BORDERS

Foreign policy is official U.S. policy designed to solve problems that take place between the United States and actors outside its borders. It is crucial to the country's domestic tranquility; without a strong and effective foreign policy, the United States' security as a rich and peaceful country could be blown away in a heartbeat.

Foreign policy, just like domestic policy, is about who gets what, and how they get it. One difference is that in foreign policy the stakes can be a matter of life and death, and we have far less control over the other actors involved. Another difference is that foreign policy is often made in secret. When foreign policy makers start responding to domestic constituencies, foreign policy can start to be made in the interests of specific groups and not in the interests of the country as a whole.

KEY POINT

U.S. foreign policy is almost always carried out for the good of American citizens or in the interest of national security. Even foreign aid, which to some critics seems like giving away American taxpayers' hard-earned

foreign policy: a country's official positions, practices, and procedures for dealing with actors outside its borders

money to people who have done nothing to deserve it, is part of a foreign policy to stabilize the world, to help strengthen international partnerships and alliances like NATO (the North Atlantic Treaty Organization), and to keep Americans safe.

TWO FUNDAMENTAL PERSPECTIVES ON OUR RELATIONSHIP WITH THE WORLD

There are two ways Americans have approached foreign policy over the years, and there remains a tension between those two perspectives today:

\#   **Isolationism** holds that Americans should put themselves and their problems first and not interfere in global concerns. The United States has tried to pursue an isolationist policy before, perhaps most notably after World War I, but this experiment was seen largely as a failure. Most recently, the events of September 11, 2001, have put to rest the fiction that what happens "over there" is unrelated to what is happening "over here." Still President Trump has been turning back in an isolationist direction, closing the door to immigrants and weakening the country's relationships with traditional allies like NATO because he doesn't feel they pay a fair share of their defense, although the NATO countries were meant to be our buffer to holding an aggressive Soviet Union at bay.

\#   **Interventionism** holds that to keep the republic safe, the United States must be actively engaged in shaping the global environment and be willing to intervene in order to shape events. The United States has had a long history of interventionism—in the Americas and Asia in the 1800s; in World Wars I and II; and, since September 11, in the Middle East, especially under President George W. Bush. Unlike Trump, President Obama had a global perspective on the United States' relationships with other countries, but he didn't think we needed to take the lead in solving every international problem.

WHAT'S FOREIGN? WHAT'S NOT?

Sometimes the distinction between "foreign" and "domestic" is not so clear. Consider, for example, how environmental policy in the United States can have foreign repercussions. American industries located on the border with Canada have been the source of some tensions between the two countries because pollution from U.S. factories is carried into Canada by prevailing

. . . .

isolationism: a foreign policy view that nations should stay out of international political alliances and activities and focus on domestic matters

interventionism: a foreign policy view that, to keep the republic safe, the United States must be actively engaged in shaping the global environment and be willing to intervene to shape events

winds. This pollution can damage forests and increase the acidity of lakes, killing fish and harming other wildlife. Environmental regulations are largely a domestic matter, but because pollution is not confined to the geography of the United States, the issue takes on unintended international importance. Still, foreign policy is generally understood to be intentionally directed at external actors and the forces that shape these actions. External actors are obviously other countries, but they are also organizations that exist across borders:

WHO ARE THESE EXTERNAL ACTORS?

- # **Intergovernmental organizations** are bodies that have countries as members, such as the United Nations, which has 193 member countries; NATO, which has 29 members from North America and Europe; the Organization of the Petroleum Exporting Countries (OPEC), which has 15 member countries from Africa, Asia, the Middle East, and Latin America; and the European Union (EU), which has 28 members from across Europe and more waiting to join.

- # **Nongovernmental organizations**, or NGOs, are organizations that focus on specific issues and whose members are private individuals or groups from around the world. Greenpeace (environmental), Amnesty International (human rights), International Committee of the Red Cross (humanitarian relief), and Doctors Without Borders (medical care) are all NGOs.

- # **Multinational corporations** are large companies that do business in multiple countries and that often wield tremendous economic power, like Nike or Apple. More and more companies outsource parts of their production, marketing, or service, so it is very difficult to find one of any size that stays strictly within the borders of one country.

- # Miscellaneous other actors are groups that do not fit the other categories, including those that have a "government" but no territory, like the Middle East's Palestinians or Ireland's Irish Republican Army, and groups that have no national ties, such as terrorist groups like al Qaeda and ISIS (although ISIS tries to claim territory like a state).

- -

intergovernmental organizations: bodies, such as the United Nations, whose members are countries

nongovernmental organizations: organizations comprising individuals or interest groups from around the world focused on a special issue

multinational corporations: large companies that do business in multiple countries

AND WHAT DOMESTIC ACTORS MAKE FOREIGN POLICY?

The question of what domestic actors make foreign policy is tricky to answer. The Constitution spreads the authority around, and when checks and balances are working as they should, the president is the chief foreign policy actor. Congress, especially the Senate, applies the brakes or encourages action.

THE BIGGEST CHEESE

The president and the executive branch. As we said, the president is the chief foreign policy maker. Presidents are more likely to set the foreign policy agenda than other actors in American politics because of their constitutional powers, the informal powers that come with this high-profile job, and the chief executive's opportunities to communicate directly with the public.

The president sits at the top of a large pyramid of executive agencies and departments that assist in making foreign policy (see the accompanying figure). If the president does not take time to manage the agencies, other individuals may seize the opportunity to interpret foreign policy in terms of their own interests and goals. In a sense, the president provides a check on the power of the executive agencies, and without the president's leadership, foreign policy can drift. President Ronald Reagan didn't pay a lot of attention to foreign affairs, and so staff members in the National Security Council began to make foreign policy themselves. The result was the Iran-Contra scandal in the mid-1980s. A similar dynamic is playing out in the Trump White House.

COMPONENTS OF THE EXECUTIVE BRANCH THAT ARE INVOLVED IN FOREIGN POLICY

Many components of the executive branch have crucial roles in foreign policy:

The **National Security Council (NSC)** is part of the president's inner circle, the Executive Office of the President. It was created in 1947 by the National Security Act to advise the president on matters of foreign policy and is coordinated by the national security adviser. By law the NSC includes the president, vice president, secretary of state, and secretary of defense. Additionally, the director of national intelligence (who is also the head of the Central Intelligence Agency) and the chair of the Joint Chiefs of Staff (the head of the commanders of the military services) sit as advisers to the NSC. Beyond this, the president has wide discretion to decide what the NSC will look like and how he or

National Security Council (NSC): the organization within the Executive Office of the President that provides foreign policy advice to the president

10.1: KEY FOREIGN POLICY MAKING AGENCIES

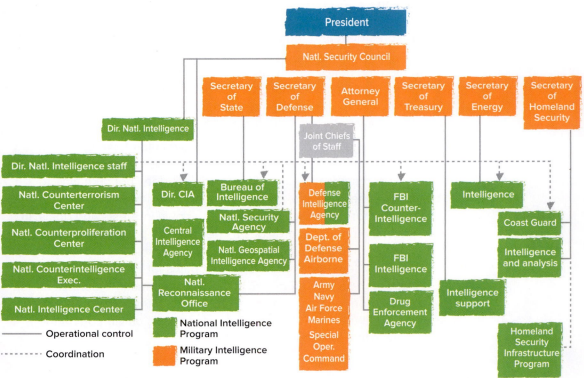

she will use it by appointing other members and deciding how the council will function.

\# The **Department of State** is charged with managing foreign affairs. It is often considered to be "first among equals" in its position relative to the other departments because it was the first department established by the Constitution in 1789. The State Department is headed by the secretary of state, who is part of the president's cabinet and fulfills a variety of foreign policy roles, including maintaining diplomatic and consular posts around the world, sending delegates and missions (groups of government officials) to a variety of international organization meetings, and negotiating treaties and executive agreements with other countries. Among the employees of the State

Department of State: the executive department charged with managing foreign affairs

Department are the foreign service officers, the most senior of which are the U.S. ambassadors.

\# The **Department of Defense**, headquartered in the Pentagon, is tasked mainly with managing American soldiers and their equipment in order to protect the United States. The Defense Department is headed by the secretary of defense, whose job in part is to advise the president on defense matters and who, it is important to note, is a civilian.

\# The **Joint Chiefs of Staff** is part of the Defense Department. This group consists of the senior military officers of the armed forces: the army and navy chiefs of staff, the chief of naval operations, the commandant of the Marine Corps, and the chief of the National Guard Bureau. The chair is selected by the president. The Joint Chiefs of Staff advise the secretary of defense, although the chair also may offer advice directly to the president and is responsible for managing the armed forces of the United States.

\# The **intelligence community** comprises several government agencies and bureaus. This community's job is to collect, organize, and analyze information. Information can be gathered in a number of ways, from the mundane (such as reading foreign newspapers) to the more clandestine (for instance, spying both by human beings and through surveillance satellites). Until 2004 the community was coordinated by the director of central intelligence, who was also the head of the **Central Intelligence Agency (CIA)**. In the wake of many studies and hearings about the events leading up to September 11, as well as current security concerns, President George W. Bush signed legislation that altered how the intelligence community is managed. The job of the director of central intelligence was limited to directing the CIA. The job of coordinating the entire network of agencies now falls to the **director of national intelligence**, who is also part of the NSC.

Department of Defense: the executive department charged with managing the country's military personnel, equipment, and operations

Joint Chiefs of Staff: the senior military officers from four branches of the U.S. armed forces

intelligence community: the agencies and bureaus responsible for obtaining and interpreting information for the government

Central Intelligence Agency (CIA): the government organization that oversees foreign intelligence gathering and related classified activities

director of national intelligence: the overseer and coordinator of the activities of the many agencies involved in the production and dissemination of intelligence information in the U.S. government, as well as the president's main intelligence adviser

THE SMALLER CHEESE

> # **Congress.** Congress has a variety of constitutional roles in making foreign policy, including the powers to make treaties, to declare war, and to appropriate money. But Congress faces obstacles in its efforts to play an active role in foreign policy. It must deal with the considerable powers of the president, for instance, and it is more oriented toward domestic than foreign affairs, given the ever-present imperative of reelection. Congressional organization also can hamper Congress's role in foreign policy. The fragmentation of Congress, the slow speed of deliberation, and the complex nature of many foreign policy issues can make it difficult for Congress to play a big role, particularly in fast-moving foreign events.

TENSIONS BETWEEN THE BRANCHES— THE STRUGGLE FOR POWER THE FOUNDERS ENVISIONED

> The foreign policy tension between the president and Congress is illustrated by the complex issues surrounding the use of military force. The president is in charge of the armed forces, but only Congress can declare war. Presidents try to get around the power of Congress by committing troops to military actions that do not have the official status of a war, but this can infuriate legislators. Presidents have sent troops abroad without a formal declaration of war on a number of occasions—for example, to Korea (1950), the Dominican Republic (1965), Vietnam (1965), Lebanon (1982), Grenada (1983), Panama (1989), the Persian Gulf (1990), Afghanistan (2001), and Iraq (2003). As the United States became more involved in the Vietnam War, however, Congress became increasingly unhappy with the president's role. When, in the early 1970s, public opinion against the war became increasingly vocal, Congress turned on the commander in chief, passing the **War Powers Act** of 1973 over President Richard Nixon's veto.

THE UPSHOT

Despite its difficulties in enforcing the War Powers Act, Congress has tried to play a fairly active role in foreign policy making, sometimes working with presidents and sometimes at odds with them. The calculation for Congress is fairly straightforward: Let presidents pursue risky military strategies. If they succeed, take credit for staying out of their way. If they fail, blame them for not consulting and for being "imperial." Either way, Congress wins politically, even if they don't get their preferred course of action.

. . . .

War Powers Act: a federal law passed in 1973 that was designed to check the president's power to commit the United States to an armed conflict without the consent of the U.S. Congress

GENGAP!

GENERATIONAL ATTITUDES TOWARD FOREIGN POLICY

It is striking how much more likely younger Americans are to favor health care for all, and to see a role for government in helping the needy. In terms of foreign policy, they are far more likely than their elders to want to see diplomatic solutions to international problems and to want to reach out to allies. What in these generations' respective histories would account for that difference? Will younger Americans' attitudes also change as they age, or are these preferences that they will carry into their own old age? How will U.S. domestic and foreign policy likely change as the older generation steps aside for younger American leaders?

FIGURE IT!

10.2: GENERATIONAL PREFERENCES FOR HEALTH CARE COVERAGE FOR ALL AND INCREASED GOVERNMENT AID FOR THE NEEDY

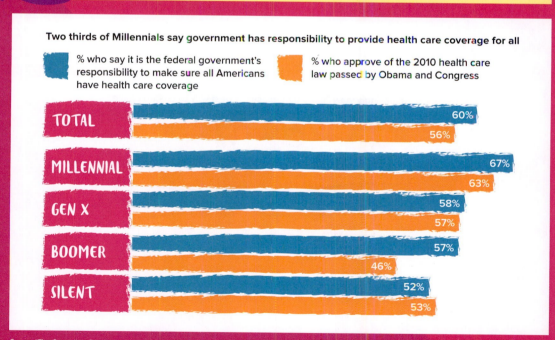

Two thirds of Millennials say government has responsibility to provide health care coverage for all

% who say it is the federal government's responsibility to make sure all Americans have health care coverage

% who approve of the 2010 health care law passed by Obama and Congress

	Government responsibility	Approve 2010 law
TOTAL	60%	56%
MILLENNIAL	67%	63%
GEN X	58%	57%
BOOMER	57%	46%
SILENT	52%	53%

Source: "The Generation Gap in American Politics." Pew Research Center, Washington, D.C. (March 01, 2018) http://www.people-press.org/wp-content/uploads/sites/4/2018/03/03-01-18-Generations-release.pdf

10.3: GENERATIONAL DIFFERENCES ON INCREASED GOVERNMENT AID FOR THE NEEDY

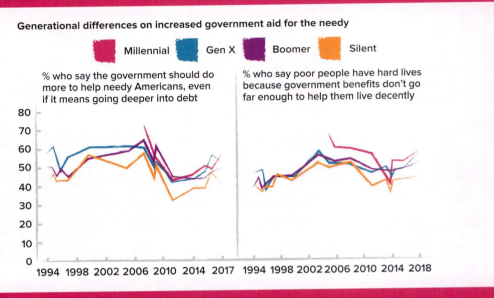

Generational differences on increased government aid for the needy

Millennial   Gen X   Boomer   Silent

% who say the government should do more to help needy Americans, even if it means going deeper into debt

% who say poor people have hard lives because government benefits don't go far enough to help them live decently

Source: Pew Research Center, *The Generation Gap in American Politics*, March 1, 2018, http://www.people-press.org/2018/03/01/3-u-s-foreign-policy-and-americas-global-standing-islam-and-violence-nafta/.

10.4: GENERATIONAL PREFERENCES FOR THE USE OF DIPLOMACY AND OTHER ASPECTS OF FOREIGN POLICY

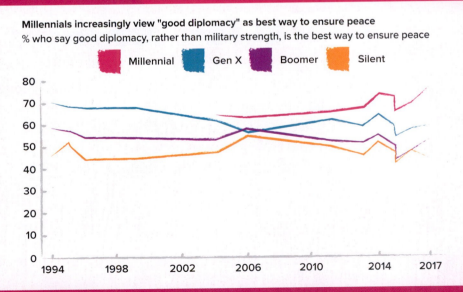

Millennials increasingly view "good diplomacy" as best way to ensure peace
% who say good diplomacy, rather than military strength, is the best way to ensure peace

Millennial   Gen X   Boomer   Silent

Source: "The Generation Gap in American Politics." Pew Research Center, Washington, D.C. (March 01, 2018) http://www.people-press.org/wp-content/uploads/sites/4/2018/03/03-01-18-Generations-release.pdf

10.5: GENERATIONAL PREFERENCES WHEN TAKING ALLIES' INTERESTS INTO ACCOUNT

% who say . . .

	Follow own national interests even when allies strongly disagree	Take into account interests of allies even if it means making compromises with them		We should pay less attention to problems overseas, concentrate on problems at home	It's best for the future of our country to be active in world affairs
Total	36	59	Total	47	47
Millennial	29	66	Millennial	51	44
Gen X	36	60	Gen X	47	47
Boomer	42	53	Boomer	44	50
Silent	43	48	Silent	42	50

Source: Pew Research Center, *The Generation Gap in American Politics*, March 1, 2018, http://www.people-press.org/2018/03/01/3-u-s-foreign-policy-and-americas-global-standing-islam-and-violence-nafta/.

TAKEAWAYS

→ **An America run by Millennials would be a very different place from the one run by the Silent Generation.** What might be some of the key differences?

→ **Given the clear generational differences in policy preferences, societal turbulence might result as one generation takes over from the other.** Do we see any evidence of that turbulence today?

→ **The generational differences in foreign policy preferences are greater for some issues (e.g., taking allies' interests into account) than for others (e.g., being active globally).** How do you explain that finding?

TYPES OF FOREIGN POLICY POLITICS

 All foreign problems are not the same, and neither are the policies that deal with them:

\# **Crisis policy** deals with emergency threats to our national interests or values. Such situations often come as a surprise, and the use of force is one way to respond. The political dynamics behind crisis policy, for instance, are dominated by the president and the small group of advisers around the Oval Office. Congress tends not to be much engaged in crisis policy but often watches with the rest of the public (and the world) as presidents and their advisers decide how to respond to international crises. The United States' response to threats by North Korea is an example of crisis policy.

\# **Strategic policy** lays out the basic U.S. stance toward another country or a particular problem. Strategic policy tends to be formulated in the executive branch, but usually deep in the bureaucratic divisions we discussed, rather than at the top levels. This gives interest groups and concerned members of Congress opportunities to lobby for certain policies. The public usually learns about these policies (and responds to and evaluates them) once the president announces them. The moving of the U.S. Embassy in Israel to Jerusalem was a strategic decision with public input.

\# **Structural defense policy** focuses largely on the policies and programs that deal with defense spending and military bases. These policies usually focus on, for example, buying new aircraft for the air force and navy or deciding which military bases to consolidate or close down. Structural defense policy, which often starts in the executive branch, is crafted largely in Congress, with much input from the bureaucracy and interest groups. When a plan to build and deploy a new fighter jet is developed, for example, it is made with coordination between Congress and the Defense Department— usually with members of Congress keeping a close eye on how their states and districts will benefit from the projects.

crisis policy: foreign policy, usually made quickly and secretly, that responds to an emergency threat

strategic policy: foreign policy that lays out a country's basic stance toward international actors or problems

structural defense policy: foreign policy dealing with defense spending, military bases, and weapons procurement

FOREIGN POLICY AT WORK—A HISTORICAL PERSPECTIVE

At the end of World War II, when the common purpose of fighting Adolf Hitler and ending German fascism no longer held the United States and the Soviet Union in an awkward alliance, fissures developed between the two largest and strongest superpowers in global politics. Nearly all of Europe was divided between allies of the Soviets and allies of the United States, a division seen most graphically in the splitting of postwar Germany into a communist East and a capitalist West.

WAR BETWEEN SUPERPOWERS, BUT WITHOUT MILITARY ACTION.

The Cold War, waged between the United States and the Soviet Union from 1945 to 1989, was a bitter global competition between democracy and authoritarianism, capitalism and communism. It never erupted into a "hot" war of military action, due in large part to the deterrent effect provided by a policy of "mutual assured destruction." Each side spent tremendous sums of money on nuclear weapons to make sure it had the ability to wipe out the other side. During this era, American foreign policy makers pursued a policy of containment, in which the United States tried to prevent the Soviet Union from expanding its influence, especially in Europe.

COLD WAR GAVE DEFINITION TO THE WORLD.

As dangerous as the world was during the Cold War, it seemed easy to understand, casting complicated issues into simple choices of black and white. Countries were either with us or against us: they were free societies or closed ones, had capitalist or communist economies, were good or bad. Although the world was hardly that simple, it seemed that way to many people, and much of the complexity of world politics was glossed over—or perhaps bottled up—only to explode after the end of the Cold War in 1989.

THE COLLAPSE OF THE SOVIET UNION, THE END OF THE COLD WAR, AND THE START OF SOMETHING MORE COMPLICATED

In 1991 the Soviet Union finally fell apart, to be replaced by more than a dozen independent states. Although most Westerners hailed the fall of the Soviet Union as an end to the tension that kept the Cold War alive, Russia inherited the Soviet nuclear arsenal, and a majority of its citizens hold a negative view of the leaders of the United States. Russians' views of American citizens have also become more critical recently. (Americans' views of Russia have also been declining, although Republicans, formerly the staunchest opponents of Russia, seem to be following President Trump into a softened stance.)

Cold War: the half-century of competition and conflict after World War II between the United States and the Soviet Union (and their allies)

containment: the U.S. Cold War policy of preventing the Soviet Union from expanding its influence, especially in Europe

WAR OF A DIFFERENT KIND

Russia's attitude toward the United States is not irrational. When the Cold War ended, many of the countries that had been under Soviet control and part of the Soviet defense alliance called the Warsaw Pact started looking to the United States and NATO for security. Over the years that followed, many of these countries joined NATO and the European Union. When the United States sought to put part of a new ballistic missile defense system in the Czech Republic, Russian leaders became particularly irritated. The prospect of Ukraine moving closer to NATO upset Russian president Vladimir Putin greatly.

Certainly the Russian invasion of our electoral system in 2016 was an act of aggression, but President Trump's inconsistent response has left the issue in foreign policy limbo. The executive branch, including the secretary of state, has acknowledged that Russia interfered in our election, but the president has often seemed not to agree.

DIG DEEPER

Watch the movie *Black Hawk Down* for a portrayal of the complexities of the post–Cold War era of foreign policy.

Go to **edge.sagepub.com/ dig-deeper**

THE UPSHOT

This post–Cold War era has eluded easy description in terms of global organization and threats to the United States, especially in the days since September 11. Who was likely to be the country's most dangerous adversary? What threats must it prepare for? How much should be spent on military preparedness? Should the United States be the world's police officer, a global banker, or a humanitarian protector?

How different presidents have answered these questions:

THE BUSH DOCTRINE

\# President George W. Bush, in 2002, asserted that the United States' role is to maintain its military supremacy and take preemptive action against hostile and threatening states. In identifying an "axis of evil" of Iran, Iraq, and North Korea, President Bush set out a vision of American foreign policy that was rooted in taking active steps to promote democracy and to use force, alone if necessary, to eliminate perceived threats before they could more fully develop. This **Bush Doctrine** joined a long list of presidential foreign policy doctrines that have tried to define and protect U.S. interests in the world.

AN EMPHASIS ON DIPLOMACY UNDER OBAMA

\# President Obama's approach was markedly different from his predecessor's. Obama emphasized diplomatic over military solutions, keeping communications channels with our enemies open and trying

Bush Doctrine: the foreign policy that supported preemptive attacks as a legitimate tactic in the U.S. war on state-sponsored terrorism

to find common interests on which to build. Although Obama pulled troops out of Iraq, a war he opposed from the start, he ramped up the war effort in Afghanistan in hopes of creating a stable system there that wouldn't provide cover to those who wish our country harm, and he stepped up the use of drone strikes and Special Forces to try to target ISIS when it was clear that the terrorist group meant harm to the United States.

A TRUMP DOCTRINE?

What shape a Trump Doctrine might take is as yet unknown: Trump's campaign positions had elements of several different kinds of foreign policy. He has rejected or weakened many of our traditional alliances, almost all of which were designed to keep us safe. He has been aggressive (toward ISIS and even China), conciliatory (such as toward Russia), and baffling (as to North Korea). He is also conducting, against the advice of most conventional advisers, a trade war that may have unpredictable economic outcomes for the entire globe.

CURRENT THREATS

At this point, almost every major nation—and some groups that are not nations—have the power to blow up large portions of the world and, by and large, no one wants to do that because of the certainty that they'd get blown up in return. The nuclear race is not paramount anymore—you can destroy the planet only so many times. For those who are not global superpowers, like North Korea, smaller-scale nuclear threats and computer hacking are the best currency they can deal with. For Russia, also not a rich global power, hacking into the United States' systems and disrupting democracy give it power on the national stage.

DIG DEEPER

Read about the challenges posed by artificial intelligence in the article "Why Technology Favors Tyranny," by Yuval Noah Harari.

Go to **edge.sagepub.com/ dig-deeper**

Not to diminish the threats from North Korea or Russia, but for major, wealthy nations like the United States and China, the new "cold war" is over cyber power and artificial intelligence, the ability to build (or steal) the technology needed to create machines that can think and solve problems better than humans do, and the ability to bring another country to a standstill with the flick of a switch.

THE UPSHOT

Automation and artificial intelligence will undoubtedly change the shape of the world in the next few decades, and both the United States and

China want to be king. It's good to be king, but it also makes you a target. How this new cold war will play out is going to be a primary challenge in the future.

Big Think

➜ How much responsibility does society bear for taking care of those who are least able to care for themselves?

➜ Who should be in charge of keeping the economy running smoothly?

➜ Are you an interventionist or an isolationist? What's likely to be the long-term outcome of such a policy?

➜ What should be America's role in the world today?

➜ What would you consider worth fighting a war over?

Key Terms

CONCEPTS

agenda setting (p. 315)

capital gains taxes (p. 327)

containment (p. 341)

crisis policy (p. 340)

deficits (p. 326)

deregulation (p. 327)

distributive policies (p. 316)

economic policy (p. 325)

entitlement program (p. 322)

Federal Reserve System (p. 326)

fiscal policy (p. 326)

foreign policy (p. 330)

health care policy (p. 323)

interest rates (p. 326)

interventionism (p. 331)

isolationism (p. 331)

means-tested programs (p. 318)

middle-class and corporate welfare (p. 320)

monetary policy (p. 326)

policy (p. 312)

policy adoption (p. 315)

policy evaluation (p. 315)

policy formulation (p. 315)

policy implementation (p. 315)

policymaking (p. 312)

progressive income taxes (p. 327)

public policy (p. 313)

redistributive policies (p. 316)

regressive taxes (p. 327)

regulatory policies (p. 317)

social insurance policies (p. 321)

social policy (p. 318)

social welfare
policies (p. 318)

strategic policy (p. 340)

structural defense
policy (p. 340)

subsidies (p. 320)

surpluses (p. 326)

tax policy (p. 327)

value-added taxes
(VATs) (p. 327)

IMPORTANT WORKS AND EVENTS

Aid to Families with
Dependent Children
(AFDC) (p. 318)

Bush Doctrine (p. 342)

Cold War (p. 341)

Medicaid (p. 323)

Medicare (p. 323)

Patient Protection and
Affordable Care Act (p. 323)

Social Security (p. 32)

Supplemental Nutrition
Assistance Program
(SNAP) (p. 320)

Temporary Assistance to
Needy Families (TANF) (p. 319)

War Powers Act (p. 336)

KEY INDIVIDUALS AND GROUPS

Central Intelligence Agency
(CIA) (p. 335)

Department of Defense (p. 335)

Department of State (p. 334)

director of national
intelligence (p. 335)

intelligence
community (p. 335)

intergovernmental
organizations (p. 332)

Joint Chiefs of Staff (p. 335)

multinational
corporations (p. 332)

National Security
Council (NSC) (p. 333)

nongovernmental
organizations (p. 332)

Glossary

accommodationists: people who want to support "all" religions equally

accountability: ensuring elected officials do what they say they are going to do

adjudication: the process of resolving disputes in court

administrative laws: laws created by the bureaucracy after legislation has been passed stating a general intent

adversarial system: a legal system concerned primarily with fairness (that is, whether a trial will be fair), trusting that a just judgment will result from a just trial

advice and consent: the Senate's constitutional obligation to approve certain executive appointments

agency capture: when a government agency begins to identify the interests of the groups they regulate as their own

agenda setting: the process through which issues attain the status of being seriously debated by politically relevant actors

Aid to Families with Dependent Children (AFDC): a New Deal–era policy designed to ensure that poor families could take care of their kids

allocative representation: congressional work to secure projects, services, and funds for the represented district

amendment process: the process by which the Constitution may be changed

amicus curiae briefs: "friend of the court" documents filed by interested parties to encourage the Court to grant or deny certiorari or to urge it to decide a case in a particular way

anarchy: no government at all, a system in which individuals are free to do as they wish

Anti-Federalists: advocates of states' rights who opposed the Constitution

appeal: rehearing a case because the losing party in the original trial argues that a point of law was not applied properly

appointment power: the president's power to select the heads of the departments (the cabinet), as well as more than 3,500 federal employees

Articles of Confederation: the first constitution of the United States, adopted in 1777, creating an association of states with a weak central government

astroturf lobbying: indirect lobbying efforts that manipulate or create public sentiment, "astroturf" being artificial grassroots

authoritarian capitalism: a system in which the authoritarian government has strong control over how individuals may live their lives, but individuals do have some market freedom

authoritarian governments: political systems in which the rulers have all of the power and the rules don't allow the people who live under them to have any power at all

authority: power that people consider legitimate, that they have consented or agreed to

bicameral legislature: a lawmaking body with two chambers

bill of attainder: a law directed at an individual or group that accuses and convicts them of a crime

Bill of Rights: ten amendments to the Constitution that explicitly limit government by protecting individual rights against it

bipartisanship: an effort that incorporates work from both sides of the aisle and produces a solution to a problem both sides can live with

black codes: a series of laws in the post–Civil War South designed to restrict the rights of former slaves before the passage of the Fourteenth and Fifteenth Amendments; denied freed blacks the right to vote, to go to school, or to own property, which re-created the conditions of slavery under another name

block grants: funds that come with flexibility for the states to spend the money as they wish within broad parameters

boycott: the refusal to buy certain goods or services as a way to protest policy or to force political reform

Brown v. Board of Education: the 1954 Supreme Court case that rejected the idea that separate could be equal in education

bureaucracy: a hierarchical decision-making structure in which unelected officials answer to the layer of people above them, and who in turn answer to the people above them, and so on

bureaucratic culture: the accepted values and procedures of an organization

bureaucratic discretion: when the bureaucracy exercises legislative power delegated to it by congressional law

Bush Doctrine: the foreign policy that supported preemptive attacks as a legitimate tactic in the U.S. war on state-sponsored terrorism

cabinet: an advisory group to the president composed primarily of the heads of the major departments of the federal bureaucracy

capital gains taxes: a tax levied on the return from capital investments

capitalism: an economic system that relies on the market to make decisions about who should have material goods

capitalist democracy: a political-economic system that grants the most individual control over both political and economic life

casework: representation that involves taking care of one's constituents' needs and problems

categorical grants: grants of money with specific instructions on how it is to be spent

caucuses: party gatherings where candidate choice is debated openly

Central Intelligence Agency (CIA): the government organization that oversees foreign intelligence gathering and related classified activities

checks and balances: the idea that each branch of government has just enough power over the others that their jealousy will guard against the overreach of the others

chief administrator: the president's role as head bureaucrat, in charge of making sure that the departments, agencies, and boards and commissions charged with enforcing the laws do their jobs

chief foreign policy maker: the president's power to formulate foreign policy and negotiate treaties

chief of staff: the person who oversees the operations of all White House staff and typically controls access to the president

citizens: individuals who live under non-authoritarian governments

civil law tradition: a legal system in which laws are passed by a legislature and written down, which gives judges less leeway

civil laws: laws that regulate interactions between individuals

civil liberties: the individual freedoms guaranteed by the Constitution that limit government

civil rights: the freedom of groups to participate fully in the public life of a nation; protected by the government primarily in the Thirteenth, Fourteenth, Fifteenth, Nineteenth, and Twenty-Sixth Amendments

civil rights movement: the group effort of African Americans to claim their civil rights through a variety of means—legal, political, economic, civil disobedience—in the 1950s and 1960s

civil service reform: efforts begun in the 1880s to ensure that the federal bureaucracy serves the interests of the public rather than the powerful

classical liberalism: an Enlightenment philosophy emphasizing individual freedom and self-rule

clear and present danger test: the rule used by the courts that allows language to be regulated only if it presents an immediate and urgent danger

clickbait: sensational headlines designed to tempt Internet users to click through to a specific web site

clientele groups: groups of citizens whose interests are affected by an agency or a department and who work to influence its policies

cloture: a vote to end a Senate filibuster; requires a three-fifths majority, or sixty votes

coattail effect: the added votes received by congressional candidates of a winning presidential party

Cold War: the half-century of competition and conflict after World War II between the United States and the Soviet Union (and their allies)

collective goods: benefits that, if the group is successful in obtaining them, can be enjoyed by everybody, whether they were members of the group and contributed to the effort or not

commander in chief: the president's power to act as the civilian head of the armed forces of the United States

commercial bias: the tendency of the media to make coverage and programming decisions based on what will attract a large audience and maximize profits

committees: small groups oriented around policy or procedural issues where the real work of Congress gets done

common law tradition: a legal system in which the decisions of judges become part of the legal tradition and those precedents have the standing of law

compelling state purpose: a fundamental state purpose, which must be shown before the law can limit some freedoms or treat some groups of people differently

compromise: the act of giving up something you want in order to get something else you want more; an exercise in determining and trading off priorities

concurrent powers: powers that are shared by the federal and state governments

concurring opinions: documents written by justices expressing agreement with the majority ruling but describing different or additional reasons for the ruling

confederation: a form of government in which all the power lies with the local units; in the American case, that's the states

conference committee: temporary committees formed to reconcile differences in House and Senate versions of a bill

Congress: the U.S. legislature, the part of government that makes the laws

congressional district: a geographic region into which state legislators divide their state for purposes of representation

congressional oversight: efforts by Congress, especially through committees, to monitor agency rule-making, enforcement, and implementation of congressional policies

conservatives: Americans on the political right who believe in less regulation of the economy

constituencies: groupings of individual constituents, or people whom an official is obligated to represent

Constitutional Convention: the assembly of fifty-five delegates in the summer of 1787 to recast the Articles of Confederation; the result was the U.S. Constitution

constitutional laws: laws that establish the legal infrastructure in the United States—how the branches relate to each other—and determine how the game of politics is played

containment: the U.S. Cold War policy of preventing the Soviet Union from expanding its influence, especially in Europe

crime: a broken criminal law, a violation against the state

criminal laws: a form of substantive law that prohibits behavior that makes collective living difficult or impossible (for example, theft, murder, rape, disrupting the peace)

crisis policy: foreign policy, usually made quickly and secretly, that responds to an emergency threat

critical election: an election signaling a significant change in popular allegiance from one party to another

cycle effect: the predictable rise and fall of a president's popularity at different stages of a term in office

dark money: campaign money that goes to nonprofits (including political groups like unions and trade groups) that can be spent to influence elections and whose donors do not need to be revealed

de facto discrimination: discrimination on the basis of life circumstances, habit, custom, or socioeconomic status

de jure discrimination: discrimination by laws

Declaration of Independence: the political document that dissolved the colonial ties between the United States and Britain

deficits: shortfalls in the budget due to the government's spending more in a year than it takes in

democracy: a type of non-authoritarian government wherein citizens have considerable power to make the rules that govern them

Department of Defense: the executive department charged with managing the country's military personnel, equipment, and operations

Department of State: the executive department charged with managing foreign affairs

departments: one of the major subdivisions of the federal government, represented in the president's cabinet

deregulation: the elimination of regulations in order to improve economic efficiency

descriptive representation: the degree to which a legislature looks like the population it represents

digital natives: people who have been born in an era in which not only are most people hooked up to electronic media, but they also live their lives partly in cyberspace as well as in "real space"

direct lobbying: lobbying that impacts public officials directly

director of national intelligence: the overseer and coordinator of the activities of the many agencies involved in the production and dissemination of intelligence information in the U.S. government, as well as the president's main intelligence adviser

discrimination: differential treatment

dissenting opinions: documents written by justices expressing disagreement with the majority ruling

distributive policies: policies funded by the whole taxpayer base that address the needs of particular groups

divided government: the situation that exists when political rule is split between two parties, in which one controls the White House and the other controls one or both houses of Congress

divine right of kings: the political culture that understood power to be vested in the king because he was God's representative on earth

due process rights: the guarantee that laws will be fair and reasonable and that citizens suspected of breaking the law will be treated fairly

earmarks: a type of legislative representation in which general taxpayer funds are used to pay for some special benefit for a member's district

economic conservatives: Americans who favor a strictly procedural government role in the economy and the social order

economic interest groups: groups that seek to influence policy for the pocketbook issues of their members, that is, for what they do

economic liberals: Americans who favor an expanded government role in the economy but a limited role in the social order

economic policy: all the different strategies that government officials employ to solve economic problems

economics: the process for deciding who gets the material resources and how they get them

election: the formal process of voting candidates into office

electioneering: nominating and electing candidates to office

Electoral College: an intermediary body that elects the president

electoral mandate: the perception that an election victory signals broad support for the winner's proposed policies

entitlement program: a federal program that guarantees benefits to qualified recipients

enumerated powers: congressional powers specifically named in the Constitution

equal opportunity interest groups: groups that seek to influence government on behalf of people who feel they are not represented on account of who they are

Equal Rights Amendment: a constitutional amendment passed by Congress but never ratified that would have banned discrimination on the basis of gender

equality: in American political culture, forms of political fairness that require minimal government intervention

establishment clause: the First Amendment guarantee that the government will not create and support an official state church

ex post facto law: a law that makes something illegal after you have already done it

exclusionary rule: the rule created by the Supreme Court that evidence seized illegally may not be used to obtain a conviction

executive: one who has the power to carry out plans, strategies, or laws

executive agreements: presidential arrangements with other countries that create foreign policy without the need for Senate approval

executive branch: the law-enforcing component of the federal government

Executive Office of the President: the agencies and advisers that help the president manage the range of issues that the White House has to deal with every day

executive orders: clarifications of congressional policy issued by the president and having the full force of law

executive privilege: the president's ability to claim that some materials relevant to his job must be kept confidential to enable him to perform his duties or for national security reasons; a right with limits, according to the Supreme Court

exit polls: polls that are taken as people leave their polling places immediately after voting

expressive benefits: the opportunity to do work for something that matters deeply to you

factions: groups of citizens united by some common passion or interest and opposed to the rights of other citizens or to the interests of the whole community

federal bureaucracy: the network of departments, agencies, and boards and commissions that make up

the executive branch at the federal level; characterized by hierarchical structure, worker specialization, explicit rules, and advancement by merit

Federal Reserve System: the independent commission that controls the money supply through a system of twelve federal banks

federalism: the horizontal division of government into layers: national (also called federal) and state

Federalist Papers: a collection of eighty-five newspaper editorials written in support of the Constitution under the pseudonym of *Publius*, whose real identity was three Federalists: Alexander Hamilton, James Madison, and John Jay

Federalists: supporters of the Constitution who favored a strong central government

feeding frenzy: excessive press coverage of an embarrassing or scandalous subject

Fifteenth Amendment: the 1870 constitutional amendment guaranteeing that the right to vote could not be denied on the basis of race

fighting words: speech intended to incite violence

filibuster: a practice of unlimited debate in the Senate in order to prevent or delay a vote on a bill

fiscal policy: the government's power to tax and spend to stabilize the economy

foreign policy: a country's official positions, practices, and procedures for dealing with actors outside its borders

Fourteenth Amendment: the 1868 constitutional amendment ensuring that southern states did not deny those free from enslavement their rights as citizens

framing: the process through which the media emphasize particular aspects of a news story, thereby influencing the public's perception of the story

free exercise clause: the First Amendment guarantee that citizens may freely engage in the religious activities of their choice

free rider problem: the social dilemma faced when people can receive a collective good without having to put in any individual resources to earn it

freedom: in American political culture, individual independence *from* government

freedom of assembly: the right of the people to gather peacefully and to petition government

freedom of expression: the ability to express one's views without government restraint

front loading: the process of scheduling presidential primaries early in the primary season

front runner: the candidate who appears to be the likeliest to win the election at a given point in time

gatekeepers: journalists and media elite who determine which news stories are covered and which are not

gender bias: systemic ways of treating women differently to their detriment

gender gap: the tendency of men and women to differ in their political views on some issues

general election: an election cycle in which presidential candidates are on the ballot

generations: groups of people born within the same general time period who share life experiences that help shape their political views

gerrymandering: the process of redistricting with political intent

get-out-the-vote (GOTV): efforts by political parties, interest groups, and the candidate's staff to maximize voter turnout among supporters

Gibbons v. Ogden: the 1824 Supreme Court decision that opened the door to federal regulation of commerce, broadly understood to mean most forms of business

glass ceiling: the invisible but impenetrable barrier that most women face when trying to ascend the corporate or political ladder

going public: a president's strategy of drumming up support with the public on an issue, with the hope of using public pressure as leverage with Congress

governing: activities directed toward controlling the distribution of political resources by providing executive and legislative leadership, enacting agendas, mobilizing support, and building coalitions

government: a system or an organization for exercising authority over a body of people

government corporations: organizations that fill some commercial functions that are important but not profitable enough for private industry to supply

government interest groups: groups hired by governments to lobby other governments

grassroots lobbying: indirect lobbying efforts that spring from widespread public concern

Great Compromise: the constitutional solution to congressional representation: equal votes in the Senate, votes by population in the House

habeas corpus: the right to be brought before a judge and informed of the charges and evidence against you

hard money: campaign funds donated directly to candidates; amounts are limited by federal election laws

hashtag activism: the forming of social movements through viral calls to act politically

head of government: the president's partisan role as head of his own party, twister of arms, maker of deals, and pusher of the party's agenda

head of state: the president's largely ceremonial, apolitical role in rallying the country together

health care policy: a country's decisions, plans, and actions designed to promote specific health care objectives

honeymoon period: the first 100 days following an election when a president's popularity is high and congressional relations are likely to be productive

horse race journalism: the media's focus on the competitive aspects of politics rather than on actual policy proposals and political decisions

house effects: the way a particular pollster's results tend to favor Democrats or Republicans

House Rules Committee: the committee that determines how and when debate on a bill will take place

hyperpartisanship: a commitment to party so strong that it can transcend other commitments, including that to the national interest

ideologies: competing narratives that explain various political disagreements

imminent lawless action test: the rule used by the courts that restricts speech only if it is aimed at producing or is likely to produce imminent lawless action

impeachment: a formal charge by the House that the president (or another member of the executive branch) has committed acts of "Treason, Bribery, or other high Crimes and Misdemeanors," which may or may not result in removal from office

implicit bias: the tendency for passing thoughts to confirm existing stereotypes in our minds, even if we quickly catch them

inalienable rights: rights that we are born with, that cannot be taken away from us, and that we cannot sell

incorporation: Supreme Court action making the protections of the Bill of Rights applicable to the states

incumbency advantage: the electoral edge afforded to those already in office

independent agencies: organizations within the executive branch that execute the law and that are separate from the departments

independent regulatory boards and commissions: government organizations that regulate various businesses, industries, or economic sectors

indirect lobbying: a type of lobbying focused on getting the public to put pressure on elected officials

individualism: a political cultural emphasis on individual rights rather than on the collective whole

information bubble: a closed cycle in which all the information we get reinforces the information we already have, solidifying our beliefs without reference to outside reality checks

infotainment: when the news is presented in a deliberately entertaining way in order to keep audiences interested

inherent powers: presidential powers implied but not stated explicitly in the Constitution

inquisitorial system: a legal system concerned primarily with finding the truth

integration: breaking down barriers (legal, cultural, economic) that keep races apart to allow the creation of a diverse community

intelligence community: the agencies and bureaus responsible for obtaining and interpreting information for the government

interest groups: groups, including corporations, that are bound by a common interest and that seek to use the political system to attain their policy goals from the outside, by persuading people in power to give them what they want

interest rates: the cost of borrowing money, calculated as a percentage of the money borrowed

intergovernmental organizations: bodies, such as the United Nations, whose members are countries

interventionism: a foreign policy view that, to keep the republic safe, the United States must be actively engaged in shaping the global environment and be willing to intervene to shape events

invisible primary: the period of time before primaries begin when candidates are sounding out support, testing the waters, and trying to decide whether to run

iron triangles: close policymaking relationships among legislators, regulators, and the groups being regulated that tend to exclude the public

isolationism: a foreign policy view that nations should stay out of international political alliances and activities and focus on domestic matters

issue advocacy ads: advertisements paid for by soft money, and thus not regulated, that promote certain issue positions but do not endorse specific candidates

issue networks: complex systems of relationships among groups that influence policy, including elected leaders, interest groups, specialists, consultants, and research institutes

James Madison: one of the founders whose key insight was to design a system that takes human nature *as it is* (self-interested, greedy, and ambitious), not as you want it to be

Jim Crow laws: laws passed after the Thirteenth, Fourteenth, and Fifteenth Amendments granted African Americans citizen rights; intended to re-create the power relations of slavery

John Locke: the British philosopher who introduced the idea that the social contract was conditional on the government's protection of rights and could be revoked if the government failed to protect those rights

John Marshall: the third chief justice of the Supreme Court; believed in the Federalist vision of a strong national government

Joint Chiefs of Staff: the senior military officers from four branches of the U.S. armed forces

joint committees: combined House-Senate committees formed to coordinate activities and expedite legislation in a certain area

journalists: professional communicators who focus on news sharing and narrative building

judicial branch: the law-interpreting component of the federal government

judicial interpretivists: supporters of a judicial approach holding that the Constitution is a living document and that judges should interpret it according to changing times and values

judicial review: the Supreme Court's power to determine if congressional laws, state laws, or executive actions are constitutional

judiciary: the law-interpreting component of the federal government

jurisdiction: a court's authority to hear certain cases

laissez-faire capitalism: a form of capitalism wherein there are no restrictions on the market at all

leaks: confidential information secretly revealed to the press

legislative agenda: the slate of proposals and issues that representatives think it worthwhile to consider and act on

legislative branch: the lawmaking component of the federal government

legislative liaisons: executive personnel who work with members of Congress to secure their support in getting a president's legislation passed

Lemon test: the three-pronged rule used by the courts to determine whether the establishment clause is violated

libel: written defamation of character

liberals: Americans on the political left who believe in greater government regulation of the economy

libertarians: Americans who favor a minimal government role in any sphere

likely voter polls: polls of respondents who pollsters have determined are likely to vote by asking questions about prior voting behavior

likely voter screens: the questions that different pollsters use to decide how likely they think a respondent is to vote

limited government: the Enlightenment idea that the power of government should be restricted to allow for maximum individual freedom

litigious system: a legal system in which parties typically settle their differences in court

lobbying: efforts by groups to persuade government officials to do something

lobbyists: professionals who are hired to persuade government officials to do something

majority opinion: the written decision of the Court that states the judgment of the majority

majority party: the political party that wins the most seats in a given chamber

Marbury v. Madison: the 1803 Supreme Court ruling holding that the Court had the power of judicial review

market: the collective decisions of multiple individuals about what to buy or sell, creating different levels of demand and supply

marriage equality: the idea that marriage should not be reserved for heterosexual couples and that all marriages should be equal before the law

material benefits: group member benefits that involve items of real monetary worth, like insurance discounts or professional paybacks

McCulloch v. Maryland: the 1819 Supreme Court ruling holding that the necessary and proper clause of the Constitution could be interpreted broadly to include many powers that are not among the enumerated powers of Congress

means-tested programs: programs that require beneficiaries to prove that they lack the necessary income or resources (means) to provide for themselves, according to the government's definitions of eligibility

media: channels of communication

media aggregators: web sites, applications, and software that cull content from other digital sources

media convergence: the merging of traditional media with digital communication technologies such as telecommunications and the Internet

mediated citizens: people who are constantly receiving information through multiple channels that can and do shape their political views but who also have the ability to use those channels to create their own narratives

Medicaid: a federally sponsored program that provides medical care to the poor

Medicare: the federal government's health insurance program for the elderly and disabled

mercantilism: an economic system that sees trade as the basis of the accumulation of wealth

middle-class and corporate welfare: a set of distributive policies that benefit the middle class and corporations

midterm loss: the tendency for the presidential party to lose congressional seats in off-year elections

Miller test: the rule used by the courts in which the definition of obscenity must be based on local standards

minority leader: the head of the minority party in either the Senate or the House

Miranda rights: the rights that a person has to resist questioning and not to incriminate oneself; the police must inform suspects that they possess these rights

modern presidency: the trend toward a higher degree of executive power since the 1930s in response to more complex social problems

momentum: a sense of forward movement and enthusiasm that candidates can get from primary wins or other positive events

monetary policy: the government's power to control the money supply by manipulating interest rates

multinational corporations: large companies that do business in multiple countries

national law making: the creation of policy to address the problems and needs of the entire nation

national nominating convention: a formal party gathering at which candidates for the general election are chosen

National Security Council (NSC): the organization within the Executive Office of the President that provides foreign policy advice to the president

natural rights: the idea that one is born with a set of rights that no government can take away

naturalized citizens: people who become U.S. citizens through a series of procedures that the law lays out

necessary and proper clause: the constitutional authorization for Congress to make any law required to carry out its powers

negative advertising: campaign advertising that emphasizes the negative characteristics of opponents rather than one's own strengths

net neutrality: the principle that Internet service providers cannot speed up or slow down access for customers or make decisions about the content they see or the apps they download

neutral competence: an ideal bureaucratic structure where power is hierarchical and rule-based, and where people are appointed because of their expertise and promoted on the basis of merit

New Deal: under Franklin Roosevelt, a series of programs that encouraged people to turn to the government for the solution to social and economic problems; made the government larger and more unwieldy and reignited a debate about the role of government

New Jersey Plan: a proposal at the Constitutional Convention that congressional representation be equal, thus favoring the small states

news management: the efforts of a politician's staff to control news about the politician

Nineteenth Amendment: the 1920 constitutional amendment granting women the right to vote

non-authoritarian governments: political systems in which the rules regulate people's behaviors in some respects but allow them considerable freedom in others

nongovernmental organizations: organizations comprising individuals or interest groups from around the world focused on a special issue

nonresponse bias: a skewing of data that occurs when there is a difference in opinion between those who choose to participate and those who do not

norms: unspoken, unwritten ideas that support the U.S. Constitution and give structure to democratic government

nuclear option: a controversial Senate maneuver by which a simple majority could decide to allow a majority to bypass the filibuster for certain kinds of votes

nullification: declaration by a state that a federal law is void within its borders

omnibus legislation: large bills stuffed with often-unrelated pieces of legislation that are voted on all at once

online processing: the experience of picking up various decision-making cues throughout the day that help you arrive at a rational conclusion even though you might not be able to re-create the process of getting there

open seat: an election with no incumbent

opinion followers: the vast majority of citizens who take their cues about what to think from opinion leaders

opinion leaders: the subset of the population who are well informed about politics and involved in civic activity

pardoning power: a president's authority to release or excuse a person from the legal penalties of a crime

parliamentary system: government in which the executive is chosen by the legislature from among its members and the two branches are merged

partisan gerrymandering: redistricting that enhances the political fortunes of one party over another

partisan sorting: the process through which citizens align themselves ideologically with one of the two parties, leaving fewer citizens remaining in the center and increasing party polarization

partisanship: one's allegiance to one's party

party activists: the most ideologically extreme of a party's voters, also called the "base"

party caucuses: a local gathering of party members to choose convention delegates

party era: a period of party dominance or party instability

party identification: the tendency of members of the public to associate themselves with a particular party because they share its values, culture, policy preferences, or social network

party machines: a system in which party leaders or "bosses" made decisions about policy and kept the loyalty of their voters by providing them with services and support

party organizations: the Democratic National Committee and the Republican National Committee, both of which are staffed with officials who are paid political operatives in charge of keeping the party infrastructure working

party platform: a distinct set of policies set forth by a political party that is based on its ideology

party primaries: elections in which candidates from each party are chosen to run in the general election

party-in-government: elected officials who are in charge of the key function of governing—filling key positions and making policy

Patient Protection and Affordable Care Act: health care legislation passed during the Obama administration designed to make health care more affordable to more people

patriotism: shared loyalty to our country and its institutions

patronage: a system in which people in power reward friends, contributors, and party loyalists for their support with jobs, contracts, and favors

permanent campaign: the idea that governing requires a continual effort to convince the public to sign on to the program, requiring a reliance on consultants and an emphasis on politics over policy

pocket veto: the presidential authority to kill a bill submitted within ten days of the end of a legislative session by not signing it

polarization: the ideological distance between the parties and the ideological homogeneity within them

policy: a prescribed course of action, a way of accomplishing a goal, or a set of operational principles

policy adoption: a phase of the policymaking process in which policies are adopted by government bodies for future implementation

policy evaluation: a phase of the policymaking process in which policymakers attempt to assess the merit, worth, and utility of a policy

policy formulation: a phase of the policymaking process in which policies are developed to address specific problems that have been placed on the national agenda

policy implementation: a phase of the policymaking process in which government executes an adopted policy as specified by legislation or policy action

policy representation: congressional work to advance the issues and ideological preferences of constituents

policymaking: the process of formulating policies

political action committees (PACs): the fundraising arms of interest groups

political culture: a set of shared ideas, values, and beliefs that define the role and limitations of government and people's relationship to that government and that, therefore, bind people into a single political unit

political efficacy: citizens' feelings of effectiveness in political affairs

political narrative: a story that is used to persuade others about the nature of power, who should have it, and how it should be used

political parties: groups that are bound by a common interest or interests and that seek to use the political system to attain their goals from inside the system by controlling government

political socialization: the process of picking up values and commitments to a regime through various social agents like family, schools, religious institutions, peer groups, and the media

politics: the way we decide who gets power and influence in a world where there is not enough power for all of us to have as much as we'd like

polling: the use of scientific methods and technology to measure public opinion

polling aggregators: analysts who combine polls by averaging or other techniques in order to minimize sampling error and make the polls more accurate

polls: the instrument though which public opinion is measured, or the place where one goes to cast a vote

popular sovereignty: the concept that the citizens are the ultimate source of political power

pork barrel: public works projects and grants for specific districts paid for by general revenues

power to persuade: the president's ability to convince Congress to support his plans

precedent: a previous decision or ruling that is binding on subsequent decisions

president: the chief executive in a presidential system

presidential branch: the bureaucracy within the White House that serves the president

presidential system: government in which the executive is chosen independently of the legislature and the two branches are separate

presidential veto: a president's authority to reject a bill passed by Congress; may be overridden only by a two-thirds majority in each house

primaries: preliminary party elections

prior restraint: censorship of or punishment for the expression of ideas before the ideas are printed or spoken

procedural laws: laws that define how the laws are used, applied, and enforced

progressive income taxes: taxing people who have more money at a higher rate

progressives: economic liberals who believe in a stronger role for the state in creating equality

public interest groups: groups that try to change policy in accordance with values that *they believe* are good for everyone

public opinion: the collective attitudes and beliefs of individuals on one or more issues

public policy: a government plan of action to solve a problem that people share collectively or that they cannot solve on their own

public-interested citizenship: citizens who put country ahead of self by putting aside their self-interest to advance the public interest

pundit: a professional observer and commentator on politics reporting

racial gerrymandering: redistricting that either dilutes or concentrates minority votes

racial profiling: when law enforcement officers base their decision to investigate a person's activities on the individual's apparent race or ethnicity

racism: institutionalized power inequalities based on the perception of racial differences

random digit dialing: the process of choosing respondents for a poll by letting a computer pick phone numbers without bias

random sample: samples chosen in such a way that any member of the population being polled has an equal chance of being selected

ratification: the process through which a proposal (such as the Constitution) is formally approved and adopted by vote

rational ignorance: the state of not engaging in politics because the payoff seems remote or insignificant

realignment: a substantial and long-term shift in party allegiance by individuals and groups, usually resulting in a change in policy direction

reapportionment: the process of reallocating seats in the House of Representatives based on population

reconciliation: a legislative process that allows certain budgetary laws to pass with a simple majority in the Senate and with limited debate

red tape: the complex procedures and regulations surrounding bureaucratic activity

redistributive policies: policies that shift resources from more affluent segments of society to those who are less affluent and less likely to participate politically

redistricting: the process of dividing states into legislative districts

regressive taxes: flat taxes, like sales taxes, that consume a higher percentage of a poorer person's money

regulated capitalism: a market system in which the government intervenes to protect rights

regulating the electorate: the practice of trying to limit the number of eligible voters by law or custom in order to maximize one's party's fortunes

regulations: limitations or restrictions on the activities of a business or an individual

regulatory policies: policies designed to restrict or change the behavior of certain groups or individuals

reporting: the action of seeking out facts to tell a complete story about a public event or individual

representation: the efforts of elected officials to look out for the interests of those who elect them

republican virtue: the idea that citizens would act in the public interest without coercion by a strong government

responsible party model: an ideal model of how parties might operate to maximize voter information and elected official accountability

revolving door: when people move from the public sector to the private sector and then sometimes back to the public sector again

right to privacy: the judicial creation from *Griswold v. Connecticut* (1965) that certain rights in the Bill of Rights protected intimate decisions like family planning from state interference

rule of law: a system in which laws are known in advance, they apply the same way to everyone, and if we feel they have been unjustly applied we can appeal to a higher authority

rule-making: filling in all the technical details in the laws Congress passes so that they can be enforced

rules: political directives that help to determine who will win or lose future power struggles

sample bias: the effect of having a sample that does not represent all segments of the population

sampling error: a number that indicates within what range the results of a poll are accurate

sedition: speech that criticizes the government in order to promote rebellion

select committees: committees appointed to deal with an issue or a problem not suited to standing committees

selective incentives: benefits offered to induce people to join groups

self-interested citizenship: citizens who are focused on their personal lives and use the political system to maximize their interests

Senate majority leader: the head of the majority party in the Senate

separate but equal: the legal principle stemming from *Plessy v. Ferguson* (1896) that segregation didn't violate the Fourteenth Amendment unless the separate facilities provided were unequal

separation of powers: the division of the government vertically into branches: legislative, executive, and judicial

separationists: people who want a separation between church and state

single member, first past the post: a system of representation in which only one person is elected from each congressional district—the person who gets the most votes

single-issue voters: voters who make electoral choices based on a particular issue

slander: spoken defamation of character

slavery: the ownership, for forced labor, of one people by another

social conservatives: Americans who endorse limited government control of the economy but considerable government intervention to realize a traditional social order; based on religious values and hierarchy rather than equality

social contract: the idea that power is not derived from God but instead comes from and is limited by the consent of the governed, who can revolt against the government they contract with if their rights are not protected if the contract is not kept

social insurance policies: programs that offer benefits in exchange for contributions

social liberals: Americans who favor greater control of the economy and the social order to bring about greater equality and to regulate the effects of progress

social policy: distributive and redistributive policies that seek to improve the quality of citizens' lives

Social Security: a social insurance program under which individuals make contributions during working years and collect benefits in retirement

social welfare policies: government programs that provide for the needs of those who cannot, or sometimes will not, provide for themselves

socialism: an economic system in which the government (a single ruler, a party, or some other empowered group) decides what to produce and who should get the products

soft money: unregulated campaign contributions by individuals, groups, or parties that promote general election activities but do not directly support individual candidates

solicitor general: the legal officer who argues cases before the Supreme Court when the United States is a party to the case

solidary benefits: group member benefits derived from an individual's desire to associate with other people who care about the same things

soundbites: a brief, snappy excerpt from a public figure's speech that is easy to repeat on the news

Speaker of the House: the head of the majority party in the House

spin: an interpretation of a politician's words or actions, designed to present a favorable image

spoils system: the practice of creating a bureaucracy that serves the president's interest

standing committees: permanent committees responsible for legislation in particular policy areas

State of the Union address: the president's constitutional obligation to regularly inform Congress of the state of the union and to recommend the measures the president considers useful or necessary

statutory laws: laws made by legislatures

stereotypes: assumptions about other people based on their race, ethnicity, gender, or sexual orientation

strategic policy: foreign policy that lays out a country's basic stance toward international actors or problems

strict constructionists: supporters of a judicial approach holding that the Constitution should be read literally, with the framers' intentions uppermost in mind

strict scrutiny: a heightened standard of review used by the Supreme Court to assess the constitutionality of laws that limit some freedoms or that make a suspect classification

structural defense policy: foreign policy dealing with defense spending, military bases, and weapons procurement

subjects: people who are bound to the will of the rulers and who have no power of their own to push back on an abusive government

subsidies: financial incentives given by the government to individuals, corporations, or other government jurisdictions or institutions usually to encourage certain activities or behaviors

substantive laws: laws that define what people can or cannot do

Supplemental Nutrition Assistance Program (SNAP): a federal program that provides vouchers to the poor to help them buy food

supremacy clause: a constitutional clause that says the Constitution itself and national laws made under it are the law of the land

surpluses: the extra funds available because government's revenues are greater than its expenditures

suspect classification: a classification, such as race, for which any discriminatory law must be justified by a compelling state interest

swing states: states in which the outcome of a general election is not easy to predict in advance

swing voters: the approximately one third of the electorate who are undecided at the start of a campaign

symbolic representation: the public role of showcasing the values of public service and patriotism

tax policy: the government's power to require that individuals and businesses contribute to collective costs

Temporary Assistance to Needy Families (TANF): a welfare program of block grants to states that encourages recipients to work in exchange for time-limited benefits

Tenth Amendment: the amendment that stipulates that any powers not explicitly given to the national government are reserved to the states

Thirteenth Amendment: the 1865 constitutional amendment banning slavery

Three-Fifths Compromise: the formula for counting five slaves as three people for purposes of representation; reconciled northern and southern factions at the Constitutional Convention

tort: a broken civil law, a violation against an individual

totalitarianism: a system that combines authoritarian government with a socialist economic system wherein the government makes all the decisions about power, influence, and money

tracking polls: polls that keep track of data over time to detect changes in support for people or issues

traditional presidency: the founders' vision of limited executive power

treaties: formal agreements with other countries; negotiated by the president and requiring approval by two thirds of the Senate

trial balloon: an official leak of a proposal to determine public reaction to it without risk

two-step flow of information: a psychological process by which opinion followers look to opinion leaders for cues on how to vote

unfunded mandates: policies requiring states to do something but without any funds provided to offset the costs of administering the policy

unitary executive: the theory that the executive, not the legislature, is at the core of American power

unorthodox lawmaking: lawmaking tactics—such as omnibus legislation or reconciliation—that bypass usual committee processes to ease the passage of laws

U.S. Census: a constitutional mandate requiring the U.S. government to count the people who live within its borders every ten years

value-added taxes (VATs): taxes levied at each stage of production, based on the value added to the product at that stage

veto: the presidential power to reject a piece of legislation by not signing it into law

Virginia Plan: a proposal at the Constitutional Convention that congressional representation be based on population, thus favoring the large states

voter mobilization: a party's efforts to inform potential voters about issues and candidates and to persuade them to vote

voter turnout: the percentage of the eligible population who turn out to vote in an election

War Powers Act: a federal law passed in 1973 that was designed to check the president's power to commit the United States to an armed conflict without the consent of the U.S. Congress

weak presidents: presidents who have difficulty getting priorities through even a friendly Congress

wedge issue: a controversial issue that one party uses to split the voters in the other party

weighting: adjustments to surveys during analysis so that selected demographic groups reflect their values in the population, usually as measured by the census

White House Office: an in-house group of advisers that includes the Office of the Chief of Staff (who also oversees the White House Office); the Communications Office, including the press secretary; the Council on Domestic Policy and the National Economic Council; the Office of the First Lady; and various political advisers

white privilege: the learned tendency to see the world through the context of white culture and power

writs of certiorari: formal requests by the U.S. Supreme Court to call up the lower court cases it decides to hear on appeal

Index

NOTE: Page references in **bold** refer to definitions; boxes, figures, and tables are identified as (box), (fig.), (table).

Afterword

Most introductory textbooks follow a more or less straight-forward formula. Books are rich in anecdote and examples and they use a lot of words to paint a picture of complex subjects and nuanced concepts. They provide the perfect context for a traditional lecture based course. For many students, that formula works.

But I have found as I have taught non-traditional students (those returning to school after some time off, students holding multiple jobs or juggling a family, international students for whom English is not their first language, or just those fitting in a class here and there in a busy life) that the conventional text, no matter how well-conceived and written, is a stumbling block. They get hit with more information than one can handle without much guidance on how to process it—this can create a real log jam. More than one student has told me they couldn't finish the reading, so they didn't start. These are not words a teacher wants to hear.

I started to think about a reconceptualized textbook for that non-traditional student. Something tightly organized with all the fat cut out, a friendly book that would not be threatening to a student facing a daunting pile of work as well as a demanding life. The book would contain "just the facts, ma'am," but with links to go deeper if the student's interest was caught. I intended to do everything I could to catch it.

I took this idea to Charisse Kiino at CQ Press. Charisse is a special friend with an eye for the golden apple. She immediately sent me to Monica Eckman, CQP's Executive Publisher. Monica, Development Editor Elise Frasier, and Content Developer Anna Villarruel have been a dream of a team to work with.

Monica is sharp as a knife, cool and astute, and funny as hell, with a full-throated laugh that embraces you and pulls you back from the cliff edge when necessary. I have come to depend on her CAPITAL LETTERS and lavish use of "!!!!!"—I worry when I get an email without them. I have known her for a little over a year and I want to write books with her forever. Elise, who I have known for years, has turned into a dear and valued friend. I want her in my life forever too. She kept this book on track—made it smarter, kept it shorter, and gave it its tagline: "*Long Story Short*." Anna has borne the brunt of my relentless compulsion to turn this into the book of my imagination, which meant mind-reading, temper-soothing, and advocating by proxy. Plus video conferencing with me in my pajamas which goes WAY above the call of duty for anyone.

What I am trying, in my goofy way to say, is that these wonderful women are a treasure—I will write a book with them anytime, anywhere.

The Wonder Women are the editorial side of the team, but they are not alone in making this book happen. Kelly DeRosa is a skilled and competent production manager who talked me down from the treetops more than once. Anthony Paular and Scott Van Atta worked tirelessly to reconceptualize the old idea of a textbook, making color and design and visual humor tools of pedagogy. Alexa Turner stepped in and worked with an illustrator to develop each of the colorful graphics in this book.

A book, no matter how cool and innovative, doesn't teach a soul if it just sits on the shelf.

Erica DeLuca and Christina Fohl have devised marketing strategies to test the book with students and faculty, coming back with the fabulous quote from one young woman who found the spiral bound format excellent because she could read the book while drying her hair.

One takes the wins where one can find them. Deepest thanks to all the reviewers and editors and designers and producers and marketers and everyone else who helped put this one together.

—Christine

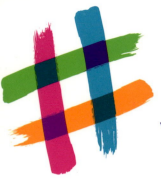

"THIS NEW AMERICAN GOVERNMENT TEXTBOOK DOES THE IMPOSSIBLE BY ACTUALLY ENGAGING TODAY'S STUDENTS."
—WILLIAM PARENT, SAN JACINTO COLLEGE, NORTH

ALL THE FUNDAMENTALS. NO FLUFF. LEARN MORE WITH LESS!

A truly revolutionary American Government textbook, **AmGov: Long Story Short**, responds to the needs of today's students and instructors through brevity and accessibility. The succinct ten chapters are separated by tabs that make it easy to skim, flip, revisit, reorient, and return to content quickly. Reading aids like bullets, annotations, and arrows walk students through important facts and break up the material in short, engaging bites of information that highlight not only what is important but why it's important. Though brief, this core book is still robust enough to provide everything that students need to be successful in their American Government course. Whether for the on-the-go student who doesn't have time to read and digest a lengthy chapter, or the instructor who wants a book that will stay out of their way and leave room for plenty of supplementary reading and activities, **AmGov** provides a perfectly simplified foundation for a successful American Government course.

SAGE coursepacks

Our Content Tailored to Your LMS

Instructors! SAGE coursepacks makes it easy to import our quality instructor and student resource content into your school's learning management system (LMS). Intuitive and simple to use, SAGE coursepacks does not require special access codes and gives you the control to focus on what really matters: customizing course content to meet your students' needs. Learn more at **sagepub.com/coursepacks**.

www.cqpress.com

CQPRESS

FSC
www.fsc.org
MIX
Paper from responsible sources
FSC® C011825

ISBN 978-1-5443-2592-7

90000
9 781544 325927